JAMES J. MURPHY is Chairman of the Department of Rhetoric at the University of California, Davis, and the author of several studies of classical and medieval rhetoric.

Medieval Eloquence

Medieval Eloquence

Studies in the Theory and Practice of Medieval Rhetoric

EDITED BY

James J. Murphy

University of California Press

Berkeley · Los Angeles · London

University of California Press
Berkeley and Los Angeles, California

University of California Press, Ltd.
London, England

Copyright © 1978 by
The Regents of the University of California

ISBN 0-520-03345-0
Library of Congress Catalog Card Number: 76-48026
Printed in the United States of America
1 2 3 4 5 6 7 8 9

Contents

Contributors

JACKSON J. CAMPBELL
University of Illinois

CHARLES B. FAULHABER
University of California, Berkeley

ERNEST GALLO
University of Massachusetts

SAMUEL JAFFE
University of Chicago

MARGARET JENNINGS, C.S.J.
Saint Joseph's College, Brooklyn

DOUGLAS KELLY
University of Wisconsin

CALVIN B. KENDALL
University of Minnesota

MICHAEL C. LEFF
University of California, Davis

JAMES J. MURPHY
University of California, Davis

M. B. PARKES
Keble College, Oxford

ROBERT O. PAYNE
City University of New York
Graduate Center and Herbert H. Lehman College

JOSEF PURKART
University of California, Riverside

ALDO SCAGLIONE
University of North Carolina

JOHN O. WARD
University of Sydney, Australia

Preface

SHORTLY after the middle of the thirteenth century, Brunetto Latini, the teacher of the poet Dante, remarked in his *Tresor* (1260) that the lore of rhetoric applied to both speaking and writing—to communication by the mouth and by the hand making letters.[1] This medieval readiness to apply the *ars rhetorica* to a wide range of uses reveals a far broader compositional spirit than Cicero or Aristotle had ever contemplated.

We are just now beginning to appreciate the richness of artistic invention which thus became available during the Middle Ages to poets, diplomats, preachers, linguists, grammarians, teachers and, indeed, to anyone interested in language or its uses in human affairs. Like the character in Molière's play who discovers to his astonishment that he has been speaking prose all his life and hasn't known it, modern scholars are discovering that they have been reading applied rhetoric in medieval texts and didn't know it. In the middle of the nineteenth century, for instance, historians began to discover that some accepted historical documents were merely model letters written as composition exercises to help users of the *ars dictaminis,* or art of letter writing.[2] Within the past half century a large number of texts,

---

1. "Or dist li mestres que le science de rectorique est en ii manieres, une ki est en disant de bouche et un autre que l'on mande par letres; mais li enseignement sont commun." *Li livres dou Tresor,* ed. Francis Carmody (University of California Press, 1948), III. iv.

2. For example W. Wattenbach, "Über Briefsteller des Mittelalters," pp. 29–94 in "Iter Austriacum 1853," *Archiv für kunde österreichischer Geschichts-Quellen* 14(1855), 1–94. The landmark collection of texts of Latin dictaminal manuals by Ludwig Rockinger in 1863 was one off-shoot of this discovery: *Briefsteller und formelbücher des eilften bis vierzehnten Jahrhunderts,* Quellen und Erörterungen zur bayerischen und deutschen Geschichte 9 (two vols., Munich, 1863; reprinted New York, 1961, two volumes in one).

translations, and studies have rolled from the presses,[3] so that we are now in a much better position to assess the real impact of rhetoric upon medieval culture. The annual bibliography of the Modern Language Association now includes "Rhetoric" as a separate category. The study of medieval rhetoric is in danger of becoming fashionable.

It is of course all too easy now to see too much where before too little was seen. As one of the essays in this volume points out, the mere making of a catalogue of rhetorical tropes and figures in the Old French *Erec* adds little to critical understanding; indeed, such catalogues "foster the false notion that definition of the device explains its function in context." Another writer points out "a number of pitfalls to avoid" in trying to apply rhetoric to Old English poetry. (An inadequate understanding of the rhetoric itself can lead to bizarre conclusions, as in the case of one earlier writer [Benjamin S. Harrison, 1934] who alleged that all the tales in Chaucer's *Monk's Tale* are examples of the figure *brevitas* because they are short!) The isolation of a single rhetorical term or concept for the purpose of "finding" it in some text is an all too common practice, it would seem; the tropes and figures in particular seem to have suffered this fate quite frequently in recent times.[4]

The solution for a modern critic would seem to be to acquire as full an understanding as possible of the rhetoric itself before attempting to apply it to a text. As Margaret Schlauch has pointed out, one cannot compare what one does not know:

> Anyone intending to apply rhetoric to literature should first study rhetoric as a separate, complete subject before attempting to apply it. Otherwise he is in danger of sporadic and incomplete references to the rhetorical aspects of a given text. He may concentrate, for instance, on shorter figures of speech while ignoring larger structures that may also be in-

---

3. See James J. Murphy, *Medieval Rhetoric: A Select Bibliography* (University of Toronto Press, 1971), and Murphy, *Rhetoric in the Middle Ages: A History of Rhetorical Theory from Saint Augustine to the Renaissance* (University of California Press, 1974).

4. For a discussion of some of the difficulties of this approach, see Murphy, *Rhetoric in the Middle Ages*, pp. 184–191. There have been some notable cautionary reactions. For instance, Sherman Kuhn (*Speculum* 42(1972), 188–206) concludes that "the so-called cursus in Old English literature is nothing more than a part of the natural rhythm of the language. It is not a rhetorical ornament either of prose or of poetry, for it appears in unpolished, non-rhetorical Old English boundary descriptions as well as in everyday speech."

debted to rhetorical models traceable, via medieval models and examples, to classical sources.[5]

This volume, therefore, provides within one cover a survey of basic medieval rhetorical theories, together with some of their applications in various literatures of the Middle Ages.

Medieval approaches to rhetoric are themselves varied, for historical reasons too complex to outline here,[6] so that a full understanding of that theory requires a grasp of what one writer here calls the "environment of discourse" in which medieval texts were produced. A mature educated man of, say, the fourteenth century, would have heard literally thousands of sermons, read (or even heard) hundreds of letters written to the format of the *ars dictaminis*, heard (or possibly read) an untold number of verse compositions affected by the advice of teachers of the *ars poetriae*, listened in church over a lifetime to a liturgy informed for centuries by rhetorical and rhythmical theories, with his understanding of the Scripture itself affected by punctuational decisions based on the commentators' concern for audience effect. His elementary education, whether he realized it or not, was an amalgam of grammatical and rhetorical processes, transformed in the twelfth century by apparently dry academic quarrels over the relation of rhetoric and dialectic.

Such a man did not live a life of isolated linguistic fragmentation. He had a rich array of language capabilities available to him, whether he used Latin or a vernacular tongue. Indeed, one of our writers asks here, how can we assess even a genius like Dante until we realize that his ideas (expressed in Latin) may have a bearing on his performance (expressed in the Italian vernacular)? The entire environment of discourse helped to shape the language usage of medieval man, and a variegated rhetoric was a major part of that environment.

In that sense this book is a demonstration of possibilities. Each writer was simply asked to say what he or she felt needed saying about

---

5. Letter from Margaret Schlauch, Warsaw, Poland, December 5, 1972. She goes on to say that studying rhetoric separately from literature proved advantageous in her own career: "It was my good fortune to study the history of rhetoric many years ago under Charles Sears Baldwin, and I was inspired by him to go on reading on my own: not only other historical treatments of the subject but also textbooks used in medieval and classical times. While I was lecturing on Old and Middle English literature I found that I was making more and more use of rhetorical doctrine for literary explication."

6. See Murphy, *Rhetoric in the Middle Ages,* esp. pp. 43–88.

a particular topic. Since "theory" tends, traditionally, to come from individual expressions by particular authors, most of the essays in the theory section of this book deal with one or another of the famous men whose individual books influenced others. Since medieval "practice" was so clearly varied over ranges of time, place, and nationality, these essays too are varied. Much has been written about rhetoric and Chaucer, for instance, so that Robert O. Payne can now contribute a critical assessment of the state-of-the-art in connection with that poet. Less has been written about German. Enough has been written about Old French to identify some underlying critical issues. Another approach identifies twelfth-century education as the key to an early Middle English poem.

We will have succeeded in opening some possibilities of further understanding if these original essays actually do awaken interest in a fundamental fact of medieval intellectual life—the prevalence and practice of rhetoric. By and large medieval men did master the challenge implied by Boethius, who is described in one of these essays as feeling that "the rhetorical practices are themselves too sprawling for a focused theory to be induced from them." They did evolve uniquely medieval rhetorical theories, and they did put them into practice. The entire aim of this book is to encourage curiosity into the ways in which that evolution/application took place. To apply to this whole book what one writer says of punctuation, this volume is offered "to stimulate further, more detailed investigation."

Part One

✤ ✤ ✤

The Theory of Rhetoric
in the Middle Ages

Boethius' *De differentiis topicis*, Book IV

MICHAEL C. LEFF

TOWARD the end of his career, Boethius wrote a treatise entitled *De differentiis topicis*.[1] He had already published separate commentaries on the *Topics* of Aristotle and Cicero, and in *De diff. top.* he set out to unify the study of topical invention.[2] Boethius based this synthesis on a careful analysis and comparison of the various topical systems known to him. He intended to show that all of these systems were reducible to the same basic set of distinctions (*differentiae*).

The treatise was divided into four books. The first defined certain terms necessary for an understanding of topical logic; the second and third explicated and attempted to synthesize the theories of Aristotle and Cicero; the fourth sought to place rhetorical topics within the

1. Anicius Manlius Severinus Boethius (c. 480–525) is best known as the author of the *Consolation of Philosophy*, one of the most widely read books of the Middle Ages. Boethius also wrote numerous treatises on theology and the liberal arts, especially on logic. He exercised a seminal influence on later medieval thought in a number of different areas. For general studies of Boethius and his significance, see: E.K. Rand, *Founders of the Middle Ages* (New York: Dover, 1957), pp. 135–80, H.F. Stewart, *Boethius, An Essay* (London: Blackwood, 1891), Howard Rollin Patch, *The Tradition of Boethius: A Study of His Importance in Medieval Culture* (New York: Oxford U. Press, 1935), and Helen M. Barrett, *Boethius: Some Aspects of his Times and Work* (New York: Russell and Russell, 1965). Although scholars disagree about the absolute date of *De differentiis topicis*, there is agreement about its relative chronology in terms of Boethius' career. The treatise is a late work, probably the last he composed before his imprisonment. See, Arthur Patch McKinlay, "Stylistic Tests and the Chronology of the Works of Boethius," *Harvard Studies in Classical Philology*, 18 (1907), 134, and L.M. De Rijk, "On the Chronology of Boethius' Works on Logic II," *Vivarium*, 2 (1964), 154. (De Rijk and several other scholars think that the proper title of the treatise is *De topicis differentiis*).

2. For Boethius' statement of purpose, see *De diff. top.*, 1173 C13–1174 C3. All citations from *De diff. top.* refer to the text in J. Migne (ed.), *Patrologia Latina* (Paris: Published by the Editor and his Successors, 1891), 64, cols. 1173C–1216D.

ambit of this synthesis. The fourth book represented an innovation, since classical theorists had treated the topics of rhetoric and dialectic separately. Boethius, however, wished to be thorough and to show that even the topics of rhetoric fit within his system.

De differentiis topicis proved to have a long, interesting, and somewhat paradoxical history during the later Middle Ages. One of the most striking features of this history was illustrated by the earliest statutes of the University of Paris. The Paris statute of 1215 prescribed what was perhaps the first "curriculum" in European higher education. Logical studies dominated this curriculum, but it also provided for lectures on "philosophers and rhetoric and the quadrivium and *Barbarismus* and ethics . . . and the fourth book of the *Topics.* "[3] Apparently the *Barbarismus* (the third book of Aelius Donatus' *Ars maior*) and the final book of *De diff. top.* were the designed texts for rhetoric. Forty years later, a new statute revised the curriculum at Paris, and it made no provision for lectures on rhetoric. *De differentiis topicis* remained as a text, but it was now listed under "The Old Logic," and only the first three books were prescribed.[4]

Taken together, the Paris statutes of 1215 and 1255 illustrated the later medieval tendency to separate *De differentiis topicis* into two discrete components. Both components exercised a significant influence on the thought of the period, but they were restricted to different fields. The first three books became part of the "Old Logic" and served as a major source for dialectical theory.[5] The fourth book became a standard reference for rhetorical theory. As such, *Topica* IV appeared in the curricula of Montpellier and Oxford as well as Paris, and it was cited regularly by writers on rhetoric from Notker Labeo in the eleventh century to Traversagni in the fifteenth.[6]

---

3. Lynn Thorndike, *University Records and Life in the Middle Ages* (New York: Columbia U. Press, 144), p. 28, and Hastings Rashdall, *The Universities of Europe in the Middle Ages,* rev. ed. by F.M. Powicke and A.B. Emden (Oxford: At the Clarendon Press, 1936), I, 440–1.

4. *Ibid.,* 442, and Thorndike, pp. 64–5.

5. See Otto Bird, "The Formalizing of Topics in Medieval Logic," *Notre Dame Journal of Formal Logic,* 1 (1960), 140–1.

6. Michael Leff, "Boethius and the History of Medieval Rhetoric," *Central States Speech Journal,* 24 (1974), 137–8. There is no detailed and systematic study of Boethius' influence on later medieval rhetorical theory. There is general agreement, however, that his influence was very great. See the references in *ibid.,* and James J. Murphy, *Rhetoric in the Middle Ages: A History of Rhetorical Theory from St. Augustine to the Renaissance* (Berkeley and Los Angeles, University of California Press, 1974), pp. 112–17, Eleonore Stump, "Boethius' Work on the Topics," *Vivarium,* 12 (1974), 79, and Aldo Scaglione, *The Classical Theory of Composition*

While this division of *De diff. top.* was well adapted to the needs of the medieval schools, it was not entirely consistent with Boethius' original purposes. In the first place, the separation of the dialectical and rhetorical sections of the work obscured the author's attempt to synthesize the theory of topics *per se.* More important, Boethius certainly did not intend to write the fourth book as an independent text on rhetoric. His objective was only to complete his study of topical logic. In fact, several passages in the fourth book explicitly warned the reader against expecting a standard textbook treatment of rhetorical theory. For example, at 1209B–C, after presenting a list of the five legal statuses, Boethius added this qualification: "To show that all these (statuses) differ from one another is a rhetorician's task, not mine. This work is intended for the examination of the learned not for the instruction of the uneducated."[7] And he made a similar disclaimer after his analysis of the rational statuses:

> All these arguments have their own variations, and hence very fine distinctions which are dealt with in greater detail in the rhetorical works written to set out and explain them. Let it suffice for the present that I have taken these observations from Cicero. For the whole purpose of the present work is directed to another end (1210B–C).[8]

Whatever Boethius' intentions, however, the educational authorities at Paris (and many other places as well) regarded *Topica* IV as an appropriate instrument for instructing those uneducated in rhetoric. This development raises some puzzling questions about the history of this short book. Despite the avowed intent of the author, the book was isolated from its context and used as a sort of rhetorical textbook. Despite its narrow, limited, and technical focus, it eventually became one of the most popular medieval texts on rhetoric. How can we account for this unexpected use of *De diff. top.* IV? What accounts for its apparent popularity? Why did it displace the more balanced rhetorical compendia of authors such as Julius Victor, Fortunatianus, Martianus Capella, and Alcuin?

---

from Its Origins to the Present: A Historical Survey (Chapel Hill: U. North Carolina Press, 1972), p. 163, n. 5. See also the essay in this volume by John O. Ward, particularly note 75.

7. Quos omnes a se differre non est nostri operis, verum rhetorici demonstrare; haec enim speculanda doctis non rudibus discenda proponimus. . . .

8. Horum vero omnium sunt propriae differentiae, atque ideo minutissimae divisiones quas rhetorum in his docendis explicandisque conscripti libri diligentius continent. Sed nos haec a M. Tullio sumpsisse sufficiat. Ad aliud enim tota operis festinat intentio.

.

In part, the answers to these questions may depend upon accidents or upon the enormous prestige that Boethius enjoyed throughout the Middle Ages. But it seems to me that there are also some larger issues involved—issues that bear on the elusive question of the "subject matter" of medieval rhetoric and on the history of the shifting relationships among the arts of the trivium. In this essay, I propose to raise these issues and to suggest some approaches for answering them based on a study of *De differentiis topicis*. To achieve this purpose, it is necessary first to examine *De diff. top.* itself and then to attempt to set it within the context of traditional theories of rhetoric.

I. DIALECTICAL TOPICS

Boethius presents his basic theory of topics in the first three books of *De diff. top.* A rudimentary knowledge of these books is necessary in order to appreciate the position Boethius argues in the fourth book on rhetoric.

Boethius repeats the standard Ciceronian definition of a topic as a seat (*sedes*) of argument (1174D, 1185A). But he also refines this definition by distinguishing between two types of topics—"topical principle" (*propositio maxima*) and "topical difference" (*maximae propositionis differentia*).[9] These are the two basic concepts upon which he constructs a system of topics.

Topical principles are the kernel units of argumentation. They are propositions that can be used to prove other propositions but do not themselves require any proof. They are self-evident, indemonstrable, and universal propositions that give support to argumentative inferences (1185D). Topical principles include propositions such as these: if the definitions of two things differ, the things themselves are different (1185D); what inheres in the individual parts must inhere in the whole (1188D); things that have natural efficient causes are themselves natural (1189C).

Evidently, the number of topical principles is very great. Yet a well-ordered science must have a limited number of basic classifications. For this reason, Boethius introduces the concept of topical

9. Bird, *Notre Dame Journal of Formal Logic*, 140 translates *propositio maxima* as "topical maxim." Eleonore Stump, however, argues that the word "maxim" in this context does not agree with the ordinary usage of the word in English. I prefer her "topical principle" as a translation of this phrase. I am very much in debt to Dr. Stump for allowing me to read a draft version of her dissertation, *Boethius' De topicis differentiis* (Cornell University, 1975).

difference as a means of arranging principles under a manageable set of headings (1186A–B). Topical differences are mechanisms for grouping principles according to the way that they differ among themselves. Once identified, the *differentiae* may be classified as topics in their own right. Moreover, since these *differentiae* are abstracted from the principles, they are more universal and thus fewer in number (1186B). Consequently, the *differentiae* offer a convenient vehicle for an orderly analysis of topical argumentation.

Following Themistius' commentary on Aristotle's *Topics,* Boethius expends most of his effort in the attempt to establish a fundamental set of *differentiae.*[10] He bases his theory of topical difference on the relationship between the nature of the inference and the terms of the proposition in question (*quaestio*). This criterion produces a three-fold division of topics as intrinsic to the subject, extrinsic to it, or intermediate (1186D).

Intrinsic topics are those that depend on the subject and predicate terms of the question. This category is further divided into topics that arise directly from the substance of the terms and those that depend on consequences intimately associated with the terms. The first class encompasses all arguments from definition and description. The class of consequents includes arguments from the whole, from the parts, from efficient causes, from matter, from natural form, and from end. A short example may help to clarify Boethius' method. Let us suppose that we are debating the question of whether justice is good. One line of argument would proceed this way: if happiness is good, then justice is good, since the end of justice is to produce happiness. This argument rests on the topical principle that all things that have a good end are themselves good (1189D). The topic is intrinsic since it relies on a consequence following from the term "justice", and the specific consequence is "from end". All topical principles that can be differentiated on the grounds that they make

---

10. Themistius' commentary on Aristotle's *Topics* is now lost. Some quotations from it, however, are found in the *Paraphrasis Topicorum* of Averroes. See Jan Pinborg, *Logic und Semantik im Mittelalter: Ein Ueberblick* (Stuttgart, 1972), pp. 23–6. There is a considerable controversy about the extent of Boethius' reliance on Themistius. For opposing views, see James Shiel, "Boethius' Commentaries on Aristotle," *Medieval and Renaissance Studies,* 4 (1958), 240–1, and Eleonore Stump, *Vivarium,* 77–93. The summary of topical theory that follows in this essay is based on book II of *De diff. top.* and deals only with Aristotelian (or, more properly, Themistian) theory. In book III, Boethius explicates Ciceronian theory and concludes with an attempt to synthesize the two topical systems. The Themistian scheme seems more important for Boethius, and for the sake of brevity and simplicity, I have summarized it alone in this paper.

use of the substance of a term of the question, or a consequence of that term, fall into the category of intrinsic topics.

Extrinsic topics draw their force from something outside the terms of the question. For example, one can argue that the heavens are spherical because all those who are expert in astronomy uphold this view (1190B–C). The principle in this argument is that one should not doubt the opinions of experts. But this principle is in no way justified by the terms of the question, since expert opinion is something quite distinct from and unrelated to the designation of the terms themselves. Thus, this topic is extrinsic. In addition to the topic "from opinion on the matter," extrinsic topics include arguments from similars, from the greater, from the lesser, from proportion, from opposites, and from transumption.

Finally, Boethius recognizes a topical division intermediate between the intrinsic and extrinsic. This category has three members—inflection, conjugates, and division (1192B). The rationale for this category is not entirely clear, but we can gather some idea of its purpose by considering the first two types of topics within it. Both inflection and conjugates are arguments based on the form of a word. For example, if we acknowledge that something done justly is good, we must admit that justice itself is good (1192A). The proof comes from a grammatical modification of the term. In such cases, Boethius contends that the argument depends neither on the substance of the terms, nor on something entirely alien to the terms, and so he must make allowance for topics that are intermediate between the two extremes.[11]

In sum, the first three books of De differentiis topicis specify two basic meanings for an argumentative topic. A topic is both an abstract premise that expresses a basic mode of inference and a heading for a class of arguments.[12] In the first sense, Boethius views topics as self-evident, indemonstrable propositions that generate further and more specific propositions; these fundamental propositions are top-

---

11. In Book III, Boethius deals with Cicero's doctrine in *Topica*. Boethius notes that Cicero lists only two basic types of *differentiae*, intrinsic and extrinsic. He then presents a detailed analysis indicating the relationship between the Themistian and Ciceronian topical systems. See 1200B–1206B, especially the diagrams at 1202C–D and 1206B. McKeon's judgment that Boethius reduces the topical schemes of Cicero and Themistius to a single system seems essentially correct. See "Rhetoric in the Middle Ages," *Speculum*, 17 (1942), p. 10.

12. Cf. Chaim Perelman and L. Olbrechts-Tyteca, *The New Rhetoric: A Treatise on Argumentation*, trans. John Wilkinson and Purcell Weaver (Notre Dame and London: U. Notre Dame Press, 1969), p. 83.

ical principles, and they serve as the atomic units of argumentation. In another sense, he views topics as *differentiae* that allow the theorists to cluster principles together into molecular structures. These topical differences provide the organizational basis for a theory of topics. Finally, Boethius subdivides *differentiae* into three classes according to whether the argument draws its strength from the terms of the question, from something beyond the terms, or from something between these two categories.

II. RHETORICAL TOPICS

The whole of book four is devoted to rhetoric. It begins with a statement of purpose:

> Any careful observer who examines the title of this work will naturally expect from us, writing as we are about topical differences, not merely an exposition of how dialectical topics are distinguished from one another, and how rhetorical topics are distinguished from one another, but also (and this is important) a differentiation between dialectical topics on the one hand and rhetorical topics on the other (1205C).[13]

To achieve this goal, Boethius proceeds by analyzing the general differences between rhetoric and dialectic as faculties. His method is based on the assumption that "once the differences and similarities between dialectic and rhetoric have been demonstrated, the points of resemblance and disparity of the topics that serve these faculties must necessarily be inferred from the faculties themselves" (1205C).[14]

At 1206D, Boethius summarizes the differences between rhetoric and dialectic:

> . . . all the differences between the two faculties lie in subject matter, methodology, and goal: in subject matter, because the subject matter of thesis and hypothesis are their respective domains; in methodology, because dialectic proceeds by interrogation, rhetoric by uninterrupted discourse and because dialectic indulges in complete syllogisms, and rhetoric in enthymemes; in goal, because rhetoric seeks to persuade the judge, while dialectic tries to extract what it wants from the adversary.[15]

---

13. Si quis operis titulum diligens examinator inspiciat, cum de Topicis differentiis conscribamus, non id a nobis tantum exspectare debebit, ut locorum inter se dialecticorum, vel etiam rhetoricorum differentias demus, verum id multo magis ut dialecticos locos a rhetoricis segregemus. . . .

14. Ostensa enim dialecticae ac rhetoricae similitudine ac dissimilitudine, ab ipsarum facultatum necesse est formis etiam locorum qui eisdem facultatibus deserviunt communitates discrepantiasque ducamus.

15. . . . omnis earum differentia vel in materia, vel in usu, vel in fine est constituta: in materia, quia thesis atque hypothesi materia quidem utrisque subjecta

The difference in subject matter (*materia*) is the most important, and we should note it carefully. Boethius maintains that the subject of dialectic is the thesis. A thesis is a question proposed for debate that makes no reference to particular circumstances. (Thesis vero est sine circumstantiis quaestio, 1205C). Rhetoric, on the other hand, deals with the hypothesis, a question that is framed by circumstances. (Rhetorica vero de hypothesibus, id est de quaestionibus circumstantiarum multitudine inclusis, tractat et disserit, 1205C). Circumstances consist of such factors as person, place, time, motive, and means, and the presence of these considerations marks the difference between dialectical and rhetorical subjects of argument. Thus, to cite a commonly used example, the question, Should a man marry?, is a thesis, but the question, Should Cato marry?, is a hypothesis. In other words, one faculty deals with abstract issues, the other with concrete issues.[16] As we shall soon observe, this basic distinction between the subject matter of rhetoric and dialectic is a crucial step in the formation of Boethius' theory of rhetorical topics.

Following the introductory remarks on the nature of rhetoric and dialectic, Boethius presents a brief summary of the art of rhetoric as a whole[17] and a conventional discussion of the status

---

est; in usibus, quod haec interrogatione, illa perpetua oratione disceptat, vel quod haec integris syllogismi, illa vero enthymematibus gaudet; in fine vero, quod haec persuadere judici, illa quod vult ab adversario extorquere conatur.

16. The distinction between the thesis and hypothesis can be traced back to the Hellenistic rhetorician Hermagoras of Temnos. See George Kennedy, *The Art of Persuasion in Greece* (Princeton, N.J.: Princeton U. Press, 1963), pp. 304–6. Hermagoras included both the thesis and hypothesis within rhetoric. In *De inventione* (I.8), Cicero attempted to refute Hermagoras by maintaining that the thesis went beyond the interests of the rhetorical theorist. In later works, however, Cicero changed his position (*Partitiones oratoriae*, 17, and *Topica*, 82). The relationship between the thesis and hypothesis became a matter of some controversy in later Latin rhetoric; see: Quintilian, III.5.10; Augustine, *De rhetorica*, 5–6, in C. Halm, *Rhetores latini minores* (1863; rpt. Frankfurt: Minerva, 1963), pp. 139–40; Sulpitius Victor, *Institutiones oratoriae*, 2–3, Halm, pp. 314–315; Isidore, *Origines*, II.15, Halm, p. 515, and the anonymous *Excerpta rhetorica*, Halm, p. 585.

17. At 1207A, Boethius notes the problem of attempting to understand the cohesiveness of rhetoric as an art (quanta enim sibimet ars rhetorica cognatione jungatur). He complains that earlier writers only give rules about details and ignore the art as a whole. Boethius then claims to present an original account of the art, dividing it into nine parts: genus, species, subject matter (*materia*), parts of rhetoric, instrument, parts of the instrument, task of the orator, duty of the orator, and goal (1206B–1209A). For comments on the significance of this scheme, see Richard McKeon, *Speculum*, 10–11. While the basic classifications in Boethius' system differ from the standard analysis of rhetoric, he retains almost all of the traditional precepts of the art. His rearrangement of categories in this section of the treatise seems far less

system.[18] He then turns to his main task, the analysis of the topics of rhetorical invention. At first reading, this section of the treatise (1212A–1215B) appears to be nothing more than a commentary on Cicero's *De inventione.* Closer examination, however, reveals that the section has an important argumentative function.

At *De inventione* I.34–43, Cicero discusses the topics of *confirmatio,* the fourth part of the forensic oration. These topics fall into two areas, the attributes of the person and of the act. The attributes of the person are divided into eleven classes,[19] and the attributes of the act into four. In the latter category, Cicero notes that some attributes are coherent with the act itself; some are considered in connection with the performance of the act; some are adjuncts of the act, and some are a consequence (*consecutio*) of the act. In analyzing the topics of rhetorical invention, Boethius follows this Ciceronian pattern very closely; he retains the same divisions and sub-divisions of the subject and sometimes even borrows phrases from Cicero. Nevertheless, he does add one further consideration, the seven circumstances involved in a rhetorical case (i.e. who?, what?, why?, how?, where?, when?, and "with what assistance?").[20] and he correlates these circumstances with the various divisions of the Ciceronian topical scheme.

Boethius spends little time dealing with the attributes of the individual. Topics within this category refer to the circumstance Boethius calls "who?". Such topics do not attempt to resolve the conjectural issue of who committed the crime, but rather bear on the character of the persons involved in the case. Boethius repeats the eleven divisions of this topic, but does not elaborate on them.

The attributes of the act, however, are the subject of detailed analysis. The first division under this heading consists of attributes coherent with the act itself (*continentia cum ipso negotio*). Topics in this category relate to what was done and why it was done (to the

---

important to me than his analysis of the relationship between rhetorical and dialectical topics at the end of the fourth book. For reasons argued later in this paper, I believe that the fixed relationship he specifies for the topics of the two faculties signaled a major departure from traditional theories concerning the nature of rhetorical argument.

18. 1209B–1210C. As Boethius acknowledges, this section of the work is based on *De inventione.* See *De inv.,* I. 10–11; 14–6, and 17–18.

19. *De inv.,* I.34. Ac personis has res attributas putamus: nomen, naturam, victum, fortunam, habitum, affectionem, studia, consilia, facta, casus, orationes. These same categories are repeated by Boethius at 1212D.

20. 1212D.

"what?" and "why?" circumstances). Such topics refer to the specific
act in question, and they focus on the actual deeds committed before, during and after the act, and the motivation for the act. Thus,
they consider those things that are implicit within the subject of the
argument.

Attributes connected with the performance of the act encompass
the four remaining circumstances, the "how?", "when?", "where?",
and "with what assistance?". Topics in this category do not consider
the deeds implicit in the act. Instead, they focus on attendant circumstances necessary for the performance of any given act. In a sense,
these topics deal with conditions that are necessary but not sufficient
causes of an action. Circumstances such as time, place, opportunity,
means, and manner can exist independent of any specific act, but
no act can occur in the absence of such conditions (1213D). Thus,
while topics in this category do not govern the consideration of the
act itself, they are intimately connected with the act. These topics,
then, are similar to dialectical topics inherent in the subject under
consideration (1214A). (Presumably, Boethius is arguing that they
are analogous to those intrinsic topics proceeding from the consequents of a substance.)

The third division, the adjuncts of the act (*adjuncta negotio*), takes
the rhetorician farther away from the specific act itself. This is a topic
of comparison in which the arguer considers other cases that bear
some relationship to the case at hand. The first two types of attributes
generate arguments based on something implicit within the act, or
something inseparably connected with it, but the adjuncts yield
proofs only on a comparative basis (1214C). Still following Cicero,
Boethius indicates that there are seven modes of drawing an inference
through comparison: from species, from genus, from opposite, from
outcome, from greater, from lesser, and from equals. These topics
are also used in dialectic, but Boethius adds the qualification that
the rhetorical arguments do not arise from "oppositeness but from
an opposite case, not from similarity, but from a similar case"
(1214C).

The final division is consequence (*consecutio*). Neither Cicero nor
Boethius provides a clear explanation of this topical heading. Cicero
maintains that this group of topics deals with things that ensue after
the event (*quae gestum negotium consequentur*, I.43). Boethius,
however, maintains that consequence refers either to what precedes

or to what follows the act (*rem gestam vel antecedit, vel etiam conse-
quitur,* 1214C). The terminology is a bit confusing, but the concept
is reasonably clear. Apparently, this category encompasses things that
occur before or after the act that have no direct bearing on the facts
of the case, but that might color our perception of it. Thus, it would
include an argument concerning the name that we should apply to
the act, since the issue in this case is semantic rather than factual.
This category also includes arguments based on what we would expect
to happen to a guilty defendant after he committed the crime.[21]

Having presented this analysis of the topics in *De inventione* I.34–
43, Boethius can argue that rhetorical topics fall under the same
categories of topical difference that operate in dialectical theory.
Topics dealing with the seven circumstances of the case are all inseparably connected with the act itself. Hence, the attributes of the
individual, the circumstances coherent with the act, and the circumstances connected with the performance of the act provide intrinsic
topics. On the other hand, the topic of consequence draws materials
from considerations outside the act and is therefore extrinsic. Adjuncts of the act generate topics based on comparison, and the comparison involves the relationship of something outside the act to the
act itself. In this sense, the adjuncts produce topics intermediate
between the other two categories.

This analysis is consistent with Boethius' intent to effect a complete
synthesis of topical theory. Even the topics of rhetoric respond to
Themistius' basic divisions since, like their dialectical counterparts,
all rhetorical topics can be classified as intrinsic, extrinsic, or intermediate in relation to the subject at hand. In dialectic, this classification depends on whether the topics bear directly on the subject and
predicate terms of the question in dispute. In rhetoric the distinction
centers on whether the arguments are drawn from circumstances
linked to the act in question or from things beyond the act. There is
a difference in subject matter, but (presumably) since the *differentiae*
accurately index types of inferential principles, topics governed by the

---

21. See Victorinus' commentary on *De inventione,* I. 28, Halm, p. 230. Victorinus
breaks the topic of consequence into two subdivisions, the one concerning the person
and the other concerning the nature of the act. In the former case, arguments are
based on what men thought of the perpetrator of the act after it was done. In the
latter, the argument is based on the inevitable consequences of certain kinds of acts
(e.g. madness that follows parricide).

same *differentiae* must be similar to each other. Thus, Boethius can assert that the affinities between rhetorical and dialectical topics are apparent: "Both faculties use essentially the same topics" (1215C).[22]

What then are the differences between rhetorical and dialectical topics? To answer this question, Boethius returns to the issue of subject matter and to his earlier analysis of the basic differences between the two faculties. Just as dialectic deals with the general question, or thesis, and rhetoric with the specific question, or hypothesis, so also "their topics are differentiated by the breadth of the one and the narrow scope of the other" (1215D).[23] Unfettered by particular circumstances, dialectical topics point to the very genus of argument *qua* argument. But rhetorical topics are circumscribed by particulars and draw their proofs from the material of the genus. Thus, dialectical topics are broader in scope and prior in nature, since the general modes of inference they indicate encompass the particular arguments used by rhetoricians. Both faculties rely on the same processes of inference, but dialectic treats the forms of inference, while rhetoric deals only with concrete manifestations of those forms.

Boethius further clarifies his point by citing a short example. Let us suppose that a man is accused of drunkenness, and we wish to defend him. One line of argument available is to assert that this man never overindulged and therefore could not have been drunk. The immediate rationale for this inference is that since drunkenness is a kind of overindulgence, where there is no overindulgence, there can be no drunkenness. As the argument stands, it is rhetorical in that it involves a specific person acting in a specific set of circumstances. But its ultimate justification rests on an abstract dialectical rule—i.e. that the genus never abandons the species. Thus, Boethius concludes: "Dialectic seeks proofs based on the qualities themselves, while rhetoric seeks proofs based on the things that partake of the quality. The dialectician's proofs are based on the quality of similarity, the rhetorician's on a similar case, that is, on something that has taken on the quality of similarity. In the same way, the dialectician works from oppositeness, while the rhetorician works from an opposite case" (1216C).[24]

---

22. . . . quidem ipsi pene in utrisque facultatibus versantur loci . . .
23. . . . ita etiam eorum loci ambitu ex contractione discreti sunt.
24. Dialectica enim ex ipsis qualitatibus, rhetorica ex qualitate suscipientibus rebus argumenta vestigat. Ut dialecticus ex genere, id est ex ipsa generis natura, rhetor ex ea re quae genus est; dialecticus ex similitudine, rhetor ex simili, id est ex ea re quae similitudinem cepit. Eodem modo ille ex contrarietate, hic contrario.

The fifteenth-century humanist Lorenzo Valla once described Boethius as "more a lover of dialectic than rhetoric."[25] Valla was referring specifically to the way in which Boethius constructed arguments, but there is nothing theoretical in De differentiis topicis that would cause us to modify his judgment. Boethius' conclusion is that rhetorical topics derive their force from the abstract propositional rules provided by dialectic. In effect, rhetorical argumentation becomes a subordinate part of dialectical theory. Dialectic governs the genus of argumentation, and rhetoric is a species of that genus.

III. IMPLICATIONS

Since rhetoric and dialectic both deal with the process of constructing arguments, they compete for the attention of students of argumentation. The rivalry between the two arts can be traced back to the time of Plato, and the controversy remains lively at least until the end of the sixteenth century. Short of an outright rejection of one of these arts, the issue allows for three possible solutions: (1) rhetoric and dialectic may be viewed as parallel and coequal arts devoted to different aspects of the same process; (2) dialectic may be subordinated to rhetoric, or (3) rhetoric may be subordinated to dialectic. The choice involved in this matter is more than a technicality, since it virtually forces a theorist to make a decision about the ultimate function of argumentative discourse.

The relationship between rhetoric and dialectic, then, raises issues of great theoretical importance for historians of rhetoric. These issues are difficult to approach in the abstract. Consequently, it is convenient to rely on an analysis that permits comparison of theories advocating alternative solutions to the problem. Furthermore, such a comparison offers an approach for setting De diff. top. IV within the context of the history of rhetorical theory. It should, therefore, aid in the attempt to understand the reason for and the meaning of the influence that this work had on later medieval rhetoric.

Since Boethius clearly advocates the subordination of rhetoric to dialectic, his position can serve as a touchstone for a comparative analysis. Aristotle, I believe, provides an example of a theory that allows for relative parity between the two arts, and certain Renaissance humanists present the third alternative, the subordination of dialectic

25. Quoted in Jerrold E. Seigel, *Rhetoric and Philosophy in Renaissance Humanism: The Union of Wisdom and Eloquence from Petrarch to Valla* (Princeton, N.J.: Princeton U. Press, 1968), p. 157.

to rhetoric. In all three cases, the role of topics seems especially important.

Aristotle's conception of the relationship between rhetoric and dialectic is complex and difficult to understand. We certainly do not have time for an adequate explanation of the issue in this essay. Nevertheless, it is fair to say that Aristotle's position differs markedly from the theory presented in *De differentiis topicis*. The contrast is indicated in the opening line of the *Rhetoric*: "Rhetoric is the counterpart of dialectic."[26] As Cope explicates the term "anti-strophos" (counterpart), it represents rhetoric as "an art independent of, though analogous to Dialectics, but not growing out of it, nor included under it. . . . The term antistrophos, therefore, applied to the two arts, seems to represent them as co-ordinate opposites, or opposites in the same row. They are sister arts, with general resemblances and specific differences."[27]

A number of these specific differences are spelled out in terms of topics. One of the most obvious of these stems from Aristotle's contention that rhetorical proof depends not only on the ability to reason logically, but also on the ability to understand human character and emotions (1356^{a}22–25). As a consequence, he devotes a good part of the second book of the *Rhetoric* to an analysis of topics designed to put the audience into "the right frame of mind."[28] These ethical and emotional aspects of rhetorical persuasion are ignored totally by Boethius.

The consideration of audience leads to an even more fundamental distinction between rhetoric and dialectic in Aristotelian theory. In dialectic, arguments are evaluated on the basis of the relationships among the terms in the propositions. In rhetoric, arguments are evaluated according to their effect on a particular audience. McKeon indicates the application of this distinction to the topics of the two faculties:

> In dialectic the principles of discussion are found in the distinction between definition, genus, property, and accident; but in rhetoric they are derived from the view of the facts that the speaker can make acceptable to the audience, and the example, enthymeme, and maxim must therefore be considered in terms of a second group of common-places

---

26. Aristotle, *Rhetoric*, 1354^{a}1.
27. Edward M. Cope, *The Rhetoric of Aristotle with a Commentary*, rev. ed. by J.E. Sandys (Cambridge: At the University Press, 1877), I, 1–2.
28. 1377^{b}24.

that bear not on the plausibility of arguments relative to their alternatives, but in their plausibility relative to the person addressed. In dialectic no separate consideration of the audience is required. . . . In rhetoric, on the contrary, the audience addressed determines both the subject matter appropriate to its interests . . . and also the principles that may be used effectively in the general common-places appropriate to arguments.[29]

Thus, Aristotle conceives of a type of argumentation in which topics refer both to the affective and cognitive states of an audience. No such conception is possible in Boethius, since his basic presuppositions require him to refer all rhetorical topics back to the propositional principles and *differentiae* that inhere in the faculty of dialectic.

Aristotle provides us with a diversified approach to the arts of argumentative discourse. He recognizes certain techniques of invention and modes of inference common to all types of argument, but he also indicates that different subject matters and different ends alter the character of arguments. Thus, he allows rhetoric and dialectic to coexist on a relatively equal footing with each other. Both arts serve important functions in dealing with different types of situations.

Humanist theorists of the fifteenth and sixteenth centuries implicitly reject this balanced perspective. Their thinking originates in presuppositions antithetical to those of Boethius, and it eventuates in an equally radical, though totally different, conception of the relationship between rhetoric and dialectic. Holding that persuasive eloquence is the highest end of discourse, the humanists place more emphasis on the social and political effects of language than on propositional consistency. Dialectical topics are useful sources for inventing arguments, but the rules of dialectic have no intrinsic value; they are important only insofar as they aid in the pursuit of eloquence. Consequently, the humanists tend to regard dialectic as ancillary to rhetoric.[30] At least this seems to be the position of Lorenzo Valla and a number of his successors.

---

29. Richard McKeon, "Aristotle on Language and the Arts of Language," in R.S. Crane, *et al.*, (eds.), *Critics and Criticism: Ancient and Modern* (Chicago: U. Chicago Press, 1952), p. 222.

30. The attempt to reform dialectic by making it more responsive to the problems of practical communication was one of the noteworthy characteristics of the humanist movement. Among other works, see: Walter Ong, *Ramus, Method, and the Decay of Dialogue* (Cambridge, Mass.: Harvard U. Press, 1958); Quirinus Breen, "The Terms 'Loci Communes' and 'Loci' in Melanchthon," *Church History*, 16 (1947), 197–209,

Valla is a particularly vehement apologist for rhetoric. In the preface to the second book of *Disputationes dialecticae*, Valla expresses his belief in the inferior status of dialectic: "Dialectic is nothing other than a type of refutation, and refutations themselves are part of invention. Invention is one of the five parts of rhetoric."[31] This argument, of course, depends upon a rather narrow definition, but it stems from a broad view of the function of human learning. In rejecting scholastic formal logic, Valla issues a call for thinkers to address themselves to problems of practical consequence. The search for metaphysical truth is futile and dangerous, futile because it sets an impossible goal and dangerous because it diverts men from the authentic problems of the community. The pursuit of knowledge should be directed toward social and political ends.

This epistemological stance lends itself to a reinterpretation of the status of rhetoric. According to the social criterion for knowledge, what people believe is far more important than what the rules of inference tell them they ought to believe. Thus, Valla believes that the rules of language and all decisions about them should belong to the people,[32] and it is persuasive eloquence, not philosophical method, that moves the people.[33]

A number of later humanists pursue the line of inquiry opened up by Valla, and the attempt to reform topical logic is one of their primary interests. In the later fifteenth century, for example, Rudolph Agricola proposes major changes in topical theory based on

---

and "The Subordination of Philosophy to Rhetoric in Melanchthon," *Archiv für Reformationsgeschichte,* 43 (1952), 13–28; James Richard McNally, "Dux Illa Directrixque Artium: Rudolph Agricola's Dialectical System," *Quarterly Journal of Speech,* 52 (1966), 337–47, and "Rector et Dux Populi: Italian Humanists and the Relationship between Rhetoric and Logic," *Modern Philology,* 67 (1969), 168–76; Cesare Vasoli, *La dialectica e la retorica dell'Umanesimo: "Invenzione" e "Metodo" nella cultura del XV e XVI secolo* (Milan: Feltrinelli, 1968); John Herman Randall, *The Career of Philosophy:* Vol I: *From the Middle Ages to the Enlightenment* (New York: Columbia U. Press, 1962), 230–55; Neal W. Gilbert, *Renaissance Concepts of Method* (New York: Columbia U. Press, 1960), pp. 67–92, and Lisa Jardine, *Francis Bacon: Discovery and the Art of Discourse* (Cambridge: Cambridge U. Press, 1974), pp. 1–58.

31. *Opera omnia,* ed. by Eugenio Garin (Turin: Monumenta Politica et Philosophica Rariora, 1962), p. 693: "Nam quid aliud est dialectica, quam species confutationis, hae ipsae sunt partes inventionis. Inventio una est ex quinque rhetoricae partibus." The passage is quoted both by McNally, *Mod. Phil.,* 171, and Seigel, pp. 161–2.

32. Valla, *Opera,* p. 685, cited by Seigel, pp. 166–7.

33. See *ibid.,* pp. 137–69.

an expanded view of the function of dialectic.[34] In Agricola's scheme of things, dialectic serves as the "leader and directress of the arts,"[35] but dialectic itself is conceived in terms alien to Boethius and the Scholastic tradition. Agricola classifies dialectic as an art directed to the "ordering of language and speech," and he asserts that the end of speech is to allow one person to share his mind with another.[36] From this perspective, the psychological and persuasive effects of discourse, areas previously reserved for rhetoric, fall within the domain of dialectic. Likewise, dialectical topics become less closely connected with abstract rules of logic and more closely associated with the psychological interests of the orator. In fact, Agricola's dialectic incorporates many of the traditional rubrics of classical rhetorical theory; e.g. the enthymeme, the example, the status system, and ethical and emotional proofs. The net result is to "rhetoricize" dialectic. As McNally observes, Agricola's extension of the confines of dialectic leads to "the absorption of dialectic by rhetoric. For with the widening of the boundaries of dialectic so as to include nonformal linguistic considerations, the formal or syntactic aspects of language, which are the proper concern of logical science, were submerged under the psychological and pragmatic considerations proper to rhetoric."[37]

This tendency to absorb dialectic into rhetoric becomes even more apparent during the sixteenth century. Vives argues that "dialectic must forsake metaphysics and become part of rhetoric,"[38] and Nizolius wishes to have rhetoricians and grammarians replace dialecticians and metaphysicians as the leaders of the intellectual community.[39] Melanchthon goes so far as to subordinate philosophy as a whole to rhetoric.[40] Agreeing with Quintilian, Melanchthon holds that the

---

34. On Agricola, see Vasoli, pp. 147–82, Ong. pp. 92–130, and McNally, *Quarterly Journal of Speech*, 337–47. The citations below from Agricola's *De inventione dialectica* were brought to my attention by McNally's article. Selected passages from Agricola's treatise are translated by McNally in *Speech Monographs*, 34 (1967), 393–422.
35. *De inventione dialectica*, II.2.
36. *Ibid.*
37. McNally, *Quarterly Journal of Speech*, 343.
38. Randall, I, 238.
39. See Breen, *Archiv*, 20.
40. See *ibid.*, 13–27. Melanchthon's position, however, did not remain consistent throughout his career. See McNally, "Melanchthon's Earliest Rhetoric," in *Rhetoric: A Tradition in Transition*, ed. by Walter R. Fisher (East Lansing: Michigan State U. Press, 1974), 33–40.

highest achievement of a man is to become an orator, and he therefore favors practical wisdom over theoretical knowledge. Furthermore,
"the items of practical wisdom are the commonplaces of human
knowledge which are to be so presented as to benefit society."[41]
These commonplaces, of course, are the audience centered topics of
rhetoric that Boethius had not even acknowledged.

It is tempting to continue this inventory of theories about the
relative merits of rhetoric and dialectic. But enough has been said to
illustrate the differences among the three basic positions and to point
out the sharp distinction between Boethius' view on the matter and
that of Aristotle and the humanists. This distinction has an important
bearing on two issues of general theoretical interest. First, it has an
obvious effect on the placement of rhetoric within the hierarchy of
the arts, a matter of concern throughout the Middle Ages and Renaissance. It also has a more subtle and fundamental significance. Owing
to the amorphous character of rhetoric itself, the art is most easily
defined in terms of its relation to some other discipline. Dialectic
offers a particularly attractive model, and for this reason, the relationship between rhetoric and dialectic often implies an operational
definition of the boundaries of rhetorical theory.

Boethius is fully aware of the difficulties involved in attempting
to establish self-contained limits for the art of rhetoric. He notes that
a consideration of "the faculty as a whole" poses a "large and difficult problem. The cohesiveness of the art of rhetoric as a unit is not
an easy problem to contemplate; one can scarcely understand it when
explained, let alone discover it for one's self." (1207A).[42] The problem still persists and a modern writer pinpoints its origin in these
terms:

> But there is a double problem. First the rhetorical practices are themselves
> too sprawling for a focused theory to be induced from them, as Aristotle
> induced a poetic form from existing poetry. The guidance of an outside
> discipline is needed. But, second, if rhetoric is simply subsumed under
> the outside discipline, the freedom and sprawl which rhetoric needs on
> pragmatic grounds can be rigidified.[43]

---

41. Breen, *Archiv*, 22.
42. Nunc paulisper mihi videtur de tota admodum breviter facultate tractandum
magnum opus atque difficile. Quanta enim sibimet ars rhetorica cognatione jungatur, non facile considerari potest, vixque est etiam ut auditu animadverti queat,
nedum sit facile repertu.
43. Harold Zyskind, Review of *Rhetorical Dimensions in Criticism* by Donald
C. Bryant, *Philosophy and Rhetoric*, 7 (1974), 264.

In order to meet the first side of this dilemma, rhetoricians frequently resort to dialectic as a fixed point of reference. This strategy seems promising for two good reasons. First, the connection between rhetoric and dialectic has a clear logical basis, since both arts prescribe rules for constructing arguments. Second, dialectic offers a corrective to the main problem in devising a theory of rhetoric, since it is a much more rigorous and systematic art. Nevertheless, a practical student of persuasion cannot ignore the other side of the dilemma. Consequently, the relationship between rhetoric and dialectic raises a delicate problem; it may be formulated in a number of different ways, and as this formulation changes, so does the nature, subject matter, and integrity of the art of rhetoric.

Aristotle's *Rhetoric* strikes a fine balance between the order needed for systematic theory and the "sprawl" needed for practical application. He achieves this compromise by drawing an analogy between rhetoric and dialectic—an analogy sufficient to impose methodological form on the art, but not so potent as to obliterate the distinctive problems of rhetorical discourse. Relying on the enthymeme, the example, and the method of topics, Aristotle can produce rhetorical counterparts to the inferential principles used in dialectic. But he does not push the analogy too far, since he recognizes that the demands of subject matter and purpose differ markedly between the two arts. In this respect, the theory of genres is especially important. Through it, Aristotle is able to construct substantive boundaries within which rhetorical method can operate. The subjects of rhetoric, that is, cover only those matters relevant to forensic, deliberative, and epideictic discourse.[44] Once these broad areas are induced from existing practice, the peculiar status of rhetorical argument emerges with some clarity. Arguments devoted to public affairs are subject

---

44. *Rhetoric*, 1358ᵃ–1359ᵃ. Cicero clearly recognized the importance of Aristotle's limitations of the subject matter of rhetoric to these three genres: ". . . We call the material of the art of rhetoric those subjects with which the art of rhetoric and the power of oratory are concerned. However, some have thought that there are more and some less of these subjects. To cite one example, Gorgias of Leontini, almost the earliest teacher of oratory, held that the orator could speak better than anyone else on all subjects. Apparently he assigned to the profession a vast—and in fact infinite material. Aristotle, on the other hand, who did much to improve and adorn this art, thought that the function of the orator was concerned with three classes of subjects, the epideictic, the deliberative, and the judicial . . . According to my opinion, at least, the art and faculty of the orator must be thought of as concerned with this threefold material." (*De inv.*, I.7, trans. by H.M. Hubbell in the Loeb edition, Cambridge, Mass.: Harvard U. Press, 1949).

to special constraints. They deal with issues that can hardly ever be "demonstrated", and they are always subject to the beliefs and emotions of a mass audience. One cannot expect the rhetorician to achieve the same precision in argument demanded of a logician or a mathematician.[45] Nor can the rhetorician hope to succeed solely on the basis of propositional consistency. Hence, the devices borrowed from the *Organon* prescribe a general pattern for rationalizing rhetoric as method, but they must be altered significantly in order to meet the problems of the orator. The contrast is evident as one moves from the topics of dialectic to those of rhetoric; it is a movement from propositional analysis to audience analysis.

Boethius approaches the problem from a different perspective. His concern for rhetoric is purely intellectual and schematic. He has no interest in practical application. Moreover, rhetoric-in-practice does not place an effective constraint on his theorizing, since the culture of Ostrogothic Italy renders oratory on public affairs trivial. The dilemma of the classical theorist (i.e. the tension between theory and practice) no longer has any effect. This leaves Boethius free to attack the relationship between rhetoric and dialectic on an entirely theoretical level. As a result, he does what is forbidden to the practical rhetorician—he subsumes rhetorical argument under an outside discipline. The simplicity and elegance of this position is possible only because it ignores the ambiguities of actual public debate. For Boethius, the coherence of rhetoric presents a problem of classification rather than a problem of constructing a theory sufficient to account for rhetorical practice.

This analysis leads us back to the question raised in the introductory section of this essay: why did *De differentiis topicis* exercise such a significant influence on later medieval rhetorical theory? The answer lies in Boethius' implicit rejection of classical models premised on the attempt to adapt theory to the practices of law courts and legislative assemblies. The other writers of the late classical and early medieval period sought to reproduce classical lore on its own terms. Their definition of rhetoric and their treatment of its precepts were still tied to the functions of the classical orator.[46] Thus, the theory they preserved was anachronistic; it described types of discourse that no

---

45. *Nicomachean Ethics*, 1094[b] 24–27.

46. The civil question and the three traditional genres of oratory remain established fixtures in most late classical and early medieval rhetorical treatises. Fortunatianus' *Ars rhetorica* (I.1, Halm, p. 81) presents a typical example.

longer had any practical use; more important, it proceeded on the assumption that rhetoric was a separate entity that governed a special class of subjects. In *De differentiis topicis* these presuppositions were unnecessary. The civil question was located and subordinated in relation to the rules of propositional analysis. Whatever the subject matter of rhetoric, its arguments could be reduced to forms that were controlled by dialectic method.

The dissociation of rhetoric from a specific subject area proved congenial to the interests of later medieval scholars. The demise of the classical forms of oratory led to the destruction of the materials essential to the classical systems of the art. Consequently, the medieval conception and use of rhetoric departed radically from the classical tradition. Rhetoric more or less lost its status as a separate discipline and became an ancilla to a number of other arts (e.g. *dictamen* or poetry).[47] There were no special subjects for rhetorical discourse; instead there were various forms of discourse to which rhetorical devices could be applied. Moreover, as a corollary to this first development, there was no single and stable body of doctrine that characterized medieval rhetoric as a whole. The precepts of the classical writers formed a common source, but they took shape only insofar as they were used to aid in theory construction in some other art. Thus, as McKeon has observed, if we conceive of rhetoric in terms of a specific subject matter, it had little or no history during the Middle Ages.[48]

For these reasons, the fourth book of *De differentiis topicis* had an influence that transcended its original purpose. Boethius' intent was to fit rhetorical topics within his general scheme of topical invention. But this seemingly narrow purpose involved a number of complications. Since topics formed the root source of invention in both rhetoric and dialectic, a comparison of the topics of the two arts required a comparison of the arts themselves. In characterizing the art of rhetoric, Boethius felt no responsibility to account for the diversity of rhetorical practice as it had been defined by the classical authorities. He, therefore, could view the topics of rhetoric as special instances of dialectical topics, emphasizing their logical form and ignoring their function in relation to the audience. And once he had taken this step, his argument implied that rhetoric was subordinate to dialectic, that rhetorical invention was coherent only in relation to

---

47. Murphy, *Rhetoric in Middle Ages,* pp. 87–8.
48. McKeon, *Speculum,* p. 3.

principles outside the art, and that rhetorical method could be derived without reference to the audience. Thus, the internal logic of the situation led to a progression from a theory of topics to an implied theory of the status of rhetoric as an art. As Boethius worked his way through this progression, he formulated a conception of rhetoric that broke with the classical tradition and anticipated the evolution of the art in the later Middle Ages.

In a seminal essay on medieval rhetoric, Richard McKeon urges scholars to expend less effort enumerating specific rhetorical devices and to pay closer attention to conceptions of the matter and function of rhetoric as they evolve through various stages of historical development.[49] If we are to accept his advice, the study of the relationship between rhetorical and dialectical topics demands careful attention. Differences between the topics of the two arts are often expressed in highly technical terms. Yet the choices that a theorist makes on this issue reveal a great deal about his conception of what subjects are proper to rhetoric and how the art ought to function. In *De differentiis topicis,* the theory of rhetorical topics indicates a severely rationalistic approach to the art of argumentative discourse. According to Boethius, rhetorical subjects are reducible to abstract propositional categories, and rhetorical arguments function as derivatives of the pure forms of inference specified in dialectical theory. Propositional logic governs the whole field of argumentation; the function of the audience is ignored. Aristotle's bifurcated application of topical theory and the rhetorically oriented theories of the Renaissance humanists both present a striking contrast to Boethius' position. The differences among these three approaches have implications that go far beyond the technical apparatus of the art of argumentation. They underscore fundamental disagreements about the nature and purpose of human discourse.

---

49. *Ibid.*

From Antiquity to the Renaissance: Glosses and Commentaries on Cicero's *Rhetorica*

JOHN O. WARD

OF ALL THE ARTS and sciences developed and given a systematic structure in antiquity, the art of rhetoric stands out today as a curious and unstable hybrid. Its birth and rapid development in the ancient world represent an intriguing phenomenon; the cultural historian is even more puzzled by the endurance of the art for well over a thousand years after the political disintegration of the Roman Empire. No less surprising, perhaps, rhetoric today is no longer the systematic study it was in ancient times. What one age, however, sees fit to develop and codify, another to study intensively and extend, and a third to abandon, will have a certain primary value as an index, a yardstick of cultural, and perhaps more broadly, social change. Rhetoric has already begun to attract historians who are aware of these historical tendencies.[1]

---

1. I have expanded a little on this subject in my doctoral dissertation, "*Artificiosa Eloquentia* in the Middle Ages," Diss. Toronto 1972, I, ch. 1, where, amongst others, the following references are cited: D. C. Bryant, ed., *The Rhetorical Idiom: Essays in Rhetoric, Oratory, Language, and Drama presented to H. A. Wichelns* (Ithaca N.Y., 1958), pp. 44, 59, 68, 69, 88, 90–1, 271 etc.; E. P. J. Corbett, *Classical Rhetoric for the Modern Student* (Oxford, 1965), pp. 544–573; W. J. Ong, "Tudor Writings on Rhetoric," *Studies in the Renaissance*, 15 (1968), pp. 45–6, 52, 64, 68 and his *Ramus: Method and the decay of dialogue* (Cambridge Mass., 1958), esp. ch. 12; I. A. Richards, *The Philosophy of Rhetoric* (1936; New York, 1965), pp. 5–6; D. E. Grosser, "Studies in the Influence of the *Rhetorica ad Herennium* and Cicero's *De inventione,*" Diss. Cornell 1953, pp., 201–59; W. S. Howell, "English Backgrounds of Rhetoric," in *History of Speech Education in America: background studies* (New York, 1954), pp. 3–47, with the same author's *Logic and*

Any first acquaintance with the classical *ars rhetorica* will immediately suggest the conclusion that it should never have survived the passing of antiquity. Even at its height it enjoyed no unchallenged and unequivocal status as a discipline. It fluctuated between a variety of roles: a total scheme of public education for the leaders of society; a system of preparation and instruction for legal advocates; a simplified set of dialectical and thematic procedures for oral delivery before popular audiences; a set of devices for adding glitter and flourish to displays of public oratory and recitations, or polish to prose and verse writing. By late antiquity the technical terminology of the art had become complicated and overelaborate, bearing unmistakable signs of the circumstances for which it had developed: it was a system peculiar to Graeco-Roman antiquity and, on the face of it, an unlikely candidate for export to another age or culture where the pressing context of popular persuasion which gave it birth was not present.[2]

In its one-thousand-year ancient life-span, rhetoric spawned a long series of textbooks and treatises, many of which have not survived. Those that have fall into two broad classes: treatises distinguished by breadth of approach or depth of analysis, which are still occasionally read with profit today; and the manuals or handbooks for day to day training: terminological jungles, each born and bred for its age, and

---

Rhetoric in England 1500-1700 (Princeton, 1956); K. R. Wallace, *Francis Bacon on Communication and Rhetoric* (Chapel Hill, 1943), pp. 7 ff, with his "Francis Bacon on Understanding, Reason and Rhetoric," *Speech Monographs*, 38 (1971) 79 ff; M. McGee, "Thematic Reduplication in Christian Rhetoric," *Quarterly Journal of Speech*, 56 (1970), 201 ff; R. M. Weaver, *The Ethics of Rhetoric* (Chicago, 1953); M. Natanson and H. W. Johnstone Jr., *Philosophy and Argumentation* (University Park Penn., 1965), pp. xii–xiii, 29–30, 56, 88–92 etc.

Whilst the reader is referred for general bibliographical orientation to J. J. Murphy, *Medieval Rhetoric, a select bibliography* (Toronto, 1971), or, more discursively (if it is accessible), my dissertation already cited, the following contain insights on which I have relied in the early pages of the chapter, and basic information on classical rhetorical theory: E. H. Gombrich, "The Debate on Primitivism in Ancient Rhetoric," *Journal of the Warburg and Courtauld Institutes*, 29 (1966), 34; N. Struever, *The Language of History in the Renaissance* (Princeton, 1970), pp. 23, 27, 118 etc.; M. Untersteiner, *The Sophists*, trans. K. Freeman (Oxford, 1954), pp. 321 ff and ch. 9; Jean-Pierre Vernant, "Greek Tragedy: problems of interpretation" in *The Languages of Criticism and the Sciences of Man: the structuralist controversy*, ed. R. Macksey and E. Donato (Baltimore, 1970), pp. 273–289; J. Martin, *Antike Rhetorik, Technik und Methode* (Munich, 1974); H. Lausberg, *Handbuch der literarischen Rhetorik* (Munich, 1960); G. Kennedy, *The Art of Rhetoric in the Roman World* (Princeton, 1972).

2. For an extreme example of the complications inherent in ancient rhetorical terminology see J. O. Ward, "The *Constitutio Negotialis* in Antique Latin Rhetorical Theory," *Prudentia* (Auckland, N.Z.) 1, No. 2 (1969), 29–48. On the "pressing context of persuasion" that gave birth to oratory in Rome, see Kennedy, pp. 74–5.

seemingly bound for dinosauric extinction once that age had passed away. In the former class fall Aristotle's *Rhetoric,* Cicero's *De oratore* and Quintilian's *Institutes of Oratory.* Among the latter group may be mentioned the minor Latin rhetoricians edited by C. Halm in 1863, their Greek counterparts, and the two Latin manuals of late Republican Rome: Cicero's youthful *De inventione* and the anonymous, approximately contemporary, *Ad Herennium.* Of all these, perhaps the least impressive candidate for survival is the *De inventione,* which Cicero himself learned to speak of with disdain. It is an incomplete statement of the *ars rhetorica*; it is bald, derivative and badly organised. It deals almost exclusively with the finding and handling of arguments suited to the issues that advocates were called upon to treat in late Roman judicial courts.

Faced with these two categories of textbook, the postantique world might have been forgiven for taking neither up. The technical obscurity and aridity of the latter kind of text was matched by the unfamiliarity of the cultural climate that gave meaning and relevance to the former kind. The sophistic inheritance which lay behind the Roman art of rhetoric assigned language and the speaker (or writer) a much higher status than truth, in any suprahuman or absolute sense.[3] In so far as medieval Christendom reversed this emphasis it was likely to find the general assumptions underlying classical rhetoric and oratory increasingly foreign.

Certainly St. Augustine, whose *On Christian Doctrine* Book IV is usually seen as the *Magna Carta* of medieval rhetoric, implies that Christians can be made eloquent "not by teaching them the rules of eloquence, but by having them read and hear the expressions of the eloquent, and imitate them insofar as they are able to follow them" (*De doctrina* 4.3.5 and cf. 4.5.8, trans. D. W. Robertson Jr., N.Y., 1958, pp. 120, 122). Augustine quarrels not so much with the use of rhetorical ornament and structures in Christian sermon or treatise, as with the premises of an educational system that placed the systematization and learning of these above the inculcation of appropriate thought and content (cf. Augustine's emphasis upon clarity, *De doctrina* 4.8.22, 4.9.23, 4.10.24, etc.). The Augustinian emphasis upon 'matter' as opposed to 'discourse' (*De doctrina* 4.12.28) disparaged both the formal study of rhetoric and the textbooks inculcating it, despite an obvious interest in use and extension of the *tria genera dicendi* of classical rhetorical theory in Christian sermon and

---

3. Untersteiner; Struever, ch. 1.

exposition. From the discussion of rhetoric in the *De doctrina*, the Christian would have been pardoned for displaying attention simply to *Ad Herennium* Book IV and ignoring the *De inventione* altogether.[4]

With these credentials classical rhetoric must have seemed ill-suited to weather the centuries; and, indeed, such postclassical 'history' as it has acquired at the hands of medieval and Renaissance scholars of the present century is more the account of its misapplications and extensions than the history of the classical discipline itself.[5] The academic world of early Christianity, it has been argued, needed only certain portions of the classical *ars rhetorica*. It needed an elementary exegetical system for the reconciliation of contradictory texts; it could use a measure of *elocutio* to spread the Gospel effectively.[6] In a world without the classical judicial system, without a measure of political liberty to encourage deliberative oratory, and with panegyric transmuted into hagiography, the classical rhetorical manuals, insofar as they survived, could perform at best a kind of caretaker role, vestigial and anachronistic; they kept alight a spark, to ignite the fires of more specialised systems of medieval public persuasion from the eleventh century onwards: letter and official document composition, the art of composing effective prayers and sermons, the techniques for writing good verse.[7]

---

4. See *De doctrina* 4.20.39 etc., and Quadlbauer (n. 14 below). In "adapting" parts of the ancient rhetorical curriculum for Christian use, Augustine was preceded by Victorinus and followed by Rabanus Maurus and other medieval Christian scholars: see below, notes 36–51. On Augustine and rhetoric see Murphy T51, T97 and T33–T56 generally. Note also E. Auerbach, *Literary Language and Its Public in Late Latin Antiquity and in the Middle Ages*, trans. R. Manheim (New York, 1965), ch. 1 and esp. pp. 33 ff.

5. I have borrowed a phrase here from R. McKeon, "Rhetoric in the Middle Ages," *Speculum*, 17 (1942), 2. This article remains today the most learned introduction to the subject.

6. See R. McKeon, "The Transformation of the Liberal Arts in the Renaissance" in *Developments in the Early Renaissance*, ed. B. S. Levy (New York, 1972), p. 164.

7. Modern attempts at a "history" of medieval rhetoric are mentioned and discussed in McKeon, "Rhetoric in the Middle Ages," pp. 1–3, and my dissertation (above n. 1), I, ch. 1. It is particularly important to note the discussion and references in Struever, pp. 33–37. Murphy's recent *Rhetoric in the Middle Ages* is not up to the standards set in McKeon, "Rhetoric," pp. 1–3, and Struever, as cited. The attitude towards the medieval study of rhetoric I am discussing dies hard: see J. Contreni's assertion in his Michigan doctoral dissertation "The School of Laon from 850–930, its manuscripts and masters," 1971, p. 124: "Rhetoric, in the classical sense, was not studied in the ninth and tenth centuries. Instead, a highly practical form of rhetoric, the *ars dictaminis*, supplanted the art of the orator." The tendency to equate medieval study of classical rhetorical theory with *dictamen* and an abuse

In drawing such a picture of the classical art of rhetoric in the Middle Ages, historians have made a lopsided trio of the fundamental medieval arts of language: grammar and dialectic, disciplines that had more to offer in the abstract pursuit of theological truth, flourished, within school and without, but rhetoric was a rubric only, a file raised and labelled but with little in it, an art with the peculiar capacity of being something else as soon as it was subjected to scrutiny.

Such a picture played into the hands of modern students of the Renaissance, who found with satisfaction that the full Ciceronian programme of *eloquentia* had indeed undergone a recess in late antiquity, from which Petrarch, Bruni, Valla and other devoted students of the classics resurrected it in the fourteenth and fifteenth centuries. In one recent formulation, the decay and subsequent revival of the classical rhetorical perspective is seen as amounting to a fundamental dichotomy between the medieval and the Renaissance perspectives, the former devaluing language as a determinant of truth, the latter rediscovering it; the former adapting the world to theory, the latter allowing the experience of the world to prompt a variety of theories and literary formulations. Seen in this way, the classical rhetorical perspective emerges as a symptom of deeper diachronic cultural change, and the historian finds himself in a difficult territory where rhetorical documents (and, in a way, all documents are rhetorical) must be used as texts bearing some distinct but as yet ill-defined relationship to the larger subterranean movements of an age.[8]

At this point the reader will demand to know upon what evidence the current interpretation of rhetoric in medieval cultural life is

---

of the *colores* is readily apparent in G. Vallese, "Retorica Medioevale e Retorica Umanistica" (originally published in *Delta*, 1952), rpt. in the same author's *Da Dante ad Erasmo, studi di letteratura umanistica* (Naples, 1962), ch. 11. A fairly typical treatment of medieval rhetoric is ch. 5 of D. L. Clark, *Rhetoric and Poetry in the Renaissance* (N.Y., 1922). Cf. also M. W. Croll, *Style, Rhetoric and Rhythm* (New Jersey, 1966), p. 264.

8. See Struever as already cited n. 1 above, and her article "The Study of Language and the Study of History," *Journal of Interdisciplinary History*, 4 (1974), 401–415. A discussion of Struever's book will be found in my dissertation (I, 31–36), and in an article by David McRuvie in *Studium (The Record of the Sydney Medieval and Renaissance Group)*, No. 2 (March 1972). Struever has elaborated some of her ideas in a review of J. Seigel's *Rhetoric and Philosophy in Renaissance Humanism, History and Theory*, 11 (1972), 64–74. There are many broadening reflections in D. Newton-de-Molina's "Reflections on Literary Criticism and Rhetoric," *The Durham University Journal*, 65 (1972), 1–40.

based. The answer must be that, as so often happens, interpretation
has preceded research. Despite a recent upsurge of interest in the
quantitative aspects of medieval cultural history,[9] we are still nowhere
near the point at which we may assess the relative intensity of the
medieval study of classical and postclassical *auctores*. In the slow,
meditative cultural world of the Middle Ages, with its powerful
emphasis upon *auctoritas* and its accompaniment of interpretative
commenta, lecturae and *glosae*, a complete record of what manuscripts were read and copied, where and by whom, would provide a
fundamental quantitative base for an interpretation of cultural
trends. If all extant medieval library catalogues were systematically
itemised, and the provenance and contents of all surviving medieval
manuscript books grouped[10] and analysed, cultural history could be

9. On the need for a quantitative approach to intellectual history see Geoffrey
Barraclough in *The New York Review of Books*, xiv, No. 11 (4 June 1970), and J.
Vicens Vives, *Approaches to the History of Spain* (University of California Press,
1967), p. xx. There is no space here to discuss the quantitative movement, but note,
for instance, the massive labours of the Kommission zur Herausgabe des Corpus der
lateinischen Kirchenväter or of those engaged in the Leonine edition of the works of
St. Thomas Aquinas, Agostino Sottili's articles on the manuscripts of Petrarch in
recent numbers of *Italia Medioevale e Umanistica*, the new periodical *Revue d'histoire des textes*, and the increasing number of special manuscript studies such as
Colette Jeudy, "L'*Ars de nomine et verbo* de Phocas: manuscrits et commentaires
médiévaux, "*Viator*, 5 (1974), 61–156, or M. A. Rouse and R. H. Rouse, "The
Texts called *Lumen Anime*," *Archivum Fratrum Praedicatorum*, 41 (1971), 5–113.
   Margaret Gibson has counted Priscian MSS., *Scriptorium*, 26 (1972), 105–124,
and Paola Piacentini Persius MSS., *Saggio di un censimento dei manoscritti con-
tenenti il testo di Persio e gli scoli e i commenti al testo* (Rome, 1973). For further
references see pp. 9–10 of E. Pellegrin et al., *Les Manuscrits Classiques Latins de la
Bibliothèque Vaticane* (Paris, CNRS, 1975). The fruits to be derived from close study
of *all* extant MSS. of a particular work in a particular period are clear; see for instance,
M. Gibson, "The Study of the Timaeus in the eleventh and twelfth centuries,"
Pensamiento, 25 (1969), 183–194 (and note also her remarks in *Viator* 6[1975] p. 12).
Specialist studies of the growth of particular libraries, according to modern standards
of manuscript research will greatly deepen our understanding of medieval cultural
life. See, for instance, R. M. Thomson's "The Library of Bury St. Edmunds Abbey
in the eleventh and twelfth centuries," *Speculum*, 47 (1972), 617–645, and note the
work of J. Contreni (cited above n. 7): "A propos de quelques manuscrits de l'école
de Laon au IXᵉ siècle: découvertes et problèmes," *Le Moyen Age*, 78 (1972), 5–39;
"The Formation of Laon's Cathedral Library in the Ninth Century," *Studi medievali* 13 (1972), 919–939.
   10. On the assumption that works grouped together in a manuscript were studied
together, or were interconnected in some way, it would seem reasonable to pay more
attention to the manuscript context of particular works than has hitherto been the
case. See my dissertation, I, 407–418; Pellegrin as cited in the previous note, pp.
16–17; E. M. Sanford, "The Use of Classical Latin Authors in the Libri Manuales,"
Transactions of the American Philological Society, 55 (1924), 190 ff; M. Parkes in

written. Such a stage, however, lies far in the future. We are still, for the most part, reduced to speculating on the influence of a text without knowing just how widespread its use was. As an instance, one could cite the formative and relevant statements on *narratio* and *narratio historica* in the *Ad Herennium* and the *De inventione*: how far were such texts built into the educational cadre and how far did they unwittingly shape the medieval attitude to history-writing?[11]

In order to aid our assessment of the intensity and scope of the medieval and Renaissance interest in classical rhetoric, the present chapter focuses on one neglected but surprisingly extensive class of manuscript and early printed source material: the medieval and Renaissance commentaries and glosses on the *De inventione* and *Ad Herennium*, the principal witness to the vitality of the medieval rhetorical teaching tradition.[12]

This teaching tradition was basic to the survival of ancient rhetorical values. Without an educational cadre in which the details of the classical rhetorical system, however dessicated and arid, could be repeatedly inculcated, to form the sensibilities and literary attitudes of each new generation, the afterlife of the *ars rhetorica* in the Middle Ages would have been at an end, except perhaps in the case of isolated, vigorous, individuals. In turn, from the viewpoint of present-day study, without a knowledge of the teaching tradition, which is an essentially conservative element in society, the novelty of great attempts to see beyond the 'world vision' of a period can scarcely be measured.[13] Yet it is exactly this teaching tradition of which we are currently in the greatest ignorance.

D. Daiches and A. K. Thorlby, *Literature and Western Civilization,* ii (London, 1973), p. 562; N. G. Siraisi, *Arts and Sciences at Padua* (Toronto, 1973), p. 45; L. D. Reynolds and N. G. Wilson, *Scribes and Scholars,* 2nd ed. (Oxford, 1974), p. 73.

11. See my dissertation (above note 1), I, 399–407 with references, and, recently, R. D. Ray in *Viator,* 5 (1974), 57–58.

12. On the importance of the gloss and commentary on classical authors, see P. O. Kristeller, *The Classics and Renaissance Thought* (Cambridge Mass., 1955), p. 31 ("the two main types of medieval scholarly literature, the commentary and the question"), and his *Studies in Renaissance Thought and Letters* (Rome, 1956), p. 569, n. 45; my dissertation, II, 1 ff.; Pellegrin (above n. 9), pp. 15–16. Three volumes of the series *Catalogus Translationum et Commentariorum: Mediaeval and Renaissance Latin Translations and Commentaries* are now available (ed. P. O. Kristeller and F. E. Cranz). See in general, R. R. Bolgar, ed., *Classical Influences on European Culture A.D. 500-1500* (Cambridge, 1971), pp. 1–25.

13. I use the term "world vision" with L. Goldman's *The Hidden God* (London, 1969), in mind.

In the field of the classical art of rhetoric we have not yet succeeded in looking behind the idiosyncratic greater writers of the day to the educational cadre that formed them. Some names have begun to emerge from the mist, some texts have been isolated; but still our understanding of the teaching of the *ars rhetorica* lags far behind our knowledge of the other six liberal arts of the Middle Ages, as well as of the three philosophies and the three major sciences.[14]

14. Some scholarship on the rhetorical commentaries/glosses is mentioned in Murphy, *Medieval Rhetoric*, R28–44. More relevant studies are those by Dickey in *Medieval and Renaissance Studies*, 6 (1968); Rev. N. Haring in *Medieval Studies* 1964; Margareta Fredborg in *Université de Copenhague Cahiers de L'Institut du Moyen-Âge Grec et Latin*, Nos. 7 (1971), 11 (1973), 13 (1974); myself in *Viator*, 3 (1972); Professor Harry Caplan in *Of Eloquence, studies in ancient and medieval rhetoric* (Ithaca, 1970), pp. 247–270; F. Quadlbauer, "Die antike Theorie der *genera dicendi* im lateinischen Mittelalter," in *Öst. Akad. der Wiss. Philos.-Hist. Klasse*, 241, 2 (1962), reviewed in *Speculum*, 39 (1964), 333–4; and M. Wisén, *De Scholiis Rhetorices ad Herennium codice Holmiense traditis* (Stockholm, 1905). Konrad Burdach, as early as 1926, in editing a "schlesisch-Böhmische" letter collection from the beginning of the fifteenth century (in a manuscript from the Premonstratensian Church of Schägl in Oberösterreich) had occasion to deal briefly with the gloss tradition and the growth of the medieval study of the text of Cicero's *Rhetorica* (especially the *Ad Herennium*), but at that stage could speak only in generalities, having no basic manuscript material to cite (with the exception of Wisén and F. Marx's *editio maior* of the *Ad Herennium*; see K. Burdach, ed., *Vom Mittelalter zur Reformation*, vol. 5 [1926], especially pp. 59–74). However, the study of the rhetorical commentaries and glosses has not yet attained the sophistication that prevails in the study of the other *artes* as a result of the researches of Grabmann, Lottin, Smalley, Hunt, Bursill-Hall, Pinborg, Van de Vyver, Haskins, Clagett, Thurot and others. It is probable that even the literary *auctores* are better served; see, for instance, the article by Professor Bischoff in Bolgar, ed., *Classical Influences on European Culture*; R. E. Clairmont, "Glose in librum de Ludo Claudii Annei Senece," in *Rivista di Cultura Class. e Med.*, 16 (1974), 235–266; A. K. Clarke and P. M. Giles, *The Commentary of Geoffrey of Vitry on Claudian De Raptu Proserpinae* (Leiden, 1973); M. C. Edwards, *A Study of Six Characters in Chaucer's Legend of Good Women with reference to Medieval Scholia on Ovid's Heroides*, B.Litt. thesis Linacre College (Oxford, 1970); L. Frati, "Pietro da Moglio e il suo commento a Boezio," *Studi Mem. per la Storia dell'Università di Bologna*, 1st Ser., 5 (1920), 237–276; M. Jennings, "Lucan's Medieval Popularity: the exemplum tradition," *Rivista di Cultura Classica e Medioevale*, 16 (1974), 215–233 (with bibliography on editions of twelfth-century Orléans glosses); R. Sabbadini, "Giacomino da Mantova commentatore di Terenzio," in his *Classici e Umanisti da Codici Ambrosiani* (Fontes Ambrosiani II, Florence, 1933), pp. 69–85.
One should also mention the labours of P. Courcelle and D. K. Bolton (see a forthcoming issue of *Archives d'histoire doctrinale et littéraire*) and others on the glosses on Boethius' *De consolatione philosophiae*; of Cora Lutz, Ann Raia (see her dissertation "Barberini MSS 57–66 and 121–130," Diss. Fordham University 1965) and Claudio Leonardi on the Martianus Capella *De nuptiis* glosses, commentaries and manuscripts; of Ruth Dean and others on Nicholas Trevet's commentaries on classical authors.
An edition of Sedulius Scotus' Donatus glosses has just appeared from the Pon-

How far is this neglect warranted by the absence of source material? How extensively was classical rhetorical theory taught in the monasteries, cathedral schools and universities of the Middle Ages and Renaissance? How far did it succeed in retaining its classical guise in this teaching? What is the long term cultural significance of the answers to these questions? These are the problems to which the rest of this chapter will be devoted. Larger questions, such as the general influence of the training based on the material shortly to be outlined, and the motivation behind the persisting medieval and Renaissance study of the classical rhetorical texts, must for the moment be left aside.[15]

First of all, a brief idea of the extent of academic rhetorical material surviving from the Middle Ages and Renaissance must be obtained. Excluding for the time miscellaneous items,[16] we possess continuous, full commentaries on the *De inventione* and *Ad Herennium*, without a text, combined texts and commentaries in alternating paragraphs,[17] texts with extensive commentaries filling the margins of the pages (= my 'major glossed texts'), texts with significant or relatively

---

tifical Institute of Medieval Studies, Toronto, and work on Peter Helias' Priscian glosses is well advanced there. We even possess an edition of Radulphus de Longo Campo's gloss on Alan of Lille's *Anticlaudianus*, ed. Jan Sulowski (Polish Academy of Sciences, 1972); see his article in J. Kellera, ed., *Katolicyzm wczesnośrednio-wieczny* (Warsaw, 1973), p. 543. Marjorie Woods, a student of Margaret Nims, is currently extending the work of Manacorda, Wilmart, Stadder and Samuel Jaffe on the glosses on Geoffrey of Vinsauf's *Poetria Nova,* and an edition of at least one gloss should emerge from recent work in the field. By contrast, the only expected edition of a *rhetorica* gloss is Margareta Fredborg's edition of the *De inventione* and *Ad Herennium* commentaries by Thierry of Chartres. For the quadrivium see now G. R. Evans, 'The influence of quadrivium studies in the eleventh- and twelfth-century schools,' *Journal of Medieval History* 1 (1975), 151–164.

15. For some orientation in these problems see the works cited in n. 7 above, and Grosser as cited in n. 1 above.

16. I hope to provide an extensive discussion of all surviving manuscript and early printed evidence of glosses and commentaries on Cicero's *Rhetorica* in some future numbers of *Mediaeval Studies.* Because of limitations of space in the present chapter, the reader is referred to these fuller studies for proper documentation of the skeleton summary presented in the following pages. I hope in these *Mediaeval Studies* articles to notice a wide variety of "miscellaneous" material which, while interesting in itself and little noticed hitherto by scholars, does not formally contribute to surviving glosses/commentaries narrowly defined. For convenience, I will refer henceforward to these *Mediaeval Studies* articles as Ward, "Sources". Ultimately, Professor Caplan and I hope to provide a summary of this material for inclusion in the series *Catalogus Translationum* (cited above n. 12).

17. Some early Victorinus MSS are presented alternately with the text of the *De inventione,* and for two interesting later examples of the practice see MSS Milan, Ambros. I.142 inf. and Rome, Vatican, Bibl. Apost. Vat., Pal.lat.1461.

extensive commentaries only partially filling the margins (= my 'minor glossed texts'), and texts with, at most, a scatter of marginal and interlinear notes and headings (= my 'slight to not significant glossed texts'). 'Introductions' or *accessus* have also survived, usually preceding a (glossed) text of the *De inventione* or *Ad Herennium,* and we have a few collections of 'notes' on one or both texts, which are insufficiently systematic, or extensive, to merit use of the term 'commentary'. My survey of European and American libraries has covered both manuscript and printed material from approximately 350 A.D. to the early nineteenth century; but after 1600 A.D. I have confined my attention to printed versions of material originally published before that date, excluding new material.

Some cautions, however, are essential: I have not seen or otherwise checked the contents of *all* extant MSS containing copies of the *Ad Herennium* or *De inventione,* nor have I taken any account of texts which my investigation or a reliable catalogue reference have shown to contain no notes, headings or glosses whatsoever. I have not had an opportunity of consulting all the printed descriptions of manuscript holdings listed in Professor Kristeller's *Latin Manuscript Books.*[18] The printed descriptions are frequently incomplete or unreliable in their listings. Numerous libraries or collections of MS material have not yet been adequately catalogued in print, or, in some cases, catalogued at all, and whilst Professor Kristeller's *Iter Italicum* is a fundamental guide to some of this material, it emphasizes the humanist, rather than the medieval contents of the holdings surveyed. Only a fraction of once extant MSS has survived the ravages of time: preliminary attempts to construct MS stemmata for commentaries surviving in more than one codex suggests that many stages in the transmission of these texts are no longer represented among our extant manuscripts. Investigation of the relationship between different MSS of surviving commentaries and major glosses, and versions of them, has only recently been undertaken. Hence, the 'statistics' advanced below must be treated with great caution.[19]

For convenience I have divided my material into two groups: manuscripts and early printed books. Under the former I have so far had to take account of some 545 separate items; that is, separate

---

18. P. O. Kristeller, *Latin Manuscript Books before 1600,* 3rd ed. (Fordham University Press, 1965). My own work on the manuscript and early printed material was carried out in Europe 1966, 1972 and 1975.

19. For a good statement of the difficulties of working in this kind of material see C. Leonardi, "I codici di Marziano Capella," *Aevum,* 33 (1959), 484–5.

'works' (commentaries, *accessus,* collections of notes, sets of glosses, even one or two glosses where they are the only sign of a student's attention to a MS for a particular period). These items represent 391 individual MSS. Fifty-nine full scale commentaries have survived, of which almost half are extant complete, 22 *accessus* / collections of notes, 20 major glossed texts (= MGT), some 60 minor glossed texts (= MiGT) and 300 slight or not significant sets of glosses (= S/NSG).[20]

The rhetorical glosses do not reach the sumptuous magnificence of, for instance, Dionigi da Borgo's fourteenth-century commentary on Valerius Maximus, but some are extremely handsomely presented.[21] Very few individual authors are known to us by name, and, to complicate matters, we know of a number of scholars who certainly wrote commentaries, but whose work cannot be recognised among our extant MSS.[22] Our present information allows us to identify an interesting spectrum of authors whose glosses have for the most part survived complete. The leading ecclesiastical academics and administrators of the twelfth-century Renaissance are well represented: Menegaldus, possibly the famous publicist of the Investiture Controversy;[23] Thierry, archdeacon and Chancellor of Chartres and the most

---

20. It is in this category that my survey is most in need of extension. When I began work I was inclined to make note only of texts that contained *significant* glosses; as my investigations proceeded I became aware of the need for a full listing of *all* extant *Ad Herennium* and *De inventione* texts, broadly divided into texts containing signs of attention by any student/scholar other than the scribe himself or containing scribal annotations/corrections, and texts which were simply clean, relatively uncorrected copies that saw no apparent use in later times. However, I have not been able, in every case, to go back over work done to lay a comprehensive foundation for such a listing. In my category "NSG" I am therefore presenting but a broad selection of MSS which contain some evidence of attention either at the hands of the scribe himself, or later generations.

21. Dionigi's commentary: Paris, BN lat. 5858; cf. *Bocace en France de l'humanisme à l'érotisme* (Paris, 1975, Cat. de l'exposition), No. 10, pp. 8–9. For a handsomely presented *rhetorica* gloss volume see MS Ghent, Bibl. der Rijksuniv. 10.

22. For instance: Anselm of Laon, Lanfranc of Bec, a certain twelfth-century Magister Guillelmus, the earliest known commentator of them all, Marcomannus (mentioned in Victorinus' *De inventione* commentary), and a host of fourteenth- and fifteenth-century Italian probables, such as Giovanni di Bonandrea, Pietro da Moglio, Bartolomeo del Regno, Giovanni Conversino da Ravenna, Pietro da Forlì. There were doubtless many others; Siraisi (above n. 10) in her appendix p. 175 lists 33 professors of grammar and rhetoric at Padua before 1350 and there must have been many more at larger centres such as Bologna. Some are most recently discussed in J. R. Banker, "The *ars dictaminis* and rhetorical textbooks at the Bolognese University in the fourteenth century," *Medievalia et Humanistica,* NS 5 (1974), 153–168.

23. See Dickey as cited above n. 14 and W. Hartmann in *Deutsches Archiv,* 26 (1970). I am preparing a short study of the MS evidence for Menegaldus rhetor,

celebrated teacher of the liberal arts in his day;[24] Petrus Helias, scarcely less famous teacher and central figure in the western study of grammar;[25] Lawrence of Amalfi, eleventh-century archbishop and one-time monk of Monte Cassino;[26] 'Alanus', possibly to be identified with the late twelfth-century poet and prolific scholar Alan of Lille, of whom contemporaries wrote that he knew whatever man could know.[27]

Among later authors we have an important series of fourteenth- and fifteenth-century Italian *dictatores* and university lecturers in *dictamen,* rhetoric and the classics; these include Bartolinus de Benincasa de Canulo, Philippus de Vicecomitibus de Pisto(r)ia, and Guarino da Verona.[28] Among the less academic Italian authors of the same period may be found the Florentine orator, diplomat and lawyer Luigi de Gianfigliazzi, and Messer Lorenzo di Antonio Ridolfi, businessman, decretalist, diplomat and statesman of the leading Florentine Ridolfi family. Clearly the seeds laid by Brunetto Latini in thirteenth-century Florence bore some fruit: Brunetto, whom both Dante and his contemporary, the Italian chronicler Giovanni Villani praised, is the earliest known Italian commentator on either the *De inventione* or the *Ad Herennium* since the time of Lawrence of Amalfi, and the first teacher to leave behind him glosses on either text in the Italian vernacular.[29] Northern humanists of the fifteenth century are represented by the French canon Jean Poulain, and the celebrated Swiss scholar, publisher and, ultimately, Carthusian monk Johannes Heynlin aus Stein (de Lapide).[30]

Three periods stand out in terms of the number of surviving MSS of commentaries: antiquity (81 MSS), the twelfth century (24 MSS,

---

entitled "The Earliest Medieval Commentaries on Cicero's *Rhetorica*; some new fragments" (from Munich).

24. See Ward and Fredborg above n. 14. Thierry's (?) important Boethius commentaries have been edited by N. M. Häring (Toronto, 1971).

25. See Fredborg's articles cited n. 14 above.

26. See F. Newton's articles in *Traditio,* 21 (1965), 445–9 and *Transactions of the American Philological Association,* 93 (1962), 277–280 etc.

27. On the Alanus commentary see Caplan as cited above n. 14. On Alan of Lille and his intellectual context see most recently W. Wetherbee's *Platonism and Poetry in the Twelfth Century* (Princeton, 1972) and his article in *Traditio,* 25 (1969).

28. A recent study of Guarino: R. Schweyen, *Guarino Veronese. Philosophie und humanistiche Pädagogik* (Munich, 1973). Sandra Wertis, a student of Professors Kristeller and Caplan, is preparing an introduction to the commentary by Bartolinus, to be submitted to the journal *Viator.* On Bartolinus see also Banker (above n. 22).

29. F. Maggini, ed., *Brunetto Latini, La Rettorica* (Florence, 1968).

30. On Johannes see M. Hossfeld in *Basler Zeitschrift für Geschichte und Altertumskunde,* VI Hft. 2 (Basel, 1907), and VII Hft. 1 (1908).

TABLE I
SURVIVAL OF COMMENTARIES AND GLOSSES BY PERIOD (LATIN)

Period	Commentaries	Accessus/ Collections of notes	MGT	MiGT	S/NSG
late s. X–end of s. XI	3	2	2	12	10
s. XII	15	2 (3 MSS)	4	12	41 (+ 4 glossed texts not seen)
s. XII–XIII (perhaps ca. 1175–1225)	3	3	—	6	23
s. XIII	1	2	2	4	53
s. XIV–XV	30	9	11	27	c. 160

MGT = Major Glossed Texts; MiGT = Minor Glossed Texts; S/NSG = Slight or Not Significant Glosses

35 if we include works which may have been written in the early thirteenth century), and the fourteenth–fifteenth centuries (63 MSS). When we consider the total survival of material (see Tables I and II), the significance of these periods stands out even further: no commentary or significant set of glosses predates the late tenth century, and between the two central periods of rhetorical commentation, c. 1080–1225 A.D. and c.1290–1500 A.D., lie but a single, inferior, Latin commentary (on part of the *Ad Herennium*)—that of the monk of Dinant named Jacques who seems to have professed rhetoric at Bologna in the later thirteenth century,[31] the Italian commentary on the *De inventione* by Brunetto Latini, already mentioned, 2 *accessus*/collections of notes, and a few glossed texts. The thirteenth century thus forms something of a hiatus in the history of medieval academic rhetorical scholarship.

Further precision is possible when we consider the survival figures for individual outstanding commentaries. Victorinus survives in 50 MSS, but, curiously, 22 MSS predate the twelfth century (s.vii–xi/xii) and 26 date from the fifteenth century: clearly the twelfth century is the period when original commentaries replaced copies of Victorinus. Thirty-one MSS of Grillius's commentary on the *De inventione*[32]

31. See Banker (above n. 22) p. 154 and references cited.
32. Seventeen contain the curious fragment which Courcelle, *Revue de Philologie*, 29 (1955), 34–38, on no very certain grounds claimed was part of Grillius' lost

TABLE II
APPROXIMATE SURVIVAL OF MSS BY CENTURY

Century	Number of MSS	Century	Number of MSS
vii	1	xii–xiii	16
ix	2	xiii	19
ix–x	8	xiii–xiv	1
x	8	xiv	32
x–xi	3	xiv–xv	11
xi	34	xv	175
xi–xii	5	post xv	13
xii	63		

Total MSS: 391. Note: this table does not include simple *texts* of the *Ad Herennium* or *De inventione* (i.e. without any marginalia etc.)

survive, more evenly spread across the centuries, but they contain only fragments of the lost original commentary. Other popular commentaries are those by Alanus (8 MSS in two main versions[33]), Bartolinus[34] (16 MSS in three main versions), and Guarino da Verona (17 MSS in five versions). Our eighteen twelfth- to early thirteenth-century commentaries survive in 21 contemporary MSS, 5 fourteenth-century MSS, and nine fifteenth-century MSS, indicating some trickle of later medieval currency. In the main, however, the fourteenth- and fifteenth-century schools made relatively little use of earlier medieval commentaries, although one fifteenth-century glossator chose Thierry of Chartres's commentary for his marginal gloss, Jean Poulain transcribes from a twelfth-century 'proto-Alanus' commentary, and the influence of the commentary currently assigned to Alanus remained considerable.

Two principal foci of medieval rhetorical interest emerge therefore: the period c.1080–1225, and 1290 to the era of printing. We are not able at the moment, however, to speak with much certainty of the provenance of these two rhetorical upsurges. The shift from northern Europe to Italy is, nevertheless, already clear. The twelfth-century commentaries are centered upon such 'foyers d'érudition' as Laon,

---

commentary. It may, however, be a medieval composition. It first appears in the eleventh century. See my dissertation, II, 522–25, and Ward, "Sources".

33. I exclude, for the present, two early (?) versions of the Alanus commentary in MSS Vienna, Nationalbibl. 240 and Venice, Marc. lat. XI, 23 (4686).

34. See above n. 28.

Rheims, the Rhineland, Chartres and Paris, with a couple of items probably to be located in Italy (Pavia/Milan? Amalfi?). The fourteenth- to fifteenth-century material, however, is overwhelmingly (though not completely) Italian in provenance. Such a pattern reinforces our present understanding of medieval and Renaissance interest in classical liberal culture[35] and epitomises the double attraction of the classical rhetorical legacy: first as a system of persuasion and communication attractive to a generation of scholars convinced of the need for theoretical knowledge to be socially relevant and devoted to a pioneering exploration of the limits and utility of knowledge and the language of science and learning (grammar, dialectic), and second as a resource to supply the later medieval schools of *dictamen* and political oratory, as a cradle for that interest in the forms and patterns of classical culture which generations of scholars have labelled 'humanism'.

The advent of printing allowed the rapid multiplication of texts of the *Ad Herennium* and *De inventione,* as it did copies of the principal commentaries and sets of glosses. Renaissance tastes did not, research suggests, alter the medieval emphasis upon the *Ad Herennium* and *De inventione* as basic rhetorical sources. All but twelve years between 1474 and 1500 saw the publication of an edition of a gloss or commentary on these texts.[36] Between 1500 and 1600 a

---

35. See my dissertation, I, 212–38, and note the interesting remark of Konrad von Mure, writing c. 1286, "And above all it is the Lombard masters and legists who excel all other nations in the construction of *arengae*" (L. Rockinger, *Briefsteller und Formelbücher des eilften bis vierzehnten Jlh,* Munich 1863/4, p. 468).

36. Some conspectus of the principal early editions of the works of Cicero will be found in F. L. A. Schweiger, *Handbuch der classischen Bibliographie . . . lateinische Schriftsteller* (A–L), Leipzig, 1832), pp. 102 ff., which must be supplemented by reference to the standard printed lists of incunabula and sixteenth-century printed books, specialist treatises on individual early printers and the printed catalogues of the major world libraries (Cosenza, *Biographical and Bibliographical Dictionary of the Italian Humanists* contains scattered information but must be checked). I have not had an opportunity of inspecting all early Cicero editions and thus have refrained from listing, among commentaries and notes, editions of Cicero's works advertised as possessing notes, emendations and variants, etc., ("castigationes") by the major editors (Denys Lambin, Aldus and Paulus Manutius, Pier Vettori, I. Camerarius etc.) or editions of the *Rhetorica* based on the *castigationes* of the above unless my own inspection or reliable witness reveals that the edition in question actually contains separate annotations on the *De inventione* or *Ad Herennium* (printed at the foot of the page, in the margins or at the end of the text). Thus my "statistics" at this point may not be complete. On early editions of the *Ad Herennium* see Marx, *editio maior* of that work, pp. 60–69. Scholderer, *Proceedings of the British Academy,* 35 (1949), 30, suggests that each edition of a printed work in the fifteenth century might have run to an average of 250 copies.

further edition of an old or new gloss, commentary, or collection of glosses / commentaries saw the light on an average of less than every two years, and thereafter editions of such material continued to leave the presses.³⁷ The majority of these works were written during the age of printing. Only two works from the era before printing received permanence by way of the printed page: Victorinus, whose popularity delayed composition of a Renaissance gloss on the *De inventione* until 1563/4,³⁸ and Guarino da Verona, whose *Ad Herennium* commentary, surviving in more MSS than any other medieval commentary, was stripped of all signs of authorship and put into service as the standard marginal gloss accompanying the early editions of the *Ad Herennium* (it saw at least seven editions).³⁹

Guarino's gloss, however, was soon succeeded by fresh compositions better suited to the exacting academic tastes of the time;⁴⁰ those, for example, of the Italian philologist and student of Lorenzo Valla, Jerome Capiduro (middle fifteenth century, fifteen editions), and the Perugian student of Greek and Latin letters, administrator, and diplomat, Francesco Maturanzio (1443–1518, eighteen editions) who became Professor of Eloquence at Perugia. The careers of these men typify the professional, academic, philological background of the Renaissance rhetorical commentaries and glosses.

We know of almost fifty separate commentaries, collections of notes and variants (often called *castigationes*), or *accessus*, to the *Ad Herennium* and *De inventione* from the era of printing (c.1474–1600 A.D.). Many saw numerous editions. The most popular were Victorinus (forty-one editions, forty before 1600), the commentary on *Ad Herennium* Bk.I by Antonio Mancinello, Italian classical scholar and teacher of the second half of the fifteenth century (twenty-nine editions), and those by Capiduro and Maturanzio already mentioned. The names of Lorenzo Valla, Georgius Trapezuntius and Jan Luis Vives⁴¹ are associated in a minor way with the *Ad Herennium / De*

---

37. I have noted fourteen down to 1830.
38. By Nascimbaenus Nascimbaenius of Ferrara, about whom very little is known.
39. See R. Sabbadini, *La Scuola e gli Studi di Guarino Guarini Veronese* (Catania, 1896), pp. 93–97.
40. The last edition of Guarino's commentary seems to be dated 1493.
41. Vives wrote a "praelectio" to the fourth book of the *Ad Herennium*; Valla's name is assigned to a Cicero "Rhetorica" commentary of 1490 by P. A. Orlandi, *Origine e Progressi della Stampa* (Bologna, 1722), pp. 61, 312 and 423, under the rubric of Venice, printer unknown; and Trapezuntius, it appears, was the author of some notes to the *Ad Herennium* included in editions of 1526 and 1531 (probably

inventione gloss/commentary literature, but in general one is struck by the absence of the great names among northern and Italian humanists of the age of printing: clearly *De inventione/Ad Herennium* scholarship was by now confined to the schoolroom and university lecture-hall.

It would obviously be impossible to characterize adequately these commentaries and glosses generation by generation in the present context. Something of their general character can be gained from such printed accounts as have already appeared, and the next few years should see much further material available in print. Some remarks on the genre must, nevertheless, be permitted.

What is at first sight surprising about this literature is the adaptability of the classical academic rhetorical tradition. Given the ready availability of Latin rhetorical manuals and the established place of rhetoric in the didactic tradition of late antiquity and the Middle Ages, this tradition could not be ignored. But each age stressed what suited the contemporary context, and, as a consequence, the scope and nature of rhetorical interest in each period serve to identify and characterize prevailing intellectual attitudes.

Rhetoric, as an art, had begun life in a strongly practical context: the overthrow of the tyrants in Syracuse during the fifth century B.C.[42] Its practical orientation received distinctive shape from a succession of socio-political circumstances: Athenian/Sicilian democracy of the fifth–fourth centuries B.C., Hellenistic autocracy, Roman republican court, political and legislative exigencies, and the courts and panegyrical requirements of the Empire, with its rhetorically trained professional civil servants. The rhetorical curriculum that evolved from these exigencies showed surprising resilience in adapting to the increasingly theoretical and intellectualised atmosphere of the later Roman rhetorical schools, an atmosphere promoted by the disappearing practical judicial and political context for the exercise of the rhetorical art. The fact, for instance, that the *De inventione* could become the basic text-book of Latin rhetoric until c.1150 A.D., despite its failure to deal with *pronuntiatio, memoria* and *elocutio*, illustrates in general the drift from practical to intellectual that

---

extracts from his *Rhetoricorum libri quinque*). On Trapezuntius' role in the rhetorical commentary tradition, see now John Monfasoni, *George of Trebizond* (Leiden, 1976) pp. 261 ff. I should like to thank Dr. Monfasoni here for his help on the subject of Trapezuntius and the *Ad Herennium*.

42. G. Kennedy, *The Art of Persuasion in Greece* (Princeton, 1963), 58–61.

characterises late antique and medieval rhetorical history,[43] just as it illustrates the versatility of the Latin rhetorical curriculum, and the extent to which early medieval logical theory relied upon rhetorical devices.[44]

In explaining the appeal of Latin rhetoric to early Christianity, we must not forget that the early Christian cultural environment was, in ways we tend to underestimate, inherently rhetorical.[45] Early Christian writers thought and argued in rhetorical modes; indeed, the very concentration on *inventio* and status-theory in the *De inventione*, far from disqualifying it as a suitable rhetorical text, gave it a positive advantage in the eyes of later antiquity and the Middle Ages.[46] The very terminology of rhetorical invention and status-theory had become an intriguing theatre of debate into which medieval scholars entered with vigour because it involved some expertise in the general problem of comprehending and analysing departments of knowledge by means of definition, *differentia*, allocation of genus and species, the use or assignment of dialectical topoi (*contrarium*, *comparatio*, argument from the greater, lesser, etc.) and other aspects of logical methodology applicable to the discussion of *res et nomina* (words as mere vocal sounds, and as signs of subsisting realities).[47]

---

43. It is no accident that all known ancient Latin rhetorical commentators chose the *De inventione* to gloss, that Boethius in the fourth book of his *De differentiis topicis* took the same text as the basis of his understanding of rhetoric, and that both Boethius and Victorinus were the prime influences shaping the medieval study of classical rhetorical theory.

44. McKeon, "Rhetoric in the Middle Ages," pp. 7–10.

45. See R. D. Sider, *Ancient Rhetoric and the Art of Tertullian* (Oxford, 1971) and other references cited in my dissertation (above n. 1), I, 73 ff. I had the good fortune to hear a paper given at the 1975 International Conference on Patristic Studies (Oxford) by G. C. Stead, entitled "Rhetorical Method in Athanasius"; Professor Stead demonstrated that Athanasius' familiarity with the structure and logical mechanism of rhetorical argumentation was so thorough that he was led, at times, into indefensible or invalid propositions. See also McKeon, as cited n. 5 above, p. 11, and the voluminous literature on rhetoric in St. Augustine mentioned n. 4 above and in my dissertation, I, 106–109.

46. P. Hadot, *Marius Victorinus, recherches sur sa vie et ses oeuvres* (Paris, 1971), p. 77, suggests that the *De inventione* suited Victorinus and his contemporaries because it was basically Greek in doctrine (a fact which the medieval commentators recognised): it formed a convenient substitute among late antique Latin-speaking pupils for Greek manuals they could not readily read. I have discussed the appeal of the *De inventione* and the *Ad Herennium* to the Middle Ages in my dissertation, I, 38–71, 84–87, etc.

47. See the article cited in n. 2 above, and a discussion of medieval views on the same thorny question in my dissertation, II, 428–459 ("The Corpus Christi Commentator and the Issue *Negotialis*"); also McKeon (n. 5 above), pp. 4–5.

The history of the academic study of the rhetorical system in the Middle Ages thus has a two-fold interest: it reveals the gradual adaptation of the classical rhetorical legacy to the intellectual needs and emphases of the Christian Middle Ages, but it also suggests a series of 'crises' in communication between individuals and classes which led contemporaries to seek a new relevance for ancient rhetorical doctrine.

The process of adaptation is most clearly visible in the commentary on the *De inventione* by Victorinus, and the fourth book of Boethius' *De differentiis topicis,* itself heavily reliant on Cicero's youthful rhetorical opus.[48] The background of Victorinus' rhetorical interests is Neoplatonic and dialectical. It is the theory of genus and species, syllogism, definition and Aristotle's ten categories, together with metaphysical concepts of time and substance, that interest Victorinus, rather than the accumulated lore of Greek rhetorical status-theory as found in the works of Hermogenes, Minucian, Grillius and many of the minor Latin rhetoricians. The human drama of the advent of civilization elaborated in the proemium of the *De inventione* becomes in Victorinus the exemplification of a cosmic dialogue between metaphysical entities: the emancipation of the soul (wisdom, philosophy, virtue, *studium, disciplina*) from its bondage to the body by way of *eloquentia.*[49] With Boethius' *De differentiis topicis* IV, the application of Neoplatonic and Aristotelian ideas of potentiality and actuality to the process whereby the *materia* of the *ars rhetorica* assumes rhetorical form sets the pattern of northern European

---

48. See Hadot, ch. 5; my dissertation, I, 87–106, 111–114; and the chapter by Michael Leff in the present volume.

49. "Sola scientia" is important for Victorinus, alongside "quae in actu sit"; the student of the *De inventione* is "qui rhetoricam scribit" or "orator rhetoricam scribens", not "qui rhetorica perorat" as one might expect (see Victorinus, ed. C. Halm, *Rhetores latini minores,* Leipzig, 1863, pp. 170.33, 36; 216.10, 244.28). For Victorinus, eloquence has become, in Hadot's phrase, "la forme de manifestation de la sagesse" (Hadot, p. 87).

For Victorinus (Halm, p. 165) the relationship between *eloquentia* and *sapientia* is the same as that between the external appearance of, say, honey (colour, aspect), and its substance (sweetness); the process Cicero describes at *De inventione* 1.2.3 (ed. Stroebel, 3b.26 ff.) as a process of political and moral decay, set in the changing dynamic of history, has become for Victorinus a disorder within a static ontological, metaphysical reality: Victorinus's dialectic is that of the soul's self-redemption, Cicero's is that of man in political life. Both have a belief in the basic goodness of man (*De inventione* 2b.29–3b.1; Victorinus, ed. Halm, 164.31 ff.) but in Victorinus the metaphysical antinomy between body and soul becomes the key organising principle.

rhetorical interests for some eight centuries.[50] By the time the ninth-century European scholars come to comment on the fifth book of Martianus Capella's *De Nuptiis*, the standard text in the *artes* for the day, the scholastic emphasis is fixed. The disposition on the part of these commentators to see rhetoric as an intellectual discipline rather than a practical one, the disposition to strip it of its distinctive features as an art (delivery, arrangement, memory, style) and to treat it as the brother-in-arms of dialectic, is at once the effect of the influence of Boethius and Victorinus and the factor responsible for it.[51] The way is clear to the eleventh- and twelfth-century schools, as we shall see in a moment.

Nevertheless, as each generation of medieval students of rhetoric succeeded another, our sources pinpoint ways in which contemporaries kept their teaching and study of the classical rhetorical corpus close to the needs of their day. Research has suggested that behind the summary rhetorical descriptions and references to the art in the works of Cassiodorus, Isidore, Alcuin, Lupus of Ferriéres, Rabanus Maurus, Notker Labeo, Abbo of Fleury, Gerbert of Rheims, Gunzo of Novara, and behind such apparently jejune abridgements as the little-known Quintilian extracts of the eighth century A.D., there lies a sense of relevance to contemporary conditions that was to reach a unique fruition in the multiplication of preaching manuals from the later twelfth century onwards, and in the blossoming of separate treatises and collections of models in *dictamen,* the *ars concionatoria* or *arengandi* (political or debate oratory) and the *ars notaria* which flourished in the sociologically complicated and distinct climate of the Italian communes.[52]

---

50. An interesting illustration of this, from the early eleventh century, is mentioned in my dissertation, I, 335 (with reference to the unpublished B. Litt. thesis of Mary Dickey, "The Study of Rhetoric in the first half of the Twelfth Century with special reference to the Cathedral Schools of North France," St. Hilda's Oxford 1953, pp. 177–8).

51. My dissertation, I, 162–170.

52. The same, I, 307–328; G. Vecchi, "Le *Arenge* di Guido Faba e l'eloquenza d'arte civile e politica duecentesca," *Quadrivium,* 4 (1960), 61–87; H. Wieruszowski, *Politics and Culture in Medieval Spain and Italy* (Rome, 1971), part II; J. K. Hyde, *Padua in the Age of Dante* (Manchester, 1966), ch. 10; Murphy, *Medieval Rhetoric,* ch. 5 (note especially D23, pp. 121 ff.) and *Rhetoric in the Middle Ages* (University of California Press, 1974), ch. 5. The best introduction to the Italy that produced and popularised the *ars dictaminis* would be J. K. Hyde, *Society and Politics in Medieval Italy* (London, 1973). I have discussed at greater length the originality of early medieval, apparently jejune, summaries of rhetorical theory in my

Symptomatic, and perhaps representative, of these early adaptations of rhetorical lore is the rhetorical brief which Gerbert of Rheims, tutor to Emperor Otto III and later Pope Sylvester II (999–1003 A.D.) despatched in 995 A.D. to Bishops Wilderode of Strasbourg and Notker of Liège, designed to set forth in the most persuasive terms Gerbert's version of the proceedings of the Council of St. Basle de Verzy (June 991) at which Arnulf, Gerbert's rival for the archbishopric of Rheims, was forced to vacate the archbishopric in favour of Gerbert himself. Gerbert's valiant attempt to endow his brief with rhetorical force by 'labelling' its various segments according to the terms and doctrines of the *Ad Herennium* / *De inventione* illustrates at once the appeal of the ancient rhetorical system in a moment of crisis, and, ultimately, its marginal relevance to the material and methods at hand.[53]

The twelfth century, as we have seen, is in some respects the apogee of the rhetorical movement in the Middle Ages. Its high points are a much expanded interest in *elocutio*, the rhetorical *colores* of *Ad Herennium* IV (e.g. Marbod of Rennes, Onulf of Speyer, Ulrich of Bamberg, etc.);[54] deepened study of the classical rhetorical system itself (e.g. Anselm of Besate, *Rhetorimachia*[55]); the harnessing of rhetoric to political purposes (e.g. the Investiture Controversy and German chancery rhetoric of the later eleventh century, the eleventh-century development of the papal *cursus*[56]); the birth of *dictamen*;[57]

---

dissertation, I, 119–238; App. B (I, 554–5); and additions, I, ii–iii. Murphy's study of Rabanus Maurus is relevant here: *Medieval Rhetoric*, T97 (*Rhetoric in the Middle Ages*, pp. 82–7); and for general further reference on early medieval uses, summaries of rhetoric, T57–T90.

53. See translation and notes in H. P. Lattin, *The Letters of Gerbert with his papal privileges as Sylvester II*, translated with an introduction (New York, 1961), pp. 236–262. Bibliography but no text in F. Weigle, *Die Briefsammlung Gerberts von Reims* (Berlin, 1966), p. 258 (No. 217). My dissertation, I, 178–183.

54. Murphy, *Medieval Rhetoric*, T89–90; my dissertation, I, 235–238, 435 etc.; E. Curtius, *European Literature and the Latin Middle Ages*, trans. W. R. Trask (New York, 1953), ch. 8 etc.; F. P. Knapp, "Vergleich und Exempel in der lateinischen Rhetorik und Poetik von der Mitte des 12 bis zur Mitte des 13 J/h," *Studi Medievali*, 3rd ser., 14 (1973), p. 449 etc. Note also the interesting article by R. M. Thomson in *Revue Bénédictine*, 84 (1974), 383 ff., on changing currents in twelfth-century monastic style.

55. Murphy, *Medieval Rhetoric*, T32; my dissertation, 223–234; McKeon as cited n. 5 above, p. 26.

56. My dissertation, I, 235–7.

57. Murphy, *Medieval Rhetoric*, D3, and "Alberic of Monte Cassino: Father of the medieval *ars dictaminis*," *American Benedictine Review*, 22 (1971), 129–46.

the reliance of early dialectical and legal studies on rhetorical texts and doctrine;[58] the use of a rhetorical system of argumentation to underpin the early scholastic study of theology;[59] and the realisation of a cross section of thinkers that learning and knowledge were and had to be rhetorically conditioned. For these latter thinkers learning and knowledge had to minister (in the phrase of Thierry of Chartres) 'to the cult of humanity', or, in the words of John of Salisbury, 'to the use of society': social *communio* (living conjointly; 'conviviality' perhaps, in Ivan Illich's language) is the 'law of human society', the pathway to *beatitudo* and *felicitas*; expression (grammar, dialectic, rhetoric) is therefore a cardinal basis and condition of all learning. Thus emerged, rephrased, the essence of the myth of civilization with which the *De inventione* opens and which was to so powerfully recommend that text to the attention of twelfth-century students.

Despite the growing links, as the Middle Ages wore on, between the study of rhetoric and the demands of an outside world, the commentaries themselves make few references to the latter. Nevertheless, there is everywhere, in the first few generations of commentary, an awareness of the controversial legal issues and situations of the day. In the later eleventh and early twelfth centuries, the com-

58. My dissertation, I, 192–212, 328–79; H. Fitting, *Die Anfänge der Rechts-schule zu Bologna* (Berlin/Leipzig, 1888), 21–24, 72.

59. Rhetoric and early scholastic theology: my dissertation, I, 242–47; McKeon (above n. 5), p. 21; J. Jolivet, *Arts du Langage et Théologie chez Abélard* (Paris, 1969). For Abelard the *De inventione* was the most studied of Cicero's works: G. d'Anna, "Abelarde e Cicerone," *Studi Medievali*, 3rd Ser., 10 (1969), 333 ff.

The humanists: I have taken certain phrases from the prologue to Thierry of Chartres' *Heptateuchon* and the introduction to John of Salisbury's *Metalogikon* (full discussion and references in my dissertation, I, 247–306, 543–553; on contemporary allusions to the *De inventione* prologue, I, 237–8, 336–7 etc.). I deal at length with the rhetorical interests of twelfth- and thirteenth-century Europe in my dissertation, I, 239–526, in relation to dialectic and theology, knowledge, and the acquisition of wisdom generally (in terms of the schemes of knowledge and the *accessus*), civil science and politics, law and advocacy, *dictamen*, the *colores* and *artes poetriae*, *ars predicandi*, the universities and mendicant *studia*, textbooks.

John of Salisbury's attitude towards language and truth is summarised in B. Hendley, "Wisdom and Eloquence: a new interpretation of the Metalogicon of John of Salisbury," Diss. Yale 1967, chs. 3–6; see also G. C. Garfagnini, " 'Ratio disserendi' e 'ratiocinandi via': il 'Metalogicon' di Giovanni di Salisbury," *Studi Medievali*, 3rd Ser., 12 (1971), 915 ff.

R. McKeon's "Poetry and Philosophy in the twelfth century: The Renaissance of Rhetoric," *Modern Philology*, 43 (1945–6), 217–34 or R. S. Crane, ed., *Critics and Criticism* (Chicago, 1952), pp. 297 ff., stresses the role of language in twelfth-century thinking.

mentaries reflect the currency of simony lawsuits and the initiation of new canon law to meet new situations (simony, schism) is used to illustrate the ancient rhetorical issue *negotialis*.[60] The earliest glosses and commentaries that we know of display an interest in congruences between the ancient legal issue of transference in which the defendant demands a postponement of time or a change of plaintiff or court or judge (*translatio, Ad Her.* 1.12.22) and contemporary situations which would merit an 'exception' or 'essoin': the inadmissability of

---

60. My dissertation, II.441–2 (cf.n.47 above); Margareta Fredborg 'Petrus Helias on Rhetoric' *Cahiers* (full title n. 14 above) 13(1974)34; Dickey (n. 14 above) pp. 15–17. The medieval commentators on Persius, Juvenal and Vergil contain more frequent reference to conditions outside the schools, perhaps because the study of the *auctores* occupied an earlier stage in the life of the student (see Bischoff as cited n. 14 above). An anonymous early twelfth-century rhetorical glossator who seems to be reporting lectures from a *Magister G.*, writes on *reprehensio* (*De inventione* 1.42.78): 'and it should be noted that *reprehensio*, though it is appropriate only to the defendant, yet, according to Master G., it is common to both plaintiff and defendant. For it is the mark of a good orator that he should be aware in advance of whatever his adversary might say. From this he will know not only how to establish his own proofs, but also how to weaken whatever arguments his adversary puts forward. To dissipate (*diluere*) is to destroy entirely, to weaken (*infirmare*) is not to destroy entirely but only in part; to parry (*alleviare*) is neither to destroy wholly nor in part, but to show to be of little weight. For it is worthy of attention that where the opposing side may cite many decisions on an issue, an orator ought not to adduce a decision which is found only once, or rarely. For, according to Master G., this is often the case in the canons: a certain ruling is found but once (a 'solitary' ruling) or twice, or three times (a 'rare' ruling), so that if a contrary judgement should be found frequently, it necessarily weakens a solitary or rare ruling'. In this kind of gloss, which can be paralleled many times, there is clearly a concern to provide some mutual interpretation between the lecture-hall instruction in classical rhetorical theory and issues or practice in the church law of the period. The lectures of Master G. do not appear to have survived, but they seem reflected in lecture traditions that have survived (cf. Menegaldus, MS Cologne Dombibl. 197 f.34r–v and 'In primis' MS York Minster XVI.M.7 f.23v). The above quotation is taken from MS Durham Cathedral Library C.IV.29 fols. 211rb–211va. (Late note: I have just received a copy of Margareta Fredborg's 'The Commentaries on Cicero's *De inventione* and *Rhetorica ad Herennium* by William of Champeaux', *Cahiers* 17 pp. 1–39; in this article Mrs. Fredborg seeks to demonstrate that the *Magister G.* cited in MS Durham C.IV.29 is the author of the gloss 'In primis', and that Master G. is in fact William of Champeaux. This confirms the ascription of the fourteenth-century MS Bruges 553, which I found in 1972 to be a truncated version of 'In primis', to 'magister Willelmus', though in the draft of my 'Sources' I was disinclined to accept the identification with William of Champeaux. Pages 33–39 of Mrs. Fredborg's article contain a text of the 'Epilogue' to the York MS of 'In primis': see n. 70 below). My own examination of this material suggests that the Magister G. of MS Durham Cathedral Library C.IV.29 is probably William of Champeaux (see my dissertation I, 150 n. 7), that this William is probably the author of the 'Epilogue' in the York MS, but that the gloss *In primis* is by a different author.

a lawsuit during Easter, for instance, the inappropriateness of a monastic regulation when applied to a cathedral canon, the impropriety of a dean referring a case to a bishop that he should handle himself. The glossators, however, were not drawn into any anachronistic equation between conditions in their own day and the customs of antiquity. An early eleventh-century commentator, noting that the classical Roman procedure for determining a lawsuit[61] usually prevented a defendant from demanding a transference, added that 'in our day, however, this is not the case, since when someone lays a charge he does not pay adequate attention to his wording and so defines the case badly, or demands a transference incorrectly'. More explicitly, over a century later, in his *De inventione* commentary, Petrus Helias, commenting on the ancient procedure for arriving at the issue for adjudication, says 'in forming the *constitutio* today, however, subterfuge is almost always employed. For when the defendant is summoned by the praetor or prince into court to hear the charges laid against him, he is prevented from making an immediate rejoinder; instead, a day is appointed by the magistrate for the rejoinder, to provide time for the defendant to consider what is most advantageous to his case. I do not know what lies behind this kind of subterfuge whereby the rejoinder is delayed, since, once the accusation has been laid, the rejoinder should be put forward at once, so that the issue to be adjudicated can be determined. There is little justice in the matter for the accuser has no power to claim a similar delay from the judge'.[62] This lack of congruence between ancient and 'modern' custom had little impact on the growth of scholarship on the thorny problem of the 'issues'. Within a few years of the completion of Petrus Helias' gloss, an extensive examination of all the ancient opinions on the nature of the 'issue' was a standard part of the curriculum, without any reference to 'modern' custom. To the end of the Middle Ages, the emphasis in the *De inventione* and *Ad Herennium* on the 'issues', with their origins in philosophical theory, continued to occupy a large proportion of the attention of the commentators, not only expounding the theory, but overcoming

---

61. Kennedy, *Art of Rhetoric in the Roman World*, pp. 8–9; MS Oxford Laud lat. 49 fol. 131vb middle bottom margin. Cf. also Wibald of Corvey, cited in Curtius *European Literature* p. 76, my dissertation I.423–34.

62. Fredborg as cited n.60 above ('Petrus Helias . . .') p. 35. A more literal translation of the last sentence: 'I, however, ask whether the plaintiff can say to the magistrate "fix a day for us on which the case will be tried, and then I will propose what I wish".'

discrepancies and shortcomings in the classical presentation of the theory. So entrenched a position did status-theory occupy in the rhetorical curriculum, from the time of Hermagoras to that of Guarino da Verona, that its influence on the legal glossators of the ancient and medieval period is pronounced.[63]

Other contemporary references in the rhetorical glosses either provide an indication of provenance[64] and suggest the scope of contemporary classroom discussions (which appear to have embraced even the topic of Greek Fire![65]), or else hint at the contemporary utilization of rhetorical theory (*dictamen*, legal pleading, assembly oratory[66]). In certain later commentaries we are given interesting

---

63. Cf. n. 47 above, and my dissertation I.339–356. B. Vonglis *La Lettre et l'esprit de la loi dans la jurisprudence classique et la rhétorique* (Paris, 1968) should be particularly noted. The 'extensive examination of the issues' occurs, for instance, in the following MSS: Venice Marc.lat. XI,23 (4686) fols. 52v–54r, Cambridge Pembroke College 85 III fol. 85ra, Oxford Corpus Christi College 250 fols. 8v–9r, Perugia Bibl. Com. 237 (D55) fols. 22v–24r. On pleading procedure, delays etc. see my dissertation I.364–380, esp. 369; T. Plucknett *A Concise History of the Common Law* (London, 1948) 108, 119–20; A. Harding *A Social History of English Law* (Penguin Books, 1966) pp. 123–26.

64. For example, in an otherwise completely anonymous *De inventione* commentary of the first half of the twelfth century (?), MS Trier Stadtbibl. 1082 (32) 8° f. 163v, the illustration 'as if we were to say "it is enough for a canon of Rheims Cathedral to aspire to a provostship (*preposituram*)—he ought not to aspire to an archbishopric", and so we dissuade him from excessive self-advancement . . .' allows us to suggest a provenance for the commentary. On the school of Rheims in the period see the articles of J. R. Williams in *Speculum* 29(1954) and *Traditio* 20(1964).

65. MS Oxford, Bodleian Library, Laud lat.49 f.141r, gloss 'k' 'hic propone tibi negocium medicinam vel ignem Grecum aut nigromantiam. . . .' MS Hereford, Cathedral Library, P.1.iv f.24r includes a discussion of royal succession and remarks that among the Franks women could not inherit the throne. The gloss is twelfth century.

66. Thierry of Chartres, for example, commenting on a passage in the *Ad Herennium* (1.8.13, *verum haec*) where the classical writer says: 'but it is in practice exercises that these types (of *narrationes*) will be worked out' (in reference to the third kind of *narratio*, based on persons), writes: 'WILL BE WORKED OUT. That is, may be said to work out (*transigere*). He speaks properly of letters' (MS Berlin Deutsche Staatsb. (now Preuss. Kulturbesitz) Lat. Oct. 161 f.41r). The fourteenth-century commentator Bartolinus, dealing with the *tria genera dicendi* of *Ad Her.* 4.8.11, tells his students how they should be employed 'in qualibet epistola et arenga': 'in any letter or public speech' (MS Milan, Ambros. D 37 inf. f.54r = Vatican, Pal. lat. 1461 f.274r). MS Durham C.IV.29 f.197ra (twelfth century) defines rhetoric as a part of civil science, and civil science as the science pertaining to the management of the affairs of citizens: architecture, building, military science, carpentry, cobbling, and also the science of pleading, that is, handling legal cases, that is, rhetoric, that is, eloquence learned by practice from rules. Here the equation between the *ars rhetorica* and at least one contemporary practical use of it is clear. In antiquity such a narrow definition of rhetoric was not common (see my dissertation I.25).

vignettes of contemporary political life. As an instance, the case of
the Count of Savoy who, coming to the papal court to secure some
favour, attempts to promote his case by liberally bribing the cardi-
nalate. The cardinals, accordingly, speak well of the Count in papal
audience, but one old cardinal, who missed out on the Count's
largess, while purportedly speaking well of the Count, lets slip the
latter's Ghibelline pretensions. At once the Count's suit fails.[67]

Until the appearance of the full-scale *Ad Herennium* commentary
in the later twelfth century, with its correspondingly fuller treatment
of delivery, memory, arrangement and style, medieval commentaries
were 'strongly influenced by Boethius and Victorinus, and preoccu-
pied with the rhetorical theory of argumentation and its affinities
with dialectic'.[68] Mrs. Margareta Fredborg's articles have admirably
pinpointed the major concerns of these commentators: the doctrine
of *circumstantiae* which gave particularity to the rhetorical *causa/
hypothesis* and distinguished it from dialectic[69] (in particular, the
difficult group of *adiuncta negotio*, which are, in fact, dialectical
topoi); necessary and probable argument; *ratiocinatio* and *inductio.*
Two examples must serve to illustrate twelfth-century preoccupations,
the first, a small 'epilogue' attached to one MS of an early twelfth-
century *Ad Herennium* commentary written, possibly, at Laon, by
a reasonably close adherent of the teaching of Magister Menegaldus.[70]
What follows is a paraphrase of the discussion.

Boethius and Cicero have different views when it comes to describing the subject-matter (*materia*) of rhetoric. Boethius, in the fourth
book of his *De differentiis topicis,* says that any business (*negotium*)
concerning which an orator intends to act in his speech is the *materia,*
and this is later endowed with demonstrative, deliberative or judicial
form. The *materia* must be some simple matter (*tegma*) not yet
imbued with demonstrative, deliberative or judicial form. But Cicero
says that nothing can be the *materia* of rhetoric if it does not already
possess deliberative, demonstrative or judicial form. One might,
analogously, say that the *materia* of Socrates is 'animal', which is

---

67. MS Oxford, Balliol College, 295 f.20vb.

68. Fredborg as cited above n.60 ('Petrus Helias . . .') p. 35.

69. Fredborg, 'The Commentary of Thierry of Chartres on Cicero's *De inventione'*, *Cahiers* 7(1971) pp. 17(241)ff; Victorinus ed. Halm 220.22ff, 206.40ff.

70. MS York, Cathedral Library, XVI.M.7 fols. 68vb–69 vb. The 'epilogue' is
found transcribed as an appendix to Mary Dickey's thesis (above n.50), but I have
used a transcription which Margareta Fredborg very kindly sent me (see now n.60
above). See Dickey as cited above n.14.

later divided into rational and irrational, or else that 'pure animal' is not the *materia* of Socrates, but 'animal' formed by rationality and death. Boethius then calls demonstrative, deliberative and judicial cases the 'parts' of rhetoric, whereas Cicero calls them the 'kinds' (*genera*). Consider the peculation of Verres. Now Verres himself can be termed 'demonstrative', insofar as there is some case possible concerning praise or blame of him. His peculation may also be termed 'demonstrative' insofar as it is shown to be praise- or blameworthy. Similarly the proposition 'Verres committed peculation' is also to be termed 'demonstrative' insofar as there is a court action concerning the things signified by those words, with a view to praise or blame. Likewise, viewed from different angles, these three things, Verres, his peculation, the proposition, can be termed deliberative or judicial. It may seem impossible that someone can 'inform' an external object by thought, but it is not so. For, just as sight imposes form on an outside object, so does thought. We can thus inform something with the properties signified by such words as 'deliberative', 'demonstrative', 'judicial'. But what reality subsists in these latter words? We may conclude that although in a strict sense these terms do not literally 'exist', yet they enjoy a kind of analogous existence, because they are capable of being named, just as we speak of a phoenix, though a phoenix does not exist: we act with regard to non-existent things, when we describe or speak of them, in the same way that we do with regard to existent things.

The rest of the epilogue asserts that it is incorrect to call Verres or his peculation the 'issue' of a case; examines how a demonstrative *genus* (someone's intention to act in regard to allocating praise or blame to Verres) becomes a demonstrative-conjectural *species* or issue when an accuser charges peculation and a defendant denies it;[71] discusses how the *circumstantiae* may be said to be present in such an apparently general *quaestio* as 'did Verres commit peculation?' (which in some respects is like the *quaestio* 'is Socrates white?'), and whether, since in the exordium, narration, partition and conclusion of a speech we do not need arguments, Cicero is correct in saying that all parts of rhetoric (*inventio, dispositio, memoria* etc.) are involved in the construction of all parts of a speech (*exordium, narratio,* etc.).

Our second example comes from the curious commentary contained in the early folios of MS Oxford, CCC 250, unique in its heavy

---

71. Such an issue, however, would remain a judicial one in the ancient system.

reliance upon Quintilian's *Institutes of Oratory*, and perhaps symptomatic of the thirteenth-century situation in its heavy dependence (often verbatim) upon Boethius, *De differentiis topicis* IV. The commentary doubtless belongs to the Alanus generation, but is, in many peculiar ways, distinct from the pattern of commentary found in our many Alanus versions.

'At this point[72] (the author writes), it is usual to ask why Cicero does not mention 'faculty' (or 'facilities', 'capability', 'opportunity') which belongs among the circumstances to do with the conduct of the act alleged. Some answer that since 'faculty' has two species, 'hope of success' and 'hope of escaping detection', Cicero mentions the two species instead of the genus. Others not unreasonably assert that 'faculty' is not a *locus* (source of argument) in itself, but only mixed with other *loci*. An argument which is drawn from place, or point of time, or duration of time, or occasion, it is argued, is drawn from 'faculty'. Thus it would seem that the *First Rhetorical Books* (i.e. the *De inventione*) are badly written, for there the *locus* from 'faculty' is made distinct from the other *loci*'. The passage illustrates one aspect of the attraction of the classical rhetorical system in the Middle Ages: the fascination of an intellectual structure and its terminology. The commentaries of the twelfth and thirteenth centuries frequently turn upon the problem of smoothing away apparent terminological inconsistencies in Cicero: the 'system', or codification of the *ars*, endowed with an *auctoritas* and intellectual reality that we today find surprising, had to be complete, harmonious, consistent.

Despite the narrow area of interest displayed in both of the above passages, it would be incorrect to suppose that the rhetorical curriculum never went beyond such topics. By the early thirteenth century the accumulated gloss on all parts of both the *De inventione* and *Ad Herennium* was extraordinarily thorough, covering elucidation, paraphrase, illustration, comparison, discussion, and extension. So comprehensive was the full curriculum that many glosses, commentaries and doubtless lecture series never completed the course: our MSS abound in unfinished work. In addition, the narrowly dialectical concentrations of the early generations of commentator gradually give way to a treatment of the classical texts oriented towards *dictamen*, the *ars arengandi*, and, finally, philological humanism.

---

72. MS Oxford, Corpus Christi College, 250 f.14va–b on *Ad Herennium* 2.4. I have discussed this commentary at length in my dissertation I.466–482, II.310–459 (including a partial text). I hope to prepare a detailed study of the use made in this MS of Quintilian's *Institutes*, in the light of the medieval knowledge of that text.

Such a scanty outline can scarcely do justice to so long and so extensive a tradition of teaching. Some space, however, must be left to indicate the numerous problems for further research that currently bedevil our attempt to comprehend the significance of the academic rhetorical curriculum of the Middle Ages. These may be conveniently discussed in four groups.

I

Were the *Ad Herennium* and *De inventione* in fact the basic rhetorical curriculum texts in the period? At present we know of teaching materials which do *not* take the form of glosses or commentaries on Cicero's *rhetorica*. We have collections of sample *exordia* to illustrate *Ad Herennium I;* we have—covering all periods—*compendia,* abridgements (often spliced with other basic texts, such as Quintilian's *Institutes,* or, later, Aristotle's *Rhetoric*), and even a versification (!) of the *Ad Herennium,* expanded lists of *capitula* to the same text, not to mention independent treatises on rhetoric (usually, however, very dependent upon the doctrine of the *Ad Herennium*). Although no systematic survey of this material has yet been made, it would seem, however, that it played a supplementary role in the classroom to the two classical texts and their glosses/commentaries. Again, although we are not yet in a position to know how extensively other classical and late classical rhetorical texts survived into, and were used by, the medieval schools, it would not appear that our impression of the primacy of the *Ad Herennium* and *De inventione* can be challenged. Of Aristotle's *Rhetorica* we speak below; the *rhetores latini minores* were used in the early Middle Ages, consulted from time to time during the central Middle Ages, and copied again in the Renaissance;[73] Quintilian's *Institutes* enjoyed

73. On the popularity of the classics in general see Wilson and Reynolds (above n. 10); R.A.B. Mynors, 'The Latin Classics known to Boston of Bury' in *Fritz Saxl Essays,* ed. D. J. Gordon (London, 1957); M. Manitius, *Handschriften antiker Autoren in mittelalterlichen Bibliothekskatalogen* (Leipzig, 1925), and Thomson, as cited above n. 9. On the *rhetores latini minores* see G. Billanovich 'Il Petrarca e i retori latini minori', *Italia Medioevale e Umanistica* 5(1962) pp. 103–64. The same journal 8(1965) 410–12, together with *Revue d'histoire des textes* 2(1972)137,139, R.Sabbadini 'Spogli Ambrosiani' *Studi Ital. di Filol. Class.* 11(1903) 276–294 and his *Le Scoperte dei Codici Latini e Greci nei secoli XIV e XV,* II (Florence, 1914) 199– 261, provide some information of the *fortleben* of the minor Latin rhetoricians to supplement data contained in Halm's 1863 edition of them (cf. n. 49 above). I use the term 'minor Latin rhetoricians' for the moment narrowly, excluding Victorinus, Grillius, Martianus Capella and the other encyclopedists, whose *fortleben* is better known than that of Julius Victor, Fortunatianus and others (e.g. on Isidore, *Traditio*

greater currency than is generally realised, the *De Oratore* was at least known[74] and Cicero's lesser rhetorical writings, especially the *Topica* (with Boethius' commentary) appeared from time to time. These texts were not, however, commented or glossed and their circulation was minimal in comparison with the massive distribution of the *Ad Herennium* and *De inventione*.

The only antique text which seems to have enjoyed a general currency approaching, but not equalling, the *Ad Herennium* and *De inventione* was the fourth book of Boethius' *De differentiis topicis*. This was commented in the later Middle Ages and appears frequently in the MSS as a separate treatise. It seems to have supplanted actual use of the two 'Ciceronian' texts in the thirteenth-century university classrooms at Paris, and possibly elsewhere. This circumstance is perhaps to be expected. The Boethian text was, after all, behind the elaborate and sometimes muddled *quaestiones* in the twelfth-century rhetorical commentaries; once these commentaries had established the dimensions of the Boethian placement and description of rhetoric, the schools could revert to the formulas of the *De differentiis topicis*, since their interests were primarily dialectical, demonstrative, scientific, theological, ethical, and, in terms of theory, political.[75]

22(1966) 440, and on Martianus Capella the article by Cora Lutz in *Catalogus* (above n. 12) II and the thesis by Raia n. 14 above). On the pseudo-Augustine *De rhetorica* see *Speech Monographs* 35(1968) 90–108. The rhetorical portion of Cassiodorus' *Institutiones* forms an extremely common introductory text, usually to the *De inventione* in the MSS (see Ward, 'Sources').

74. In the twelfth/thirteenth century the rhetorical commentator 'Alanus', author of the most successful of the medieval *Ad Herennium* commentaries, wrote of the 'librum de oratore quo nos caremus', MS London, British Museum, Harley 6324 f.2vb. The textual survival of the *De oratore* is discussed in A. S. Wilkins' 1895 Oxford edition I, 64–72 and C. H. Beeson, *Lupus of Ferrières as Scribe and Text Critic* (Cambridge, Mass., 1930). For Quintilian in the Middle Ages see Wilson and Reynolds p. 237, M. Winterbottom in T. A. Dorey *Empire and Aftermath, Silver Latin II* (London, 1975) pp. 92–97, and, for recent evidence, Zinn in *Viator* 5(1974) 224–5. I have, however, attempted to extend our understanding of this subject in my dissertation I.64–71, 82–87, 136–150, 418–82, II.310–378, 402–416 etc. Although Professor Caplan in the introduction of his Loeb *Ad Herennium* translation says that there are probably over 100 extant MSS of the treatise, the figure is more likely to be closer to 1,000. The combined MS survival of both *Ad Herennium* and *De inventione* might lie between 1,000 and 2,000 copies, making them the major works of Latin antiquity for the Middle Ages. The figures presented in Clark (above n. 7) pp. 64–5 are quite inadequate.

75. See my dissertation I, 482–526; the principal evidence for the apparent replacement of the Ciceronian texts by Boethius' *De differentiis topicis* is: surviving commentaries on the text from the 13th and 14th centuries (see *Traditio* 28(1972) 299, 29(1973)111, MSS Brussels B.R. 3540–7, Erlangen Univbibl. 213, Paris B.N.

In connection with the latter emphases, it should also be remembered that Aristotle's *Rhetorica* (in Latin translation) enters the university curriculum in the later part of the thirteenth century and thereafter: more than one hundred MSS of Moerbeke's translation survive, many with substantial marginal glosses, an *index alphabeticus* for the work was compiled towards 1300, and commentaries on it were written by such men as Albertus Magnus, Boethius of Dacia, Giles of Rome, Jean Buridan, John of Jandun; at least one of these commentaries survives in as many as 20 MSS.[76] It is interesting that Buridan deals most extensively with the place of rhetoric in relation to dialectic, as a special argumentative system for a particular context (ethics, moral questions, emotional 'public' issues). Robert Kilwardby, the indefatigable thirteenth-century Oxford Dominican, similarly, in his *De ortu scientiarum*, is concerned to fix the place of rhetoric, 'a conjectural science, which ought not unsuitably be placed between ethics and the mechanical arts, since it is devoted to the service of the field of political ethics (in the areas of *elocutio* and *pronuntiatio*) and is totally bound up with human affairs as far as they are engaged in any civil controversy'.[77] It is curious that these

lat. 16617 etc.), the University of Paris statutes for the thirteenth century (ed. Denifle and Chatelain, Paris, 1891; and see G. Leff *Paris and Oxford Universities in the Thirteenth and Fourteenth Centuries* (Wiley, 1968) pp. 137–160), Robert Kilwardby's *De ortu scientiarum* (shortly to be published by the British Academy (*Auctores Britannici Medii Aevi* IV) and the Pontifical Institute of Medieval Studies, Toronto, ed. A. G. Judy), and the MS Barcelona Ripoll 109 (Archivo de la Corona de Aragón) discussed by M. Grabmann in *Bay. Akad. d. Wiss. Philos.-Hist. Sitzungsb.* 1939 Hft.5 ch.vi pp. 112–6 and *Mittelalterliches Geistesleben* II (Munich, 1936) 183–99. Further MS detail will be found (not always accurately) in P. Glorieux, *La Faculté des Arts et ses Maîtres au XIIIᵉ Siècle* (Paris, 1971). I have to thank Margareta Fredborg for information on this topic. See also the essay by Michael Leff in this volume.

76. I owe this information to the kindness of Margareta Fredborg, whose paper on Buridan's 'Questions on the Rhetoric of Aristotle' is to appear in *Museum Tusculanum* (Copenhagen, 1976): The Logic of John Buridan, Acts of the Third European Symposium on Medieval Logic, Copenhagen 16–21 Nov. 1975. See also the articles by Boggess and Lohr in *Viator* 2(1971) and *Traditio* 24(1968: pp. 191–2 on Guido Vernani de Arimino). Mrs. Fredborg was kind enough to send me a typescript of her material on Buridan prior to its publication. The oldest MS containing indices to the works of Aristotle (MS 124 of the Seminary Library in Pisa) contains an alphabetical subject-index to Boethius' *De differentiis topicis*.

77. I have drawn this sentence from sections 638, 643 and 647 of Kilwardby's *De ortu* in the edition cited n. 75 above. Dr. R. W. Hunt was kind enough to show me proofs of this edition prior to its publication. On the general relationship between the Latin rhetorical tradition in the Middle Ages and the Aristotelian, see Murphy *Medieval Rhetoric* R18, R20, R21, R27, S. Robert in *New Scholasticism*

northern preoccupations, which resulted in texts of Aristotle's *Rhetorica* being included for the most part in manuscripts with a political/ethical emphasis, are not duplicated below the Alps: there, although Aristotle's *Rhetorica* was known, the Ciceronian works formed the basis of instruction, in an overtly rhetorical context, on a scale that dwarfed the northern attentions to Aristotle Rhetor.

In grammar, as is well known, the study of certain 'moderni' came to supplant or supplement attention to Priscian and Donatus as basic curriculum texts in the thirteenth and fourteenth centuries.[78] In rhetoric no such development seems to have taken place: if the commentaries by Alanus, Bartolinus and Guarino da Verona achieved a certain currency, this did not reduce—indeed, it enhanced—the primacy of the 'Ciceronian' texts. In view of their general appeal to an age that believed its preparatory *artes* should be systematic, well sign-posted, neatly interlocking and finite, these texts deserved their popularity.

II

What is the relative significance of the *rhetorica* glosses? As noted earlier in this chapter, we are not yet in a position to compare the long tradition of *rhetorica* glosses with the medieval and Renaissance commentation of other classical authors. The major classical poets (Vergil, Persius, Juvenal for instance) were taught, glossed and commented for as long a period of time as the *rhetorica* texts, and lesser lights, such as Lucan and Ovid, did not lag far behind. In the earlier medieval period the encyclopaedic texts (Boethius *De consolatione philosophiae*, Martianus Capella *De nuptiis*, Macrobius *Somnium Scipionis*) were much taught and glossed. Donatus and Priscian, supplemented in the later Middle Ages by Alexander de Villedieu, Geoffrey of Vinsauf and others, accumulated a further store of

---

31(1957)484–98 and M. T. D'Alverny in *Archives d'hist. doctr. et litt.* 35(1968) 314–326 on the mixed Greek and Latin rhetorical contents of MS Toledo Bibl.Capit. 47.15 (= no. 1234 in G. Lacombe *Aristot. Lat. Cod. pars post.* (Cambridge, 1955) p. 853 and see Ch. Faulhaber in *Ábaco* IV p. 173, with p. 202 of the volume cited in Murphy item R20). I provide some remarks in my dissertation I.509–12. Note too A. M. Patterson, *Hermogenes and the Renaissance* (Princeton, 1970), G. L. Kustas 'The Function and Evolution of Byzantine Rhetoric' *Viator* 1(1970) and the same author's *Studies in Byzantine Rhetoric* (Thessalonica, 1973).

78. Alexander de Villedieu *Doctrinale* and Évrard de Béthune *Graecismus*, for instance. See L. J. Paetow (Murphy *Med.Rhet.*B85) and Murphy *Rhetoric in the Middle Ages* pp. 138–39 etc.

marginal learning, *lecture* and *glosule*. The massive efforts of the glossators in logic, theology, biblical scholarship and law are better known.

How does the *rhetorica* corpus compare with these other departments of learning, in quantitative and qualitative terms? It is too early to tell. At this stage we can only point to the fact that the interest of the *rhetorica* gloss tradition lies not so much in its size or scope, but in its very existence. Glosses on the *Ad Herennium* and *De inventione* were strictly speaking unnecessary, at least after the middle of the twelfth century, when law and logic were fully emancipated from their rhetorical aegis and when disciplines making secondary use of classical rhetorical theory had all come to acquire their own, more specialised manuals (*artes poetriae, dictaminis, predicandi* etc.). Yet the birth of full scale *Ad Herennium* commentation dates from the second half of the eleventh century and only achieves primacy over *De inventione* usage in the second half of the twelfth. Thereafter, commentaries and glosses on the text burgeon magically. Why? The *Ad Herennium* is not a literary classic; it could not serve the needs of general education as well as texts like the *De nuptiis*, the *Aeneid* or Boethius' *Consolations of Philosophy*. Neither it nor the *De inventione* offered the scholastic or the humanist much insight into classical law, life or thought that could not be derived more successfully from other sources, and they could not compete for the attention of the *dictator, predicator* or *poetista* against the more specialised professional manuals. Wherein lies the secret of the 'vita nuova' of the classical rhetorical texts after the mid-twelfth century?

III

How do the *rhetorica* glosses fit into the university trivium curricula? We are for the most part ignorant of university or cathedral school syllabi, methods of study and curriculum requirements, as they relate to the teaching of the rhetorical texts. Certain celebrated indications exist for the earlier period, such as Richer of Rheims' description of the teaching methods of Gerbert, and John of Salisbury's remarks on teaching at Chartres. Later materials are few and difficult to interpret: the 'list of text-books' ascribed to Alexander Neckam by C. H. Haskins, the MS Ripoll 109 (Barcelona) 'Quaestionensammlung' for examination use from the University of Paris towards the middle of the thirteenth century, and the university statutes themselves.[79] Writers like Alan of Lille and his commentator Radulphus de Longo Campo, for example, acquired a thorough formal grounding in classical rhetorical theory that could only have been obtained at the university (of Paris), and the numerous *rhetorica* commentaries and glosses themselves bear witness to considerable, though perhaps not overly tightly organised study in the pre-university period, and a long tradition of ordinary and extraordinary lectures, especially in Italy, in the universities and *studia*.[80] Two aspects of this teaching curriculum are currently in perplexing confusion. The first, classroom technique, will be noticed at once, the second, the status of rhetorical teaching in the universities, will be mentioned again under IV below.

Medieval teaching was predominantly oral, and, as a consequence, we are not certain of the actual circumstances under which glosses, commentaries, lectures were written down in the first place. What purpose were they supposed to serve? Why are some unfinished, some sketchy, and some massive? Why do the same selection of glosses (mostly from Victorinus) appear in so many tenth- to eleventh-century MSS? Why did eleventh- to twelfth-century scholars decide to replace Victorinus with *De inventione* commentaries of their own? Why was Victorinus so popular in the immediate post-Carolingian period, and again in the Renaissance? Why did one fifteenth-century student choose to copy the scrappy thirteenth-century commentary of Jacques de Dinant, and why did another copy out (an older MS of) Petrus Helias, ascribe it to Augustine, and accompany it with some of the *rhetores latini minores*? Why did Jean Poulain, in the fifteenth century, use a 'proto-Alanus' *Ad Herennium* commentary and not one of the later (?) and better-known versions of the Alanus commentary, such as were in common use south of the Alps? Why do we find two MSS identically splicing an early version of the popular commentary by the early fourteenth-century Bolognese lecturer Bartolinus, with an earlier (?) commentary, ascribed to 'Alanus', yet almost certainly not Alanus, or at least not any of the so far recognised 'Alanus' or 'proto-Alanus' versions

---

79. Cf. n. 75 above. The Neckam list will be found in C. H. Haskins' *Studies in the History of Medieval Science* (New York, 1924) ch.18. Richer: *Histories* III.46–8 (my dissertation I.178ff); John of Salisbury: *Metalogikon* I.24.

80. Radulphus: n. 14 above. Ordinary and extraordinary lectures: H. Rashdall, *The Universities of Europe in the Middle Ages* I (Oxford, 1936, ed. Powicke-Emden) pp. 205–07, Gordon Leff (above n. 75) p. 149 etc.

in our MSS? What factors governed the selection of material? Some scholars (Thierry of Chartres, Petrus Helias) make a conscious attempt to clear out the warehouse of rhetorical wisdom, some (like Alanus) attempt to produce a master 'glossa ordinaria' and some (like Jean Poulain) are content to work up a stated and unstated mosaic of material across the centuries. Half a millenium, a millenium, is as nothing in the life-cycle of a *rhetorica* gloss. In the schoolroom, the Renaissance dawns late.

It is perhaps not surprising that in general teachers were reluctant to stake individual claims to their shares of the gloss potpourri. Nearly all commentaries and glosses are anonymous, though admiring copyists and redactors sometimes tell us whose lectures they are preparing. Occasionally, personal circumstances will provoke an author to identify himself (for example Thierry of Chartres) or humble pride in humble work (for example Jean Poulain). Even the greatest of the *magistri* seem to have taken little trouble to secure the survival of their work: Alan of Lille, if his is the commentary ascribed in some versions to 'Alanus', was careless of fame, and no less a scholar than Guarino da Verona left the task of editing his *Ad Herennium* gloss to his pupils—and their pupils.

Consequently, the accumulating mass of rhetorical wisdom came to form a kind of anonymous pool, from which pitchers were drawn almost at random: some commentaries, as we have seen, exist in many versions; some MSS float uneasily between two or more versions, two or more authors, two or more MSS themselves made up of two or more versions or authors; we possess massive compilations from many sources, scant pastiches of a single author, and a bewildering variety of prefaces that serve to disguise many a reworking of a standard gloss.

What factors, we may finally ask, governed the survival of material to our own day or determined whose lectures became part of the 'standard gloss' and whose did not? How far were glosses from one center circulated in others? How easy was it for writers such as Alanus or Jean Poulain to assemble MSS of the major commentaries of previous generations, as they appear to have done?

IV

The mists of time will no doubt hide forever from us the answers to most of the foregoing questions. Certain outstanding problems, however, may one day be capable of solution, and certain basic tasks completed. The initial work before students in this field concerns proper study of the surviving MSS: working out their correct date, authorship, identity, provenance and relationship. This will enable any interested person to trace the development of ideas on particular doctrines and on such topics as the understanding of antiquity in the Middle Ages.[81] By comparing the commentation of major writers on select significant passages of the *Ad Herennium* and *De inventione,* it will be possible to plot and measure the movement of the corporate academic mind, as it reflected the concerns and emphases of the day, from the fourth to the seventeenth century A.D. Few other texts remained in vogue in the schools for so long a period.

Particular outstanding problems can then be tackled. We are, for instance, fairly well aware of the origins of *De inventione* commentation: Victorinus, Boethius, Grillius and the first, tentative, marginal glosses of the tenth and eleventh centuries. But what of the *Ad Herennium? Ad Herennium* commentation appears fully grown, as it were, in the eleventh century.[82] Was there a late antique/early medieval *Ad Herennium* gloss? Certain scholars have thought so; and the thirteenth-century bibliophile Richard de Fournival, from whose library many of the manuscripts of the Sorbonne, and ultimately, the Bibliothèque Nationale, are derived, claims he owned a Grillius and a Victorinus commentary on the *Ad Herennium.*[83]

The origin of full-scale *Ad Herennium* commentation in late thirteenth- to early fourteenth-century Italy is a more interesting subject of research of some currency today.[84] The thirteenth century, as we have seen, is almost devoid of commentaries and major glosses on the Latin rhetorical texts. One or another of the 'Alanus' versions *may* be early thirteenth-century in date; and at the other end of the century, in Italy, we appear to have a fragmentary *Ad Herennium* commentary by the northerner Jacques de Dinant and, possibly, the first major Italian *Ad Herennium* commentary of the Renaissance,

---

81. The detailed analysis, for instance, of patristic and medieval commentation on Romans xiii, 1–7 noted by Beryl Smalley, *The Becket Conflict and the Schools* (Oxford, 1973), p. 52, n. 50, is an example of this type of research in another field.

82. I hope to deal with this at greater length elsewhere (cf. n. 23 above).

83. See Wisén cited n. 14 above, the introduction to J. Martin's edition of Grillius' *De inventione* commentary (Paderborn, 1927), and my 'Sources' (above n. 16) for details. I refer to items 32 and 36 of Richard de Fournival's *Biblionomia* (ed. L. Delisle, *Cabinet des MSS. de la B.N.* v.2).

84. See Banker and Wertis, cited notes 22 and 23 above, for instance.

surviving in four MSS and known from its incipit as *Plena et perfecta*, close in content to the Alanus versions, and ascribed to Alanus in one of the Bartolinus commentary versions. The first half of the fourteenth century, by contrast, is crowded with glosses and commentaries (Italian), and thereafter a steady stream left the schoolrooms. Very little of the fourteenth- to fifteenth-century material I have surveyed can with any certainty be ascribed to the northern academic environment. The fourteenth-century Italian commentaries reveal a ferment of academic opinion on the correct method of introducing, subdividing and lecturing on the *Ad Herennium*; they show considerable familiarity with the scholastic techniques of lecturing and commentation used in the thirteenth-century northern schools, on the *artes* and the Bible.

What circumstances explain the sudden burgeoning of *Ad Herennium* commentaries in fourteenth-century Italy? To what extent are these commentaries based on (lost) northern *Ad Herennium* commentaries and to what extent do they represent an importation into Italy of northern university lecturing and commentary techniques? What relation do they bear to contemporary Italian intellectual ferment, 'prehumanism' as it is sometimes called?[85] What status did this rhetorical teaching occupy in the universities of the time? Was it a kind of advanced resource study designed to deepen the more elementary lectures on *dictamen* and preaching, or on the art of political address? Was it merely part of an upsurge of interest in the classical *auctores*? Was the *Ad Herennium* glossed simply because it was thought to be a work of no less an author than Cicero himself? What was the relation between the study of the *Ad Herennium* and the study of grammar, dialectic, Geoffrey of Vinsauf's *Poetria nova* and other linguistic texts that seem to have attracted attention in the universities and *studia* of the period?[86] Was the *Ad Herennium* (and the bulk of the fourteenth- to fifteenth-century Italian commentaries concern the *Ad Herennium* rather than the *De inventione*) a basic requirement of the contemporary curriculum in

---

85. The literature on this subject is enormous: see Struever (above n. 8) ch. 2 and the writings of Renucci, Kristeller, Simone, Billanovich, Weiss, Wieruszowski (n. 52 above), the notes to Wertis' paper, etc. Of importance too is Beryl Smalley's *English Friars and Antiquity* (Oxford, 1960), especially ch. 12.

86. See for example G. Manacorda 'Fra Bartolomeo da S. Concordio grammatico e la fortuna di Gaufredo di Vinesauf in Italia', *Raccolta di Studi di Storia e Critica Letteraria ded. a Francesco Flamini* (Pisa, 1918) 139–152.

the *artes*, or was it a 'special option'? One fourteenth-century commentary, surviving in a Milanese MS, puts forward novel and strongly contentious ideas on the way to divide the text of the *Ad Herennium*, and how to blend it with what is relevant from the *De inventione*: these ideas are neither paralleled nor referred to in other MSS of the time. Why?

These problems introduce us to the chief topic of research in the area of medieval and Renaissance rhetorical studies: how far is the shift from 'medieval' to 'Renaissance', as conventionally understood, apparent in the rhetorical commentaries? Rhetoric lies at the center of recent assessments of the transition from the Middle Ages to the Renaissance:[87] do the commentaries argue for continuity or discontinuity? Do the commentaries support the recent emphasis upon the place of linguistic and rhetorical preoccupations in the literary consciousness of the time?[88] To what extent is the controversy between Guarino da Verona and Poggio Bracciolini on Caesar and Scipio simply a sign of the conservatism of the schoolroom pitted against the freshness of the humanist rhetorical insight?[89] Is there any substantial difference between John of Salisbury's comprehension of the myth of civilization in the opening pages of the *De inventione* and Petrarch's?[90] Both the twelfth and the fourteenth centuries were marked by an intensive study of the Latin *rhetorica* texts; the extent to which certain individuals in each age understood and attempted to recreate the contentious position of Cicero in his late Republican intellectual context may not materially advance our understanding of the intellectual temper of each age. It may be more to the point that Cicero, John of Salisbury, Petrarch, the *dictatores*, Leonardo Bruni and Poggio himself, were 'novi homines', or moved around the margins of the established intellectual patterns of their

---

87. Struever and Seigel (above n. 8) and references cited Struever pp. 41–2. McKeon (above n. 5) has perceptive remarks, e.g. pp. 2, 10 and see also his article cited above n. 6. Tateo (cited Struever p. 42) sees as one criterion of the 'Renaissance' the emancipation of poetry from rhetoric and its development as a witness to the earthly destiny of man and his creative capacity, as a science dealing with human activity on a par with politics and philosophy, as a human creation, the unique form of creation conceded to man, in which is displayed the nobility of his finer nature. Tateo calls this poetry 'la poesia civilizzatrice'.

88. See no. 8 above.

89. Struever pp. 161, 179 and, for the details, J. W. Oppel 'Peace vs. liberty in the Quattrocento: Poggio, Guarino and the Scipio-Caesar controversy', *The Journal of Medieval and Renaissance Studies* 4(1974) 221–265.

90. Seigel (above n. 8) ch. 6, my dissertation I, 31–33.

day, or belonged to a profession that needed intellectual legitimization, or were unstable personalities: the attraction of the rhetorical mode, or cast, was therefore pronounced, but how far each 'typified' his age is debatable.[91]

In a sense, and some ruminations on this point must close this overlong chapter, the role played by classical rhetorical theory in society and learning does tend to reinforce the distinction between 'medieval' and 'Renaissance', or, better, between the intellectual priorities of the class most concerned with theoretical learning in medieval society and its counterpart in the world of the later medieval Italian communes. Contrasts, however, should not be exaggerated. Although humanist attention to the sources of classical rhetorical theory was marked by a philological accuracy and thoroughness unknown earlier, it was not until very late in the humanist 'vogue' that this accuracy and thoroughness were sufficiently attuned to spot the anomalies attendant upon the acceptance of the *Ad Herennium* as the work of Cicero. This is an academic point, however, and ought not concern us: medieval estimation of the value of the *Ad Herennium* is not altered by the quibbles concerning its authorship. Of more significance for our present theme is the static, Christianised educational pattern that overshadowed the study of classical rhetorical theory in the Middle Ages. In this static pattern, which bore no specific relation to any particular sociological situation, rhetoric, in the manner of a fossil, occupied a fixed position, of which the origins lay far in the past. The intellectual context that gave relevance to this educational pattern, revivified as it was in the writings of Augustine, stressed life on earth as a time for scriptural preparation for the afterlife, or at least as a time for the attainment of a state of earthly beatitude that imposed considerable restrictions upon the free play of economic, social and political forces. Within this framework, classical rhetoric enjoyed a surreptitious existence, partly because it shared the unimpeachable *auctoritas* of antiquity, and partly because it acted as a source for largely extraneous technical disciplines which made no particular direct use of the Ciceronian theory of the primacy of oratorical eloquence: the derived arts of letter/document composition, poetry-writing, preaching, praying, pleading. From its somewhat ambivalent position in the educational cadre of the period,

---

91. Struever's portrayal of Poggio Bracciolini's rhetorical cast of mind is enticing (Struever ch. 4).

rhetoric exercised almost accidentally a broader influence on the processes of argument, the canons of interpreting laws and scripture, and the classification of legal issues. For a moment, in the twelfth century, when the social impact of higher learning was first intensively felt, it assumed something of its ancient significance as a program setting appropriate aims and limits to the acquisition of learning. The details of the program, however, differed duly from antique realisations of theory, just as the classes concerned and the political, juridical and legal framework of the two ages differed. John of Salisbury's *Metalogicon* deals more with the dialectical content of the *trivium* than with rhetoric conventionally received, partly because he was not writing a rhetorical textbook: he had other purposes in mind. He was addressing (or thought he was addressing) the intellectual leaders of medieval western Christendom, and he had reformist ambitions.

At bottom, however, in medieval times, rhetoric in the schoolroom remained a series of observations based on, derived from, or designed to elucidate either the *De inventione* or the *Ad Herennium*. Neither text gave much space to the concept of eloquence as Queen of the Sciences, however much they assumed it. Medieval Christian learning, despite the attacks of heretics, mystics and social reformers, remained elitist and hierarchical: it could not, therefore, adopt the principal tenets of an art that assumed a more popular focus of learning and was initially designed for theatres other than the schoolroom. Fragments of rhetorical wisdom spun off into nonacademic areas of medieval intellectual endeavour, in the course of the centuries, but it is only in later medieval Italy that one can see a fully developed academic, scholastic tradition of classical rhetorical study, serving something like the social and vocational spectrum at which the ancient Latin rhetorical manuals were aimed. Yet, and here is the relevant point, rhetorical theory continued to be of use to medieval man, in roughly its ancient dress, because he continued to be confronted by situations that required persuasion at a nontechnical level. The intensity of these situations varied. Clearly, the circumstances that provoked Alcuin to his dialogue on rhetoric, Gerbert to the composition of his epistolary defence, the eleventh-century *dictamen* writers to the systematisation of their art, the early twelfth-century thinkers to their articulation of the implications of the *De inventione* proem were of a more critical nature than those that sustained the ordinary rhetorical teaching of the cathedral and monastic schools of quieter times. This in itself suggests a law of value in the study of medieval intellectual history. All study of rhetoric in medieval times was motivated by more than inertia or antiquarianism or a socio-vocational structure that paid a class of people to think, write and teach more or less what they wished to. A heightened interest in the full apparatus of classical rhetorical theory, or, at least, in any part or parts of the *De inventione* and *Ad Herennium* other than the passages on *elocutio*, a near staple in the slow moving, meditative Latin culture of the time, suggests a crisis of communication: between king and adviser, between opposed political or religious parties or factions, between personal enemies, between educationalists with conflicting views, between conflicting professional classes and social groups, between the bearers of Christian truth, their opponents, and the bulk of mankind.[92]

The use made of classical rhetorical theory is thus a yardstick in intellectual history. More important, perhaps, it is a yardstick of that way of looking at mankind and learning which we label 'classical humanism'. In his *De officiis* (1.16.50) Cicero had written that the first and most basic bond which can be perceived in the social patterns of the entire human race was that between speech (*oratio*) and the power to reason, systematise and organise (*ratio*). This bond is the cement of human fellowship and society: by teaching, learning, communicating, instructing and judging (*docendo, discendo, communicando, disceptando, iudicando*), it makes peace between men and encourages their joint activity in a kind of social intercourse that conforms to all the intentions of nature. In these terms, when medieval scholastics cultivated *ratio* to the neglect of *oratio*, it could be said that they manifested essentially antihumanist characteristics: they concerned themselves increasingly with God, truth and a narrow elite of university trained theologians and *artes* lecturers, rather than with the bulk of mankind, or the concerns of its dominant classes. At such times, rhetoric, in its classical formulation, faded away in the university curricula, was glimpsed through a glass darkly by way of Boethius' *De differentiis topicis*, was converted by the mendicants

---

92. Compare the situation that faced Tisias and Corax (above n. 42) with that described in Galbert of Bruges' chronicle of the murder of Charles the Good, Count of Flanders (1127), trans. J. B. Ross (New York, 1959) sect.1 p. 84, sect.2 p. 85, sect. 7 p. 96 etc. (my dissertation I, 336–8).

into a tool for the inculcation of intellectual absolutism (preaching) or assigned a sinecure in the field of moral philosophy and ethics (as taught rather than practised).

In itself, such a development represented no great loss: classical rhetorical theory was, after all, but one particular realisation of the art of communication, if as useful as any and more thorough than most. Of more significance is the philosophy that lay behind the systematization of classical rhetorical theory: the conviction that the art of communication could be reduced to rules, was above all else worthy of study, and formed the basis of human society. It is the sporadic appearance of this philosophy, despite the adverse influence in the Middle Ages of absolutism in both political and theological systems, that fascinates. Political autocracy and intellectual authoritarianism cannot encourage rhetorical study since they inhibit the free exchange of ideas between men and the consequent possibility of altering fixed attitudes.[93] In the twelfth-century debate over wisdom and eloquence, dialectic or human studies, the myth of civilization as it is found in the *De inventione* or the mouthings of Cornificius, the author of the anonymous *Metamorphosis Goliae*,[94] is in some respects making the point that each generation will reinterpret and reexamine even religious truth. This is a natural process: knowledge as such does not exist; only human beings make knowledge possible or relevant. Knowledge is a series of conceptions communicated, and the act of communication, together with the circumstances in which the act is performed, makes inevitable a gradual process of modification to those conceptions. To attempt to arrest this process is to belie the nature of man. Thus monastic sentiment must not be allowed to oppose the free play of *sermo* and *ratio*.

The long night of classical rhetorical precepts in the Middle Ages prompts a final thought. That these rules continued to attract attention testifies to the medieval faith in the attempt to institutionalise the modes of communication between men by the use of rules extraneous to the subject-matter to be communicated, in areas not directly affected by absolutism in political practice and intellectual systems. Medieval faith in these rules is the measure of the influence

93. See Kenneth Burke, *A Rhetoric of Motives* (New York, 1950) p. 50 'Persuasion involves choice, will.......'

94. See *Viator* 3(1972)221ff; the latest discussion of the *Metamorphosis Goliae* (in a relatively narrow context) is by Benton (*Speculum* 50(1975)199ff). See also references cited above n. 59.

of classical rhetorical humanism. In a real sense the *dictator* is the ancestor of the Florentine civic humanist. Not only did he keep alive a sensitivity towards style, latinity and language, and demonstrate the ability of the word to shape, determine and fix social hierarchies,[95] but he continued and handed on to his successors the vestigial medieval understanding of the classical attempt to institutionalise human relationships and thus to translate into a programme of education the twin capacities of *ratio* and *oratio*.[96]

---

95. Cf. Albert of Samaria: 'rhetorica vero distincte, ornate, expolite componere unicuique sexui et persone et etati necnon ordini et dignitati congrua accidentia distribuere, ordinem et modum discernere' (cited Kantorowicz, *Medievalia et Humanistica* I p. 53). I think also of Giovanni di Bonandrea's *Brevis introductio ad dictamen*: J. R. Banker in *Manuscripta* 18(1974)12. I am much indebted to Dr. Banker for the gift of a copy of his doctoral dissertation on Giovanni's *introductio* (University of Rochester, 1971).

96. The humanist and the dictator: Seigel (above n. 8) ch. vii, *Past and Present* 36(1967)3ff, H. H. Gray 'Renaissance Humanism: the pursuit of eloquence' in P. O. Kristeller and P. P. Wiener ed. *Renaissance Essays* (New York, 1968). Much of the debate over the intellectuals of the Italian Renaissance as committed humanists or professional *dictatores* must remain without fruit until we know more fully the mechanism and significance of diachronic change between the vocational and intellectual structure of one generation and that of the next or subsequent generations, until we can free the texts we use as documents from their inferred context of intention and immediate human motivation.

I should like to thank Dr. R. W. Hunt and Mrs. Margareta Fredborg for very carefully reading through this chapter and making many corrections and suggestions for improvement, most of which I have been able to incorporate. The remaining deficiencies are, of course, entirely my own.

The *Poetria nova*
of Geoffrey of Vinsauf

ERNEST GALLO

THE MOST POPULAR of the medieval arts of poetry was Geoffrey of Vinsauf's *Poetria nova*. Bernard Silvester had apparently written an earlier art of poetry, but it has not come down to us. Bernard's pupil, Matthew of Vendôme, wrote his *Introductory Treatise on the Art of Poetry* around 1175. Around 1210, Geoffrey of Vinsauf wrote his *Poetria Nova* in Latin hexameters and dedicated it to Pope Innocent III. Geoffrey recast his work into a prose form, the *Documentum de arte versificandi,* adding some valuable explanations of certain points in the poetic version.[1] Of Geoffrey's life we know very little except that he lived in London before going to Rome during the pontificate of Innocent III.[2]

The *Poetria nova* was widely circulated. Prof. John Conley, who is completing a definitive edition of the text, reports that the work exists in over 200 MSS.[3] He has pointed out that in the codices the

1. The texts of most of the medieval arts of poetry are available in E. Faral, *Les arts poétiques du XIIᵉ et du XIIIᵉ siècle* (Paris, 1924; reprinted Paris, 1958). The *Poetria nova* is in Faral, pages 197–262, and exists in several translations: Margaret F. Nims. *Poetria nova* (Toronto, 1967); Jane B. Kopp, *Poetria nova,* in *Three Medieval Rhetorical Arts,* ed. James J. Murphy (Berkeley and Los Angeles, 1971), pp. 32–108; and Ernest Gallo, *The Poetria nova and Its Sources in Early Rhetorical Doctrine* (The Hague, 1971). Matthew of Vendôme's *Ars versificatoria* is in Faral, pp. 109–193, and is translated by Ernest Gallo, "Matthew of Vendôme: Introductory Treatise on the Art of Poetry," *Proceedings of the American Philosophical Society* 118 (February 1974), 51–92. Geoffrey of Vinsauf's *Documentum de arte versificandi* is in Faral, pp. 265–320, and is translated by Roger Parr, *Instruction in the Method and Art of Speaking and Versifying* (Milwaukee, 1968).

2. For the life of Geoffrey of Vinsauf, see Faral, pp. 15–18; see also Josiah Cox Russell, *A Dictionary of Writers of Thirteenth Century England* (London, 1936), s.v. Geoffrey de Vinesauf.

3. Prof. Conley informs me that Sr. Nims uncovered many of these manuscripts and generously shared her knowledge with him.

Poetria nova is found in distinguished company, being very often bound together with Horace's *Art of Poetry*, Boethius' *Consolation of Philosophy*, or Virgil's *Georgics*. It is found once with a commentary on Dante's *Paradiso*, and several times, interestingly enough, with Bernard Silvester's *De mundi universitate*. However, there was one segment of its audience with which the work was not popular: Professor Conley has pointed out that, in the *Morales scolarium*, John of Garland says that boys not only scorn grammar but think ill of the wholesome works of Geoffrey of Vinsauf.

In his own *Poetria*, John of Garland shows considerable debt to Geoffrey of Vinsauf, as does Eberhard the German's *Laborintus*. The latter work almost certainly refers to the *Poetria nova* when it speaks of the *Ars nova scribendi* as a work that shines with a special merit.[4] Gervais of Melkley also praises Geoffrey of Vinsauf, together with Matthew of Vendôme and Bernard Silvester.[5] Prof. George Engelhardt has pointed out that, in a letter to Cornelius Gerard, Erasmus places Geoffrey of Vinsauf in the distinguished company of Horace and Quintilian.[6]

The *Poetria nova* opens with a well-known passage about the necessity of planning one's work beforehand and of predetermining the limits of its subject matter.[7] The passage is well known because Chaucer translates it in part in *Troilus and Criseyde*, I. 1065–1069. In the *Poetria nova*, the passage reads as follows:

> If anyone is to lay the foundation of a house, his impetuous hand does not leap into action: the inner design of the heart measures out the work beforehand, the inner man determines the stages ahead of time in a certain order; and the hand of the heart, rather than the bodily hand,

---

4. *Laborintus*, lines 665–666, in Faral, p. 360.

5. Gervasius of Melcheley, *Ars poetica*, ed. Hans-Jürgen Gräbener (Münster, 1965), p. 1.

6. George Engelhardt, "Mediaeval Vestiges in the Rhetoric of Erasmus," *PMLA* 63 (June 1948), 739–744.

7. Following is an outline of the major topics of the *Poetria nova*, with corresponding line references:

   I. Introduction; Divisions of the art of rhetoric (1–86).
   II. Arrangement, including the natural and artificial openings (87–202).
   III. Amplification and Abbreviation (203–741).
   IV. Stylistic ornament (742–1592).
   V. Conversion (1593–1765).
   VI. Determination (1766–1846).
   VII. Miscellaneous advice on choice of words, humor, faults to avoid (1847–1973).
   VIII. Memory and delivery (1974–2070).

forms the whole in advance, so that the work exists first as a mental model
rather than as a tangible thing.

(*Poetria nova*, lines 43–48)

Of interest here is the notion of the mental model, the *archetypus*,
to which we will return later. I will suggest that it is precisely the
archetypus which is to be expressed in the opening lines of the poem.

Geoffrey makes a distinction between the natural order and the
artificial or artistic order. A poet uses the natural order if he starts his
poem at the beginning of a sequence of events. He uses the artificial
order if he starts at the middle or the end of the action, or if he begins
the poem with a proverb or an example. Further, the poet can begin
his poem at the middle with the use of a proverb, and so on. This
procedure yields eight possible ways of employing an artificial opening, and of course one way of employing the natural opening.
Geoffrey says that the artificial opening is always preferable. The
entire doctrine is quite curious to say the least, and we will return to
it later on.

Geoffrey then proposes methods of amplification and abbreviation. Given a subject matter, one may either treat it at great length
or dispose of it very quickly. In order to draw out a subject at length,
the poet may use the eight methods of amplification, namely, refining or dwelling on a point; periphrasis; comparison; apostrophe;
prosopopeia; digression; description; and opposition. Geoffrey composes many illustrations of these processes. His top-to-toe description
of a beautiful woman is fairly well known. And to provide examples
of apostrophe, he composes a lament on the death of Richard the
Lion Hearted, during the course of which he manages to apostrophize
Friday, the venemous day of Venus on which Richard supposedly was
shot; the soldier who shot him; sorrow; death; Nature; and God. This
poem was popular and enjoyed a separate circulation; and of course
it is this poem that Chaucer parodies in the *Nun's Priest's Tale* in a
series of heartfelt apostrophies on the capture of Chantecler by
the fox.

Now one can also condense a tale or an incident in a tale, by the
use of several methods, the most interesting of which involves simply
conjuring up in mind the key words of the story, and then building
a very few lines of verse around these key words. Geoffrey takes his
example from the story of the snow child, which was apparently a
favorite subject in the Middle Ages for the double treatment of
amplification and abbreviation.

Having determined the scope of the subject matter, we adorn the matter with words. Stylistic ornament must be chosen with discretion. Fancy words are not enough; there must be inner substance. And the expression should match the substance. Adornment should be functional and not merely decorative.

Geoffrey distinguishes between *ornatus gravis* and *ornatus levis*. He uses *gravis* to mean 'difficult, serious, dignified,' and *levis* to mean 'easy, pleasant, light.' *Gravitas* is to be achieved by using the ten tropes listed in the *Ad Herennium*. These tropes are distinguished from other figures by the fact that they will use a word, as Geoffrey says, "under an alien meaning, one not properly its own" (965). However, the tropes should never be obscure but should illuminate the subject. The labor of *gravitas* should be the poet's, not the reader's.

The chief trope is of course metaphor. In order to help the student to form metaphors, Geoffrey suggests that certain parts of speech be used as topics of invention. For example, the verb can be used metaphorically in connection with its subject (*The winds grow silent*) or with its complement (*Your words inebriate the ears*), and so forth. Erasmus' *De duplici copia* seems to have borrowed some suggestions from this method.

The *ornatus levis* includes the figures of diction and of thought given in the *Ad Herennium*. These figures are for the most part nonmetaphorical. Geoffrey does not define the figures of diction but gives examples of each in the same order in which they appear in the *Ad Herennium*. In a virtuoso display, he weaves each of these figures into a discourse on the Fall and Redemption of man. He then defines the figures of thought and places them also into a similar discourse.

Next appears the doctrine of conversion, a systematic method of varying a given sentence so that one may choose its most pleasing form. The method is to take an important noun in the sentence and vary its cases. If the basic sentence is *Splendor illuminates his features,* we can ring the changes this way: *His face dazzles with the light of splendor* (genitive); *His face is wed to splendor* (dative); and so forth. In the *Documentum* Geoffrey commends this process as helping the inexperienced poet to cast his lines into a pleasing shape (Faral, pp. 304–309).

The next doctrine is that of determination, which consists primarily of creating a long sequence of brief phrases. Geoffrey identifies this style as the manner of Sidonius and says that "Such a piling up of

expressions suits the verse for praise and blame. In praise it heaps up
applause and in blame it provides the means of striking frequent
blows." The style is a familiar one in medieval Latin poetry, and we
can give an example from Matthew of Vendôme's *Introductory
Treatise*:

> Davus is the dishonor of the world, a vexing plague,
> instigator of crime, the dregs of the world . . .[8]

The remaining doctrines are treated very briefly in the *Poetria
nova*. Words are to be chosen according to the persons and actions
described. Humor generally avoids the use of ornament; but the
Documentum adds that *occupatio, praecisio,* and *correctio* are appropriate for humor (Faral, p. 317). Geoffrey then mentions certain
faults to be avoided: excessive alliteration, overly long periods, and
so on. For correcting one's work he recommends reliance on the ear
as well as the mind. Geoffrey commends the use of memory systems
only for those who like them, for only delight will foster memory. In
delivery, one must follow the sense, imitating in a controlled manner
the emotions called for by the text.

Some of these doctrines are the concern of rhetoric, and some are
in the province of grammar. The line of demarcation between grammar and rhetoric had for long been indefinite and fluctuating. Both
of these liberal arts taught composition and taught the student to
examine the diction, figurative language, and meters of the curriculum authors who were to serve as models for imitation. However,
Prof. Douglas Kelly has pointed out that certain concerns differen-
tiate these two subjects.[9] The *Poetria nova* devotes a great deal of
space to the use of figurative language: to that extent, it shares a
concern with grammar. However it was rhetoric and not grammar that
was concerned with invention of subject matter and with disposition
or organization of the work—two of the chief concerns of the *Poetria
nova*. And finally, Geoffrey's brief comments on memory and
delivery also show the relation of his work to areas that are traditionally the concern of rhetoric.

We have to ask ourselves how we are to understand the doctrines
of the *Poetria nova*. We must not consider them simply as establish-
ing procedures which every right-thinking medieval poet strove to

---

8. Faral, p. 125, trans. Gallo, p. 68.
9. "The Scope and Treatment of Composition in the Twelfth- and Thirteenth-
Century Arts of Poetry," *Speculum* 41 (1966), 261–278.

follow. Rather, we will have to question the doctrines for the implications, the assumptions, that stand behind them. In doing so we may have to turn to other medieval arts of discourse, and we will certainly have to consider the actual practice of medieval poets.

At present I want to examine the implications of two of the major doctrines of the *Poetria nova*: the use of natural and artificial openings, and the processes of amplification and abbreviation. I will try to suggest some of the implications of these doctrines and draw some conclusions about the medieval notion of poetic discourse. One question that arises is why Geoffrey preferred the artificial order to the natural order. There is an illuminating comment in the *Dictaminum radii* of Alberic of Monte Cassino:

> The writer should above all give careful consideration to beginning from a point that will not obscure his subject matter but rather from one which will so to speak infuse it with light. It is therefore necessary to choose a point from which you can quickly bring the listener to an understanding, *a point from which virtually nothing of the narrative is omitted* [emphasis added]. Place the middle in the opening position when, as though it were the primary opening, it seizes upon the reader and illuminates everything beforehand, as in a mirror.[10]

The mirror (*speculum*) is the model, the idea, wherein the object is presented in all of its lucidity. Geoffrey refers to this model as the *archetypus* which the poet consults before he sets to work. The *speculum* presents not an individual phenomenon but its model in its most comprehensible form. One should begin the poem at the precise point which most lucidly summarizes the meaning of the sequence of the action.

Both classical and medieval commentators use the *Aeneid* as the standard example of a poem that begins in the middle: it does not start with the fall of Troy, but with the shipwreck of Aeneas on the shores of Carthage. Tiberius Claudius Donatus (fourth century) tells us that Virgil's intention in the *Aeneid* is to praise its hero, in doing which Virgil proves himself a master rhetorician: "As is characteristic of a consummate orator, he admits those points that cannot be denied; he first dispels the accusation and then transforms it into praise."[11]

---

10. Alberic of Monte Cassino, *Flores rhetorici,* ed. D. M. Inguanez and E. H. M. Willard (Monte Cassino, 1938), p. 35. Translations are mine except where otherwise indicated.

11. *Interpretationes Vergilianae,* ed. Henricus Georgius (Leipzig, 1905), Vol. I, 3.

This purpose informs the whole work and determines the character of its opening lines: "And so he composes not, as some think, the opening of the poem but, as we maintain, its theme (*carminis thema*) with such artful subtlety that within it, as brief as it is, he demonstrates the vast breadth of the work to come" (p. 3). Donatus' commentary on the opening of the *Aeneid* may be outlined as follows:

I. The arms, that is the deeds, of Aeneas.
II. The man: indicating not Aeneas' sex but rather that he was the man who
    A) could wield such mighty and such beautiful arms
    B) was worthy to found Rome
    C) overcame the hostility of Juno and her party among the gods
    D) bore so many adversities
       i)   on land
       ii) at sea
       iii) forced by fate (a fact which frees Aeneas from blame)
       iv) overcoming fate (a fact which redounds to Aeneas' praise).

Fulgentius, a Christian writer of the second half of the fifth century, similarly finds the opening of the *Aeneid* to be heavy with implication. His *De continentia Virgiliana* recounts a vision in which the shade of Virgil appears and deigns to explain that the *Aeneid* is an allegory of the life of man, proceeding through all the stages from helpless infancy to wise old age.[12] The wisdom of old age is the fruit of a life-long *psychomachia* against the destructive forces which try to overwhelm the soul. To introduce this pageant of the human condition, Virgil opens with the words *Arma virumque cano,* implying strength in *arma* and wisdom in *virum.* And so we find that the first two words of the *Aeneid* correspond to an intellectual schema (*fortitudo* and *sapientia* as the two fundamental virtues of the epic hero). Further, that schema presents us with an exhaustive division, "for all perfection abides in strength of body and wisdom of mind" (p. 87).

Although logically substance should be represented before accident, Virgil has placed *arma* before *virum.* Thus the basis of merit precedes the man, just as in letter-writing we first set down "to my worthy lord" and only later add the name of the letter-writer. Virgil's reference to fate and the power of the gods is intended to demonstrate that not Aeneas but fortune is to be blamed for his mishaps. Fulgentius then proceeds to analyze the opening of the *Aeneid* according

12. *Opera,* ed. R. Helm (Leipzig, 1898), pp. 84 ff.

to a tripartite schema: "There are three stages in human life: the first is to have; then to rule what you have; and third to decorate what you rule" (p. 89). The third stage is represented by *primus*, that is, *princeps*. There is a natural order in the progress of human life: we all start with human nature, then acquire wisdom, then obtain happiness. These three are the sources of all good (pp. 89–90). Fulgentius provides several schemata, the various parts of which are homologous with one another. We may outline his analysis as follows:

I. *Arma: strength*, related to *Nature*; pertains to the *body*, which we have.

II. *Virum: wisdom*, related to *Learning*; pertains to the *intellect*, by which we *rule*.

III. *Primus: sovereign*, related to *Happiness*; pertains to *ornamentation*, by which we *are adorned*.

Thus we have what centuries later, in the arts of preaching, was to be called the "explanation of parts." Not content with foreshadowing this much of the thematic sermon, Fulgentius proceeds to confirm his threefold division by a reference to Plato (recte Tertullian), thereby supplying what was later to be named the "confirmation of parts":

"All goods arise, or are learned, or are gathered": for they arise from nature, are learned from instruction, are gathered from advantage. (p. 90)

Has it been observed that this fifth-century literary analysis contains all of the characteristics of the method of the thematic sermon, "invented" eight centuries later? In each mode of analysis we have a short theme *in which the entire discourse which follows is supposed to be contained* (compare the medieval attitude toward the artificial opening of the poem, as expressed by Alberic, above). In each mode of analysis, the opening statement, the theme, is divided into parts according to a rational schema; and that schema is shown to parallel various other schemata which thereby validate it. And the division is further validated by reference to an authority.

Fulgentius' interpretation of the *Aeneid* is adopted by John of Salisbury[13] and forms the basis of Bernard Silvester's lengthy *Commentary* on the first six books of the *Aeneid*.[14] Bernard writes his introduction in the scholastic manner. He will confine himself to

---

13. *Polycraticus* 1. 8. 24, ed. Clemens C. I. Webb, 2 vols. (Oxford, 1909).

14. *Commentum Bernardi Silvestris super sex libros Eneidos Vergilii*, ed. G. Riedel (Greifswald, 1924).

three topics: Virgil's intention, his method of procedure (*modus agendi*), and the profit arising from the work. Knowledge of these three subjects will respectively render the reader receptive, well-disposed, and attentive.

However, Virgil writes as both poet and philosopher. Hence each of these three headings must receive a twofold treatment.

Bernard's explanation of the difference between the natural and artificial order is the usual one we find in the later Middle Ages: if we follow the chronological sequence of events, we follow the natural order. If, however, we begin in the middle of the sequence of events and only later explain what had happened earlier, we follow the artificial order.

As a poet, Virgil intends to set forth the misfortunes of Aeneas and the other Trojans, and to give an account of their labors in exile. His method of procedure is in accordance with the artificial order, for he departs from chronological sequence by beginning with Aeneas' shipwreck and only later recounting the fall of Troy. The usefulness of the work is twofold: as a model of composition it teaches writing skills, and through example and exhortation it teaches prudence in action.

As a philosopher, Virgil intends to describe the nature of human life. The method of procedure is in accordance with the natural order, for he describes the course of human life from its very beginning, the "shipwreck" of birth. The usefulness of the work is that it teaches us to know ourselves.

It is apparent, then, that Virgil was thought (at least by Fulgentius) to have implanted a complex intellectual schema in the supposed allegory foreshadowed in the opening lines of the *Aeneid*. It is further apparent that Virgil is considered a master rhetorician. His purpose is to write a poem in praise of Aeneas; and in the first four lines, Virgil has manipulated the facts of the case so as to amplify the good qualities of Aeneas and to diminish the impact of certain facts that seem to detract from the hero's glory. The poet's aim is that of the orator: each is arguing a case. The artificial opening—here achieved by starting at the middle, at the precise point that throws light on the meaning of the text—has been carefully wrought to suggest the entire argument of the poem, and to manipulate the reader's responses.

The desire for clarity and lucidity, the desire to control the impact of the subject matter of the poem, is also the motive for opening the poem with a proverb or an example. In this method the point, again, is to throw light on, or to control, the meaning of the sequence of events, this time by distancing oneself from them long enough to invoke a generalization through which the events may be understood. Geoffrey of Vinsauf's language is significant here. He says

> If you should wish the opening to send forth a greater light, without disturbing the natural order of the theme, let the sentiment you begin with not sink to any particular statement but rather raise its head to a general pronouncement. With this new grace it is unwilling to think of the matter at hand, but almost disdainfully refuses to remain in its bosom. Let it stand above the given subject; pondering thereon but saying nothing, let it gaze with brow uplifted.
>
> (*Poetria nova*, lines 126–131)

The posture Geoffrey describes is a contemplative one. And just like the proverb, the example serves to generalize by comparing the narrative to an authoritative parallel case, a precedent taken from nature, or perhaps from the classics, or from Scripture.

The artificial opening, then, renders a mass of particular facts comprehensible. The poet can control our response to his material by starting in a way that will lead us to see the subject matter in just the way that he wants us to see it. In short, poetry is essentially rhetorical; the poet is arguing for a certain point of view.

We are fortunate in having a contemporary analysis of an important medieval poem, an analysis which emphasizes the importance of the opening. The poem is the *Canzone d'Amore* of Guido Cavalcanti (which Pound found sufficiently interesting to translate three separate times); and the commentary is by Dino del Garbo.[15]

In the opening lines of the *Canzone*, Dino finds, by implication, the four Aristotelian causes.[16] Why does Cavalcanti say that a "lady"

---

15. Otto Bird, "The Canzone d'Amore of Cavalcanti according to the Commentary of Dino del Garbo," *Mediaeval Studies* 2 (1940), 150–174 and 3 (1941), 117–160.

16. I here provide (with the kind permission of the editors) Otto Bird's translation of the first two stanzas of Guido's poem (*Mediaeval Studies* 2 [1940], 157–158).

I
A lady asks me that I would tell
of an accident which is often fierce
and is so great that it is called love;
so that if anyone denies it, let him hear the truth.
And for the present I seek men of understanding,
for I do not hope that one of base heart
could bring understanding to such reasons;
for without natural demonstration
I have no desire to try to prove

asks him? Because women are the appropriate objects of love, and, perhaps, he is in love with this lady, whom he thus compliments by designating her as the efficient cause of his poem.

But in saying *Donna me prega,* and not *me comanda,* Cavalcanti indicates that he will write in a scientific manner, as a magister who proposes solutions, and not as one who writes simply to win the object of his desires. This "scientific and veridical method, drawn from the principles of natural and moral science" (p. 160) is the formal cause of the poem, the method of treatment. This *forma tractandi* defines the author's attitude toward the lady, who is the efficient cause, and also defines the subject matter of love; for the poem is to show that love relinquishes all of its passional elements as it enters the intellect.

The final cause of the poem is the satisfaction of the lady's petition. That petition is worthy (and hence deserves a response from the poet) since it fulfills these two requirements for a just petition: it is presented by one who understands the nature of the request, and who is a worthy person. Now the word *donna* implies a woman of mature knowledge, and one of worthy character.

The material cause, the subject matter, of the poem is love, but love as apprehended by the soul, wherein it is subjected to successive stages of abstraction from matter. This abstraction is performed first by the various powers of the sensitive soul, and then by the powers of the rational soul. As Dino points out, the order of the stanza

---

where it is posited and who makes it created,
and what its virtue is and its power,
its essence and its every movement,
the pleasingness which makes it called loving,
and whether one can show it by sight.

II

In that part where memory is
it [love] takes its state so formed as
a diaphan by light from an obscurity.
It comes from Mars and makes its rest.
It is created and has a sensible name,
a habit of the soul and will from the heart.
It comes from a seen form which is understood,
which takes its place and rest
in the possible intellect as in a subject.
In that part [the intellect] it never has any power,
because the intellect does not descend from quality;
it shines in its own perpetual effect,
and has no delight but consideration,
so that it cannot grant a likeness [to love as a passion].

follows this order of apprehension from a lower to a higher degree of abstraction—with one important exception. Cavalcanti *begins* his discussion of his subject matter (stanza 2, line 1) with the memory, which is not the lowest power of the soul but rather an intermediate power. That is, Cavalcanti has here employed the "artificial" opening.

To what end has he done so? Dino's answer is that the poem (after the prologue has ended) opens *in medias res,* with memory, because memory, being related to both the intellect and the senses, implies the dual nature, the ambivalent nature, of love.

The *species* (i.e. apprehended form, at whatever degree of abstraction) of the beloved is first apprehended by the sight (*vien da veduta forma*): the other senses play a role, but sight is preeminent. This sensible *species* is then apprehended by the imagination (which Dino assigns to the *communis sensus*),[17] the lowest of the interior powers of the soul, whose function it is to grasp the *species* as an imaginable form. Although the imagined *species* still is somewhat material (possessing, for example, color, shape, and so on), it is less material than the *species* apprehended by sight, which perceives the *species* as individuated by matter.

The cogitative power then perceives the apprehended form as something to be desired or avoided. The perception here is still somewhat material, but now a qualitative judgment is formed which is not dependent on the data of corporeal matter.

The *species* then enters the memory, which is capable of conserving it even in the absence of the object. (When the lady is absent, the lover can prove that his continued devotion is independent of his sensible apprehension of the lady.)

The form created by the memory is yet a sensible one: it is rendered intelligible by the operation of the active intellect, which finally frees the *species* from all remaining associations with matter and individuality. The resulting concept is delivered to the potential intellect— the highest cognitive power of the soul, according to Dino and Guido. The active intellect thereby actualizes the power of the potential intellect to become the intelligible *species,* and thus to comprehend it.[18]

Such is the order of apprehension, and such the order of the second stanza (lines 19–28). However, that stanza deviates from the natural

---

17. The *sensus communis* puts together our individual perceptions—e.g. of color, taste, touch—and forms of them a coherent perception of a unified object. It is also the seat of recollection (Aristotle, *De anima* 3.2. 425 b 12).

18. Compare the treatment in Aristotle, *De anima* 3.5. 430 a 17 ff.

order in one respect, and Dino finds that deviation fraught with meaning. The second stanza *begins* by saying that love is formed in the memory, because by so beginning, Guido implies the double nature of love, which, like memory, exists between two worlds, the sensual and the spiritual.

Memory, like love, participates in both the sensitive and rational powers of the soul. The sensual movement begun in the imagination comes to rest in the memory, which presents desire with a completed *species* of the beloved. That *species* or representation is still dependent on matter for its representation but not at all for its perception, its conservation in the memory. The memory receives the beloved as still implicated in matter; it preserves the beloved in a condition freed from matter. The poem opens with the memory since that power of the soul reflects the dual nature of love, which is the chief subject of the poem—and which therefore determines the attitude of the speaker in the poem.

Love is a passion of that sensitive appetite which wars against reason, man's proper perfection. The speaker of the poem therefore speaks not as a lover but as a *magister,* who reveals the dual nature of love. It is a passion which occupies all of one's intellectual energies and may end in death. The first stanza shows us the range of love in perception, a range that spans the worlds of intellect and of sense. The following two stanzas detail the strife that naturally exists between these two worlds. The entire movement of the poem is implied in the poet's first placing love in the memory, and only later describing its movement from low to high, in the natural order of apprehension.

In addition to the artificial opening, the poet has another very effective means of controlling his material, and that is the use of amplification and abbreviation. Amplification is achieved by lengthening material, spinning out that which was lucidly and succinctly expressed in the beginning. Abbreviation, on the other hand, is the condensation of lengthy material. As Geoffrey says,

> Your way is twofold, either wide or narrow, a rivulet or a stream; you will either . . . check off an item briefly, or treat it in a lengthy discourse. The passage through each way is not without labor.
>
> (*Poetria nova,* lines 206–210)

Geoffrey's first method of amplification is refining, that is, restating the theme in different ways. The presentation should be varied and yet the same. The ideal is diversity in unity. Now this ideal may tell us something about medieval poetry. If the poem has lucidly made its essential statement at the very beginning, then the precise task of the poet must be to restate the theme, refine upon it, and draw from it all of its implications and meanings. We should consider how fond medieval poets are of such restatement, how they go round about a single point as though to draw all possible meanings from it. Consider the movement of the Middle English *Pearl,* which consists of a series of such *morae* ("delays"), to use Geoffrey's term. The movement of the *Pearl* is not linear but circular; the poem ends where it began, having drawn out the implications contained in its initial theme.

In classical rhetorical theory, amplification was a method of enhancing the emotional impact of a statement. Medieval arts of poetry have often been accused of forgetting this original and sensible function of amplification, and of treating it as a kind of mindless padding of the material. But I do not think that such was Geoffrey's purpose. In classical practice, the speaker amplified facts that helped him make his case, and he abbreviated or played down facts that weakened his case. Medieval practice was essentially the same. For the medieval poet, the facts of the case, so to speak, were those delivered to him by literary tradition. Take, again, the case of Aeneas, a man who overcame many obstacles, including the hatred of Juno and the love of Dido, in order to found Rome. From Virgil's point of view, Aeneas is a hero. From other points of view—Dido's, for example—Aeneas is a villain; and poets such as Chaucer were free to present Dido's point of view.

The poet has to work more or less within the traditional framework, but he is free to make it new, to elicit possibilities left undeveloped by earlier writers and to abbreviate material not relevant to his new purpose. In the *Documentum,* Geoffrey makes it clear that the function of amplification and abbreviation is to give new meanings to old materials. Citing Horace's statement that "it is difficult to treat common material in an individual way" (*Ars poetica,* line 128), Geoffrey adds that "although it is difficult, it is possible." The first method of doing so, he says, is "not to delay where others have delayed, but to skip over what they expand, and expand what they skip over."[19]

---

19. *Documentum,* in Faral, p. 309.

After one has outlined all of the doctrines contained in the *Poetria nova*, the *Documentum de arte versificandi*, and for that matter, all of the medieval *poetriae*, the work has just begun. The important question is how to apply these doctrines to the practical criticism of, elucidation of, medieval works of literature. In short, after the work of scholarship is done, the labor of criticism begins; and it is my opinion that the former is quite meaningless without the latter. But in applying the principles of medieval discourse to the practice, we run into formidable problems. In some ways these problems are similar to those inherent in applying *any* document to the criticism of a poem to which it is related. Here we have a letter of Keats; there we have a poem of Keats. How do we use the former to elucidate the latter? Paradoxically, the task may be the more difficult and require the more critical tact, the closer the document is related to the poetry. We are fortunate enough to have the *Poetria nova*, a work which tries to teach nothing less than how to write a poem. But can it really teach us anything about how to *read* medieval poetry?

One possible approach is very simple: it is to locate the doctrine in the poetry. Geoffrey of Vinsauf teaches that it is good to open a discourse with a proverb, and lo! such-and-such a medieval poem doth open with a proverb. Alternately, the critic can go through a poem to ferret out all the examples of figurative language. Many supposed works of rhetorical criticism (in both medieval and Renaissance studies) are simply figure-hunts (often very gracefully done), as though the mere location of figures were an end in itself. The spirit is that of E. K.'s gloss to the *Shepherd's Calendar*: "A prety Epanorthosis in these two verses, and withal a Paronomasia. . . ." What hard heart could forbear to cheer? In fact, to induce cheers is the purpose of such a gloss, which conveys no genuine critical information but does rather attractively reveal the scholiast's enthusiasm for the work upon which he is commenting.

Such application of rhetorical doctrine to poetic practice is, by itself, overly simple, and may account for the objections of those who feel that *no* application can or should be made. "After all, rhetorical doctrine cannot account for the genius of a Chaucer." "Geoffrey of Vinsauf is teaching grammar school children how to compose school exercises." "The treatise is, after all, simpleminded: who could take seriously the doctrine of amplification, which simply teaches padding?" (The answer to this last question is "Erasmus.")

We may characterize such statements as belonging to the "after all" or "tut tut" school of criticism. Still, these objections cannot be dismissed lightly. Is it really necessary to defend the depth and wisdom of the *Poetria nova* before we can use it as a critical tool? I think not, if we use the *Poetria nova* to provide us with a certain kind of evidence. The medieval *poetriae* may have laid down preceptive principles for the poet to follow; but I don't think the modern critic should be content simply to trace out the poet's obedience to the doctrine. I believe that he should treat the doctrine primarily as data, as evidence of medieval attitudes towards poetry and its functions. Further, such data will be in no way more compelling or authoritative than the data to be gathered from the poems themselves. Principles and practice are to be examined together, side by side.

To review an example given above: it is not enough to note that the *Poetria Nova* advises opening the poem with a proverb: we must seek out the assumption that underlies that doctrine. Fortunately, we can find analogues to that doctrine in commentaries on the *Aeneid*, in the medieval thematic sermon, in Alberic of Monte Cassino, and in Dino's commentary on the *Canzone d'Amore*. And from all this we draw certain conclusions as to what habit of mind underlay the doctrine. But we can be reasonably sure of our conclusions only if we find that habit of mind at work in the poetry.

This question of habit of mind is extremely important. If we open a modern handbook of composition, we do not expect to find an eternally true set of principles, but an approach which betrays some specifically modern assumptions and attitudes concerning discourse. We will find such information whether or not the handbook we open is hackwork or an inspired text. And on this assumption it simply does not matter whether one considers Geoffrey (or Matthew of Vendôme and all the rest) to have been grammatical hacks or wise and witty mentors. In either case, we may legitimately examine what they say to discover their principles and assumptions.

In conclusion, I would like to suggest some of the directions that I believe rhetorical criticism may take, although I am not at all certain that the following comments will command universal agreement. I believe that rhetorical criticism will very likely emphasize formal and conventional elements at the expense of the realistic. Consequently, rhetorical criticism may rescue us from some tempting but erroneous approaches to medieval literature.

Take, as an example, the Reeve's self-portrait in the *Canterbury Tales* (A 3864–3898). The Reeve has been insulted by the Miller's story about an old and doting cuckold. The Reeve prepares to get

his revenge: he prefaces his tale with a sharp and disagreeable portrait
about the vices, not of Millers, but of old men like himself. In real
life, that tactic would demand explanation. Is it a rather low bid for
sympathy? Does it reveal a bitter, self-destructive nature? (And if
we say it does, it is only a short step to finding that the Reeve's *Tale*,
which is a rollicking bit of hilarity, is dripping with spite and im-
potent fury.) Is there an alternative? Does the text simply provide
us with a portrait of old age—a superb example of such portraits,
written by a great poet, but still one composed in accordance with
a recipe as old as Horace? Is the voice really not that of the Reeve but
that of Chaucer? Perhaps we have here not the realistic baring of a
soul, but a purely formal description, made because the medieval
reader delighted in *notatio*? Such an approach of course is open to
the charge that it fragments the poem—that it treats the *notatio* as a
separate piece of description made virtually for its own sake and not
related *organically* to what precedes and what follows. That is indeed
what I am suggesting. Medieval poets never heard of organic form,
and they did quite well without it. The skeptical reader is invited to
try to analyze the imagery in, for example, troubadour verse, on the
assumption that these poems are "organic" (that is, that there is an
essential and mutually illuminating interplay among all the images).

   Robert Jordan, in *Chaucer and the Shape of Creation*,[20] contends
that medieval art is essentially inorganic, and he has examined some
of Chaucer's poems from that point of view. Jordan finds in the
Timaeus, and also in Gothic architecture, a theory of number as
structural principle. But Jordan does not maintain that Chaucer's
poetry is numerically organized; rather, he first seeks the principle
behind numerical composition, finds it to be what he calls inorganic
form, and finds that this principle is also at work in Chaucer's poetry.
I believe that Jordan's conclusions are relevant to rhetorical criticism.
I suggest that the immediate rhetorical impact of certain moments in
a medieval work may often be of more importance than that mutual
interplay of all parts that we call organic unity. I do not know whether
Jordan would agree with this characterization of inorganic form. But
I believe that we would gain much by reading medieval poetry from
this perspective, rather than with purely modern expectations.

---

   20. *Chaucer and the Shape of Creation: The Aesthetic Possibilities of Inorganic
Structure* (Cambridge, Mass., 1967).

The *Summa dictaminis* of Guido Faba*

CHARLES B. FAULHABER

It is one of the paradoxes of the history of rhetoric that what was in Antiquity essentially an oral discipline for the pleading of law cases should have become in the Middle Ages, in one of its major aspects, a written discipline for the drawing up of quasi-legal documents.

The process which produced this transformation in the millenium between Quintilian and Alberic of Monte Cassino is too complicated to be summarized here. Even the early history of the *ars dictandi* must be omitted. Let it suffice to say that the theory of letter-writing, born in early twelfth-century Bologna and given a classicizing up-bringing in late twelfth-century France, came to a triumphant maturity in the early thirteenth century, once again in Bologna.[1]

The Bolognese maturity of *dictamen* is associated with the names of three masters, Boncompagno of Signa (ca. 1165–ca. 1235), Bene of Florence (fl. 1220), and most especially Guido Faba. The doctrines they advocate are essentially Boncompagno's, elaborated by Bene, Guido, and later *dictatores* but (so far as can be judged in the absence of editions of key works) basically unchanged throughout the later Middle Ages until they were overwhelmed in the fifteenth century by the rising tide of Ciceronian rhetoric popularized by the humanists.

---

*This paper is a considerably expanded version of the one read at the Kalamazoo conference on medieval rhetoric in 1974.

1. The general outlines of this process have been known for almost a century, but the details remain very obscure. We still lack adequate editions of most of the works involved, as well as stylistic and source studies. For a good review of the history of the *ars dictandi* as presently understood, see James J. Murphy, *Rhetoric in the Middle Ages: A History of Rhetorical Theory from Saint Augustine to the Renaissance* (University of California Press: Berkeley and Los Angeles, 1974), pp. 194–268.

Of all the authors of *dictamen,* the most influential and imitated in the later Middle Ages was Guido Faba.[2] Why this should be so is a result both of Guido's own qualities as a writer and of his place within the Bolognese tradition. In contrast to the sometimes extravagant theorizing of his predecessor and rival Boncompagno, Guido never forgot that *dictamen* was an eminently *practical* discipline. Everything he wrote was designed to reflect that fact. His major theoretical work, the *Summa Dictaminis,* is organized not as a complete treatise of dictaminal theory (like Boncompagno's *Rhetorica Antiqua* and *Rhetorica Novissima* or the *Candelabrum* of Bene), but rather as a practical handbook with a limited number of short and succinct precepts. Unlike early collections of models, which usually offered a mere handful of sample letters, Guido, in his *Dictamina Rhetorica,* presented the busy secretary with hundreds of model letters on the most varied of topics.[3] And, coming at the end of over a century of intense activity in the field of *dictamen,* Guido, at the very heart of that activity, was in a position to distill the collected

2. That Guido was influential is virtually an article of faith among modern scholars. Gaudenzi's statement, that "non v'è quasi biblioteca d'Europa, che non possieda manoscritta la *Somma di dettato ei Dettati rettorici* di Guido Fava" (*Lo studio di Bologna nei primi due secoli della sua esistenza* [Bologna: R. Università di Bologna, 1901], p. 17) has been echoed by almost all of his successors: N[oël] Denholm-Young, "The Cursus in England," in *Oxford Essays in Medieval History Presented to Herbert Edward Salter* (Oxford: At the Clarendon Press, 1934), pp. 68–103; p. 83 (repr. in his *Collected Papers on Medieval Subjects* [Oxford, 1946], pp. 26–55); Ernst H. Kantorowicz, "An 'Autobiography' of Guido Faba," *Mediaeval and Renaissance Studies,* 1 (1941), 253–280; pp. 253–254; Helene Wieruszowski, "Ars Dictaminis in the Time of Dante," in her *Politics and Culture in Medieval Spain and Italy.* Storia e Letteratura, Raccolta di Studi e Testi, 121 (Rome: Edizioni di Storia e Letteratura, 1971), pp. 359–377 (repr. from *Medievalia et Humanistica,* 1 [1943], 95–108), p. 363.

    Yet concrete information about the extant MSS and Guido's influence in the later Middle Ages is surprisingly hard to come by. Thus Virgilio Pini, in his edition of Guido's *Summa de Vitiis et Virtutibus,* notes but 16 MSS of Guido's works (*Quadrivium,* 1 [1956], 41–152; pp. 58–80). Paul Oskar Kristeller offers an additional 17 (*Iter Italicum. A Finding List of Uncatalogued or Incompletely Catalogued Humanistic Manuscripts of the Renaissance in Italian and Other Libraries.* Vol. I: *Italy. Agrigento to Novara.* Vol. II: *Italy. Orvieto to Volterra; Vatican City* [London-Leiden: The Warburg Institute-E. J. Brill, 1963–1967]), to which may be added the seven listed in my "Retóricas clásicas y medievales en bibliotecas castellanas," *Abaco,* 4 (1973), 151–300; pp. 216–221. There are undoubtedly many more. We urgently need a complete census, as well as detailed studies of Guido's influence on theoretical works and letter collections.

    3. Augusto Gaudenzi, "Sulla cronologia delle opere dei dettatori bolognesi da Boncompagno a Bene di Lucca," *Bullettino dell' Instituto Storico Italiano,* 14 (1895), 85–161; pp. 86–87, 137–138; Wieruszowski, "Ars Dictaminis . . . ," 364–365.

wisdom of his predecessors into a concentrated essence which was accepted by both contemporaries and successors as the definitive statement of the Bolognese school.

Few documented facts are known about Guido Faba, but the broad outlines of his life are fairly certain.[4] He was probably born in Bologna, around 1190, and by 1210 had completed the arts course (the *trivium*) at the university.[5] He was thus Boncompagno's junior by some twenty-five years. After finishing his basic studies, he must have spent several years studying law—a not unusual practice in Bologna—or, as student slang put it, "laboring in the smithies."[6] But he found that the study of law was causing him to lose what rhetorical skill he had, so he gave it up to return to the arts, probably as a teacher. Finding his duties singularly unremunerative, he finally embraced the profession of notary, which he exercised at least as early as 1219. He served the city of Bologna in this capacity during 1219–1220 and then took service with the Bishop of Bologna, also as a notary, a position which he held for several years.[7] Around 1223 he must have been named professor of *dictamen* at the chapel of San Michele di Mercato di Mezzo in Bologna;[8] and here he appears to have remained for the rest of his life, except for a possible stint at the nascent Ghibelline *studium* of Siena around 1242.[9] He was dead very shortly after this date; in a manuscript written not much later than 1245 a cross is found beside his name, the equivalent of *requiescat in pace.*[10]

Guido wrote eight major works, all of them dealing with *dictamen*.[11] In chronological order, as near as can be established, they are:

---

4. The essential sources remain Gaudenzi, "Sulla cronologia . . . ," 118–150, and Kantorowicz.

5. Gaudenzi deduces both the date of birth and his academic career from the fact that his name first appears (as witness to a leasehold) in 1210, already as "Magister Faba" (119).

6. Kantorowicz, 267–268. This article, based on a close reading of the prologue to Guido's *Rota Nova* and an unparalleled knowledge of the intellectual climate of early thirteenth-century Bologna, is a masterly study.

7. Ibid., 276.

8. Ibid., 272, 277.

9. At least his *Parlamenta et Epistole* seem to have been written there (Gaudenzi, "Sulla cronologia . . . ," 148–149).

10. Ibid., 150.

11. There are a number of minor works attributed to him as well; but without a close study of the MS tradition it is impossible to say which are really his. Gaudenzi mentions a *Summula magistri Guidonis* ("Sulla cronologia . . . ," 140); Kantorowicz, *De Sapientia Salomonis* and *De Proverbia Salomonis* (263). The latter are probably sections II.clsv–clxvi of his *Summa Dictaminis*. The works found in Oxford,

1) *Exordia*.[12] A collection of 330 *sententiae*, divided into nine groups according to the theme of the letter or the person to whom it was addressed, to be used at the beginning of the letter as a *captatio benevolentiae*. The original version of this work was followed by a series of *continuationes exordii*, transitional phrases used to link the *exordium* to the *narratio*. A second version, ca. 1229, collapsed the two works together, so that each *exordium* was followed immediately by its respective *continuatio*.[13]

2) *Summa de Vitiis et Virtutibus*.[14] This, the only one of Guido's works to have merited an adequate edition,[15] is a collection of *exordia* organized according to the vices and virtues, an idea which appears to be original with Guido.[16] After definitions of them, Guido gives six *exordia* and *continuationes,* with their Italian translations, for each one.

3) *Arenge*.[17] Again, this is a collection of *exordia*, but to be used in speeches—by ambassadors, *podestà*, judges—as well as in letters. A second redaction, ca. 1240–1241, offered complete speeches.[18]

4) *Gemma Purpurea*.[19] Yet another collection of *exordia*, in Latin and Italian, to be used in letters to members of various social classes.

New College MS. 255, particularly the *Rota Nova* and the letters addressed to the students of Bologna, deserve to be studied in some detail for the information they may yield about Guido's life and the evolution of his dictaminal works. The *Rota Nova* is a preliminary version of the *Summa Dictaminis,* written c. 1223; and it seems evident that the letter collections represent the lectures given during a sequence of academic terms (see Denholm-Young, pp. 94–95). A. Y. [A.P.?] Campbell has been working on an edition in conjunction with V. Pini; see the former's "The Perfection of *Ars Dictaminis* in Guido Faba," *Revue de l'Université d'Ottawa,* 39 (1969), 103–139, and "*Ars Dictaminis*: Order, Beauty, and Our Daily Bread," *Humanities Association Bulletin* (Canada), 22 (1971), i, 13–21.

12. Partially ed. by Oswald Redlich, *Eine wiener Briefsammlung zur Geschichte des deutschen Reiches und der österreichischen Länder in der zweiten Hälfte des XIII. Jahrhunderts,* Mittheilungen aus dem Vaticanischer Archive, II (Vienna: In Commission bei F. Tempsky, 1894), pp. 317–331. The *continuationes* are lacking.

13. Gaudenzi, "Sulla cronologia . . . ," 140; Pini, in his edition of the *Summa de Vitiis et Virtutibus,* 49.

14. Gaudenzi thought this to be Guido's first work (124), but it must postdate the *Exordia*, since, as Pini points out in his edition (82), the *Exordia* are mentioned in the *Summa* (ibid., 101).

15. Ed. Pini (see n. 2, above).

16. Ibid., 50.

17. Giuseppe Vecchi announced (in his "Le *Arenge* di Guido Faba e l'eloquenza d'arte, civile e politica duecentesca," *Quadrivium,* 4 [1960], 61–90) the publication of an edition in Bologna, 1954; in fact, that announcement was premature. The promised edition still has not appeared (private communication).

18. Gaudenzi, "Sulla cronologia . . . ," 145–146.

19. The Italian portions of this work have been edited frequently; the Latin parts remain unedited, except for the excerpt entitled *Doctrina ad inveniendas incipiendas*

The vocabulary used in these phrases and expressions is chosen very carefully—*ipse dixit*—to reflect the rank of the recipient of the letter. 5) *Dictamina Rhetorica* (ca. 1226–1227).[20] Guido's major collection of model letters, with a total of 220 examples showing how correspondents of varying social levels and estates, secular and ecclesiastical, should phrase requests of various kinds and how these requests should be answered: A son studying at Bologna asks his parents for more money because of the high price of food (i); a wife requests her husband to return home after an absence of five years (xliii); he replies that he cannot, since he has gone back to his first wife, whom he had thought dead (xliv); a merchant asks a friend to invest 100 £ in marketable fabrics (lxvii); a bishop writes to the pope for the absolution of an excommunicate (cxxviiii); a cathedral chapter writes to an archbishop to seek confirmation of an episcopal election (cxxxvi); the emperor promises the pope that he will join the crusades (clxxxxiii). The collection is remarkable for the complete absence of the imaginary letters so common in Boncompagno and the French school of *dictatores*.[21]

---

et formandas materias (ed. Ludwig Rockinger, in his *Briefsteller und Formelbücher des eilften bis vierzehnten Jahrhunderts,* Quellen und Erörterungen zur bayerischen und deutschen Geschichte, 9 [Munich: 1863–1864; repr. Burt Franklin Research and Source Works Series, 10, New York: Burt Franklin, 1961], pp. 185–196). For the Italian see Ernesto Monaci, "Su la *Gemma purpurea* e altri scritti volgari di Guido Faba o Fava, maestro di grammatica in Bologna nella prima metá del secolo XIII," *Rendiconti della Reale Accademia dei Lincei,* 4 (1888), ii, 399–405, and *La Gemma Purpurea del maestro Guido Fava ricostituita nel testo volgare con l'aiuto di quattro codici,* [Nozze Spezi-Salvadori] (Rome: Forzani e C., 1901); Angelo Monteverdi, "Le formule epistolari volgari di Guido Fava," in his *Saggi neolatini,* Storia e Letteratura, 9 (Rome: Edizioni di Storia e Letteratura, 1945), pp. 75–109; and Arrigo Castellani, "Le formule volgari di Guido Faba," *Studi di Filologia Italiana,* 12 (1955), 5–78.

There is some controversy concerning the date of the *Gemma Purpurea,* which Gaudenzi assigns to the year 1226. Apparently unaware that the *Doctrina* ed. by Rockinger forms part of the *Gemma Purpurea,* he gives to it the date of 1237 on the basis of historical references ("Sulla cronologia . . . ," 142). It is possible that, like some of Guido's other works, there was a second recension. That there are problems with the textual tradition is indicated, for example, by the fact that MS. 43–4 of the Chapter Library of Toledo (Spain) contains a copy of the *Gemma Purpurea* (ff. 32r^a–37v^a) which omits the Italian material but adds a complete exposition of all parts of the letter.

20. Ed. by Gaudenzi, from four MSS, in *Il Propugnatore* (N.S.), 5 (1892), i, 86–129, ii, 58–109; see id., "Sulla cronologia . . . ," 133, for the date.

21. Thus in the French formulary found in MS. 227 of the Chapter Library of Tortosa (Spain) and attributed to a pupil of Bernard of Meung there are letters from Pyramus to Thisbe (f. 105r^b), from the Soul to God and from God to the Body (f. 107r^a), and, best of all, from the Pygmies to the King of Spain, seeking his aid against the storks (f. 107v^b). For an examination of the letter collections from the

Wieruszowski sums up the influence of the *Dictamina*:

> Most of the *Artes dictaminis* written after Guido's two works [she refers
> to his later *Epistole* as well] adopted the exterior form of these models:
> entire letters fitted to the requirements of the students, ordered according
> to the correspondents, and provided with headings which facilitated
> their use.[22]

6) *Summa Dictaminis* (ca. 1228–1229).[23]

7) *Petitiones* (ca. 1230). These models are more narrowly concerned with canon law, particularly with appeals to the pope.[24]

8) *Parlamenta et Epistole* (ca. 1242–1243).[25] Like the *Arenge*, the
Parlamenta et Epistole were designed as models for both letters and
speeches. Like the *Gemma Purpurea*, they were written in both Latin
and Italian. For each speech, written in Italian, there are two letters
on the same subject, written in Latin.[26]

Guido's authorial activity can be fixed roughly in two periods, the
middle and late '20's of the thirteenth century, when the bulk of his
works—including the most influential—were written; and the late

---

school of Bernard of Meung see Franz-Josef Schmale, "Der Briefsteller Bernhards
von Meung," *Mitteilungen des Instituts für österreichische Geschichtsforschung*, 66
(1958), 1–28, and Walter Zöllner, "Eine neue Bearbeitung der 'Flores Dictaminum'
des Bernhard von Meung," *Wissenschaftliche Zeitschrift der Martin-Luther Universität Halle-Wittenberg. Gesellschafts- und Sprachwissenschaftliche Reihe*, 13 (1964),
335–342.

22. "Ars Dictaminis . . . ," 364; see also Gaudenzi, "Sulla cronologia . . . ,"
137–138: "I predecessori di Guido, ed egli stesso prima di allora, si erano contentati
di scrivere degli schemi di esordi, o di conclusioni di lettere. Il pregio dei *Dettati*
consistè in questo, che essi erano vere lettere, appropriate a tutte le circonstanze
possibili della vita. Ma mentre le lettere che si trovano sparse nelle opere di Buoncompagno sono tutte prolisse, contorte e oscure, e portano la impronta strettamente
personale dell'autore, quelle di Guido sono brevi, semplici e chiare, e s'ispirano
sempre, non ai sentimenti dello scrittore, ma alle circonstanze che le hanno
suggerite."
The *Epistole*, which survive in only one MS—so far as is known—, contain another
105 sample letters exactly similar to those of the *Dictamina Rhetorica*. Gaudenzi
dates them ca. 1239–1241 ("Sulla cronologia . . . ," 145) and edits them in *Il Propugnatore* (N.S.), 6 (1893), i, 359–390, ii, 373–389.

23. Ed. by Gaudenzi in *Il Propugnatore* (N.S.), 3 (1890), i, 287–338, ii, 345–393,
on the basis of four MSS. Given the importance of this work, we are badly in need of
a well-edited and well-annotated edition. For the date see Gaudenzi, "Sulla cronologia . . . ," 139.

24. Ibid., 141.

25. Partially ed. by Gaudenzi, in his *I suoni, le forme e le parole dell'odierno
dialetto della città di Bologna* (Turin: E. Loescher, 1889), 127–160. For the date
see his "Sulla cronologia . . . ," 148–149.

26. Ibid.

1230's and early 1240's, when he revised several of them (*Arenge*, possibly *Gemma Purpurea*) and wrote the *Parlamenta et Epistole*. His first works are all collections of models for the beginning of the letter.[27] Of the rest, only the *Summa Dictaminis* is theoretical in nature. The other works are again collections of models, but now models of *complete* letters or speeches. It seems obvious that Guido was consciously trying to reduce the theoretical complexity of *dictamen* to a minimum in order to make it more accessible to the student and the practicing notary.

The *Summa Dictaminis* itself is the best evidence for this attempt to clear out the dead wood of dictaminal theory. Unlike the vast majority of similar treatises, which usually begin with the most universal question—*quid sit dictamen?*—and then work down through increasingly narrow definitions of the letter and its various parts,[28] Guido commences with a list of vices to be avoided in writing the letter and only afterwards goes into the basic definitions.[29] He seems to be putting the cart before the horse. Not so, however, for the *Summa* was designed as a handbook, to be used not only by the beginning student but also, and perhaps more importantly, by the man of affairs. Both would appreciate a practical guide to the more common epistolary errors at the beginning of the treatise, where it could be easily consulted.

To understand the articulation of the treatise, a comparatively detailed analysis is necessary. The *Summa* begins with a short and typically virtuoso prologue, inviting all those who wish to find the gifts of wisdom to come into the "viridarium magistri Guidonis."[30]

---

27. There is no individual treatise on the *salutatio*; but this is in keeping with Guido's thesis that the letter has only three principal parts (*exordium, narratio, petitio*) and that the salutation is secondary (*Summa Dictaminis*, II.iv).

28. Cf., e.g., the rubrics of the anonymous *Rationes Dictandi* of ca. 1135: "Quid sit dictamen; Diffinitio epistole; De partibus epistole; Quid sit salutatio" (Rockinger, pp. 9–11); or the *Summa Dictaminum* of Ludolf of Hildesheim (ca. 1239): "Primo igitur videamus quid sit dictamen, quid dictare, et quot sint partes dictaminis" (ibid., 359).

29. I do not know whether this is original with Guido. Kantorowicz writes in 1943: ". . . it is impossible to tell, at the present stage of investigations, what in Guido Faba's writings is his own invention and what must be considered Bolognese school tradition" (253n). Thirty-five years later we are still lacking something so basic as a source study of the *Summa Dictaminis*. Gaudenzi speaks in very general terms of a dependence upon Boncompagno and of a direct influence from the third and last part of Bene of Florence's *Summa Dictaminis* ("Sulla cronologia . . . ," 139, 160).

30. Ed. Gaudenzi (see n. 23, above), p. 287; further references will be incorporated into the text.

Wieruszowski points out that Guido plays on the fact that the course in *dictamen*—and it should be remembered that the *Summa* is essentially a set of lecture notes which have been polished for publication—began in the spring, and so compares the colorful flowers of the young year to the *colores* and *flores* of rhetoric.[31] Like the *exordium* in the letter itself, this prologue serves as a *captatio benevolentiae* of the reader and also as an example of the author's rhetorical prowess, a sample of the style which the diligent student himself might one day command.

That style is designed to be impressive, and it achieves that design through the use of the curial *stilus altus*, which combines the rhythmical *cursus* (see below, pp. 100–103) with biblical reminiscences ("'Quasi modo geniti infantes" = 1 Peter 2.2; "ianua dictaminum sit pulsantibus aperta" = Matthew 7.7–8, Luke 11.9–10; *Summa*, pp. 287, 288), and figurative language ("In hoc siquidem tante felicitatis loco [viridario] sunt dictamina purpurata, colores reperiuntur rethorici, et iuxta platanum ad fluentia aquarum sedet sapientia Salomonis," p. 288): a classic *locus amoenus* adapted to practical purposes.

The style changes but slightly in the introduction to the first part of the work, *De vitiis evitandis et virtutibus inserendis*, p. 288), which starts with a pithy *exordium*, "quia scire malum non est malum," to justify Guido's explanation of the vices of style, and compares him to the farmer who clears the land of thorns before planting, or to the cook who washes out a bowl to prepare it for the "novi saporis dulcedinem." So too Guido must extirpate stylistic faults before explaining the rules of *dictamen*.

The style turns abruptly more prosaic, matter-of-fact—and clear—in sections I.ii–vii, where Guido gets down to the meat of his treatise, taking up first errors of diction, chiefly the unnecessary repetition of the same sound or word. Thus *alliteration* is to be avoided as well as *cacophony* and *hiatus* (the repetition of the same vowel or consonant at the end of one word and the beginning of the next). The same

---

31. "Arezzo as a Center of Learning and Letters in the Thirteenth Century," in her *Politics and Culture in Medieval Spain and Italy*, pp. 387–474 (repr. from *Traditio*, 9 [1953], 321–391); 443–444. Guido is not alone in such comparisons. Boncompagno's prologues are notorious for their florid style, and other *dictatores* are scarcely less extravagant. As Francesco Di Capua points out, "il prologo è sempre fittamente intessuto e riccamente cosparso dei colori retorici più sgargianti e dei ritmi più sonori" ("Appunti sul 'cursus' o ritmo prosaico nelle opere latine di Dante Alighieri," in his *Scritti minori*, 2 vols. [Rome: Desclée e C.—Editori Pontifici, 1959], I 564–585 [orig. pub. Castellamare di Stabia, 1919]; 564).

word repeated frequently "fastidium generat, ut ibi: 'cuius rationis ratio non extat, ei rationi ratio non est fidem adhibere' " (I.vii). The example is taken from the pseudo-Ciceronian *Rhetorica ad C. Herennium* (4.12.18).

Rhymed prose is specifically condemned, but final syllable rhyme may be allowed provided that the penultimate syllables differ. Later on, in the section on the *exordium,* Guido will use, somewhat immodestly, the following example: "Magister Guido ubique diligĭ*tur,* quia sua dictamina comprobán*tur"* (II.lxix; my accents and italics).[32]

As far as composition is concerned, there are four principal faults: first, when the parts of the letter do not follow one another logically; second, when the writer strays from his subject into irrelevancies; third, when the letter is so short that it cannot be understood; fourth, when a mixture of styles is used in the same letter (I.ix).[33]

Guido ends the section on *vitia* with a brief outline of the vices associated with the principal parts of the letter, the *exordium, narratio,* and *petitio.* Among incorrect *exordia* are to be placed those, for example, which do not render the reader "benivolum, docilem vel attentum" or which are so general that they can apply to any subject (I.x). The *narratio* is faulty if it is too prolix, or too confused, or if it omits pertinent details (I.xi). Guido refers the vices of the *petitio* to the definition which he will give in part II: if it does not ask for that which is "utile, necessarium vel honestum," it is defective (I.xii).

After having set forth the most common errors in writing letters, Guido finally gets down to defining the threefold requirements for a perfect prose style: "bonam gramaticam, perfectum sensum locutionis, et verborum ornatum" (I.xiv). He goes on to say that at the very least *latinitas* should not be lacking nor *sententia generosa,* i.e., a grammatically constructed and nobly proportioned statement.

---

32. These strictures form a marked contrast to the highly rhythmical prose written under the influence of the *stilus isidorianus,* which specifically permits, indeed encourages, the use of rhyme. See *The Parisiana Poetria of John of Garland,* ed. Traugott Lawler, Yale Studies in English, 182 (New Haven and London: Yale University Press, 1974), pp. 104–108, 256–258; Di Capua, "Lo stile isidoriano nella retorica medievale e in Dante," *Scritti minori,* II, 226–251 (repr. from *Studii in onore di Francesco Torraca* [Naples, 1922], pp. 233–259); and J. Fontaine, "Théorie et practique du style chez Isidore de Séville," *Vigiliae Christianae,* 14 (1960), 65–101.

33. The example of the fourth fault is worth citing: "Exemplum: 'Celestis altitudo consilii mundo pereunti consuluit, cum per incarnati verbi mysterium a nexibus diabuli hominem liberavit. Inde est quod ipsius amore vos rogo, ut mei semper memoriam habeatis'. Ecce quomodo stilus fuit in prima parte turgidus et inflatus, in secunda cecidit in aridum et exanguem" (I.ix). Literally, from the sublime to the ridiculous.

The second part of the work, *De omnibus regulis que faciunt ad artem utiliter adnotatis,* begins with a lofty-sounding introduction similar to the prologue of the entire work: "Properate sitientes ad fontem gratulanter, et bibite confidenter omnes qui cupitis rethorice venustatis dulcedine satiari" (p. 295). Here the fountain from which the sweetness of rhetorical beauty will flow is obviously Guido himself.

Guido starts with a definition of *dictamen* as "ad unamquamque rem, idest ad unamquamque materiam, competens et decora locutio" (II.i) and then, as was customary, divides this definition into its component parts and defines each of them in turn.[34] Unlike his predecessors, however, he makes not even a bow in the direction of other sorts of *dictamen* (*metricum, rythmicum*). He defines the letter in similar fashion: It is a *libellus*—technically a legal petition—sent to one who is absent (II.ii). Letters were invented to convey secrets between friends and because messengers, not being divine, have fallible memories (II.iii).

Next comes the division of the letter into its principal parts. Although the standard medieval division is into five parts, Guido says that there are but three (*exordium, narratio, petitio*), comparing the composition of a letter to that of a house, with its foundation, walls, and roof. And just as in the house there are many secondary constituent parts, so too are there in the letter; since the letter (of the alphabet), the syllable, or the word are considered to be such secondary parts. The *salutatio* is not, strictly speaking, part of the letter; but since it precedes the letter proper, it is taken up first (II.iv). The *conclusio* is not even mentioned.

In this attempt to impose a tripartite division on the letter, Guido

---

34. There are some problems with this definition, which does not appear to be articulated so carefully as that of other theoreticians. The passage begins with a definition of *pronuntiatio,* which is dropped immediately without linking it to *dictamen.* Then, after explaining the various terms used in the definition quoted in the text, Guido adds: "Dicitur autem *prosaycum* a *proson,* quod est *longum,* quia, nec legi metrice vel rythmice subiacens, congrue se potest extendere" (II.i). This presupposes the previous definition of *prosaicum dictamen* (cf. the *Rationes Dictandi*: "Prosaicum dictamen est . . ." [Rockinger, p. 101]), which, however, appears nowhere in Guido's text.

Three possible explanations for the anomaly suggest themselves: 1) Gaudenzi's edition is defective—which would not be very surprising; 2) The lack of logical sequence shows that the *Summa* had its origin in a set of lecture notes. Presumably, this passage would have been more extensive in the oral version; 3) Or we have another indication of Guido's relative lack of interest in questions of theory which lack immediate, practical application.

is following Bolognese school tradition,[35] but it does lead to a paradoxical situation: Over thirty percent of his treatise on the art of
letter-writing is devoted to the *salutatio*, which is not even part of the
letter. Furthermore, eight times more space is dedicated to the *salutatio* than to the *exordium, narratio,* and *petitio* taken together. This
disproportion is not uncommon in the *artes dictandi,* possibly because the *salutatio* lent itself to that rational development of first
principles so dear to the intellectual of the period.

The salutation tells us whom the letter is from and to whom it is
directed.[36] It derives its name, according to Guido, from SALU*tis
op*TATIO—and we are reminded of the importance of etymology as a
source of knowledge in the Middle Ages—for we greet him for whom
we desire health (II.v). In general the *salutatio* must take into account:
1) the person of the sender; 2) the subject of the letter; 3) and particularly the social status of the recipient, which should be alluded
to by the descriptive adjectives used in the *salutatio*. Thus a soldier
ought to be described in terms of "strenuitate et fortitudine [. . .],
ut videre poteritis in salutationibus infrascriptis" (II.vi). Guido's
theory never strays very far from his practice. But the sender should
not praise himself, in keeping with the biblical injunction: "Os
alienum te commendet, non tuum" (Proverbs 27.2).

The *Generalis doctrina omnium salutationum* then sets forth basic
rules, founded primarily on rank. If one equal writes to another, it is
more polite to put the recipient's name first; if an inferior writes to
a superior, or a superior to an inferior, the superior's name goes first.
When declared enemies correspond, the sender's name goes first
and instead of wishing his opponent health, he desires him *merorem*.
If, however, the animosity is concealed, a normal salutation is to be
used (II.viii). These rules allow for a great deal of variation in the

---

35. Hugh of Bologna (ca. 1119–1124) implicitly rejects the *salutatio* as part of the
letter ("Et quia salutationis ordinem ad unguem usque perduximus, ad epistolas
transeamus . . ." [Rockinger, p. 56]), accepting only the *exordium, narratio,* and
conclusio (ibid.). Boncompagno advocated at different times two different schemas:
"In the *Palma* he names the three parts as *salutatio, narratio, petitio*. In the *Rhetorica novissima* he declares that the three integral parts are *exordium, narratio,* and
petitio" (Murphy, p. 255). The *Rhetorica Novissima* may have been influenced by
Guido's *Summa,* since the latter antedates the former by some years (1229 vs. 1235).
Could the insistence on a tripartite division reflect religious motives?

36. For a study of *salutatio* practice, see Carol D. Lanham, *Salutatio Formulas in
Latin Letters to 1200: Syntax, Style, and Theory,* Münchener Beiträge zur Mediä-
vistik und Renaissancen Forschung (Munich: Bei der Arbeo-Gesellschaft, 1975).

salutation, variation nicely calculated to express exactly the relationships between sender and receiver—and in the highly-structured
society of the Middle Ages, these relationships were of the utmost
importance and their proper expression crucial for the accomplish-
ment of the sender's desires.

After telling the reader that the sender's name should be given
in the nominative case and the recipient's in the dative, Guido turns
to the *Specialis doctrina omnium salutationum,* examples of salutations designed for specific people. He starts out with family and
friends and moves on to a variety of common relationships—subject
to lord (II.xxx), lover to his lady *ante factum* (II.xxxiv) and *post
factum* (II.xxxv)—before taking up the secular and ecclesiastical
hierarchies, moving up through the former from *potestates* to the
emperor (II.xxxvi–xli) and then down through the latter from the
pope to monks and hermits (II.xlii–lvii).

Each of these sections gives a series of sample salutations specifically tailored to the relationships existing between the two parties.
Thus the *salutatio* to a woman *ante factum* is broken down into four
phrases: The first praises the recipient, giving two examples ("Nobili
et sapienti domine, vel nobilissime ac sapientissime domine"); the
second is simply the name of the lady; the third, that of the lover;
the fourth, with six examples, indicates the lover's devotion (" 'se
ipsum totum' vel 'quicquid sibi' vel 'quicquid poterit' vel 'si aliquid
valet salute pretiosius inveniri' vel 'salutem cum fidelissimo servitio'
vel 'salutem et quicquid fidelitatis et servitii potest' " [II.xxxiv]).
The chiastic arrangement is customary.

There is, I think, a deliberately comic contrast between the relative
curtness of these salutations and those which follow immediately,
suggested for use in a letter to a lady *post factum.* The lady has become "anime sue dimidio, pre cunctis viventibus diligendi" or
"amice dulcissime forme, sensu et genere decorate"; while the lover
pledges not only "quicquid potest," as previously, but "quicquid
potest, et si ultra posset" and sends "tot salutes et servitia quot in
arboribus folia, quot in celo fulgent sidera, et quot arene circa maris
littora" (II.xxxv).[37] This is the only expression in the *Summa Dictaminis* of that playfulness which found such free rein in Boncompagno
and the earlier French *dictatores.*

---

37. The *topos* goes back to classical antiquity; see H. Walther, "Quot-Tot. Mittelalterliche Liebesgrüsse und Verwandtes," *Zeitschrift für deutsches Altertum und
deutsche Litteratur,* 56 (1928), 257–289.

The theory of the *salutatio* closes with further general remarks on: people who ought not to be greeted, such as excommunicates, Moslems, and Jews (II.lxii); letters in which greetings should be omitted, as when treason, theft, murder, or some other shameful subject is contemplated, or when a churchman or secular dignitary writes a woman, "et tunc per occulta signa debet proprium nomen sub imagine representare" (II.lxiii);[38] letters in which the name of the recipient may be omitted, as when writing to a particular office, e.g., to the Bishop of Bologna, rather than to a specific holder of that office (II.lxv); honorifics appropriate to the higher ranks of society ("papa et imperator debent dici superillustres" [II.lxvi]); and finally, the factors which the letter-writer should keep in mind: the relationship between sender and recipient (with the implication that the author of the letter is *not* the same as the sender, i.e., that he is a secretary), the fortune and condition of each, etc. (II.lxvii).

Guido next takes up the *exordium,* defining it in terms specifically cited from the *Rhetorica ad Herennium* (1.4.7): its purpose is to render the reader docile, attentive, and benevolent (II.lxviii). But the further definitions and examples which follow show that Guido, like his predecessors, conceived of its practical value in quite different terms: it is a means of leading into and giving point to the specific facts of the *narratio* by linking them to some general principle, frequently stated in the form of a proverb or biblical citation.[39] Moreover, far from occurring exclusively at the beginning of the letter— where it ought to be found (*exordior* 'to begin'), and where it would logically have to be placed were its function indeed to seize the reader's attention and render him well disposed toward the following *narratio*—, the *exordium* may in fact be placed in the middle or even at the end of the *narratio.*[40] The letter thus becomes a sort of enthymemic argument from authority, with the *exordium* serving as the major premise, the *narratio* as the minor premise, and the *petitio* as the conclusion.

---

38. This reminds one forcibly of the *senhal* used in the old Provençal *canso* in order to conceal the name of the lady to whom the poem is written.

39. See Francesco di Capua, "Sentenze e proverbi nella tecnica oratoria e loro influenza sull'arte del periodare (Studi sulla letteratura latina medioevale)," in his *Scritti minori,* I, 41–188 (orig. pub. Naples, 1947); p. 165.

40. An example of the *exordium* after the *narratio* is the following: "Si vere sc[i]entie cupis acquirere margaritam, peccatum fugias et consortia malignorum [narratio]; nam cuius mens est vitiorum tenebris offuscata, non potest splend[o]re sapientie luminari [exordium]" (II.lxix; my emendations).

The *exordium* is to be stated in the third person, as befits its status as a basic principle not limited by specific circumstances; and its gravity may be enhanced by the use of imperfect rhyme (see above, p. 93).

Following the *exordium* in Guido's exposition come the *arenga* and *proverbium,* presumably as possible alternatives to the former. The *arenga* is used by the Lombards and the Roman church in letters and speeches. It is like the *exordium* in that it must cohere with the *narratio* but different in that it takes the first and second persons rather than the third (II.lxx). Thus it loses the force of a general statement of principle but gains in immediacy. As for the *prover- bium,* it is an "oratio sententiam continens ante productam, vel consuetudinem approbatam" (II.lxxi).[41]

Only a paragraph apiece is given over to the *narratio* and the *petitio,* probably because they vary so much that no specific rules can be adduced. The former, the statement of facts in the letter, should be brief, lucid, and plausible, as the *Rhetorica ad Herennium* states (I.9.14). The *petitio* should seek only what is just, useful, necessary, and honorable, and should follow naturally from the *nar- ratio* (II.lxxiii–lxxiv).

After a discussion of how the parts of the letter should be arranged and whether any of them can be omitted (II.lxxv–lxxvi), Guido passes from the basic organization of the letter to the subtler nuances of its composition with a series of precepts—which could apply to any written work, not only to letters—on what we may call, without too much impropriety, "style."

To begin with, he distinguishes between the *thema* of the letter, its subject matter, and its *materia,* the "plena et artificiosa verborum ordinatio ex hiis que in themate assumantur" (II.lxxvii), roughly form and content.[42] But *materia* is something more than form, as he goes on to explain more fully in the next section. He says that the wise *dictator* should seek "materiam suo ingenio congruentem,"

----

41. For a general survey of the question, see Giuseppe Vecchi, "Il 'proverbio' nella pratica letteraria dei dettatori della scuola di Bologna," *Studi Mediolatini e Volgari,* 2 (1954), 283–302.

42. The examples given to illustrate the two terms show this clearly. If the *thema* is "Scias quod Bononienses contra Mutinenses exercitum iam fecerunt," then the *materia* would be the artful development of this statement: "Sciatis quod Bono- nienses, amicorum vocata multitudine copiosa, contra Mutinam iverunt cum suo carrocio tam magnifico quam potenter, et in obsidione castri Bafani diutius commo- rantes ad propria sani et incolumes sunt reversi, sed nec ipsum expugnare castrum, nec aliquem habere victoriam potuerunt" (II.lxxvii).

and, having found it, should seek to order it properly and then adorn
it with the colors of rhetoric (II.lxxviii). In a passage based on this
section of Guido's *Summa,* Konrad von Mure (c. 1276) gives an
illuminating illustration: "... materia est id, ex quo aliquid fit,
sicut ligna et lapides domus construende. Set aliud est materia
remota, aliud propinqua. Materia remota sunt rudes lapides et inex-
politi et ligna nondum dolata, nondum levigata. Set materia propinqua sunt lapides et ligna bene preparata, ut in structura domus,
prout expedit, componantur."[43] The *thema* is the subject matter;
the *materia* is the raw materials, *already shaped to the writer's purpose* in the form of rhetorical topoi, which will serve to construct the
letter around a given *thema.* Thus the first part of the *dictator*'s task
consists in the identification of appropriate *topoi* to use in the composition of the letter, then ordering them properly and adorning
them suitably. The question of what is suitable adornment will be
resolved by taking into account what the sender of the letter would
say to the recipient if the latter were present.[44] The concept of *decorum* is introduced, although not in so many words. The style of the
letter should reflect not only the subject matter, but also, and perhaps
more importantly, the rank of the sender and his relationship with
the recipient; just as the latter establish, although far more rigor-
ously, the terms of the *salutatio.*

After these animadversions, our author turns to questions of word
order and rhythm within the sentence itself, although he introduces
this section with four paragraphs on punctuation (II.lxxx–lxxxiii)
which, at first glance, do not appear relevant. In fact they could not
be more apposite, since the division of the sentence into clauses, the
primary purpose of punctuation, is a *sine qua non* for that ordered
variation of rhythmical clause endings known as the *cursus.*

Before taking up the latter, however, Guido discusses natural and

---

43. *Die Summa de Arte Prosandi des Konrad von Mure,* ed. Walter Kronbichler,
Geist und Werk der Zeiten, Heft 17, Arbeiten aus dem historischen Seminar der
Universität Zürich (Zurich: Fretz und Wasmuth Verlag AG, 1968), pp. 66–67. I am
indebted to Prof. Douglas Kelly for an illuminating conversation on this point.

44. Exemplified as follows: "Aliquis vult scribere suo domino vel amico ut possit
a curia litteras impetrare. Qualiter simpliciter diceret, si personaliter in presentia sua
foret? 'Ego rogo dominationem vestram de qua multum confido, ut dignemini mihi
adiutorium vestrum dare, ita quod in tali causa quam habeo cum Petro possim
habere litteras a domino papa'. Ecce, habes *materiam*: recurre igitur ad *disposi-
tionem* ipsius hoc modo: 'Dominationem vestram, de qua gero fiduciam pleniorem,
humili prece rogito incessanter quod mihi vestre liberalitatis et gratie taliter dignemini subsidium impartiri, quod in tali causa, vestra potentia faciente, litteras aposto-
licas impetrare valeam et habere' " (II.lxxviii; italics mine).

artificial word order: natural word order is Subject-Verb-Object, "ego amo te," whereas artificial word order is "illa compositio que pertinet ad dictationem, quando partes pulcrius disponuntur" (II. lxxvix [sic; r. lxxxiv]). As examples he offers the separation of a preposition and its object ("*de* Guidonis *bonitate* confido" [II.lxxxv; my italics]) and the separation of an adjective from the noun it modifies; but only if confusion is not caused thereby. Other devices of great elegance are: systematic variation in the place of the verb; the placing of a relative pronoun before its antecedent;[45] the placing of the relative immediately before the verb in the relative clause;[46] the ending of a sentence with two inflected verbs.[47]

The *dictator* must be mindful not only of word order, but also of the sorts of words he uses. Thus the more elegant words should be placed at the beginning and end of the sentence, "medium vero locum teneant minus digne" (II.lxxxviii). Even word stress must be taken into account. Too many "fast" words (proparoxytones) lead to "magnam deformitatem." Similarly, too many "slow" words (paroxytones) "cursum impediunt et ornatum" (II.lxxxvi). True grace requires a balance of both.[48]

The last part of this section is given order to the rules of the *cursus* "qui debeat hodie observari" (II.lxxxviii), the rules for combining the last two words of a clause in accentually euphonious combinations.[49] These combinations served as formal markers of the internal

---

45. "*Qui* penitentiam non egerit in presenti, *peccatori* venia negabitur in futuro" (II.lxxxvii; italics mine).

46. "In errorem non de facili labitur *qui* metitur rerum exitus sapienter" (ibid.; italics mine).

47. "Celestis pietas, dum peccatores *corrigit, consolatur,* et eorum qui *ceciderunt miseretur*" (ibid.; italics mine).

48. In the following example the accentual dactyls give a markedly singsong effect: "Íllius ieiúnia ad níhilum profíciunt, qui vítiis déditus, se mínime córrigit." Similarly, the accentual spondees of the second example slow the rhythm of the phrase down extraordinarily: "Vitiórum purgatiónem requiríti ieiuniórum sacrátus advéntus" (II.lxxxvi; my accents). Francesco di Capua notes that the examples given treat fasting because the lecture was given during Advent ("Per la storia del latino letterario medievale e del 'cursus'," *Scritti minori,* I, 524–563 [repr. from *Giornale Italiano di Filologia,* 4 (1951), 97–113]; pp. 548–549).

49. There is an enormous literature on the *cursus.* See the bibliographies in Gudrun Lindholm, *Studien zum mittellateinischen Prosarythmus. Seine Entwicklung und sein Abklingen in der Briefliteratur Italiens,* Acta Universitatis Stockholmiensis, Studia Latina Stockholmiensia, X (Stockholm: Almqvist & Wiksell, [1963]), and Tore Janson, *Prose Rhythm in Medieval Latin from the 9th to the 13th Century,* ibid., XX (Stockholm: Almqvist & Wiksell International, [1975]), two recent studies which have done much to put both theory and practice of the *cursus* into a better historical perspective. The latter, in particular, is of first importance

divisions of the sentence—which was less tightly organized than in classical Latin[50]—and thus had a practical as well as an aesthetic importance.

There were three primary forms of the *cursus—planus, tardus,* and *velox—*, all of which are explained and illustrated by Guido, although without using those terms. The basic principle is simple. The clause must end with a word of three or four syllables. If it ends in a trisyllable, then the preceding word must have the *same* stress pattern (i.e., both words must be either paroxytones or proparoxytones). If it ends with a word of four syllables, then the preceding word must have the *opposite* stress pattern (i.e., a proparoxytone

for its introduction of a statistical methodology (based on χ^2 analysis) which permits us, for the first time, not only to determine the proportions of *cursus* usage in a given text but also to gauge the extent to which that usage is consciously sought.

The accentual *cursus* was developed in the third and fourth centuries A.D. as a continuation of the metrical *cursus* of classical Latin prose. Although the links between late Antiquity and the Carolingian period are obscure, Janson shows that by the ninth century at least there was a tradition of rhythmical prose in France and Italy, and in later centuries several different traditions. Furthermore—and in opposition to the traditional view that the *cursus* was introduced into the papal chancery by John of Gaèta, chancellor of Urban II, in 1088 (see Murphy, *Rhetoric in the Middle Ages . . .* , pp. 249–250)—he also shows that it was used in papal documents well before that date (pp. 45–48, 60–63).

Cursus theory, however, was a relatively late development. Indeed, the first theoretical statements date only from the 1180's, and, as Murphy points out, were grafted whole onto the existing body of dictaminal doctrine, which was modified very little to accomodate them (ibid., pp. 250–253). From the very beginning these statements describe two quite different forms of the *cursus,* that of the papal *Curia*—which eventually triumphed—and that of the Orleanese school of *dictamen* of the late twelfth century. The relationships between the two schools have yet to be elucidated, but Marian Plezia has attempted to show that the French school advocated a complete theory of rhythmic prose couched in metrical terminology (spondees, dactyls) derived ultimately from the classical grammarians studied in northern France, which "degenerated" at the papal Curia into a simpler system which required the *cursus* only at the ends of clauses ("L'Origine de la théorie du *Cursus* rhythmique au XIIe siècle," *Archivum Latinitatis Medii Aevi,* 39 [1974], 5–22). Janson's study shows, however, that the two systems developed more or less independently; although he does recognize the classical influence on the French system and also shows that in certain aspects (such as *consillabicatio* [see below, n. 56]) France was ahead of Rome. More work is needed, particularly analyses of contemporary texts from the schools of late twelfth-century Bologna and Orléans.

The existence of these two competing schools of *dictamen* (whose differences went beyond *cursus* usage) was very much a live issue in early thirteenth-century Bologna. Both Boncompagno and Bene of Florence attack the French theories in some detail. Guido, as usual, simply suppresses such theoretical controversy and reduces the practice of the Roman Curia to a few simple statements.

50. See Luigi Malagoli, "Forme dello stile mediolatino e forme dello stile volgare," in *Studi Letterari. Miscellanea in onore di Emilio Santini* (Palermo: U. Manfredi Editore, 1956), pp. 57–86.

must be preceded by a paroxytone, and vice versa).[51] The clause endings given by these rules all have two primary accents (since each type is composed of two words) and either two or four unstressed syllables between the primary stresses.[52]

Let us examine Guido's specific examples. The *cursus planus* is composed of two paroxytones, the last of which must be trisyllabic: "Contagione *delictórum purgáta,* gratia *celéste donánte,* munera *virtútum adcréscant.*" The *cursus tardus*—which was less popular than the other two and not even mentioned by some writers[53]—has two forms, depending on whether the final word has three or four syllables: 1) a trisyllabic proparoxytone is preceded by another proparoxytone: "De alto *córruit Lúcifer,* qui coequari *vóluit Dómino*"; 2) a quadrisyllabic proparoxytone is preceded by a paroxytone: "Non est ieiunium commendandum, quod elemosinis *caróre dignóscitur.*" Finally, the *cursus velox* is composed of a four-syllable paroxytone preceded by a proparoxytone: "Qui digne Deo militare desiderat, negotiis non debet *secularibus implicári* (II.lxxxviii; italics and accents mine). The rhythmical patterns advocated can by symbolized as follows:

cursus planus		´ ˘ / ˘ ´ ˘
cursus tardus	Type 1	´ ˘ ˘ / ´ ˘ ˘
	Type 2	´ ˘ / ˘ ´ ˘ ˘
cursus velox		´ ˘ ˘ / ˘ ˘ ´ ˘

Guido's presentation is succinct and clear; in fact, "it is with Guido that the later statement of the Cursus in a few simple phrases originates."[54] To the rules set forth above, he adds two more, that

51. Francesco Di Capua, *Fonti ed esempi per lo studio dello "Stilus Curiae Romanae" medioevale,* Testi Medioevali per uso delle Scuole Universitarie, N. 3 (Rome: Prof. P. Maglione—Editore, 1941), pp. 64–67; Denholm-Young, "The Cursus in England," 71.

52. Mathieu G. Nicolau, *L'Origine du "cursus" rythmique et les debuts de l'accent d'intensité en latin,* Collection d'Etudes Latines . . . , V (Paris: Société d'Edition "Les Belles Lettres," 1930), pp. 2–3. There existed also a *cursus trispondaicus,* in which a quadrisyllable paroxytone was preceded by another paroxytone (*ésse videátur*). It was advocated by the French school and was so named by modern scholars because it seemed to be composed of three spondees, assuming a secondary accent: *ésse / vide átur* (ibid., pp. 1–2).

53. For example, Albert of Morra, John of Garland, Boncompagno (ibid., pp. 145–146). In the papal chancery, the *cursus tardus* all but disappears by the end of the twelfth century (Janson, pp. 70–71).

54. Denholm-Young, p. 74.

the end of a period should always be marked by *cursus velox*,[55] and that through the process of *consillabicatio* several shorter words may be combined as the rhythmical equivalent of one longer one.[56] The *cursus* is undoubtedly a mechanical procedure which lends itself easily to abuse in the hands of a mediocre writer. The need to end periods with the "correct" rhythmical pattern becomes responsible for all sorts of unusual and ill-considered inversions; the very consistency of the *cursus* becomes monotonous and leads to what has been called "inane richezza."[57] But this does not have to be the case. Guido himself uses it with grace, restraint, and clarity in the very passage in which he explains its rules;[58] and it is applied with the same clarity and consistency in his model letters.

---

55. Guido followed this rule quite strictly in his own works. Thus Vecchi found that the more than 200 sentence endings in the *Arenge* are all marked by *c. velox* ("Le *Arenge* . . . ," 76). F. Di Capua states that the *c. velox* "è sempre la clausola più lodata dai maestri [. . .]. Vi furono degli scrittori che usarono quasi solo questo" ("Lo stile della Curia Romana e il 'cursus' nelle epistole di Pier della Vigna e nei documenti della cancelleria sveva," in his *Scritti minori*, I, 500–523 [repr. from *Giornale Italiano di Filologia*, 2 (1944), 97–116]; p. 504).

56. Thus a monosyllable and a disyllable can be combined to form a trisyllable ("Illud ieiunium divinis auribus est acceptum, quod eleemosynarum *pietáte non-vácat*" [c. planus]; two disyllables or a monosyllable and a trisyllable, to form a quadrisyllable ("Pro salute gentium animam suam debet *pónere bonus-pástor*" [c. velox], "Pro tuenda iustitia sapiens se *oppónere non-formídet*" [c. velox]). (II.lxxxix)

There are other nuances to the use of the *cursus* which Guido follows in his own prose but does not explain in the *Summa Dictaminis*. For example, a compound *cursus* can be created by linking three words together, the first and second forming one *cursus*, the second and third, another, as in the following example from the prologue, ". . . de ignorantie vel cecitatis fermento massa *véstre prudéntie corrumpátur*" (p. 287; my italics and accents), which contains a *c. tardus* (type 1), *véstre prudéntie*, followed by a *c. velox*, *prudéntie corrumpátur*.

57. Vecchi, "Le *Arenge* . . . ," 75–76.

58. "Nota quod pulcriores dictiones locari debent in
princípio et-in-fíne: (c. velox consillabicatus)
medium vero locum
téneant minus-dígne;   (c. velox consillabicatus)
nec ad tam nobilissimum edificium omnes dictiones
indifferénter sumántur,   (c. planus)
sed ille
dumtáxat accédant,   (c. planus)
que maiores verborum et sententiarum
páriant venustátem.   (c. velox)
Nec finem usurpare presumant alique dictiones nimia longitudine vel
brevitáte defórmes.   (c. planus)
Attende igitur, dictator, quod taliter ad ornatum dictiones debes in
distinciónibus ordináre: (c. velox)

After the sections on sentence order and rhythm, Guido turns to what are essentially grammatical considerations, although they are again motivated by his desire that the letter-writer avoid undue repetition. He gives sets of causal and illative conjunctions to link *exordium* and *narratio* or *narratio* and *petitio* (II.lxxxix–lxxxxii), and, after a short reminder (which seems out of place) to be brief, but not obscure, passes on to the regimen and construction of participial and nominal phrases (II.lxxxxiv–lxxxxv). He gives rules for the concordance of verb forms with a double subject, and for adjectival gender when the nouns modified differ in gender (II.lxxxxvi). He states that metaphors should *not* be used in letters unless they are very common, such as "pratum ridet" or "litus aratur"; nor, since they are indicated by the verb forms, should first and second person pronouns be employed, unless it be to avoid confusion (II.lxxxxvii). He lays down the rules concerning the use of nominal constructions to avoid ambiguity and notes that most words usually have either positive or negative connotations (e.g., *extorquere* is usually pejorative; II. lxxxxviii–lxxxxix).

After sections on the use of participles instead of inflected verbs "ornatus de causa" (II.ci), and on the correct use of relative pronouns and correlative conjunctions (II.cii–ciii), Guido turns to more purely rhetorical considerations:

> [. . .] nota, quod summa urbanitas est rethoricorum colorum flosculis dictamina purpurare, et circumvallare proverbiis sapientum, et maiorum doctorum auctoritatibus insignire; nec alicuius urbanitatis pretextu auctoritatis verba debes transponere vel mutare (II.ciii).

The height of elegance is to be obtained through two processes: the use of the colors of rhetoric to, literally, "empurple" the letter; and its fortification (note the military connotations of *circumvallare*

---

nam si finalis dictio fuerit trisillaba cum penultima longa, precedens dictio suam *penúltimam longam-préstet."* (c. velox consillabicatus). (II.lxxxviii)

Of nine clauses, all but one end with some form of *cursus*. The *c. velox* predominates, but in the five examples of it there are three different types. Of the three examples of *c. planus*, one is found, contrary to precept, at the end of a sentence: Guido does not hesitate to break a rule in the interests of clarity. Similarly, he allows the next-to-last clause to end without any form of *cursus* ("penultima longa") for the same reason, even though it would have been relatively easy to produce a canonical ending: *fuerit cum penultima lónga trisíllaba* (c. tardus). But the resulting word order would have been awkward and confusing in addition to producing the least-favored of the three types of *cursus*. The use of the *cursus* in the passage from the *Summa* quoted in n. 44 above has been analyzed by Di Capua ("Appunti sul 'cursus' . . . ," 575).

and *insignire*) with the proverbs of the wise. If the two conflict, ornament yields to authority. Guido then provides the aspiring *dictator* with the raw materials for both of these activities, giving him first a list, with examples, of the rhetorical colors, and then a list of proverbs, taken from the wisdom books of the Bible.

The list of rhetorical colors follows a general explanation of the primary qualities of prose style, *elegantia, compositio,* and *dignitas,* as defined in the *Ad Herennium* (II.ciiii; *Ad Her.* 4.12.18). The list itself consists of fifty-eight rhetorical devices, in the order found in the *Ad Herennium,* from *repetitio* to *demonstratio* (II.cv–clxiii; *Ad. Her.* 4.13.19–55.68): twenty-nine figures of speech, ten tropes, and nineteen figures of thought. Five figures of speech are omitted, for no good reason that I have been able to discover.[59] In many cases Guido substitutes his own examples for those found in the original, Christianizing them or making use of moralizing maxims.[60] It is impossible to gauge the extent to which Guido follows the *Ad Herennium* directly. It may be that he is simply imitating Bolognese school tradition not only in his examples but also in his omission of certain figures.

Immediately following the figures begins the list of biblical sentences, a total of 104 separate citations from the Books of Wisdom (6),[61] Proverbs (62), Ecclesiastes (7), and Ecclesiasticus (28). They are chiefly maxims in praise of wisdom, generosity, prudence, poverty, and the like, particularly suitable for use in the *exordium* (II. clxv–clxviii).

Then, after telling the reader that capitals should be used at the beginning of letters, clauses, and the names of people and places, Guido propounds a series of exercises for the systematic variation of the parts of speech, to give the student some idea of "quas dictiones incipere valeant et per quas sua dictamina debeant terminari" (II.

---

59. The figures omitted are *interrogatio* (4.15.22), *conpar* (4.20.27–28), *adnominatio* (4.21.29–23.32), *subiectio* (4.23.33–24.34), and *transitio* (4.26.35). The absence of *conpar* (the use of clauses of equal length) and *adnominatio* (paronomasia) is particularly surprising, given the medieval fondness for wordplay and for devices which (like the *cursus*) accentuate the relationship among the various clauses of a sentence.

60. Thus Guido's example for *complexio* (the repetition of one word at the beginning of successive clauses and of another at the end) is religious in nature: "Quis liberabit nos de manu hostis? Christus. Quis pro nobis apud Patrem continuo intercedit? Christus." etc. (II.cvii); the *Ad Herennium*'s, political: "Qui sunt, qui foedera saepe ruperunt? Kartaginenses." etc. (4.14.20).

61. I have not been able to find the following maxim there: "Thesaurus desiderabilis in ore sapientis quiescit, vir autem stultus deglutit illum" (II.clxv).

clxix).[62] He starts off with nouns, using as his base the statement, "Petrus lator presentium honorabilis civis noster, nobis *conquerêndo mostrâvit* (II.clxx—note the *c. planus*), and then varying the case of *Petrus* without changing the basic idea. Thus in the genitive we find "Petri querelam *recêpimus continêntem*" (*c. velox*), and so through the rest of the declension in the canonical order. Similar exercises are given to show how to end clauses with a noun in any case, how to begin a sentence with a verb in any tense or mood, with a participle or personal pronoun in any case, or with any of a number of prepositions and adverbs (II.clxxi–clxxvi). Every example ends with a *cursus,* usually a *c. velox.*

As Di Capua points out, these exercises might appear "pedestri e quasi puerili,"[63] but assiduous practice in the composition of short periods was absolutely necessary in order for the student to acquire the mental agility necessary to "stendere ritmicamente un lungo documento, un'epistola imperiale, una bolla papale, e, se il tempo e le circonstanze lo favorivano, comporre ritmicamente un'opera di più ampia mole."[64] Furthermore, such drills were sanctioned by a scholastic tradition going back at least to Rome. They are mentioned by Quintilian, and examples are given in the *Ars Grammatica* of the late fourth-century grammarian Diomedes.[65]

To this set of exercises, generally applicable to letters of any kind, Guido appends four "decursus epistolarum" (II.clxxvii), four sets of phrases specifically designed for letters to friends, to "sublimes personas," to prelates, and to subjects (II.clxxvii–clxxx). Each set is designed to show the "venustem varietatem verborum omnem" (II.clxxvii) or the "ornatum verborum" (II.clxxviii) which ought to be used in such letters. For each part of the letter Guido gives a set of possible phrases, so that a reasonably correct and coherent letter might be written by simply choosing one phrase from each set. Thus, he gives three examples of how a letter to a great lord might begin:

[1] Ad hoc dominus vestram imperialem maiestatem preesse *vôluit super têrras* (c. velox), ut universorum iura pie sub *vêstro munîmine conservêntur* (tardus + velox);

---

62. These have been analyzed in penetrating detail by Di Capua, "Per la storia . . . ," particularly section III, "Una lezione del maestro Guido Fava all' Università di Bologna," pp. 538–544. See also the treatment of this same process in Geoffrey of Vinsauf's *Poetria nova,* discussed above by E. Gallo (p. 71).
63. "Per la storia . . . ," 539.
64. Ibid., 540.
65. Ibid., 544.

[2] divina misericordia providit *pópulo christiáno* (velox), cum vestram personam ad decus et *decórem impérii preelégit* (tardus + velox);

[3] ad hoc divina clementia serenitatem vestram *órbi prepósuit univérso* (tardus + velox), ut per eam imbecilles et dispensatores ministeriorum Dei a *pravórum incúrsibus tuerétur* (tardus + velox). (II.clxxviii; italics and accents mine)

It was this section of what was, in the last analysis, nothing more than epistolary formulas, rather than examples of the sort of elegant variation which the diligent *dictator* might invent for himself, which was imitated in whole treatises by later *dictatores,* and particularly in the *Practica sive Usus Dictaminum* of Laurence of Aquilegia (ca. 1300).[66]

At the very end of the *Summa Dictaminis* (II.clxxxi), Guido dips his toes briefly into the sea of *ars notaria,* the rules for drawing up legally valid documents, discussing and giving examples of both ecclesiastical and imperial privileges. In the short shrift afforded notarial matters, the *Summa Dictaminis* varies noticeably from later thirteenth-century treatises, which became progressively more interested in technical notarial problems at the expense of literary considerations.[67]

Guido ends his treatise with a letter of dedication to Aliprando Fava, *podestà* of Bologna, his homonym although probably not his kinsman.[68]

After this analysis of the *Summa Dictaminis,* two important questions need to be asked: Why was it so successful? More broadly, why were the *artes dictandi* in general so enormously popular in the Middle Ages? The first question is the more difficult. The heterogeneous nature of the *Summa Dictaminis,* its apparent lack of any organizing principle, its relative lack of originality, would all seem to

---

66. See Murphy, pp. 258–263.

67. Cf. the *Rhetorica Novissima* of Boncompagno (ed. by Augusto Gaudenzi in his *Bibliotheca Iuridica Medii Aevi,* vol. II (Bologna: In aedibus Petri Virano olim fratrum Treves, 1892; rep. Turin: Bottega d'Erasmo, 1962), pp. 249–297, the *Summa Prosarum Dictaminis* (ca. 1235–1240), the *Summa Dictaminum* of Ludolf of Hildesheim (ca. 1240–1260) (both ed. by Rockinger, pp. 201–398), or the *Summa de Arte Prosandi* of Konrad of Mure (ca. 1276; ed. Kronbichler [cf. n. 43 above]).

68. Since Aliprando was from Brescia and Guido from Bologna; although Guido could, of course, have been of Brescian ancestry. It is on the basis of this letter that Gaudenzi dates the *Summa* in 1229, the year in which Aliprando occupied the office of *podestà* ("Sulla cronologia . . . ," 139). Di Capua shows how biblical references are used in the *exordium* of this letter as a means of giving it a properly elevated expression ("Lo stile della Curia Romana . . . ," 512).

militate against its success. But in reality the very heterogenous nature of the work was probably in itself an asset, in the sense that Guido concentrated on those aspects of *dictamen* which presented the greatest difficulties for his students, without overly concerning himself about the internal articulation of the treatise. A case in point is his break with tradition in putting the section on vices of style and composition at the beginning of his treatise instead of burying it at the back. Another point in the treatise's favor is the fact that it is eminently readable, because Guido, ironically enough, eschews rhetoric—after the obligatory flourishes in his Introduction—in favor of a very simple style of concise, declarative prose. Then, too, Guido reduces his theoretical exposition to the minimum, making his points instead with an abundance of examples and completely eliminating any reference to extra-epistolary prose or to fictitious letters. It is a thoroughly practical treatise. Finally, the other side of Guido's unoriginality is his fidelity to the Bolognese school tradition. Coupled as it was with the preeminent law school of Europe, the mature doctrines of the Bolognese school of *ars dictandi* exercised an authority not to be challenged by treatises of lesser provenience or greater originality.[69]

The answer to the second question is in essence the same as the answer to the first, writ broad: the *artes dictandi* were useful. Their study formed an indispensable step in the training of all those who made their living running the administrative machinery of church and state. Lawyers, notaries, secretaries—all had to be familiar with the rules for drawing up formal documents as well as official and private letters (which accounts for the near-fusion of *dictamen* and *ars notaria* in later periods). Practitioners of *dictamen* were much in demand, and their positions were lucrative.[70] It is not to be wondered that the *ars dictandi* was popular.

---

69. Although I consider it unlikely, the popularity of Guido's *Summa* may turn out to be a mirage of modern scholarship, which has based itself more on the number of extant MSS than on any thorough study of the work's influence in the Middle Ages. It may well be that the number of MSS reflects the popularity of Guido's *Dictamina Rhetorica*, with which the *Summa* is invariably coupled, rather than that of the *Summa* itself. See Murphy, p. 258.

70. Most students of *dictamen* have stressed its practical importance: Louis John Paetow, *The Arts Course at Medieval Universities with Special Reference to Grammar and Rhetoric*, University of Illinois, The University Studies, vol. III, no. 7 (Urbana-Champaign: University Press, 1910), pp. 28–29; Charles Sears Baldwin, *Medieval Rhetoric and Poetic (to 1400) Interpreted from Representative Works* (New York: The Macmillan Co., 1928; repr. Gloucester [Mass.]: Peter Smith, 1959), p. 208;

This popularity in the Middle Ages explains why the *artes dictandi* should be better known among modern students of that period. They are primary material for the intellectual historian interested in tracing the vicissitudes of the liberal arts during this period. In their authors are to be sought the forerunners of the Italian humanists, who occupied exactly the same positions and carried out exactly the same kind of activities that the *dictatores* did.[71] In the doctrines advocated in the *artes*, the diplomatic historian can find material for distinguishing authentic documents from forgeries.[72] The letter collections which frequently accompany the theoretical treatises offer to the

---

Hastings Rashdall, *The Universities of Europe in the Middle Ages,* ed. F. M. Powicke and A. B. Emden, 3 vols. (Oxford: At the Clarendon Press, 1936), I, 110–111. The writers of the treatises themselves were not above advertising the rewards their students would reap. Thus in his *Candelabrum* Bene of Florence writes: "Dictamen a cunctis sequitur, facundiam auget, gratiam promeretur, honores amplificat, et sepe inopes locupletat" (cited by Vecchi, "Le *Arenge* . . . ," 64).

71. This thesis has been argued most forcefully by Paul Oskar Kristeller in "Humanism and Scholasticism in the Italian Renaissance," *Byzantion,* 17 (1944–1945), 346–374 (repr. most recently in his *Renaissance Thought: The Classic, Scholastic, and Humanist Strains,* Harper Torchbooks/The Academy Library [New York: Harper and Row, (1961)], pp. 92–119.) It has not met with universal approval: see Giulio Vallese, "Retorica medievale e retorica umanistica," *Delta* (N.S.), 1 (1952), ii, 39–57, and Hanna H. Gray, "Renaissance Humanism: The Pursuit of Eloquence," in *Renaissance Essays from the* Journal of the History of Ideas, eds. Paul Oskar Kristeller and Philip P. Wiener (New York and Evanston: Harper and Row, 1968), pp. 199–216.

72. I am thinking primarily of the *cursus.* The *Libellus de Arte Dictandi* attributed to Peter of Blois (an attribution which Janson, pp. 96–98, has shown cannot be correct) claimed that it was kept secret by the papal chancery as a means of distinguishing authentic letters from forgeries: "Huiusmodi distincionum fines vocant notarii Romane curie cadencias quas velut sanctuaria celantes nulli volunt penitus revelare; per illas etenim suas literas ab adulterinis discernunt" (ed. by Janson, p. 120). While this treatise in fact represents the theory of the French school of *dictamen,* it is still likely that at some point in the history of the papal chancery the *cursus* was seen as one of a number of diplomatic details useful as a means of authenticating letters (see Reginald L. Poole, *Lectures on the History of the Papal Chancery down to the Time of Innocent III* [Cambridge: At the University Press, 1915], pp. 95, 151–160). For the modern historian it will be helpful as a means of authenticating official documents in the measure that we have studies of its usage along the lines of those of Lindholm and Janson.

Since *cursus* usage varies both geographically and chronologically, it may also be instrumental as a means for dating and placing anonymous works, both literary and nonliterary, or of deciding among various attributions. A similar kind of statistical analysis of forms of versification has been signally successful in both deciding attributions and dating plays supposedly written by the seventeenth-century Spaniard Lope de Vega (see S. G. Morley and C. Bruerton, *The Chronology of Lope de Vega's Comedias, with a Discussion of Doubtful Attributions, the Whole Based on a Study of His Strophic Versification* [New York, 1940]).

110   CHARLES B. FAULHABER

political, social, and economic historian a myriad of details on medieval life, ranging from the activities of the most humble to those of
popes and emperors. The historian of the medieval Latin and vernacular literatures will find the *ars dictandi* of unusual interest for
the study of the development of prose style and the establishment of
critical editions of many prose texts. It has long been known that both
Dante and Boccaccio practiced the *cursus* in their Latin writings,[73] and
that *dictatores* like Guido Faba wrote not only in Latin but also in
Italian.[74] Historians of Italian literature have been engaged in tracing
the connections between the two since the nineteenth century.[75]
Franco-Latin and Hispano-Latin literature could also be studied from
the point of view of the *ars dictandi.*

The other vernacular literatures, Romance, Germanic—possibly
even Slavic—offer points of comparison as well.[76] The same influences

---

73. See, for example, Ernesto Giacomo Parodi, "Intorno al testo delle epistole di
Dante e al cursus," *Bullettino della Società Dantesca Italiana* (N.S.), 19 (1912),
249–275, and "Osservazioni sul 'cursus' nelle opere latine e volgari del Boccaccio,"
Miscellanea Storica della Valdelsa, 21 (1913), 232–245; Paget Toynbee, "Dante and
the *Cursus,"* in his edition *Dantis Alagherii Epistolae* (Oxford: At the Clarendon
Press, 1920; repr. 1966), App. C, pp. 224–247, and "The Bearing of the *Cursus* on
the Text of Dante's *De Vulgari Eloquentia,"* *Proceedings of the British Academy,*
[10–11] (1921–23), 359–377; Di Capua, "Appunti sul 'cursus' . . . ," (see n. 31
above); Aristide Marigo, "Il 'cursus' nella prosa latina dalle origini cristiane ai
tempi di Dante," *Atti e Memorie della R. Accademia de Scienze, Lettere ed Arti
in Padua* (N. S.), 47 (1930–31), 321–356, and "Il 'cursus' nel 'De Vulgari Eloquentia' di Dante," ibid., 48 (1931–32), 85–112; and Pio Rajna, "Per il cursus medievale
e per Dante," *Studi di Filologia Italiana,* 3 (1932), 7–86.
74. See the works cited in n. 19 above.
75. "L'applicazione fatta da Guido [Faba] degli adornamenti retorici alla parlata
volgare interessano direttamente lo studioso delle origini della prosa d'arte italiana;
soprattutto l'applicazione al volgare delle leggi della *compositio,* anzi della *compositio artificialis* con le sue cadenze ritmiche, le quali suggeriscono al volgare raffi-
natezze melodiche e intervengono nella conformazione strutturale sintattica del
periodo" (Vecchi, "Le *Arenge* . . . , 78). See also Paul Oskar Kristeller, "The
Origin and Development of the Language of Italian Prose," in his *Studies in
Renaissance Thought and Letters,* Storia e Letteratura, Raccolta di Studi e Testi,
54 (Rome: Edizioni di Storia e Letteratura, 1969 [1956]), pp. 473–493; Luigi Peirone,
"Dante, i trovatori e le 'artes dictaminis'," *Giornale Italiano di Filologia,* 16 (1963),
193–198; and especially Alfredo Schiaffini, *Tradizione e poesia nella prosa d'arte
italiana dalla latinità medievale al Boccaccio* 2, (Rome: Edizioni di Storia e Letteratura, 1969 [1943]).
76. See, for example, Morris W. Croll, "The Cadence of English Oratorical
Prose," *Studies in Philology,* 16 (1919), 1–55 (repr. in his *Style, Rhetoric, and
Rhythm. Essays,* ed. J. Max Patrick *et al.* [Princeton: Princeton University Press,
1966], pp. 299–359); G. H. Gerould, "Abbot Aelfric's Rhythmic Prose," *Modern
Philology,* 22 (1925), 352–366; Sherman H. Kuhn, "Cursus in Old English: Rhetorical Ornament or Linguistic Phenomenon," *Speculum,* 47 (1972), 188–206; Marçal

affected them that affected Latin literature; the same writers contributed to both. That those writers *were* exposed to the *ars dictandi*, and in all probability influenced by it, is self-evident. Since there was no such thing as a "professional" writer, every author had to make his living at some other job, quite frequently as a notary or secretary. Thus in the thirteenth century the first Spanish poet known by name, Gonzalo de Berceo, served as a notary in his monastery; two centuries later the poet Juan de Mena was secretary for Latin letters to King John II of Castile.

How should the modern critic put his knowledge of the *ars dictandi* to use in the study of such authors? E. Gallo (above, pp. 83–84) suggests that it is at best simplistic, at worst illusory, to try to find direct influence of theory on practice; rather both should be evaluated as examples of the habits of mind and presuppositions about literature which the medieval poet or theorist brought to his task. This approach is also valid for the *ars dictandi*; indeed, many of the precepts (on rhetorical invention, the use of proverbs, definitions of figures, etc.) are the same as those found in the *artes poetriae*.

What does assume extraordinary importance for the modern critic, however, are precisely those doctrines which are *not* shared with the *ars poetriae* and at the same time *not* limited exclusively to the letter (as, for example, the salutation is). Any sort of fine-meshed analysis of medieval prose style, Latin or vernacular, must take such doctrines into account—particularly those which have to do with the rhetorical tactics, rather than strategy, of composition, with the rhythm and organization of the sentence (*cursus,* word order, etc.) rather than with the work as a whole—not as "habits of mind," but as precepts faithfully followed by generations of medieval writers.

Olivar, "Notes entorn la influència de l'*Ars dictandi* sobre la prosa catalana de cancilleria de finals del segle XIV: El Ms. Y-129-7 de la Biblioteca Colombina," *Estudis Universitaris Catalans,* 22 (1936), 631–653 (= *Homenatge a Antoni Rubió i Lluch. Miscellània d'estudis literaris, històrics i lingüístics,* 3 vols. [Barcelona, 1936], III, 631–653); and Jordi Rubió i Balaguer, "Guillem Ponç, secretari del rei Martí, contemporani de Bernat Metge," *Estudis Romànics,* 9 (1961 [1966]), 67–84.

The *Ars componendi sermones* of Ranulph Higden

MARGARET JENNINGS, C.S.J.

ALTHOUGH Robert of Basevorn's *Forma Praedicandi*[1] has frequently been used as the exemplar for medieval Arts of Preaching, it is possible to advance several arguments for extending exemplar status to the *Ars componendi sermones* of Ranulph Higden, a much shorter treatise composed about 1340. Reasons for extolling Higden's work include its overall compositional unity, its clarity of illustration, its tightness of structure, and, from the editor's viewpoint, its author's very "unmedieval" ability to bring his discussion to a speedy close.[2]

---

1. Edited by Th. Charland, *Artes Praedicandi* (Ottawa: Publications de l'Institut d'études médiévales d'Ottawa, VIII, 1936).
2. Higden's organizational ability is clearly demonstrable in a comparative outline of the initial sections of his and Basevorn's treatises:

Higden: *Preface*	Basevorn: *Prologue*

Treatise is founded on scriptural and practical principles	Exposition of equations:
	  bad logic = bad reasoning
	  bad form = bad preaching

Three things required in the person preaching:
  rectitude of intention
  holiness of association
  aptitude for presentation
	Lengthy discussion of the need for this treatise
	
	"Bold" presentation of the four causes:
	  final: God

Three things required in the sermon:
  congruence of theme
  propriety of division
  utility in development
	efficient: God and the preacher
	  material: the form of preaching
	  formal: orderly procedure in 50
	  chapters

True preaching is thematic and provides motivation and example; though public persuasion, it should not use scholastic methodology.	*Chapter One* What in the proper sense is preaching and how much time one sermon should take
True preaching excludes both the	Explication of the definition of preaching What is not preaching

But tempting as the project may be, I do not intend to formulate an apologia for Higden's *Ars* since my purpose is to analyze this singularly well made guide to the preacher's rhetoric.

From among many possible approaches I have chosen the one which seems most useful to the student of medieval rhetoric—that of comparative analysis. While it can be valuable to question whether Higden's tract is directly related to classical rhetorical tradition (the relationship is more tangential), whether it follows the major outlines for thematic sermon construction[3] (it does), or whether it encompasses a wide range of favorite topics in fourteenth-century sermonalia (it treats only a few), this treatise is best viewed through its connections with, and differences from, other medieval *artes praedicandi*. Discernible as a distinct rhetorical entity about 1200, these explications of the *forma* rather than just the *materia* of sermon composition were popular throughout the Middle Ages. A survey of celebrated texts would comprise those of Alain of Lille, Humbert of Romans, Guibert of Nogent, Antonius of Florence, Jean of la Rochelle, William of Auvergne, "Albertus," "Aquinas," "Henry of Hesse," Martin of Cordoba, Michael of Hungary, Thomas of Todi, Jacobus or James of Fusignano, and several anonymous authors, all of whom were well-known contributors to the continental preaching tradition; from England would be listed the tracts of Alexander of Ashby (ca. 1200), Thomas of Salisbury (ca. 1215), Richard of Thetford (ca. 1250), John of Wales (ca. 1275), Hugh of Sneyth (ca. 1290), Robert of Basevorn

---

insignificant and the excessive.
Four causes as related to preaching:

final: three ends
material: *verba casta*
efficient: "Deus originaliter et ipsi
   predicans ministraliter"
formal: the definition of preaching

What actions make a preacher
What length a sermon ought to be

3. Detailed analyses of the thematic sermon are provided in Dorothea Roth, *Die Mittelalterlichen Predigtheorie und das Manuale Curatorum des Johann Ulrich Surgant, Basler Beiträge zur Geschichtewissenschaft* (Basel and Stuttgart, 1956), LVIII, and in Charles Smyth, *The Art of Preaching*, 747–1939 (London: Society for Promoting Christian Knowledge, 1940). For rhetorical influences see Harry Caplan's studies: "Rhetorical Invention in Some Medieval Tractates on Preaching," *Speculum*, II (1927), 284–295 and "Classical Rhetoric and the Medieval Theory of Preaching," *Classical Philology*, XXVIII (1933) 73–96. A comprehensive survey of the entire *ars praedicandi* tradition is James J. Murphy's *Rhetoric in the Middle Ages* (Berkeley and Los Angeles: University of California Press, 1974), pp. 269–355.

114   MARGARET JENNINGS, C.S.J.

(ca. 1322), and Thomas Waleys (ca. 1338).[4] Yet, when all of this
activity in the writing of thematic sermon treatises has been assessed,
Higden's *Ars componendi sermones*[5] still emerges as one of the most
clear, unified, and convincing statements of concern for preaching
instruction in the medieval centuries.

Constituted largely on the definitions of its forebears, Higden's
work can be effectively analyzed only when the positions taken by
contemporary and later manualists are understood. For, in conjunction with its easily discernible structure and its obvious relationship
to the "typical" *ars praedicandi* format—both of which are outlined
in the accompanying Appendix—the *Ars componendi sermones*
demonstrates a confluence of traditional modes of explication and
illustration. It is through concentration on these traditions and on
their shaping influence in the construction of a thematic sermon
manual that the main lines of the *Ars'* development become exposed.
Consequently, a comparative analysis of standard thematic sermon
components such as preaching and its functions, the preacher and his
attributes, types of sermons, the theme, the protheme, the introduction of the theme, its division, and its dilation, will provide a useful
vantage point for focusing on Higden's treatise.

Many authors of longer tracts on preaching began by defining and
exploring the nature of this pastoral activity. John of Wales in his
Ars praedicandi had explained succinctly that preaching consisted in
invoking God's aid and then clearly and devoutly expounding a
proposed theme by means of division, subdivision, and concordance—the aim of such an exercise being the catholic enlightenment
of the intellect and the enkindling of emotion through the action of
grace.[6] There are, certainly, many points of contact between this

---

4. General surveys of the English preaching scene are available in Gerald R. Owst,
Preaching in Medieval England (Cambridge: Cambridge Univ. Press, 1926) and in
Woodburn O. Ross, ed., *Middle English Sermons*, Early English Text Society, CCIX
(London: Oxford Univ. Press, 1940). A more detailed listing is available in the
compilation by James J. Murphy, *Medieval Rhetoric: A Select Bibliography* (Toronto:
Univ. of Toronto Press, 1971). Specific references to important texts can be found
below.

5. See "A Critical Edition of the *Ars componendi sermones* of Ranulph Higden,"
ed. Margaret Jennings, C.S.J. (Ph.D. Dissertation, Bryn Mawr, 1970).

6. "Predicatio est invocato divino auxilio dividendo, subdividendo, & concor-
dando propositi thematis clara & devota expositio ad intellectus catholicam instruc-
tionem & affectus caritativam informationem." From Mazarine MS. 569, fol. 81va
and Basel MS. A, VIII, 1, fol 148r. This definition was adopted, in a somewhat
modified form, by later writers and is consistently found in the many anonymous
abbreviations of the John of Wales tract.

definition and the one that Alain de Lille had proposed some three-quarters of a century earlier: "Praedicatio est manifesta et publica instructio morum et fidei, informationi hominum deserviens, ex rationum semita et auctoritatum fonte proveniens,"[7] but there is no absolute congruence. The author of the "Aquinas" tract (probably fifteenth century) borrows Alain's definition yet also maintains that "preaching is the fitting and appropriate dispensation of God's word.[8] About 1320, Robert of Basevorn had emphasized the more pragmatic aspects of the preaching office in his insistence that it lead many to virtue in a modicum of time;[9] twenty years later Ranulph Higden claimed that this definition was more applicable to the words of lecturers and disputants in the schools than to those of preachers, and he defined preaching more in the style of John of Wales:

> Predicatio est invocato dei auxilio, thema proponere, propositum dividere, divisum subdividere, auctoritates confirmantes cum racionibus et exemplis adducere et adductas explanare ad divini cultus ampliacionem, ad ecclesie militantis illustracionem, ad humani affectus erga deum inflamacionem.[10]

When Martin of Cordoba was compiling his *ars* towards the latter part of the fifteenth century, he chose to define *sermo* rather than *praedicatio,* and yet he continued directly into an explanation of the four causes as they apply to preaching—an explanation that had authority from John of Wales onward.[11] The actual specification of these causes, nevertheless, was not uniform; although all agreed that the *causa efficiens* was God, Robert of Basevorn, Ranulph Higden, the author of the "Aquinas" tract, and Martin of Cordoba had also added the preacher as a kind of instrumental or secondary efficient

---

7. "Preaching is clear and public instruction about morals and faith, being of service for the information of men, arising out of the path of principles and the fount of the authorities." *Summa de arte praedicatoria,* PL 210, 111.

8. Harry Caplan, "A Late Medieval Tractate on Preaching," *Studies in Rhetoric and Public Speaking in Honor of James A. Winans,* ed. A. M. Drummond (New York: Russell & Russell, 1962), p. 72.

9. "Est autem predicatio pluribus facta persuasio ad merendum, moderatum tempus retinens" in Charland, p. 238.

10. "Preaching is, having invoked the help of God, to propose a theme, to divide the proposed text, to subdivide the division, to adduce confirming authorities with reasons and examples, and to explain those things adduced for the extension of divine adoration, for the adornment of the church militant, for the inflamation of the human disposition toward God." Jennings, ibid., p. 67.

11. "Sermo est oratio informativa ex ore predicatoris emissa, ut instruat fideles quid credere, quid agere, quid cavere, quid timere, quid sperare debeant" states Martin. See Fernando Rubio, ed., "Martin of Cordoba: *Ars Praedicandi,*" in *La Ciudad de Dios,* CLXXI (1959), 330.

cause.[12] While the formal cause remained constant—the procedure of the art of preaching—both final and material causes were defined differently by the different authors: John of Wales summed up the whole material cause in his *thema*; Robert asserted that the form of preaching was the matter; Ranulph located it in the *verba casta* which were to announce virtues, vices, punishments, and joys.[13] Another diversity in opinion is expressed in the formulation of the final cause: here John specified it as a *salus animarum*, Robert as *deus ipse*, Ranulph as "ipsius predicatoris excitacio, ipsius auditoris edificatio et creatoris honoracio"[14]—by far the most inclusive. As the fourteenth century wore on, these theoretical explanations of the office and function of preaching tended to be lost as a great number of the preaching manuals concerned themselves almost exclusively with practical precepts.

Another body of traditional matter grew up around the attributes and person of the preacher. When Ranulph Higden schematizes his treatment of the *praedicator* under three headings (*intencionis rectitudo, conversacionis sanctitas, prolacionis aptitudo*), he is merely compressing and combining the elements of a long tradition. Humbert of Romans had counselled that a preacher must apply himself fully to a study of whatever is needed for the proper execution of his office and had written at length on the necessity for relevance, clarity, and brevity in the preacher's delivery.[15] William of Auvergne had been even stricter in his definition of who might preach: "doctor qui doctrine sue fuerit factor et potens in opere et sermone, faciendo et sciendo,"[16] and he had insisted after the fashion of Gregory the

---

12. Mention of these causes can be found in Higden's *Prefacio* (Jennings, p. 68), Basevorn's Prologue (Charland, pp. 234-5), the "Aquinas" tract (Caplan, p. 73), and Martin of Cordoba (Rubio, pp. 331-32). Jacobus de Fusignano (MS. Munich 5983, fol. 105 and MS Merton 102, fol. 278) and the anonymous author of Munich MS. 14634 (XVth cent.) fol. 94r also concern themselves with expositions of the Aristotelian causes as they apply to preaching.

13. Martin of Cordoba develops his own discussion of the *materia sermonis* along the lines indicated by Higden but at much greater length; see Rubio, pp. 331-32.

14. Actually Alain de Lille had also distinguished a final cause in his *Summa* but his ignoring of the other three causes does not permit a valid comparison. He did, however, specify that "informationi hominum deserviens, significatur causa finalis, sive utilitas praedicationis" (col. 112).

15. See Part I, chapter VI, "Difficulties of the Office of Preacher" in the translation of the *Treatise on Preaching by Humbert of Romans*, tr. by Dominican Students and ed. by Walter M. Conlon (Westminster Md., 1951), pp. 31-35 and Part VI, chapter XXIV, "Causes of Sterility," p. 96.

16. A. dePoorter, "Un Manuel de Prédication Médiévale," *Revue Neo-scolastique*, XXV (1939), p. 196.

Great upon the preacher's consideration of the *statum auditorum,* an insistence that was echoed by Alexander of Ashby, Alain de Lille, Jacques de Vitry, and most of the compilers of *artes praedicandi* in the fourteenth and fifteenth centuries. The personal habits of the preacher had also been considered: the divine rhetors gave much thought to *pronuntiatio* and expatiated on such "vices" as uncontrolled gestures, excessive speed, noisiness, remote digressions, slurred speech, and the like.[17] Thomas Waleys felt it incumbent on him to discourse at length on what must be avoided in the preacher's manner as well as in the matter of his appearance and company. Some authors, such as Antonius of Florence, concerned themselves only with the qualities which are desirable and necessary in a preacher ("dilectionem ardentem, exterius conversacionis relucentem, et cognicionem sciencie competentem"[18]), while others, such as Robert of Basevorn, also investigated the legal and canonical bases of the preacher's office. These latter considerations remained peripheral, however, because the main function of the preacher *a propria persona* could be expressed through the centuries in the words of Alain de Lille: "praedicator debet captare benevolentiam auditorum . . . per humilitatem et a rei quam proponit utilitate."[19]

Perhaps because of the broad areas included in "preaching" and "preachers," there was some confusion in the traditions surrounding the subject "types of sermons" or "types of preaching," but there is always some *Fortleben* for the various schemas proposed. Alain de Lille related his three species very closely to the person of the preacher when he named them *in verbo, in scripto, in facto.*[20] Though this classification is repeated in the "Aquinas" tract and its teaching is

---

17. In fact, *pronuntiatio* is given consideration comparable to that of the Roman progenitors of rhetorical doctrine. Most of these mediaeval rhetoricians set forth aids to delivery and a few issue precautions for the preacher to keep in mind during the actual delivery itself; for example, St. Bonaventure in the *Speculum Disciplinae ad Novitios (Opera Sancti Bonaventurae: Opuscula,* Vol. XIII [Venice, 1756], pp. 59ff.) sets down the desirable qualities which should be found in a preacher's personality and habits: he should be young, but boyish neither in appearance nor in manner; he must have no bodily deformities, and be strong, of competent eloquence, well-trained in grammar and Holy Scripture, and able to speak without error or confusion; for his persuasive purpose, he ought to be irreproachable in life and habits, industrious, prudent, and not given to contention.

18. Antonius treats this point fully in his *Summa Theologica,* Pars III, cap. iii, section 2 (Venice, 1478).

19. PL 210, col 113. Munich MS. 5966, fol. 58v, and the following discourses at length on like qualities in the preacher.

20. PL 210, ibid. Alain "proves" these by means of scriptural texts. Cf. Murphy, *Rhetoric in the Middle Ages,* pp. 303–09.

incorporated in spirit in every major effort to construct an *ars,* it did not survive as a useful way of discussing sermon types. The categorization proposed by John of Wales underwent a similar metamorphosis. As he set it up in the beginning of his *ars praedicandi*:

> Quattuor sunt genera predicationis. Primum genus est quando concordatur realiter et vocaliter. Secundum est quando solum concordat realiter et non vocaliter. Tertium quando vocaliter solum et non realiter. Primum . . . subtilius, . . . Secundum . . . facilius. . . . Tertium . . . curiosius. . . . Quartum devotius sicut sunt sermones factorum qui leguntur in ecclesia.[21]

John of Wales proceeds to amplify and illustrate these four definitions and in doing so he eventually specifies the time and place of their appearance: consequently, ''quartum genus predicandi servaverunt antiqui patres et doctores sancti'' who gave inspiration to the body of the church without using division, subdivision, or any system of concordances; yet ''nunc secundum primum modum precedunt moderni auctores qui subtiliter procedunt'' (fol. xviii). As the necessity for concordance gained in stature through the investigations and explications of authors of *artes praedicandi,* John's ''real'' and ''verbal'' began to be located under discussions of concordance, and his specification of these kinds of sermon construction with regard to person, place, and time began to assume the properties associated with separate topics. The transformation is seen in Robert of Basevorn, who distinguishes the ancient and modern types of sermonizing and treats verbal concordance in a separate section. Ranulph Higden, too, shows the effects of this changed point of view; like Basevorn he treats ancient and modern methods, separating the latter into the *modus Parisiensis* and the *modus Oxoniensis,* but he is clearer than his predecessor in handling the subject ''Quod thema concordiancias admittat.''[22] In addition, it is possible to trace some of the later developments in discussions of types of sermons to Robert of Basevorn's description of the methods of preaching employed by Christ, St. Paul, St. Augustine, St. Gregory, and St. Bernard. When generalized and condensed, these descriptions appear in the ''Aquinas'' tract as 1) the ancient method (also called the laical, beautiful, and popular); 2) the smooth and simple—a variation of the thematic with divisions but without distinctions; and 3) the modern or

---

21. John of Wales, *Ars praedicandi* (?Ulm, 1480), fol. xvii v and fol. xviii r. John's *Ars* is contained in a treatise attributed to Albert the Great.
22. See Chapter X of Higden's *Ars,* Jennings, pp. 98–99.

thematic.[23] In the "Albertus" tract, they show up as the homily, preaching through syllogisms and distinctions (equivalent to the modern and thematic), and preaching through poetic fictions.[24] In a like vein, the author of the "Henry of Hesse" tract knows four kinds: the *postillatio* or mystic interpretation of the terms of a text; the modern or thematic method; the ancient or homily type; and the *subalternus* (a mixture of the homily and modern methods).[25] Several other authors offer schemes of preaching modes but they are, in general, species of the general categories which have been defined above or methods of procedure which are better related to the parts of the thematic sermon.

Certainly the most complete set of traditions surrounds the parts of the thematic sermon. Fortunately, the various expositors of thematic sermon construction (Gilson, Ross, Charland, Smyth, Roth, Murphy) have provided numerous cross references for the parts of the theme and protheme as they are set forth in the larger manuals and I do not wish to repeat them here.[26] There are, however, interesting variations in the traditions connected with the introduction of the theme, its division and its dilation, which should be discussed. In the introduction especially, a process of agglutination seems fairly evident. John of Wales had made provision for the existence of the introduction of the theme but emphasized the necessity for keeping it "parvus" in order that it would not delay the preacher's approach to his division and discussion. When speaking "de introitu," John mentioned only three methods of procedure: "vel accipiendo auctoritatem canonis, vel alicuius sancti, vel aliquod commune proverbium."[27] How these processes mushroomed into as many as ten seems to have puzzled even some of the authors of the *artes*: Thomas Waleys remarks concerning this section "cuius causam non plene comprehendo," but he supposes that it afforded the preacher an opportunity to catch the attention of his audience and to make clear

---

23. Caplan, "Aquinas," pp. 88–90.

24. Caplan distills these categories from the text of the *De faciebus* of William of Auvergne. See MS. Bodley 281 and Caplan, "Classical Rhetoric," p. 87.

25. Harry Caplan, "Henry of Hesse on the Art of Preaching," *PMLA*, XLIII (1933), 347 ff.

26. In addition to the treatments of Ross and Charland which I have mentioned previously, an earlier and still useful introduction to the technique of medieval sermon construction is that of Etienne Gilson in "Michel Menot et la Technique du Sermon Médiéval," *Les Idées et les lettres* (Paris, 1932), pp. 93–154.

27. Fol. xx.

his purpose.²⁸ The author of B.M. Additional MS. 24361 shows greater consciousness of the function of the *introductio thematis* and devotes one-third of his treatise to its explication. He concludes that five methods of introducing a theme can be employed: "per manuduccionem, per simile in natura, per sacram scripturam, per scripturam sanctorum, per auctoritatem philosophorum et poeticorum."²⁹ Robert of Basevorn incorporates these methods into his discussion but his is a more logically organized approach; the introduction, he says, can be formed in three ways: by authority, by argument, by both at the same time. An authority forming an introduction can come from something original, from a philosopher or a poet, or from one of the *auctores*, provided that it is not from scripture or from the "apocrypha" which are incorporated into the Bible. The second method (argument) clearly reflects the dialectical emphasis of the universities and provides for such processes as induction, example in art, nature, and history, syllogism, and enthymeme. Basevorn particularly commends the Parisians because no matter what kind of argument they use for the introduction, all parts are confirmed by the authority of Sacred Scripture. For introductions to themes of two or more significant words, any or all of these methods can be employed; for those of just one explicit statement (for example, *intellige*), he recommends that an authority be first introduced and that three members which correspond to the feast and the theme be immediately drawn from it.³⁰ Thomas Waleys, who wrote shortly after Robert of Basevorn, is even more schematic: he begins by explaining accidental and essential diversity and divides the latter into narrative and argument, from which standpoint he proceeds to outline the several processes of *introductio thematis*.³¹ At the other end of the spectrum from the tight order prescribed by Waleys is the sprawling outline given by Alphonsus d'Alphran: the introduction of the theme can be accomplished "per syllogismum, per consequentiam, per induccionem, per exemplum, per originale, per auctoritatem philosophie, per divisionem, per distinctionem, per figuratam, per questionem."³² Between these two poles, Ranulph Higden charts

28. *De modo componendi sermones*, Charland, p. 356.
29. Fols. 52r through 53r.
30. Basevorn incorporates this discussion into two chapters; see Charland, pp. 268–273. A useful outline of Basevorn's treatise is in Murphy, *Rhetoric in the Middle Ages*, pp. 344–55.
31. Charland, pp. 357–368.
32. MS. Hamilton 44, fols. 188r–197v.

a middle course in stating that the introduction is able to be made "multis modis."[33] He allows the use of scriptural interpretation as the first of these modes following, no doubt, the lead of some of the manuscripts of John of Wales,[34] and by leaving his initial definition somewhat vague ("per scripturam"), Ranulph is able to include here also the writings of the saints, those of poets, and those of philosophers. Under his second heading, *augmentum*, he discusses inductive reasoning, the syllogism, and the enthymeme as modes of introduction, and he also commends the Parisian emphasis on authorities. The next two categories which are mentioned in the beginning of the chapter, "per exemplarem manuduccionem" and "per simile in natura" are handled in an easily decipherable manner by Ranulph, though his reflections "per exemplum in arte" and "per exemplum in historia" are indiscriminately tacked on to the section on similarities in nature. Except for an aside on the vagaries of Guy d'Evereux, his discussions of proverbial introductions and of those stemming from a theme of only one word follow Basevorn's fairly closely. It must be borne in mind, however, that the traditional methods of introducing a theme were not uniformly picked up by contemporary and later writers; the author of the "Aquinas" tract omits all reference to this part; the "Henry of Hesse" tract ignores the terminology but classifies scriptural interpretation as a type of division. Martin of Cordoba recounts ten methods of introducing a theme (similitude, quality, historical narrative, questioning, application of fables, fictional discussion, proverbs, experiences undergone, original texts, and moral declarations), but they do not completely correspond to any of those detailed above.[35] Thomas of Todi outlines six, but again they represent a composite of several systems.[36] It is

---

33. See the chapter *De thematis introductione,* Jennings, p. 116.

34. This is actually a telescoping of John of Wales' entire discussion of the introduction of the theme into one category. However, even manuscripts that are largely abbreviated from John's work enlarge upon this section. For example, see Woodburn O. Ross, "A Brief *Forma Predicandi,*" *Modern Philology,* XXXIV (1937), 342 and Additional MS. 21202, fol. 71v.

35. See Rubio, pp. 334-7.

36. The six are: 1) "per auctoritatem unam vel plures inter quas et thema est aliqualis conformitas quaerenda et reperienda" 2) "per divisionem factam circa principalem materiam thematis vel principalem partem eius" 3) "per quaestiones" 4) "per figuram" 5) "per consequentiam" 6) "per syllogismum." The *Ars Sermocinandi ac etiam Collationes Faciendi* of Thomas of Todi was edited from MS. Bibl. Nat. 15965 by June Babcock (M.A. Thesis, Cornell University, 1941): see especially pp. 42-66.

indeed this section of a typical *ars praedicandi* which best shows the working and meaning of "tradition" as it is used in this paper: a small opening is made wider through the addition of wedges similarly constructed; the several parts are enlarged and schematized under the impetus of a certain time and place; the various elements that comprise the traditional matter are, however, never set in a single mould, and so they are available for selection, imitation, or dismissal in other writers.

The many modes of division which can be traced in one form or another in the *artes praedicandi* are again sufficiently documented in already-printed texts. There is, however, one aspect of this tradition which requires further discussion: the place of *distinctio*. In the twelfth century, distinction and typological/allegorical exposition were the only real possibilities for construction of a sermon; hence the multiplication of series of *Distinctiones* on the basis of biblical texts which characterizes the preaching theory of this period.[37] As the more formally constructed *ars* appeared, however, the method of *distinctio* began to assume a rather equivocal position since it could be related under certain circumstances to division and under others to dilation. Some theorists refused to face this dilemma and proceeded to treat *distinctio* as a completely separate process, either before or after their treatment of *divisio*.[38] The effort, unfortunately, was never tremendously successful and *distinctio* became progressively vaguer. A few authors, such as Robert of Basevorn and Martin of Cordoba, found a place for it under the general heading of "methods of continuation," and they particularly felt that distinction was the proper method to use when addressing an uneducated audience.[39]

---

37. M.-M. Lebreton, "Recherches sur les principaux thèmes théologiques traités dans les sermons du xiie siècle," *Recherches de Théologie—Ancienne et Médiévale,* XXIII (1956), pp. 7 ff. Perhaps the most useful discussion of these *Distinctiones* is that of André Wilmart in "Un Répertoire d'Exégèse Composé en Angleterre vers le début du xiiie siècle," *Memorial Lagrange* (Paris, 1940), pp. 307–346. See also the methods described by Homer Pfander in "The Medieval Friar and Some Alphabetical Reference Books for Sermons," *Medium Aevum,* III (1934), 9–29.

38. MS. Balliol 179, fol. 324r seems more interested in keeping *distinctio* in a place of minimal confusion than in integrating it into the sermon manual proper. In this it is practically a copy of the connecting section between the *Omnis tractatio* (or division) and the treatise on dilation, all of which are labelled "ars concionandi." The connecting section legislates concerning distinction that it be brief, founded upon the theme, and consonant in meaning, use, reason, and vocabulary with the previous division. See *Bonaventurae Opera Omnia,* Vol. IX (Guaracchi, 1882–1902), p. 16.

39. Distinction in this sense is not subdivision. Charland (p. 152) says of a true subdivision: "l'autorité est confirmative [correspond] à la façon dont la division

Ranulph Higden briefly presents a kind of *distinctio* in his chapter "De clavibus divisionis" but never employs the term. Only "Henry of Hesse" seems to have recognized the original scholarly purpose of this method of construction. In discussing the *modus antiquus,* he first defines the term and then proceeds to outline its fourfold function in distinguishing *termini a termino, clausule a clausula, termini a clausula, clausule a termino.* He is probably the only author in the later period who understood the inherent parallelism between the methods of division and distinction and who could, consequently, state a *regula generalis:* "divisio et distinctio similiter et subdivisio et subdistinctio differunt solum ratione signorum."[40]

While the traditions surrounding *distinctio* tended to become less understood as the centuries progressed, those surrounding *dilatacio* caught the imagination of almost every sermon theorist. Scholars generally trace the formulation of the eight methods of dilation specifically intended for preaching to Richard of Thetford and from him back to the *artes poeticae,* but the line of descent is neither clear nor linear. Though direct copies of the Thetfordian text can be found in the thirteenth, fourteenth, and fifteenth centuries, variations appear with almost as great a consistency as imitations. An anonymous thirteenth-century treatise offers ten modes which all relate directly to the Thetford text but which illustrate how the eight methods were not mutually exclusive and how they admitted differing interpretations and divisions.[41] Again and again, the vagaries of "tradition" can be illustrated from the preaching manuals: MS.

---

partage la thème; tandis que la distinction et l'acceptation de pluralité se greffent sur un mot du thème (ou de l'autorité confirmative) correspondant à un membre de la division ou de la subdivision." For Martin of Cordoba's opinion of distinction, see Rubio, pp. 341–3.

40. "Henry of Hesse" included his discussion of distinction under the *Modus antiquus* and devoted several pages to its explication; see especially Caplan, "Henry of Hesse," pp. 353–6. In Simon Alcok's *De divisione thematis* (edited by Mary Fuertes Boynton in *Harvard Theological Review,* XXXIV [1941], 201–216), the eclipse of *distinctio* is quite apparent. "Potest thema etiam dividi distinguendo alique, terminum in themate in modos multiplices. Exemplum in themate predicto: *Te salvum fecit.* Potest considerari per sententiam scripturarum multiplex salvatio, scilicet salvatio reparationis, ereptionis, sanationis, reconciliationis, et confirmationis. Et iste modus aliquando coincidit cum divisione per accidentia." This discussion is placed under the general heading "Varius"; see p. 210.

41. Richard of Thetford's eight modes are interpretation, division, ratiocination, concordance of authorities, radical agreement with comparative differences, metaphor, fourfold exposition (as in the scriptures) and cause and effect. Cf. MS Bodley 848, fols. 5v–10v and Murphy, *Rhetoric in the Middle Ages,* pp. 326–29. Gonville MS. 439 agrees with the Thetfordian text in modes one through five but then reads:

Harley 1615 repeats the ten methods of MS. Gonville 439; Jacobus de Fusignano outlines twelve; Jean de Chalons, fourteen; Antonius of Florence describes eight, but they are not the same as Thetford's; Ranulph Higden discusses ten, but they do not correspond with Gonville and Harley; Michael of Hungary selects certain aspects of the eight Thetfordian methods which he wishes to emphasize in his own eight;[42] Thomas Waleys singles out a rather arbitrary method of development which appears again in Thomas of Todi;[43] and the list could go on. As the diversity here documented exemplifies, the several traditions which may be distinguished in the *artes praedicandi* do not in themselves form that pyramidlike pattern of which Ranulph Higden wrote so well.[44] What they do accomplish is the sketching in of the background out of which an achievement such as Higden's can be understood. For, from a goodly array of sources and traditions, he chose only those which resulted in the clarity, unity, and completeness of his *Ars componendi sermones*.

"per proprietates rei apositae in themate; . . . per causas et effectus; . . . per expositionem termini quadriplicem; . . . procedendo gradatim continuando litteram sequentem cum praecedenti; . . . per quadruplicem combinationem partium copulatarum vel disiunctarum in themate assumpto." See Servus Gieben, "Preaching in the Thirteenth Century," *Collectanea Franciscana* XXXII (1962), 313–16. Another mode of *dilatacio* which shows the expansion of the forty-five sections of an eight-line hexameter verse appears as late as the fifteenth century in Alcok's tractate, ed. Boynton, ibid.

42. MS. Harleian 1615, fols. 2–3; for Jacobus de Fusignano, see Munich MS. 5983, fols. 113r–130r; for Antonius see the *Summa*, ibid., cap. V; Charland discusses Jean de Chalons and Higden's text is available in Jennings, pp. 157–167. For Michael of Hungary, see the *Evagatorium Genemy* (Hagenau, 1499), particularly the first part of the section entitled *Optimus predicandi modus*.

43. For an illustration and a critique of this mode which appears in both these widely separated authors, see Charland, p. 204.

44. I refer to Ranulph Higden's description of the shapes of sermons which can be achieved through the use of various patterns of division and subdivision. Of the pyramid-like construct, he remarks how the first member of the division might be divided into three, the second into two parts and the last left undivided thus forming a kind of pyramid "habens basem, latera tendens in conmuni" (Jennings, p. 153). The "tendens in conmuni" is not characteristic of the confluence of traditions in the thematic sermon, however.

APPENDIX

"TYPICAL" *Ars Praedicandi*	HIGDEN'S *Ars componendi sermones*

Introductory Material:
  Variable in length and subject
  matter
	Introductory Material:
	  I. Required in person preaching:
	    A. Rectitude in intention—
	      developed in Chapter II
	    B. Holiness of life—developed
	      in Chapter III
	    C. Aptitude for presenting
	      truth—developed in
	      Chapter IV
	  II. Ingredients for successful ser-
	    mon—developed in Chapter
	    V: *De dicendi circum-*
	    speccione
	  Summary approach to rest of
	  treatise
	  III. Definition of preaching aposto-
	    late
	  IV. Four Aristotelian causes as
	    related to preaching

Discussions of:
  I. Choice of theme
    A. Congruent to matter and
      time of sermon
    B. Taken from Scripture
    C. Sufficiently long to accom-
      modate divisions
	Chap. VI: *De thematis congruitate*
	Chap. VII: *Quod thema congruat*
	    materie proponende
	Chap. VIII: *Quod thema sit de biblia*
	Chap. IX: *Quod thema sufficienter*
	    dividatur

II. Protheme or Antetheme
    A. Similar to, same as, or
      related to principal theme
    B. Culminating in prayer for
      grace
	Chap. XI: *De prothematis extrac-*
	    cione
	Chap. XII: *De oracionis premissione*
	    et gracie impetracione

III. Introduction of theme
    A. By narration
    B. By argumentation
	Chap. XIII: *De auditorum alleccione*
	Chap. XIV: *De thematis introduc-*
	    cione

IV. Division of theme
    A. Separation of theme by
      various modes into several
      principal parts
    B. Confirming or adducing
      "authorities" for these
      parts
      1. Use of concordance
	Chap. XV: *De thematis divisione*
	Chap. XVI: *De clavibvs divisionis*
	
	Chap. X: *Quod thema concordancias*
	    admittat

APPENDIX Continued

"Typical" *Ars Praedicandi*	Higden's *Ars componendi sermones*
2. Use of rhetorical colours	Chap. XXI: *De coloracione membrorum*
V. Subdivision of theme (Similar procedure to division of theme)	Chap. XVIII: *De membrorum subdivisione*
VI. Dilation or extension of various sermon parts	Chap. XVII: *De sermonis dilatacione*
A. By "confirmations" and rational arguments	Chap. XIX: *De dilatacione facienda per auctoritates*
B. By exempla, commentary, application	Chap. XX: *Regule circa dilatacionem*

Punctuation, or Pause and Effect[1]

M. B. PARKES

PUNCTUATION is one of the medieval contributions to literate civilization. In ancient times most manuscripts seem to have been written in *scriptura continua*,[2] although among the very few surviving fragments of Latin manuscripts from the first century we find not only *apices* (points inserted between words) but also isolated examples of other signs which reappear later as marks of punctuation.[3] Punctuation was developed when it became necessary for people to acquire Latin as a learned language, a situation in which aids to the reader became very important.

It is often assumed that medieval punctuation was essentially bound up with pronunciation. Evidence to support this view can be found in medieval sources. In the sixth century Cassiodorus defined punctuation as 'clear' (or in later manuscripts 'apt') 'pausing in

---

1. This paper has grown from a lecture given to various audiences, and I am indebted to them for stimulating questions and discussions. I am grateful to Dr P. Chaplais, Dr R.W. Hunt, Dr N.R. Ker, and Professor A.G. Rigg who have read drafts of this paper at various stages and who have made valuable criticisms and suggestions. Dr Hunt and Dr A.B. Scott have kindly checked my translations from the Latin. I must also thank Miss R. Zim who helped me to clarify both my thought and my prose in the final draft. I am solely responsible for the errors, omissions, and for the views expressed.

2. For observations on the reading of texts written in *scriptura continua* see W.G. Rutherford, *A Chapter in the History of Annotation, Scholia Aristophanica*, iii (London, 1905), 47 ff.

3. The best account of punctuation in late antiquity is by R.W. Müller, *Rhetorische und syntaktische Interpunktion: Untersuchungen zur Pausenbezeichnung im antiken Latein* (Tübingen, 1964). This work seems to have been unknown to the writer of the most recent account: E.O. Wingo, *Latin Punctuation in the Classical Age* (The Hague, 1972). For a brief general account of punctuation, see the article 'Punctuation' by T. Julian Brown, *Encyclopaedia Britannica*, 15th edition, (1974).

well-regulated pronunciation'.[4] In the ninth century Hildemar, writing to Bishop Ursus of Benevento about the art of reading, emphasized the relationship between punctuation and accentuation. He said that prose is split up by three points, adding

> Non ergo miremini, quod in medio sensu notam acuti accentus fecerim, quoniam ut ab eruditis didici viris, his tribus punctis tres aptantur accentus: id est usque ad medium totius sententiae sensum gravis; in medio quoque tantummodo sensu acutus; deindeque usque ad plenum sensum circumflexus.

> Do not be amazed that I have placed a sign of an acute accent in the middle of the sense, since, as I have learned from learned men, to these three points three accents are appropriate: the grave as far as the middle of the *sensus* of the whole *sententia*, the acute only in the middle of the *sensus*, and then the circumflex up to the full *sensus*.[5]

The fact that Hildemar expected the Bishop to be amazed suggests that perhaps the system described was already unfamiliar, or obsolescent. However, Hildemar also incorporated this letter into his commentary on the Rule of St. Benedict,[6] where it forms part of the exposition of Chapter 38 which prescribes and regulates reading aloud to the community in the refectory. Hildemar, therefore, seems to be referring to reading aloud in special circumstances and not to reading in general. Later, the thirteenth-century writer, Bonus of Florence, in that section of the *Candelabrum* which deals with punctuation, ridiculed the notion that punctuation should attempt to reflect pronunciation:

> Nam si iuxta pronunciationum modos puncta scripturalia volumus variare, antiphonarium videbitur.

---

4. *Cassiodori Senatoris Institutiones,* ed. R.A.B. Mynors (Oxford, 1937), II, i, 2. The earliest manuscripts of the first recension read *aperta.* The later recensions Φ and Δ, recorded mainly in mss of saec.xi and later, read *apta.* This later variant may reflect changes in the nature of punctuation—the adoption of the ecphonetic system. See further M.B. Parkes, 'Medieval Punctuation: a Preliminary Survey', *Codicologica,* vi, ed. A. Gruijs & J.P. Gumbert, which is to appear in the series Litterae Textuales.

5. Printed in *Monumenta Germaniae Historica, Epistolae,* v, 320. On Hildemar, possibly a monk from Corbie, see W. Hafner, *Der Basiliuskommentar zur Regula S. Benedicti,* Beiträge zur Geschichte des alten Mönchtums und des Benediktinerordens, xxiii (1959), pp. 96 and 146.

6. The letter is incorporated in the copy of the commentary now preserved in Paris, Bibliothèque Nationale, MS lat. 12637 (from Dijon): see Hafner, *Der Basiliuskommentar,* p. 26. Mr David Ganz kindly examined the manuscript for me.

If we wish to vary the points in our writing according to the manner of pronunciation, it would look like an antiphonary.[7]

It is possible to overemphasize the relationship between medieval punctuation and pronunciation,[8] particularly since a change in reading habits took place during the course of the Middle Ages,[9] a change which is reflected in changes in the appearance of books.[10]

Other evidence indicates that punctuation or the indication of pauses was regarded primarily as an aid to the understanding of a text. Jerome tells us that he introduced the system of laying out the text *per cola et commata* into his translations of *Isaiah* and *Ezekiel* for the convenience of readers, to give a clearer understanding of the sense.[11] Cassiodorus elsewhere in the *Institutiones* stated that *positurae* or *puncta* (the punctuation marks)

quasi quaedam viae sunt sensuum et lumina dictionum, quae sic lectores dociles faciunt tamquam si clarissimis expositoribus imbuantur.

are, as it were, paths of meaning (*sensus*) and lanterns to words, as instructive to readers as the best commentaries.[12]

For Cassiodorus reading meant reading aloud to bring out the sense

---

7. Printed by C. Thurot, 'Extraits des divers manuscrits latins pour servir à l'étude des doctrines grammaticales du moyen âge', *Notices et extraits des manuscrits de la Bibliothèque Impériale*, xxii (1868), part 2, p. 415.

8. As, for example, by P. Clemoes, *Liturgical Influence on Punctuation in Late Old English and Early Middle English MSS* (Cambridge, 1952), who seeks to relate the use of *positurae* to intonation patterns.

9. For example, the change from the monastic *lectio* to the scholastic *lectio*. On the habit of reading aloud in the early Middle Ages (the monastic *lectio*) see J. Leclercq, *The Love of Learning and the Desire for God* (New York, 1961), pp. 19 and 89; also J. Balogh, 'Voces Paginarum', *Philologus*, lxxxii (1926–7), pp. 84–109, and 202–240 (and especially the evidence from patristic writings cited on 202–5). On silent reading and reading aloud in the monastery see Lanfranc's *Monastic Constitutions*, ed. D. Knowles (London, 1951), p. 3. On the more ratiocinative scrutiny of the text required in a scholastic context see M.-D. Chenu, *Introduction à l'étude de S. Thomas d'Aquin* (Paris, 1954), pp. 118–9.

10. For the effect of changes in reading habits on the appearance of books see M.B. Parkes, 'The Influence of the Concepts of *Ordinatio* and *Compilatio* on the Development of the Book', *Medieval Learning and Literature: Essays presented to R.W. Hunt*, ed. J.J.G. Alexander and M.T. Gibson (Oxford, 1976), pp. 115–141.

11. In the prologue to *Ezekiel* Jerome observes that '. . . per cola scriptus et commata manifestiorem legentibus sensum tribuit'. (printed *Patrologia Latina* accurante J.P. Migne, 28, 939); and in his prologue to *Isaiah* '. . . nos quoque utilitati legentium providentes, interpretationem novam, novo scribendi genere (i.e. *per cola et commata*) distinximus' (printed *Patrologia Latina*, 28, 771).

12. *Institutiones*, I, xv, 12.

for oneself and not for oratorical delivery. In the thirteenth century
Roger Bacon remarked that

> quia non servatur punctatio recta, mutatur ordo rectus sententiae, et
> sensus perit cum litera.
>
> (when) correct punctuation (*punctatio*) is not observed the true order of
> the *sententia* is changed and the sense perishes with the letter.[13]

Because punctuation was primarily an aid to the understanding of
the text, it received a good deal of attention from those who were
responsible for correcting manuscripts. The importance of the corrector in a scriptorium, especially up to the second half of the twelfth
century, must be emphasized: he was a specialist reader whose
activity reflects not only literacy but learning, and frequently his
additions and corrections to the punctuation left by the original scribe
indicate a conscious interpretation of the text according to a specific
point of doctrine. In the rest of this paper I wish to suggest, albeit
tentatively, some of the ways in which punctuation was used as an
aid to the elucidation of prose texts.[14]

The general repertory of medieval punctuation marks grew out
of the combination of elements drawn from different systems of aids

---

13. *Opus Tertium*, printed in *Rogeri Baconi opera quaedam hactenus inedita*,
i, ed. J. S. Brewer, Rolls Series (London, 1859), 250.

14. It is not possible to discuss the punctuation of verse adequately here, as a large
number of plates would be necessary to illustrate the principal variations in layouts.
In the earliest surviving codices containing both prose and verse scribes deployed
features of layout to indicate the major divisions of a text, and marks were gradually
introduced to indicate pauses within these divisions. From late antiquity, therefore,
layout and marks function together as punctuation in the widest sense of the term.
In the Middle Ages a distinction arose between the punctuation of prose and that
of verse. In prose, layout was used to indicate the beginnings and ends of chapters
and paragraphs, and marks were used to indicate pauses within those divisions—to
identify the *sententiae* and to elucidate the *sensus*. In verse, both layout and marks
were used to indicate the metrical form. According to the grammatical theory
transmitted to the West by Isidore of Seville each *versus* formed a *periodus* ('Totus
autem versus periodus est': *Etymologiae* I, xx; printed *Patrologia Latina*, 82, 96). In
most manuscripts each *versus* was placed on a line of its own. Sometimes each line
was followed by a mark, but more frequently the layout alone was sufficient to
indicate the metrical form, and in such cases a mark (such as the *punctus elevatus*)
was placed at the end of a line only if the *sensus* was incomplete. Marks were frequently placed at the ends of lines to indicate the ends of stanzas or verse paragraphs, but in manuscripts produced from the thirteenth century onwards it became
customary to place a paragraph mark in the margin at the beginning of a new stanza
or paragraph. Marks were used within a line of verse to indicate a *caesura*. Where
verse was written continuously marks were used to indicate the end of each *versus*,
or, in vernacular verse, a corresponding metrical unit. Elaborate verse forms were
often indicated by elaborate layouts.

to the reader.[15] Some of these systems were handed down from antiquity and modified in the process of transmission; others were evolved during the course of the Middle Ages. All these systems, and the general repertory which emerged, set out to distinguish *sententiae* as well as other units of the *sensus*. These units were separated from each other by means of graded pauses in order to achieve greater clarity or to indicate differences of emphasis. The terms *sensus* and *sententia* are medieval ones which are not necessarily equivalent to the modern English 'sense' and 'sentence'. Moreover, the terms could mean different things at different times during the Middle Ages. In the twelfth century Hugh of St. Victor defined *littera, sensus,* and *sententia* as follows:

> Littera est congrua ordinatio dictionum quam etiam constructionem vocamus. Sensus est facilis quaedam et aperta significatio quam littera prima fronte prefert. Sententia est profundior intelligentia quae nisi expositione vel interpretatione non invenitur.

> The letter (*littera*) is the proper arrangement of words which we also call construction. The sense (*sensus*) is a straightforward and open interpretation which the letter offers at first sight. The sentence (*sententia*) is a deeper understanding which is discovered in no other way except by exposition or interpretation.[16]

Behind this lies the distinction made earlier by William of Conches between the *sententia* and the *continuatio litterae* in his definition of the differences between a 'gloss' and a 'commentary':

> Commentum enim est solum sententiam exequens, de continuatione vel expositione litterae nihil agit. Glosa vero omnia illa exequitur.

> A commentary only considers the *sententia*, but has nothing to do with the syntactical structure (*continuatio*) or explanation of the literal text. Indeed a gloss considers all these things.[17]

In such circumstances the pointing of *sententiae* could be related more to the interpretation of doctrinal content than to syntactic structure. However, in the fourteenth century Nicholas of Lyra

---

15. On the development of the general repertory of punctuation marks see M.B. Parkes, 'Medieval Punctuation: a Preliminary Survey'. See also the Appendix, below, p. 139.

16. *Didascalicon,* iii, 9 (*Patrologia Latina,* 176, 771). The first sentence recalls Priscian, *Institutiones Grammaticae,* II, 15 'Oratio est ordinatio dictionum congrua, sententiam perfectam demonstrans'.

17. See E. Jeauneau, 'Deux redactions des gloses de Guillaume de Conches sur Priscien', *Recherches de théologie ancienne et médiévale,* xxvii (1960), 212–247 (especially p. 225).

distinguished between the *sensus literalis* of scripture, which is that signified by the words of the text alone, and the *sensus spiritualis,* which is more obscure because the words designate things which are themselves significative (that is to say signifying other things, qualities or principles). Following Aquinas, he lays great stress on the importance of the *sensus literalis*:

> . . . necessarium est incipere ab intellectu sensus literalis: maxime cum ex solo sensu literali, et non ex mystico, possit argumentum fieri ad probationem.

> It is necessary to start from an understanding of the literal sense: especially since only from the literal sense, and not from the mystical, can an argument be adduced for proof.[18]

Clear pointing of the *sensus literalis* is therefore important, and Lyra continues:

> Sensus literalis a quo est incipiendum, ut dictum est, videtur multum obfuscatus diebus modernis: partim scriptorum vitio . . . , partim imperitia aliquorum correctorum, qui in pluribus locis fecerunt puncta, ubi non debent fieri; et versus inceperunt, vel terminaverunt, ubi non debent incipi et terminari: et per hoc sententia literae variatur.

> The literal sense (*sensus literalis*) from which one should begin, as has been said, seems to be much obscured in modern times: partly through the errors of scribes . . . , and partly through the lack of skill of some correctors who have made points in many places where there ought not be any, and who have begun or ended verses where they ought not to have been begun or ended: and through this the profound meaning of the literal text (*sententia literae*) is subject to variation.[19]

A corrector who followed the principles of Nicholas of Lyra is likely to have used punctuation to emphasize the literal sense. Moreover, what Nicholas of Lyra here calls the *sententia literae* is closely related to the syntactical structure (called the *continuatio litterae* by William of Conches) whereas that which William and Hugh of St. Victor had called the *sententia* is not. In such circumstances the *sententiae* indicated by punctuation from the fourteenth century onwards are likely to be different from those indicated by twelfth-century punctuation.

Thus different factors are likely to govern the use of punctuation at different periods within the Middle Ages. Even within a given

---

18. *Postilla,* second prologue, quoted here from the text printed in *Biblia Sacra cum Glossa Ordinaria . . . et Postilla Nicolae Lirani . . .* (Antwerp, 1634).

19. Ibid.

period of time other factors are also important—the nature of the text to be pointed; the different ways in which the text was read and understood by different scribes, correctors and readers; and the way in which the text was used.

One of the functions of medieval punctuation, especially in manuscripts up to the end of the twelfth century, is to emphasize the *sensus* as an aid to the interpretation of the doctrinal content. Different methods of pointing a particular passage from the Bible reflect different readings of the *sensus* of the passage in the light of commentaries and glosses on it; hence, even the divisions into *sententiae* differ. My examples are from manuscripts chosen at random. The first two passages I have chosen are from the beginning of John's Gospel. The first is from an eleventh-century manuscript; the second is from a manuscript of about 1160:

A. In principio erat uerbum. Et uerbum erat apud deum et deus erat uerbum.[20]

B. In principio erat uerbum. et uerbum erat apud deum ⁊ et deus erat uerbum.[21]

Example A is divided into two *sententiae* whereas B is pointed as a single *sententia*. As a result, in A the word *verbum* occurs once in the first *sententia* and twice in the second, but here the word *deus* also occurs twice. In B, however, since the passage is pointed as a single *sententia*, the word *verbum* occurs three times whereas *deus* occurs only twice. In this example it seems that the punctuation places more emphasis on the word *verbum*.

If we turn to the gloss on this passage we observe that one of the *auctoritates* is drawn from Augustine:

The Greek word 'logos' signifies both Word and Reason. But in this passage it is better to interpret it Word; as referring not only to the Father, but to those things created by the operative power of the word.[22]

Thus Augustine places more emphasis on *verbum* than on *deus*, and it seems to me that this emphasis is brought out in the punctuation of B.

Lest this appear too fanciful let us look at the treatment of the fifth verse. One manuscript has

20. Oxford, Bodleian Library, MS Bodley 155.

21. London, British Library, Additional MS 17738.

22. This translation is based on the gloss printed in *Biblia Sacra cum Glossa Ordinaria* (Antwerp, 1634).

C. Quod factum est in ipso uita erat ⁞ et uita erat lux hominum. Et lux
in tenebris lucet ⁞ & tenebrae eam non comprehenderunt.[23]

putting a major medial pause after *erat* and concluding the *sententia*
at *hominum*. But in the gloss Augustine has quite a lot to say about
this passage:

> The passage can be punctuated thus: *What was made in Him was life.*
> If the passage were read in this way, then the whole universe is life: for
> what was there not made in Him? He is the Wisdom of God, as is said,
> 'In Wisdom hast Thou made them all'. All things therefore are made in
> Him, even as they are by Him. But, if whatever was made in Him is life,
> the earth is life, a stone is life. We must not interpret it so unsoundly,
> lest the sect of the Manicheans creep in upon us, and say, that a stone
> has life, and that a wall has life; for they do insanely assert so, and when
> reprehended or refuted, appeal as though to Scripture, and ask, why
> was it said, *That which was made in Him was life*? Read the passage then
> thus: make the pause after *What was made,* and then proceed, *In Him
> was life*.[24]

In D (from the same manuscript of 1160 as B above) we see the scribe
pointing this passage according to the precept of Augustine:

D. Quod factum est ⁞ in ipso uita erat. Et uita erat lux hominum ⁞ et lux
in tenebris lucet. Et tenebrae eam non comprehenderunt.

The third example

E. Quod factum est in ipso uita erat et uita erat lux hominum. et lux
in tenebris lucet. et tenebrae non comprehenderunt.[25]

is less committed to any one reading and allows the reader greater
freedom of interpretation.[26]

Alterations and additions to existing punctuation can indicate the
pointing of a later reader in the light of his reading of a particular

---

23. Oxford, Bodleian Library, MS Auct. D. 2. 15.

24. From the gloss printed in *Biblia Sacra cum Glossa Ordinaria* (Antwerp, 1634).

25. Oxford, Keble College, MS 20, fol. 522, a thirteenth-century Bible produced
in France, with the order of books and the chapter divisions commonly found in
manuscripts produced there at that time, and with the common set of 64 prologues
(cf. N.R.Ker, *Medieval Manuscripts in British Libraries,* i [Oxford, 1969], p. 96).

26. In the earliest surviving copy of the Vulgate Gospels (St Gall, Stiftsbibliothek,
HS 1395) the first five verses of John's Gospel are treated as a single *kapitulum*. An
annotator contemporary with the text (on whom see B. Bischoff, 'Zur Rekonstruk-
tion der ältesten Handschrift der Vulgata-Evangelien und der Vorlage ihrer Mar-
ginalien', in his *Mittelalterliche Studien,* i [Stuttgart, 1966], 101–111) uses the term
kapitulum in a marginal note on page 95 of the manuscript to refer to the equivalent
of the modern verse *Matthew,* 23, 14.

commentary or gloss. This is borne out by the evidence of manuscripts like Oxford, Keble College, MS 22 where alterations to punctuation occur most frequently in passages to which a gloss has been added (see plate). These alterations are often in the same ink as the added gloss.

The examples from *John* 1 have illustrated the way in which punctuation as a form of exposition has stressed the different interpretations of the *sensus* of a passage in the context of its doctrinal content. The next set of examples, from the beginning of Paul's *Epistle to the Romans*, illustrates that there are yet other ways of reading an identical text:

F. Paulus seruus cristi iesu uocatus apostolus · segregatus in euangelium dei. Quod ante promiserat per prophetas suos in scripturis sanctis de filio suo . qui factus est ei ex semine dauid secundum carnem. Qui predestinatus est filius dei in uirtute · secundum spiritum sanctificationis . ex resurrectione mortuorum iesu cristi domini nostri · per quem accepimus gratiam & apostolatum ad obediendum fidei < > in omnibus gentibus pro nomine eius. in quibus estis et uos uocati iesu cristi ։ omnibus qui sunt rome dilectis dei uocatis sanctis Gratia uobis et pax a deo patre nostro et domino iesu cristo;[27]

G. Paulus seruus cristi iesu. uocatus apostolus. segregatus in euuangelium dei. quod ante promiserat per prophetas suos. in scripturis sanctis. de filio suo. qui factus est ei ex semine dauid. secundum carnem. qui predestinatus est filius dei in uirtute secundum spiritum sanctificationis ex resurrectione mortuorum iesu cristi domini nostri. per quem accepimus gratiam. 7 apostolatum. ad obediendum fidei. in omnibus gentibus pro nomine eius in quibus estis et uos uocati iesu cristi domini nostri [.] omnibus qui sunt rome. dilectis dei. uocatis sanctis. gratia uobis et pax a deo patre nostro. et domino iesu cristo.[28]

I wish to comment on two features only. First, there is a fundamental difference between F, where the scribe's division of the passage into three *sententiae* indicates that he regarded it as containing three points of doctrinal significance, and G, where the passage is seen primarily as the protocol, or *superscriptio*,[29] in which the whole forms

---

27. Oxford, Keble College, MS 22 (s. xi ex.). See below Note to the Plate, p. 140.
28. Oxford, Bodleian Library, MS Auct. D.4.20 (s. xii–xiii).
29. The formulae used at the beginning of a document or similar instrument, as distinct from the text which contains the subject-matter. The formulae comprise the names, titles, and qualities of the person from whom the document originates, those of the persons to whom the document is addressed, and the greeting or salutation. See further P. Chaplais, *English Royal Documents 1199–1461* (Oxford, 1971), p. 13.

a single *sententia*. Secondly, this difference of attitude is reflected in the medial pauses of G, which do not occur in F. The points after *dilectis dei* and *uocatis sanctis* suggest that these two phrases were seen as if they were titles of the persons addressed and treated as such, like other lists, or nouns in apposition.[30]

The beginning of I *Corinthians* is more straightforward than that of *Romans* as the scribes seem to have been agreed that it contained little of doctrinal import. Most of the scribes have seen it as the protocol ending with a salutation clause. Nevertheless it presented them with difficulties and was often corrected. For this reason it is a useful example to introduce problems of punctuation in other, non-biblical texts. The insertions in the manuscripts are indicated by bolder marks.

In the first passage the scribe, sensing the difficulties, has left out almost all the punctuation:

H. P(aulus) vocatus apostolus cristi iesu per uoluntatem dei et sostenes frater ecclesie dei que est corinthi sanctificatis in cristo iesu uocatis sanctis cum omnibus qui inuocant nomen domini nostri iesu cristi in omni loco ipsorum et nostro. Gratia uobis et pax a deo patre nostro et domino nostro iesu cristo.[31]

However, this is not common, and the other examples are all punctuated:

I. Paulus uocatus apostolus cristi iesu per uoluntatem dei · & sostenes frater ecclesie dei que est corinthi. sanctificatis in cristo iesu uocatis sanctis cum omnibus qui inuocant nomen domini nostri iesu cristi. in omni loco ipsorum & nostro ⁏ Gratia uobis et pax a deo patre nostro & domini iesu cristo.[32]

J. Paulus uocatus apostolus iesu cristi per uoluntatem dei [.] & sostenes frater · ecclesie dei que est corinthi · sanctificatis in cristo iesu ⁏ uocatis sanctis. cum omnibus qui inuocant nomen domini nostri iesu cristi in omni loco ipsorum et nostro ⁏ gratia uobis & pax a deo patre nostro & domino nostro iesu cristo.[33]

K. Paulus uocatus apostolus cristi iesu per uoluntatem dei . 7 sostenes frater ⁏ ecclesie dei que est corinthi. sanctificatis in cristo iesu ⁏ uocatis sanctis. cum omnibus qui inuocant nomen domini nostri iesu cristi in

---

30. See also N.R. Ker, *English Manuscripts in the Century after the Norman Conquest* (Oxford, 1960), p. 47.

31. Oxford, Bodleian Library, MS Barlow 26 (s. xii in.).

32. Oxford, Keble College, MS 22 (s. xi ex.).

33. Oxford, Bodleian Library, MS Auct. E. inf. 2 (s. xii med.).

omni loco ipsorum. 7 nostro. Gratia uobis et pax a deo patre nostro et domino nostro iesu cristo.[34]

L. Pavlvs uocatus apostolus cristi iesu per uoluntatem dei. 7 sostenes frater : ecclesie dei que est corinthi. sanctificatis in cristo iesu. uocatis sanctis cum omnibus qui inuocant nomen domini nostri iesu cristi. in omni loco ipsorum 7 nostro. Gratia uobis et pax a deo nostro. domino iesu cristo.[35]

Again I wish to comment on two features only. In I we see the first instance at which confusion may arise in this text. The epistle is from both Paul and Sosthenes to the Church at Corinth, but by placing a point after *dei* and omitting the point after *frater* the scribe allows the reader to construe *ecclesie* as a genitive instead of a dative, and thus the sense is altered drastically from 'Paul and Sosthenes *to* the Church at Corinth' to 'Paul and Sosthenes *of* the Church at Corinth to those sanctified'. In J the corrector has erased the point inserted by the scribe after *dei* in order to emphasize the point after *frater*. In K the corrector has added a *punctus elevatus* after *frater*, indicating a greater pause than that after *dei*, and this is the punctuation followed by the thirteenth-century scribe of L. Another instance at which confusion can arise can be seen in J and K where the original scribes placed a point between *uocatis sanctis* and *cum omnibus qui inuocant nomen*. In both examples the corrector has converted the *punctus* preceding *uocatis sanctis* into a *punctus elevatus*. This had become necessary because without this greater pause the reader could have been misled into thinking that *cum omnibus qui inuocant . . .* was part of the address (i.e., 'to the Church at Corinth . . . together with all those who call on the name of Christ') whereas the corrected punctuation and the punctuation of the other examples suggest that it was to be read 'called saints with (i.e., as are) all those who call . . .'.

These examples indicate what seems to me to be an important characteristic of medieval punctuation, which is that scribes punctuated and correctors corrected where they thought that confusion was likely to arise in the minds of the readers for whom the text was prepared. The examples also illuminate Roger Bacon's remark 'When correct punctuation is not observed the true order of the *sententia* is changed and the *sensus* perishes with the letter'.

This characteristic can be observed more clearly in the following

---

34. Oxford, Bodleian Library, MS Auct. D.1.13 (s. xii med.).
35. Oxford, Bodleian Library, MS Auct. D.4.20 (s. xii–xiii).

examples which are of particular interest, because the first, M, is from
an eleventh-century manuscript of Augustine's *De civitate Dei* (xix,
1) and the second, N, is from a fourteenth-century copy made from
this exemplar:

M. Quoniam de civitatis vtrivsque. terrenae scilicet et caelestis. debitis
finibus deinceps mihi uideo disputandum ⁚ prius exponenda sunt
quantum operis huius terminandi ratio patitur. argumenta morta-
lium. quibus sibi ipsi beatitudinem facere in huius uitae infelicitate
moliti sunt. ut ab eorum rebus uanis spes nostra quid differat quam
deus nobis dedit. & res ipsa hoc est uera beatitudo quam dabit ⁚ non
tantum auctoritate diuina. sed adhibita etiam ratione qualem propter
infideles possumus adhibere. clarescat.³⁶

N. Quoniam de ciuitatis vtriusque terrene scilicet et celestis. debitis
finibus deinceps mihi uideo disputandum ⁚ prius exponenda sunt
quantum operis huius terminandi racio patitur . argumenta morta-
lium. quibus sibi ipsi beatitudinem facere in huius uite infelicitate
moliti sunt · ut ab eorum rebus uanis spes nostra quid differat / quam
deus nobis dedit et res ipsa / hoc est uera beatitudo / quam dabit /
non tantum auctoritate diuina · sed adhibita eciam racione / qualem
propter infideles possumus (adhibere) clarescat ·³⁷

The fourteenth-century copyist follows the punctuation of the exemplar except at one place: he omits the *punctus elevatus* after *dabit*
in the sixth line. This has been replaced by a *virgula suspensiva* inserted by the scribe (or perhaps a corrector). But the scribe or corrector
has added punctuation where confusion is likely to arise in the difficult and confusing part of the *sententia* beginning at *ut ab eorum
rebus*. It helps the reader to construe the passage more easily (pointing, as it were, the *sensus literalis* and reflects the fourteenth-century
view about the function of punctuation found in Nicholas of Lyra).
However, in spite of his concern with the *sensus literalis,* the scribe
or corrector has *not* inserted punctuation in the earlier part of the
passage.

It seems to me that from examples like those in I to N one might
adduce a general principle about medieval punctuation. Medieval
scribes and correctors punctuate where confusion is likely to arise (if
their Latin is sufficient to recognize the fact) and do not always punctuate where confusion is not likely to arise, even when they are

36. Durham, Dean & Chapter Library, MS B.II.22.
37. Durham, Dean & Chapter Library, MS B. II. 24. On the relationship between
the two manuscripts see R.A.B. Mynors, *Durham Cathedral Manuscripts to the
End of the Twelfth Century* (Durham, 1939), p. 35, n. 33.

concerned with the *sententia literae*. Because scribes and correctors were also readers they were concerned primarily with interpretation, especially with elements which might be subject to confusion. Elements which may have a similar syntactic function or convey similar meaning, and which are punctuated in one context, need not be punctuated in another when the context ensures that confusion is not likely to arise. This factor helps to explain why some modern scholars have regarded medieval punctuation as 'irregular'.[38] Moreover, as I have attempted to show elsewhere,[39] many of the punctuation marks were regarded as interchangeable. One is sorely tempted to measure medieval punctuation in terms of units of 'confusibles'.

I suggest that the key to the understanding of medieval punctuation lies not in grammatical theory, nor in the analysis of syntactical or intonation patterns, but in the concern of the scribe or corrector to elucidate the text transmitted to him according to the needs of his own audience. He seems to have realized that he could achieve the desired effect by means of punctuation: that the adroit use of pauses would ensure that his readers followed what the punctuator regarded as his own correct interpretation of the text. This hypothesis is offered tentatively to stimulate further, more detailed investigations of the practices of individual scribes and correctors in medieval manuscripts.

APPENDIX

The principal marks of punctuation drawn from what I have called the general repertory of punctuation that emerged during the course of the Middle Ages, and mentioned in this paper are:

The *littera notabilior* was an enlarged letter—usually drawn from square capital, rustic capital, uncial, or a decorative display script—used to indicate the beginning of a new chapter, paragraph, *sententia*, or *versus*.

The *punctus elevatus*, ⸵ , was used to indicate a major medial pause, the *punctus versus*, ; , was used to indicate the final pause at the end of a statement, and the *punctus interrogativus*, ⸮ , was used to indicate the final pause at the end of a question. Variant forms of these marks exist, depending on when and where the manuscripts

---

38. For example, by R. Priebsch and W.E. Collinson, *The German Language* (London, 1958), p. 430.
39. M.B. Parkes, 'Medieval Punctuation: a Preliminary Survey'.

were copied. These signs (which, in the Middle Ages, were frequently called *positurae*) were all derived from the system of ecphonetic notation which originally indicated the appropriate melodic formula to be used in the liturgy (which in different contexts required different melodic phrases). The melodic formulae indicated by the different signs were applied at the various logical pauses in the *sensus* of the liturgical texts. With the development of musical notation these signs lost their neumatic significance, and were absorbed into the general repertory of punctuation. The signs are found in non-liturgical texts from the eighth century onwards.

The *punctus*, · , originally belonged to the system of *distinctiones*, a system which required that *punctus* be placed at carefully graded heights to indicate the nature of different pauses: a low point to indicate a pause where the *sensus* is incomplete, a medial point to indicate a pause where the *sensus* is complete but the *sententia* is not, and a high point to indicate the completion of the *sententia*. The difficulty of placing *punctus* at the correct height in a minuscule script, and, more important, the difficulty of reading them, led to the abandoning of the system of *distinctiones*. Scribes often used the *punctus* (placed indiscriminately at various heights) to indicate all pauses, but with the development of the general repertory of punctuation it was frequently used in association with marks from other sources, such as the *punctus elevatus* and the *punctus interrogativus*, and the *litterae notabiliores*, which help the reader to identify the significance of the *punctus* in its context: to indicate nouns in apposition, to indicate a minor medial pause, or, when placed before a *littera notabilior*, to indicate a final pause.

The *virgula suspensiva*, / , was often used interchangeably with the *punctus*, but more frequently it was used to indicate a medial pause when the *punctus* was used to indicate a final one.

NOTE TO THE PLATE

Oxford, Keble College, MS 22, fol. 58ᵛ. *Epistolae Pauli cum commentariis*: the plate illustrates I *Corinthians*, 16, verses 10–17. The manuscript was produced at Salisbury in the second half of the eleventh century (see N.R. Ker, 'The Beginnings of Salisbury Cathedral Library', *Medieval Learning and Literature: Essays Presented to*

enim dñm opaꝛ̄ ·ſicut & ego ; neqꝛ̄

q̄ illũ ſpnaꝛ · Deducite autē illũ

ĩpaco: ut ueniat adme · Expecto

enim illũ cũ frib; · De apollo autē

frē notũ uobiſ facio · qm multũ

rogaui eũ · ut uenireꝛ aduoſ cum

frib; & utiꞅ; nonfuiꝛ uoluntaſ

ei ut nunc uenireꝛ · Veniet autē

cum ei uacuum fuerit · Vigilate:

ſtate infide · uiriliter agite · con —

fortamini · Omnia ura incariꝛate

fiant · Obſecro autē uoſ frēſ noſtiſ

domũ ſtephane & fortunati · qm

ſunt primitie acaie · & ... mini —

nſteriũ ſcoy ordinauerunt ſe ip

ſoſ · ut & uoſ ſubditi ſitiſ eimodi ·

& omni cooparti & laboranti; Gau —

deo autē ĩ pſentia ſtephane · & for

tunati · & achaici · qm id qd̄ uobiſ

deeraꝛ: ipſi ſuppleuerunt · Refecer

Oxford, Keble College, MS 22, fol. 58ᵛ

R.W. Hunt, ed. J.J.G. Alexander and M.T. Gibson (Oxford, 1976), pp. 34–49, and especially pp. 39, 42).

Note the alterations to the punctuation in lines 11 and 12, which bring the reading of the text into line with the interpretation of the added glosses. The original scribe copied verse 14 'Omnia uestra in caritate fiant' as a *sententia,* beginning it with a *littera notabilior* and placing a *punctus* after it. The glossator has understood this verse as complementing the sense of verse 13, 'Vigilate, state in fide, uiriliter agite, confortamini'. He has therefore added a 'tick' over the *punctus* after 'confortamini' turning the mark into a *punctus elevatus,* and added a 'comma'-shaped stroke below the *punctus* after 'fiant' turning it into a *punctus versus,* thus pointing the whole of verses 13 and 14 as a single *sententia.* This is in accordance with his moral interpretation of the text revealed in his glosses: 'uiriliter agite' is glossed 'et supra fidem bona opera insistite', and 'omnia uestra in caritate fiant' is glossed 'in eo sitis perseuerantes, et cum hec (sic) feceritis, non faciatis propter humanam fauorem'.

Further examples of inserted punctuation in this manuscript are visible on the page reproduced by Dr Ker, plate V, lines 4 and 6, where a *punctus* has been corrected to a *punctus elevatus* in each case.

Part Two

❖❖❖

The Practice of Rhetoric
in the Middle Ages

Bede's *Historia ecclesiastica:*
The Rhetoric of Faith

CALVIN B. KENDALL

ALTHOUGH the Venerable Bede's *Ecclesiastical History of the English People*[1] commands nearly universal respect, commentators typically feel obliged to justify or explain the presence in it of what Colgrave calls "wonder tales."[2] No one wishes to dispense with these marvellous stories of the miracles associated with local saints; still, it does not sort well with our expectations to find the sober, reliable historian of one chapter becoming in the next a credulous, if engaging, storyteller. We see a double image. There is the dispassionate, scientific observer, meticulously sifting the evidence of the past, and there is also the child of the Dark Ages, embracing the most superstitious elements of popular legend. But can Bede really be performing two separate functions in the *History*? Perhaps our conception of the medieval historian needs refinement. A better understanding of Bede's intention could help bring the double image into a single focus.

Bede conceived the *History* as a record (or, more accurately, a verbal imitation) of the "sixth age" of mankind, in Britain. The

---

1. The standard edition is now *Bede's Ecclesiastical History of the English People,* ed. by Bertram Colgrave and R.A.B. Mynors, Oxford, 1969, which includes an English translation of the Latin text. All references are to this edition. (Even-numbered page references are to the Latin text; odd-numbered to the English translation.) Charles Plummer's classic edition, *Venerabilis Baedae Opera Historica,* 2 vols., Oxford, 1896 (reprinted 1956), remains invaluable for its introduction and notes.

2. See, for example, Colgrave's remarks in the Historical Introduction, pp. xxxiv–xxxvi; also, Plummer, Introduction, pp. lxiv–lxv. Benedicta Ward, S.L.G., has recently made the same point I make here in a paper entitled, "Miracles and History: A Reconsideration of the Miracle Stories used by Bede," in *Famulus Christi: Essays in Commemoration of the Thirteenth Centenary of the Birth of the Venerable Bede,* ed. Gerald Bonner (London, 1976), pp. 70–76.

sixth age is the time of grace extending from the advent of Christ to the second coming and the last judgment.[3] The story of that age is coextensive with the story of the Church, since the temporal significance of both is that they allow for the fulfillment of the Pauline mission, the carrying of the gospel to the nations of the world. The English Church was at once a local institution and part of the universal Roman Church, for which, by synecdoche, it could stand. By what surely struck Bede as providential coincidence, the political history of Britain began with the coming of the Romans at the start of the sixth age. Political and ecclesiastical history were therefore inseparable.

The sixth age, however, introduced a new element into human experience. As a result of Adam's fall, brother had been set against brother, tribe against tribe, nation against nation. Sin and sorrow, pain and death were conditions shared by all. But the sixth age added a hopeful paradox: for the faithful, death would be the gateway to eternal life. This paradox engendered a discontinuity in man's experience of himself. The inner self became the chief actor in a drama that went on independently of the strife and discord of public life. So desperate was the struggle of the soul to acquire an adequate faith that some men and women turned away from the world altogether in order not to be distracted from it.

Historical narratives of public affairs, whether of church or state, belonged to an established genre. Bede had a variety of models before him. But the narrative of the private self was another matter. It had developed comparatively recently in response to the Christian personality and took the form of the saint's life. Early saints' lives seem artless and naïve partly because they are a new kind of writing and open up a new area of experience. If, in addition to public affairs, the *History* was to reflect man's inner experience in the sixth age, Bede had little choice but to work with the narrative conventions of hagiography.

Whatever their reservations about miracle stories, however, readers are not likely to be bothered by an awkward disparity of styles in the *History*. They may be conscious of the juxtaposition of what we can loosely call historical and hagiographical narrative. But once the

---

3. The division of history into six ages is Augustinian. See, for example, *De civitate dei* XXII. xxx. Plummer, Introduction, pp. xli–xlii, and Charles W. Jones, ed., *Bedae opera de temporibus* (Cambridge, Mass., 1943), p. 345, provide essential information concerning Bede's use of the doctrine.

juxtaposition is seen as an accurate reflection of the discontinuity of the sixth age, conditioned by preexisting narrative conventions, the magnitude of Bede's achievement becomes apparent. The *History* is a finally unified vision of the totality of man's experience from the mundane to the miraculous, in and beyond time. The instrument which enabled Bede to hold in suspension the most diverse materials relating to the internal and external dramas of life without losing control, and thus to project the shape of faith in the sixth age, was the Latin rhetoric of the early Middle Ages. My purpose is to examine some features of Bede's use of this instrument in the *History*. In particular, I wish to suggest that Bede's conception of rhetoric in terms of "figures" was a prime element in the making of a style which mirrored his vision of experience. It is a style grounded on the premise of a real correspondence between language and physical reality. It can contain contradictions and distort language without losing clarity. By imposing a higher order upon the flux of words, it points constantly to a level of meaning beyond the confusion of the physical world.

Latin rhetoric had undergone a sea change since its heyday in the last decades of the Roman Republic. Then, as a discipline, it claimed to impart knowledge about, and to promote skill in, public speaking. The relationship between rhetoric and oratory progressively weakened in the early centuries of the Christian era to the point where Bede could ignore it entirely. Classical rhetorical theory reached the early Middle Ages in a severely attenuated form. The rhetorical treatises of late Latin antiquity were for the most part the briefest of digests. Isidore of Seville provided a fundamental source in his universal encyclopedia, the *Etymologies*. His treatment of rhetoric (*Etym*. II. i–xxi) occupies less than twenty-one pages in Lindsay's edition.[4] Classical theory isolated for the purpose of analysis five essential elements of organized discourse: *inventio*, the selection of material (in Roman judicial oratory this meant finding the appropriate arguments for a case); *dispositio*, the arrangement of the material; *elocutio*, the manner or style of its presentation; *memoria*, memory; and *pronuntiatio*, delivery. Let us see what Isidore does with them.

All that remains of *inventio* is a classification of the kinds of cases, the status of cases, and controversies (sections iv–vi). *Dispositio*

---

4. *Isidori Etymologiarum libri XX,* ed. Wallace M. Lindsay. Two vols. (Oxford, 1911).

merits a single section in which Isidore reduces the six parts of a speech as established by the Ciceronian tradition to four: *exordium, narratio, argumentatio, conclusio*. The whole of what he has to say on this topic is as follows:

> The first of these [*exordium*] catches the attention of the listener, the second [*narratio*] explains the matter at hand, the third [*argumentatio*] gives credence to our assertions, and the fourth [*conclusio*] sums up the entire speech. We ought to begin, therefore, by making our listener favorably disposed to us, receptive, and attentive: favorably disposed by our self-deprecatory manner, receptive by offering him instruction, attentive, by arousing his interest. Our narrative should be spoken briefly and clearly. We should argue first in order to prove our own assertions, and second to demolish those of our opponent. Our conclusion should arouse the listener to do what we say. (II.vii)

Next, there are sections on the five kinds of cases (viii), syllogisms, or the finding of proofs (ix), the law (x), *sententia* (xi), proof and disproof (xii), *prosopopoeia*, or personification (xiii), *ethopoeia*, or character delineation (xiv), and the kinds of questions (xv). It would be difficult to say, from Isidore's summary of these topics, what relation, if any, they bear to *dispositio*. He repeats the treatment of *prosopopoeia* and *ethopoeia* in the section on figures of speech and thought (xxi), which is where they are found in the pseudo-Ciceronian *Ad Herennium*.

Finally, Isidore comes to *elocutio*, or style (xvi–xxi).[5] Here at last we encounter material that would have been of more than hypothetical interest in the early Middle Ages. Though Roman judicial oratory is still the basis for the discussion, the elements of style easily detach themselves from that moribund genre. Isidore turns to other genres, both in prose and verse, for his illustrations. In sections xvi–xxi there are more quotations of Vergil (16) than of Cicero (14). Other illustrations are taken from Ovid and Terence, from Petronius, and, significantly, from a letter of St. Jerome and from the Bible (*Ecclesiasticus*). His method of selection is completely unhistorical. It presumes an ideal of a single style appropriate to all genres and in all periods.

---

5. Section xvii, on the three kinds of speaking, is Isidore's gesture in the direction of the fifth part of classical rhetoric, delivery. It represents an amalgamation of the theory of the three levels of style—high, middle, and low (the earliest surviving threefold division of style is the *Ad Herennium* IV. viii. 11–14)—with discussions of the tone of voice appropriate to different oratorical situations (cf. *Ad Her.* III. xi–xv). Isidore has nothing to say on the subject of memory.

Section xxi, on the figures of speech and thought, is by far the most extensive in Isidore's rhetoric (six and one-half pages in Lindsay's edition). The theory of figures encompasses the study of unusual arrangements of words (as when the adjective is separated from its noun, or when several words alliterate), affected language (such as the rhetorical question, or the apostrophe), and the use of words in other than their literal sense (broadly speaking, metaphor). Quintilian applied the Greek term "schemes" to the first two groups (*Instit.* IX. i. 1) and "tropes" to the third (VIII. vi. 1). An unusual arrangement of words is a *figura verbi*; a case of affected language is a *figura sententiae* (IX. i. 15–17).[6] In practice, the lines between the three groups proved hard to draw, as Quintilian noted (IX.i.3). Distinctions were further blurred when the epitomizers separated the Greek terms from the Latin. This led to inclusive discussions of "schemes and tropes," and of "figures of speech and thought" (*figurae verborum et sententiarum*). In addition, no doubt as a concomitant of the decline of oratory, the study of "figures" came to be seen as part of the basic study of language and literature, as a function of "grammar." Thus we find in book three of Donatus' *Ars grammatica* a section, *De schematibus,* and following it, *De tropis.*[7] The same sections appear in book one (*De grammatica*) of the *Etymologies.* There (I. xxxvi–xxxvii) Isidore devotes almost twice as much space to *De schematibus* and *De tropis* (11 pages) as he does to *De figuris verborum et sententiarum* in book two.

The theory of figures proved to be the one element of classical rhetoric that could be utilized effectively in the early Middle Ages. Because the Romans had focussed their study of rhetorical theory on judicial oratory, their analysis of invention, disposition, memory, and delivery could not be transferred readily to other literary forms. Discussion of these topics became perfunctory or disappeared altogether. But figures could be found everywhere, and St. Augustine argued that the study of tropes was essential for a mature understanding of the Bible (*De doctrina christiana* III. xxix).[8] This was the

---

6. Erich Auerbach's account of the development of these terms and the distinctions between them is fundamental. See his essay "Figura" in *Scenes from the Drama of European Literature,* reprinted Gloucester, Mass., 1973, esp. pp. 24–27.

7. Heinrich Keil, ed. *Grammatici latini* (Leipzig, 1864), IV, 397–402.

8. Although St. Augustine's original and speculative treatment of rhetoric in *De doctrina christiana* was not imitated, the book was known. M.L.W. Laistner lists it among the works in Bede's library, and adds: "The end of Book iii of the *De doctrina christiana* is transcribed by Bede in a somewhat abbreviated form in the

wedge which kept the door to rhetoric ajar. Whatever was contained in the sacred Scriptures was a proper object of study. Cassiodorus pointed out countless figures in his commentary on the Psalms.

Bede's own rhetoric, *De schematibus et tropis,* is a logical outgrowth of the tendencies I have described. It is deliberately limited in scope, a textbook designed for the needs of monastic education. In form, it is an adjunct to his larger textbook on poetry, *De arte metrica.* Bede compiled his list of figures and their definitions from similar lists in Donatus, Diomedes, and Isidore, where they occur in the same, or nearly the same, order,[9] but he substituted illustrations from the Bible for their citations of classical authors. No vestige of the five-part division of classical rhetoric remains, nor does Bede present his schemes and tropes as part of "grammar." He organized intelligently those elements of rhetoric which were known to him. Still, there is no disguising the fact of a precipitous decline in rhetorical theory from the age of Cicero to the beginning of the eighth century in Britain.

However, Bede's use of rhetoric in the *History* shows that classical rhetoric could still exert, at least on a vigorous mind, more of a creative influence than these brief treatises might suggest. Consider the rhetorical sophistication that went into the creation of an appropriate narrative voice for the *History.* The *persona* of the narrator appears in the Preface, which, in the form of an epistle dedicatory to King Ceolwulf, serves as an *exordium.* Bede, a servant of Christ, addresses himself to the most glorious king, who, in his zeal to hear not only holy Scripture, but also the words and deeds of the famous men of his own people, has expressed a wish to receive a copy of the *History.* Bede is pleased to comply but at the same time is concerned "to remove all occasions of doubt" (p. 3) about what he has written. Therefore he lists the sources from which he has obtained his infor-

---

long introduction to his commentary on the Apocalypse." *Bede: His Life, Times, and Writings,* ed. A. Hamilton Thompson, (1932; rpt. New York, 1966), pp. 263 and 250.

9. Donatus, Keil, IV, 397–402; Diomedes, Keil, I, 443–449; 456–464; Isidore, *Etym.* I. xxxvi–xxxvii. For detailed information on Bede's use of these and other sources, see my edition of *De schematibus et tropis* in *Corpus christianorum series latina* CXXIIIA, 142–171; see also Gussie Hecht Tannenhaus, "Bede's *De schematibus et tropis*—A Translation," *Quarterly Journal of Speech* XLVIII (1962), 237–253: reprinted in *Readings in Medieval Rhetoric,* edited by Joseph M. Miller, Michael H. Prosser, and Thomas W. Benson, Bloomington (Indiana) and London, 1973, pp. 96–122; Ulrich Schindel, "Die Quellen von Bedas Figurenlehre," *Classica et Mediaevalia* XXIX (1968), 169–186.

mation. Foremost among his *auctores* is Albinus, the abbot of a monastery outside Canterbury; it is chiefly at Albinus' urging that he has *dared* to undertake the task. For his own part, Bede has labored carefully and diligently to gather and record his materials, but he has accepted what he has read "in simple faith" (p. 7).[10] Therefore he humbly (*suppliciter*) begs the reader to excuse any error, since he has "simply sought to commit to writing" (p. 7) the report of fame. Likewise he humbly begs his audience to petition for divine mercy for his "weaknesses both of mind and body" (p. 7). Such pious intercession will be the fruit of his labor.

The elements which here make up the *persona* of the humble narrator are entirely conventional from the salutation to the *captatio benevolentiae,* or appeal to the goodwill of the reader, at the end. Bede employs these conventions skillfully. The salutation reads: *Gloriosissimo regi Ceoluulfo Beda famulus Christi et presbyter* (p. 2). Nothing would seem simpler; yet the form merges a "formula of submission" with a "devotional formula" in a way peculiarly appropriate to the narrative task at hand.[11] A submission formula, by which "a subject calls himself the thrall, slave, or servant of the king,"[12] is prepared for in the phrase *Gloriosissimo regi* and seems to be completed in the word *famulus*—the juxtaposition of "most glorious king" with "servant." But, of course, Bede is not the king's servant, he is Christ's; he is dependent not on Ceolwulf, but on God. In fact *famulus Christi* is a devotional or authority formula, "which expresses the idea that the drawer owes his earthly mission to the grace of God."[13] Bede's merger of the formulas of submission and devotion preserves the humble decorum appropriate in an address to secular authority, while affirming the existence of a higher authority whose voice Bede will be.[14]

---

10. He is referring in particular to a Life of Cuthbert written by the brothers of Lindisfarne.

11. The distinction between the formula of submission and the devotional formula is made by Ernst Robert Curtius in *European Literature and the Latin Middle Ages,* trans. Willard R. Trask (New York, 1953), pp. 407–413.

12. Curtius, p. 407.

13. Curtius, p. 407, quoting H. Bresslau. Although the devotional formula is in origin an extension of a secular, oriental submission formula, it enters Christian literature through the letters of St. Paul as a way "in which Paul's apostolic and hierarchic consciousness of authority finds expression" (Curtius, p. 408).

14. Papal salutations to royalty provided Bede with his model. Of the salutations which he reproduces in the *History,* the closest to his own is that of Pope Boniface to King Edwin: *Viro glorioso Eduino regi Anglorum Bonifatius episcopus seruus*

Bede's posture of humility is sustained by two "modesty formulas" in the body of the Preface. One is his reference to his "weaknesses both of mind and body"—a formula of self-disparagement. The other is his statement that it is chiefly at the encouragement of Abbot Albinus that he has dared to write.[15] His humility is restrained, however; there is no trace of servility in his tone.

Though the *persona* of the narrator is simple and humble, his words are authoritative. Bede calls himself "a truthful historian" (*uerax historicus,* iii. 17: p. 264), whose duty it is to relate matters in a plain style (*simpliciter, ibid.*). He distances himself from his material by *prosopopoeia*: "Should history tell of good men . . . ; should it record the evil ends of wicked men . . ." (p. 3). Error must be attributed to the "true law of history" (*uera lex historiae,* p. 6) which dictates the transmission of the "common report, for the instruction of posterity."[16] The *historicus* is the scribe, his voice belongs to *historia.* The distance between them lends an air of impersonal authority to the work.

So far as I am aware, none of the treatises available to Bede provide more information on the topic of the *exordium* than Isidore does in the paragraph I have quoted above. Those few, spare phrases could not by themselves carry the tradition exemplified in Bede's letter. Teachers must have elaborated upon them in the classroom, of course. But the most important carriers had to be the literary models which were considered exemplary. For Bede, these included Augustine, Jerome, and above all Gregory the Great.

SCHEMES

Bede thought of rhetoric in terms of "figures." We may follow his lead and examine certain features of his rhetorical practice in the

---

seruorum Dei (ii. 10: p. 166); the more characteristic form weakens the formula of submission still further by styling the king "son," thus insisting on the hierarchical relationship between pope and king (e.g., ii. 17). Bede gains his peculiar effect by transposing his title *presbyter* to the end.

15. On modesty formulas, see Curtius, pp. 83–85. Curtius finds examples of "the statement that one dares write only because a friend or a patron or a superior has expressed such a request or wish or command" in Cicero, Vergil, and Pliny the younger.

16. C.W. Jones has shown that these phrases (*uerax historicus, uera lex historiae*), which derive from Jerome's explanation that the evangelists sometimes expressed themselves according to the popular understanding, as when they called Joseph the father of Christ, reflect Bede's organizational plan of the *History,* which was to fuse popular hagiography with factual chronicles. *Saints' Lives and Chronicles in Early England* (Ithaca, N.Y., 1947), pp. 80–85.

History according to his division of the subject in *De schematibus et tropis* (hereafter referred to as *DST*).

Schemes involve abnormal or stylized syntactic constructions. Bede lists seventeen of them in *De schematibus et tropis*. Some are unusual constructions that occur rarely, if at all, in his own prose and do not require comment. Others are put to significant use. The one which, more than any other, gives Bede's prose its distinctive flavor, is *hyperbaton*,[17] or artificial word order. Oddly enough, the Latin rhetoricians, Bede included, classified *hyperbaton* as a trope. The reason, as Quintilian explains, is that in *tmesis* (a variety of *hyperbaton*) "the meaning is not complete until the two words have been put together." Otherwise, he says, *hyperbaton* would more appropriately be regarded as a verbal figure (or scheme, see above, p. 149) (*Instit.* VIII. vi. 62–67).[18] Prose writers in the classical period used *hyperbaton* chiefly to achieve pleasing rhythms or to avoid offensive ones, and to point up sentences by the effective placement of prominent words. Bede organizes his rhythms spatially, to please the eye, rather than temporally. As with his other uses of rhetoric, the effect often is to point toward the paradoxical resolution of the contradictions of earthly life in the vision of life eternal.

The simplest form of *hyperbaton* occurs when the "natural" order of two adjoining words is reversed. Bede calls this variety *anastrophe* (*DST* II. x). The placement of a monosyllabic preposition between the adjective and the noun (reversing the order of the preposition and the adjective) was common in classical Latin prose. In a few stereotyped phrases it became virtually obligatory (e.g., *quem ad modum, magno cum metu*). From *anastrophe,* there is a continuum of increasing complexity, not precisely delineated by rhetorical terminology, leading to *synchisis,* or thoroughly confused word order (*DST* II. x. 125–172).

Bede was particularly fond of two varieties of *hyperbaton.* In both, a phrase is interrupted by another word or phrase in such a way that two words which would normally stand together are separated. The first, which is the more frequent, is the adjective-noun phrase (a) in which the adjective is separated from the noun. The second is the prepositional phrase (b) in which the preposition is separated from

---

17. Spellings of the figures of rhetoric have been standardized on the basis of the entry-forms in Richard A. Lanham, *A Handlist of Rhetorical Terms,* Berkeley and Los Angeles, 1968.

18. Trans. by H.E. Butler, Loeb Classical Library, III, 339.

its object. An examination of four passages in the *History* of approximately equal length[19] reveals four distinct patterns of (a) and (b) which can be arranged in order of increasing complexity as follows:

1. *Simple hyperbaton.*[20] A phrase ((a) or (b)) is interrupted by another word or single integral phrase (such as an adjective-noun phrase, a compound verb, a prepositional phrase, a subject and verb, or two nouns in apposition). Examples (the intervening word or phrase is enclosed in parentheses): (a) *ad aeternam (regni caelestis) sedem* (p. 122), *pulchro (uitam suam) fine* (p. 418); (b) *per studiosae lectionis (roboraret) alloquium* (p. 124), *in episcopatus (consecratus est) gradum* (p. 232).

2. *Compound hyperbaton.* A phrase ((a) or (b)) is interrupted by two or more words not in themselves forming a single integral phrase. Examples: (a) *latiorem (in nostra historia ecclesiastica) (facere) sermonem* (p. 122), *caelestem (ei) (a Domino) (concessam esse) gratiam* (pp. 416–418); no examples of (b).

3. *Complex hyperbaton.* Two phrases interlock ((a) = two interlocked adjective-noun phrases, (b) = a prepositional phrase interlocked with an adjective-noun phrase). Examples (the second

---

19. The first passage (645 words) is from Bede's account of the life of Pope Gregory the Great (ii. 1): *His temporibus* (p. 122) . . . *resuscitator existeret* (p. 126), excluding *At nunc ex occasione . . . quod porto* (p. 124), and *Palpate et uidete . . . uidetis habere* (p. 126). The second (651 words) is the story of King Cenwealh of Wessex (iii. 7), together with two sentences about King Eorcenberht of Kent (iii. 8): *Eo tempore* (p. 232) . . . *auctoritate praecepit* (p. 236). The third (648 words) is from the miracle of Caedmon (iv. 22[24]): *In huius monasterio* (p. 414) . . . *induci solebant* (p. 418). The fourth (651 words) is the story of the layman, whose name Bede does not record, who saw in a vision his wicked deeds written in a black book (v. 13), together with the first two sentences of a similar story (v. 14): *At contra* (p. 498) . . . *conuerti ammonebatur* (p. 502), excluding *Beati quorum . . . sunt peccata* (p. 502). The excluded sentences are direct quotations of the Bible and of Gregory.

20. Some constructions are so common in all periods of Latin prose that to include them would obscure the distinctive characteristics of Bede's usage. Therefore, in counting the instances of hyperbaton, I have put the restriction on both (a) and (b) that the intervening word or phrase not be a preposition, conjunction, adverb, or interjection. As a result, such a simple *anastrophe* as *quem ad modum* would not be counted. I have put the further restriction on (b) that the intervening word or phrase not modify the object of the preposition. This excludes dependent genitives that wholly precede the object (e.g., *ex magnae humilitatis intentione* is not counted, although *ex magnae intentione humilitatis* would have been). Finally, I have arbitrarily excluded from *simple* and *compound hyperbaton*, but not from *complex* and *compound-complex hyperbaton*, all adjective-noun phrases in which the adjectival form is a participle, a cardinal or ordinal numeral, or any of the following adjectives of quantity: *aliquot, magnus, maior, maximus, minimus, minor, multus, nullus, omnis, paruus, plurimus, plus, quantus, solus, tantus, tot, totus.*

interlocking phrase is enclosed in brackets): (a) *ad nanciscendam* [*supernae*] *gloriam* [*dignitatis*] (p. 122), *inprouiso* [*mortis*] *articulo* [*praeuenti*] (p. 502); (b) *ad* [*caelestis*] *exercitia* [*uitae*] (p. 124). It should be noted that a single transposition accounts for each of the examples given here. This is normally true of *complex hyperbaton*, although I include figures like *de* [*propriae*] *quondam quiete* [*conuersationis*] (p. 124), because *quondam* is an adverb and therefore, under the restrictions I have imposed (see note 20), ignored. Otherwise this figure would be classed as (4b).

4. *Compound-complex hyperbaton*. Two phrases interlock, one of which is also interrupted by one or more additional words or phrases ((a) based on (3a), (b) based on (3b)). Example: (a) *librum (beati Iob)* [*magnis*] *inuolutum* [*obscuritatibus*] (p. 126); no examples of (b), but see comment under (3b).

The four passages were selected as representative of the stylistic range of the *History*. Bede's account of Gregory the Great's life (ii. 1) is notably solemn and elevated in style. On the other hand, Bede tells us that he wrote "simply," just as he heard it, the story of the layman who had a vision in which a devil showed him a black book in which all his evil deeds were recorded in an ugly handwriting (v. 13). If there is such a thing as a "plain style" in the *History*, this must be it. These two chapters illustrate the extremes of style in the *History*. The remaining passages were chosen to compare the two principal types of narrative—the political narrative, centered on the public lives of high-ranking secular and ecclesiastical rulers, and the personal narrative of holy dying (or the reverse), focussed on the most intimate moments of persons whose social and political ranks were of no consequence. The story of King Cenwealh of Wessex (iii. 7) illustrates the former type; the miracle of Caedmon (iv. 22(24)), the latter.[21] The data are best presented in tabular form (Table A).

Some tentative conclusions are warranted. In regard to the use of *hyperbaton*, the passages from the accounts of the sinful layman, King Cenwealh, and Caedmon are much alike. *Simple hyperbaton* is a relatively constant feature. There is an increase in the number of the more complex forms in the Caedmon passage, but not enough

---

21. The distinction here proposed is not based on the sources of these particular narratives (see note 16 above). Though in general the political narrative will depend on such secular and ecclesiastical records as chronicles, regnal and episcopal lists, etc., and the personal narrative on saints' lives, the source of iii. 7 is uncertain (*Saints' Lives*, pp. 190–192), and Jones remarks of the story of Caedmon, "There is nothing hagiological about this story" (*ibid.*, p. 185).

Table A

		Gregory the Great (ii. 1) 645 words	King Cenwealh (iii. 7) 651 words	Caedmon (iv. 22(24)) 648 words	Sinful layman (v. 13) 651 words	Average 648.75 words
1. Simple hyperbaton	a	9	6	6	5	6.50
	b	1	1	0	0	0.50
2. Compound hyperbaton	a	6	0	3	1	2.50
	b	0	0	0	0	0.00
3. Complex hyperbaton	a	1	0	0	1	0.50
	b	3	0	1	0	1.00
4. Compound-complex hyperbaton	a	1	0	0	0	0.25
	b	0	0	0	0	0.00
Totals:		21	7	10	7	11.25

The number of occurrences of four kinds of *hyperbaton* in four selected passages from the *History* of approximately equal length. (a) = *hyperbaton* in an adjective-noun phrase; (b) = *hyperbaton* in a prepositional phrase.

to alter one's intuitive judgment that all three passages are representative of a uniform stylistic level. The Gregory passage differs markedly, both in the frequency of *simple hyperbaton* and particularly in the number of the more complex forms. A look at the contexts of all the figures reveals that the more complex forms, unlike *simple hyperbaton*, are found, almost without exception, in moments of high religious seriousness. It would appear that the norm in the *History* is a "plain style" which is occasionally elevated, and that the relative frequency of *hyperbaton* is an indicator of stylistic level. Moreover, Bede tends to use the more complex forms, not to present what we might call "straight" historical narrative, but to secure a pious tone or to assert matters of faith.

Hyperbaton, being a Greek stylistic device, was unknown in early Latin. It began to appear about the beginning of the first century B.C. It spread slowly in classical Latin prose; rapidly in poetry.[22] By and large, prose writers confined themselves to the simple forms, like *anastrophe*. Cicero was fond of the monosyllabic preposition inserted between adjective and noun. There are occasional instances of *complex hyperbaton* in his prose.[23] Such devices, however, are far more common in verse. A "golden line" (*complex hyperbaton*) appears on the average once in every thirty lines in the *Georgics* and the *Aeneid*.[24] A comparison of selected passages from several authors and periods—Cicero and Livy, Augustine and Gregory, the Vulgate *Genesis* and *I Corinthians*, and Vergil—with the Bede passages will give an idea of how much his practice differed from earlier usage.[25] Again, the comparison is best displayed in tabular form (Table B).

Despite the enormous influence of the Vulgate on Christian-Latin writers from the fifth century on, it is interesting to note that in respect to this figure Bede and Gregory have moved away from Biblical style rather than toward it. Only Gregory falls within the range of the Bede passages. Both in absolute numbers and strikingly

---

22. Summarizing L.P. Wilkinson, *Golden Latin Artistry* (Cambridge, 1963), p. 213.

23. Wilkinson cites two examples, p. 215.

24. Based on figures given by Wilkinson, p. 216. Bede favored the "golden line" in verse: see *De arte metrica* XI. 23–37.

25. The seven passages for comparison are: Augustine, *De civitate dei* XVIII. liv (the first 646 words to *magister et noster*, excluding quotations from the Bible); Cicero, *De oratore* I. i–iii. 10 (the first 637 words); Gregory, *Moralia in Iob, Epistola missoria* I–II. iv (the first 629 words); Livy, *Ab urbe condita* XXVIII. i–iii. 2 (the first 641 words); Vergil, *Aeneid* I. 1–101 (659 words); the Vulgate, *Genesis* i–ii:7 (the first 661 words); the Vulgate, *I Cor.* vii:1–39 (the first 649 words).

Table B

		The Vulgate Genesis 661 words	The Vulgate I Corinthians 649 words	Augustine, De civitate dei 646 words	Livy, Ab urbe condita 641 words	Cicero, De oratore 637 words	Gregory, Moralia in Iob 629 words	Bede, average of four passages of History 648.75 words	Vergil, Aeneid 659 words
1. Simple hyperbaton	a	0	1	3	4	5	8	6.50	20
	b	0	0	1	0	0	0	0.50	0
2. Compound hyperbaton	a	0	0	0	1	0	2	2.50	9
	b	0	0	0	0	0	0	0.00	0
3. Complex hyperbaton	a	0	0	0	1	1	1	0.50	0
	b	0	0	0	0	0	0	1.00	0
4. Compound-complex hyperbaton	a	0	0	0	0	0	0	0.25	1
	b	0	0	0	0	0	0	0.00	0
Totals:		0	1	4	6	6	11	11.25	30

The number of occurrences of four kinds of *hyperbaton* in a selected passage from each of seven works compared with the average number in four passages from the *History* (from Table A). (a) = *hyperbaton* in an adjective-noun phrase; (b) = *hyperbaton* in a prepositional phrase.

in respect to the more complex forms of *hyperbaton,* Bede and Gregory stand midway between the range of earlier prose styles sampled here and the artifices of classical poetry, represented by Vergil.

Paroemion (= *paromoeon, DST* I. xi), or alliteration, is another scheme which figures prominently in Bede's style. Since alliteration occurs naturally in language, it is impossible to give objective criteria for its deliberate employment as a figure. We can be sure that the alliteration on *a* in *Auctor ante omnes atque adiutor opusculi huius Albinus abba reuerentissimus* (Preface, p. 2) was intended as a studied compliment to Albinus. (It is remarkable that there are no initial consonants before *reuerentissimus,* setting aside the *h* of *huius.* The Germanic principle of vocalic alliteration may be an influence here.) Normally Bede avoids piling up alliteration like this. The alliteration in the phrase *Defunctus est autem* Deo *dilectus pater Augustinus* (ii. 3: p. 142), which begins a paragraph on the death of St. Augustine of Canterbury, is almost as certainly deliberate. So, too, is the alliteration in the final clause of a sentence in which Bede praises the rule of Bishop Leuthere: *qui consecratus in ipsa ciuitate multis annis episcopatum Geuissorum ex synodica sanctione solus sedulo moderamine gessit* (iii. 7: p. 236). The context of each of these is honorific. On the other hand, Bede likes to use a short staccato phrase to point up a condemnation. He skewers the apostate, King Raedwald of East Anglia, on an alliterating antithesis: *natu nobilis, quamlibet actu ignobilis* (vocalic alliteration?). Since Raedwald began as a pagan, was converted, and then went astray, his end was worse than his beginning: *habuit posteriora peiora prioribus* (ii. 15: p. 190).

One wonders whether Bede, having in mind the stressed alliterative patterns of Anglo-Saxon poetry, might not have shifted on occasion from strict *paroemion,* where the alliteration falls on the first syllable regardless of stress (e.g., *Defúnctus . . . Déo diléctus*), to alliteration on the first stressed syllable. He illustrates *paroemion* in *De schematibus et tropis* with two quotations from the book of Psalms. In the first, stress and alliteration coincide, and the compound *benediximus* looks as though it participates in the alliteration: *Benedíximus uos de dómo Dómini; Déus Dóminus et inluxit nobis.* However, stress is clearly disregarded in the second: *Ira illis secúndum similitúdinem serpéntis, sicut aspidis súrdae.* On the whole, the deliberate patternings in the *History* appear to be restricted to *paroemion,* though one is tempted to see stressed alliteration playing a subordinate role.

In a sentence like this, describing Aidan's elevation to the bishopric: *Quo audito omnium qui considebant ad ipsum ora et oculi conuersi, diligenter quid diceret discutiebant, et ipsum esse dignum episcopatu, ipsum ad erudiendos incredulos et indoctos mitti debere decernunt, qui gratia discretionis, quae uirtutum mater est, ante omnia probabatur inbutus; sicque illum ordinantes ad praedicandum miserunt* (iii. 5: p. 228), in which the alliterative rhythms are fluid and leisurely, we can no longer speak solely in terms of *paroemion*. Notice how the dominant vocalic alliteration (whether thought of as a figure or not) is crossed by the alliterating *d*'s (and perhaps *p*'s), and the two firmly interwoven in the central phrase *ad erudiendos incredulos et indoctos,* which expresses Bede's confidence in the power of a rational faith to overcome the darkness of ignorance and unbelief.

Homoioteleuton, in which successive clauses end in like syllables, is another scheme that is a natural function of language. Sometimes it costs more effort to avoid it than to secure it. The like syllables result from parallelism—the placing of words of the same part of speech in the same positions. Thus *homoioteleuton* is an effective way of producing antithesis. Bede remarks in *De schematibus et tropis* (I. xii. 125–127) that Gregory made frequent use of the figure. With this encouragement we might expect to encounter it often in the *History.* Actually, Bede is rather cautious about using it. He generally introduces slight shifts to avoid exact parallelism. It takes a moment to spot the *homoioteleuton* in a sentence such as this: *Siue enim historia de bonis bona referat, ad imitandum bonum auditor sollicitus instiga*tur; *seu mala commemoret de prauis, nihilominus religiosus ac pius auditor siue lector deuitando quod noxium est ac peruersum, ipse sollertius ad exsequenda ea quae bona ac Deo digna esse cognouerit, accendi*tur (Preface, p. 2). Antithetical clauses are concluded by *instigatur* and *accenditur,* but the clauses are of unequal length and the verbs belong to different conjugations. Furthermore, what we might call "internal" *homoioteleuton* is avoided by the different order of the two phrases which depend on *historia: de bonis bona referat* (prepositional phrase, object, verb), *mala commemoret de prauis* (object, verb, prepositional phrase).

The same sentence in the Preface illustrates another scheme which Bede occasionally employs to good effect—*polyptoton,* or the use of one word in several cases. Here in the first clause we find the sequence *bonis, bona, bonum,* but again notice how Bede avoids excessive parallelism by finding an alternative to the antithetical sequence *malis, mala, malum.* In book three, Bede tells how Oswald, before going into battle against Caedwalla, the king of the Britons, set up a cross in a place called *Heaven*field. The name proved prophetic, and Bede expresses the wonder of ensuing events by means of *polyptoton*: *Vocatur locus ille lingua Anglorum* Hefen*feld, quod dici potest latine* Caelestis *Campus, quod certo utique praesagio futurorum antiquitus nomen accepit; significans nimirum quod ibidem* caeleste *erigendum tropeum,* caelestis *inchoanda uictoria,* caelestia *usque hodie forent miracula celebranda* (iii. 2: p. 216).

Paronomasia, or punning, resembles *polyptoton* insofar as it in-volves a change of a single letter or syllable, but it brings two different words into relationship. Speaking of a scarlet dye which had the property of improving with age, Bede says, *sed quo* uetustior *eo solet esse* uenustior (i. 1: p. 14). The figure has nothing to do with humor. In this case, the "real" relationship between beauty and age in the dye is expressed by the "real" relationship between the words (*uetustior/uenustior*) which express it. There is a one-to-one corres-pondence between the physical world and the verbal. The mingled awe and love of the people for King Edwin is captured in *parono-masia*; Bede speaks of the magnitude of their fear and love: *uel* timoris *eius . . . uel* amoris (ii. 16: p. 192). The most famous puns in the *History* are the three which Gregory is said to have uttered on seeing English boys put up for sale in a market in Rome. Someone told him the boys were English (*Angli*). " 'Good,' he said, 'they have the face of angels [*angelicam habent faciem*], and such men should be fellow-heirs of the angels [*angelorum*] in heaven.' " On learning they came from the province of Deiri, " '*Deiri,*' he replied, '*De ira*! good! snatched from the wrath [*de ira*] of Christ and called to his mercy. And what is the name of the king of the land?' He was told that it was Ælle; and playing on the name, he said, 'Alleluia! the praise of God the Creator must be sung in those parts' " (ii. 1: pp. 134–135). The point of this story, which Bede ascribes to the "tra-dition of our forefathers" (p. 133), is not that Gregory was blessed with a ready wit, but that the relationship between these words, whatever the truth of the story itself, cannot be accidental and is, in fact, a verbal mirror of the providential events leading to the establishment of the English Church.

TROPES

The function of rhetoric in mediating between the contradictions of human experience and the harmony of the divine plan by imposing, as it were, a higher order on the flux of language, and thereby pointing the way to the vision of God, becomes still more obvious when we move from schemes to tropes. Tropes belong to the area of semantics, since they have to do with the metaphoric use of language.

Bede's view of the nature of things was, inescapably, dualistic. Man's native home was in the kingdom of heaven.[26] Life on earth entailed separation; division. The holy men who voluntarily exiled themselves to remote and isolated places for the sake of the kingdom of heaven made themselves visible metaphors of the human condition.[27] All men and women were pilgrims on a difficult, treacherous journey back to their native place. Augustine of Canterbury's plea to Gregory, about the English mission which he and his fellows were charged with undertaking—that they ought not to be made to enter upon "so dangerous, wearisome, and uncertain a journey," *ne tam periculosam, tam laboriosam, tam incertam peregrinationem adire deberent* (i. 23: pp. 68–69; notice the fine rhetorical balancing of the clause, the triple cola, the *homoioptoton*, or use of similar cases, the *asyndeton*), suggests a failure of nerve in the face of life itself—how could anyone escape the pilgrimage of life? Gregory, in his vigorous way, would have none of it. Go to it, he replied, "and grant that I may see the fruit of your labours in our heavenly home" (i. 23: p. 71).

Rhetoric provided a means by which the unifying beatific vision could be apprehended intellectually, because the universe itself was verbal. "In the beginning was the Word, and the Word was with God, and God was the Word" (Joh. i:1). The gospel was the *uerbum uitae,* the word of life (e.g., i. 25, i. 26, *et passim*). The physical universe was metaphoric; images like fire, water, tempest, harvest, poison, famine, light, dark, and plague, were realities in the physical

---

26. The phrase *regnum caeleste* or one of its close variants, e.g., *regnum caelorum, regnum in caelis,* occurs 46 times in the *History.* See Putnam Fennell Jones, *A Concordance to the Historia Ecclesiastica of Bede* (Cambridge, Mass., 1929), s.v. *regnum.* There are, of course, several other ways of expressing this idea.

27. Ireland was the favorite resort for the English; Egbert went there (iii. 4), as did Æthelhun (iii. 27), Wihtberht (v. 9), Black Hewald and White Hewald (v. 10), and many others (iii. 27).

world and figures as well. In the final analysis, no distinction could be drawn between verbal metaphors and physical signs, since physical signs were the metaphors by means of which God communicated with man.

Let us examine these propositions in more detail. In a series of responses to questions put to him by Augustine of Canterbury (i. 27), Gregory explains how the teaching of the Old Law and the Old Testament must be understood in a spiritual sense, by means of allegory (a trope). He extends the application of the method to include our understanding of events in the physical world: "Consider then, most beloved brother, that all that we suffer in this mortal flesh through the infirmity of nature is ordained by the just judgement of God as a result of sin. For hunger and thirst, heat, cold, and weariness are the result of the infirmity of our nature" (p. 93). Heat and cold, hunger and thirst, sickness and frailty are palpable signs, a physical allegory, of God's judgment of man. He adds, in a letter to King Æthelberht of Kent (i. 32), that great disturbances of nature, "changes in the sky and terrors from the heavens, unseasonable tempests, wars, famine, pestilence, and earthquakes" (p. 113), are "signs of the end of the world" (p. 115).

Whether they are afflictions of the body, or natural or social disasters, the images we encounter are figures in God's rhetoric. St. Augustine provides a rationale in his treatment of "things" and "signs" in *De doctrina christiana* (I. ii. 2):

> All doctrine concerns either things or signs, but things are learned by signs. Strictly speaking, I have here called a "thing" that which is not used to signify something else, like wood, stone, cattle, and so on; but not that wood concerning which we read that Moses cast it into bitter waters that their bitterness might be dispelled, nor that stone which Jacob placed at his head, nor that beast which Abraham sacrificed in place of his son. For these are things in such a way that they are also signs of other things.[28]

All words are signs. Signs, in turn, "are either literal or figurative" (II. x. 15).[29] A word is used literally when it refers to the thing for which it was designed. If, however, the thing designated by the word is a sign of something else (Augustine uses the example of the ox

---

28. Trans. by D.W. Robertson, Jr., *On Christian Doctrine* (Indianapolis, 1958), p. 8.
29. *Ibid.*, p. 43.

which symbolizes the evangelist), then the word is used figuratively. Once we learn how to read these figures either in nature or in a book, we can perceive some part of God's plan.

The signs that Gregory referred to are rooted in the assumption that there was a time, before the fall of man, when nature was uniformly orderly. Though that order was broken, it was not destroyed. Christian history reveals both the consequences of the fall and the plan of redemption. The promise of grace fills history with meaning and affects every aspect of the human personality in consequence. The image or sign of the introduction of division or evil into the natural world is poison, the venom of the serpent. And the human dream of an end to the divisions of experience emerges in the image of the world without poison, the Promised Land, the celestial Jerusalem.

Bede's metaphors of alienation derive from this aspect of God's rhetoric: poison, tempest, famine, plague, madness, ruin, fire, disease. Sometimes the affliction is literal; that is, the image belongs to natural rhetoric. At other times, it is metaphorical, and the image is part of the verbal rhetoric. The primal harmony of nature is depicted in the *copia* of i. 1. We hear not only of the generous abundance of nature in Britain, but also of Ireland, the land without snakes. Practically anything Irish is an antidote to poison. Caesar's introduction of Roman power into Britain is accompanied by two violent storms (i.2). A "storm of persecution" afflicts the primitive church of the Britons (i. 8). England's protomartyr, St. Alban, suffers on a hill of ideal beauty, at the top of which a perpetual spring miraculously gushes forth (i. 7).[30] These events are followed by the plague, the madness, the poison of the Arian heresy, which is the precursor of heresies to come. The accumulation of metaphors testifies to the horror of the time: "The churches of Britain remained at peace until the time of the Arian madness which corrupted the whole world and even infected this island, sundered so far from the rest of mankind, with the poison of its error" (i. 8: p. 35).

One group of metaphors of alienation can be subsumed under the heading of antithesis. The dualism of Greek thought infused Christian teaching. Body and soul not only separated, they became hierarchically ordered. Though there was never any question in orthodox Christianity but that all God's creation was good, nonetheless,

---

30. The account of St. Alban is based on a *Passio Albani*, see *History*, p. 28, note 2.

as a result of the fall, the spirit felt itself an alien in a hostile body, caught in the bondage of the flesh, an exile from its true home in another world. Things like body and soul, which ranked comparatively as the good and the better, were reordered unconsciously as the bad and the good. Paired metaphors proliferate: light and dark, heat and cold, freedom and bondage, cleanliness and dirt.

Bede's account of Gregory is typical:

> He promptly renounced his secular habit and entered a monastery, in which he proceeded to live with such grace and perfection—as he used afterwards to declare with tears—that his soul was then above all transitory things; and that he rose superior to all things subject to change. He used to think nothing but thoughts of heaven, so that, even though still imprisoned in the body, he was able to pass in contemplation beyond the barriers of the flesh. He loved death, which in the eyes of almost everybody is a punishment, because he held it to be the entrance to life and the reward of his labours. . . . Once, for instance, when he was talking privately with his deacon Peter and enumerating the former virtues of his soul, he added mournfully that now on account of his pastoral cares, he had to trouble himself with the business of men of this world, and after the enjoyment of peace so lovely, he was soiled by the dust of earthly activities. After dissipating his strength on outward things by descending to the affairs of all and sundry, even when he sought the things of the spirit, he inevitably returned to them impaired. (ii. 1: pp. 123–125)

The passage is built on a series of antitheses—soul, body; heaven, earth; life, death; freedom, bondage; reward, punishment; progress, loss; peace, distraction; inward, outward. Hierarchical ordering is reinforced by images of motion up or down: earthly things are "falling" or "slipping" (*labientia*); Gregory "stood above" them (*emineret*); he dissipated his strength "by descending" (*pro condiscensione* [*sic*]).

Such antitheses and the metaphors associated with them are pervasive. For example, the metaphor of the flesh as the prison-house of the soul appears in connection with Eorcengota ("Hurrying out to discover what was the matter, [the brothers of the monastery] saw a very great light coming down from heaven, which bore away the holy soul, now freed from the bonds of the flesh, to the eternal joys of the heavenly country," iii. 8: p. 239); Chad ("his holy soul was released from the prison-house of the body," iv. 3: p. 343); Æthelburh ("the mother of the congregation, Æthelburh, beloved of God, was taken from the prison-house of the flesh," iv. 9: p. 361);

Torhtgyth ("she was loosed from the bonds of the flesh and her infirmities and entered upon the joys of eternal salvation," iv. 9: p. 363); Caedwalla ("he hoped that, soon after his baptism, he might be loosed from the bonds of the flesh and pass, cleansed as he was, to eternal joy," v. 7: p. 471); and Theodore (a line from the epitaph inscribed on his tomb: *Cum carnis claustra spiritus egreditur*, "When from the [bondage of his] flesh his spirit took its way," v. 8: pp. 474–475). It is but a step from this metaphor to that of the bondage of sin. The devout Irishman, Adamnan, who "longed to get free as quickly as possible from the inward bonds of sin which weighed him down," mortified his flesh by eating only twice a week, on Thursdays and Sundays (iv. 23[25]: pp. 423–425). The equation of the body with evil is obvious.

There are, of course, real bonds in the world. These "things" may also be "signs" in God's rhetoric. A dramatic case is the story of the brothers, Imma and Tunna. Imma was a thegn of Ælfwine, brother of King Ecgfrith of Northumbria. Tunna was a priest and the abbot of a monastery. During a battle between the Northumbrians and the Mercians, Imma was wounded, taken captive, and brought to a *gesith* of King Æthelred of Mercia. He pretended to be a poor peasant bound by the chain of marriage (*uxoreo uinculo conligatum*). After his wounds had started to heal, the *gesith* "ordered him to be bound at night to prevent his escape. However, it proved impossible to bind him, for no sooner had those who chained him gone, than his fetters were loosed." Meanwhile, his brother Tunna, hearing that Imma had been killed, went in search of his body. Finding one that looked like it, "he carried it to the monastery, buried it with honour, and took care to offer many masses for the absolution of his soul [*pro* absolutione *animae eius*]. It was on account of these celebrations that . . . no one could bind Imma because his fetters were at once loosed [*nullus eum posset uincire, quin continuo* solueretur]." The *gesith* questioned Imma closely, and he finally replied, " 'I have a brother in my country who is a priest and I know he believes me to be dead and offers frequent masses on my behalf; so if I had now been in another world, my soul would have been loosed from its punishment [solueretur *a poenis*] by his intercessions' " (iv. 20[22]: pp. 402–403).

If we consider the images of binding and loosing, it becomes apparent that the most "real" of them is the one that is hypothetical in terms of the story. That is, if Imma were dead, his soul "really" would be subject to binding, because that is the general proposition that is universally true in the Christian metaphysics within which Bede worked. The chains in the physical world are a sign of that reality; their failure to hold is a sign that the purgatorial[31] bonds are loosed by the intercession of prayers for the dead. Even the apparently irrelevant detail—Imma's false claim of marriage—[32] in which marriage is referred to by a metaphor of binding, seems to mirror, though darkly, the ultimate reality.

No discussion of the metaphorics of the *History* would be complete without reference to the symbolism of numbers.[33] This is a habit of mind that can be traced back to Pythagoras. Early Christian thought assimilated it to the words of Solomon: *omnia in mensura et numero et pondere disposuisti* (*Sap.* xi:21). As Augustine puts it (*De civitate dei* XI. xxx):

> And, therefore, we must not despise the science of numbers, which, in many passages of holy Scripture, is found to be of eminent service to the careful interpreter. Neither has it been without reason numbered among

---

31. There is no explicit reference in the *History* to the doctrine of purgatory. It is clearly implied here. In the vision of Dryhthelm (v. 12), the conception of purgatory is spelled out in detail. Dryhthelm's guide explains to him the meaning of one of the places he has seen: " 'The valley that you saw, with its awful flaming fire and freezing cold, is the place in which those souls have to be tried and chastened who delayed to confess and make restitution for the sins they had committed until they were on the point of death; and so they died. But because they did repent and confess, even though on their deathbed, they will all come to the kingdom of heaven on judgement day; and the prayers of those who are still alive, their alms and fastings and specially the celebration of masses, help many of them to get free even before the day of judgement.' " Gregory had proclaimed the doctrine in the *Dialogues*: "Yet there must be a cleansing fire [*purgatorius ignis*] before judgment, because of some minor faults that may remain to be purged away" (IV. xli: trans. by Odo John Zimmerman, *The Fathers of the Church* XXXIX [New York, 1959], 248).

32. Bede's audience would probably assume that, as a thegn in the service of Ælfwine, Imma was no more married than he was a poor peasant, since young men of rank served, among other reasons, in order to gain the rewards that would enable them to marry. See Dorothy Whitelock's comment on a passage in Bede's letter to Egbert, *The Beginnings of English Society* (Baltimore, Maryland, 1965 [revised]), p. 36.

33. Extended treatment of this topic will be found in Vincent F. Hopper, *Medieval Number Symbolism: Its Sources, Meaning, and Influence on Thought and Expression*, New York, 1969. The chapter on "The Early Medieval Period" in Christopher Butler, *Number Symbolism*, New York, 1970, is useful, as are the summaries in Curtius, *European Literature*, pp. 501–509, and Peter Gay, *The Enlightenment: An Interpretation* I (*The Rise of Modern Paganism* [New York, 1967]), 250–252. Plummer treats Bede's use of number symbolism in his Introduction, I, lx–lxi, as does Claude Jenkins in his article, "Bede as Exegete and Theologian," in *Bede: His Life, Times, and Writings*, ed. A. Hamilton Thompson, esp. pp. 173–180.

God's praises, "Thou hast ordered all things in number, and measure, and weight."[34]

The entire created universe seemed to reflect a numerical harmony ordained by God. Wherever number was found in the natural world, it was incumbent upon men to seek its mystical properties.

Numbers, like words, therefore, are signs that may have figurative as well as literal meaning. In *De doctrina christiana*, Augustine speculates on the spiritual significance of numbers in the Bible. Moses, Elias, and Christ each fasted for forty days. What does the number forty mean? Augustine analyzes it. Forty is built of four tens. Four signifies the knowledge of things that move in time, because both the day and the year are divided into four parts—the day into morning, noon, evening, and night; the year into the four seasons. Ten is made up of three plus seven and thereby signifies a knowledge of the Creator (3) and the creature (7). "Thus when the number ten is suggested to us with reference to time, or, that is, when it is multiplied by four, we are admonished to live chastely and continently without temporal delight, or, that is, to fast for forty days" (II. xvi. 25).[35]

Bede took pains to interpret numbers in his commentaries on the Bible.[36] He does not in the *History*. Rather, what happens is that events, particularly events of an edifying nature, attract significant numbers to themselves, which then become part of the meaning of those events.

Time is the phenomenon most likely to be measured. Three, seven, and nine are the common units of perfection. Bishop Wilfrid put an end to a three-year period of drought and famine in the kingdom of the South Saxons by converting the people. On the day he washed them in the waters of baptism a gentle rain soaked the earth (iv. 13). Queen Æthelthryth died three days after a tumor was removed from her jaw (iv. 17[19]). King Sebbi of the East Saxons died three days after receiving a comforting vision which foretold the time of his death (iv. 11). Æthelthryth held the rank of abbess for seven years (iv. 17[19]); the body of her aunt, Æthelburh, who held the same rank, was dug up seven years after her death and found to be incorrupt (iii. 8). Angels revealed to Chad the exact time of his death, promising to return after seven days to lead him into heaven (iv. 3).

---

34. Trans. by Marcus Dods, *The City of God* (New York, 1950), p. 375.
35. Trans. by Robertson, p. 52.
36. See Claude Jenkins, in *Bede: His Life, Times, and Writings*, pp. 173–180.

Oswald, "the most Christian king of Northumbria" (p. 241), is said to have ruled for nine years by a curious method of reckoning which assigns to him an ill-omened year in which his two immediate predecessors reverted to idolatry and were destroyed (iii. 1; 9).

There are one or two stories in which the mystical properties of the number three appear to have been imposed upon events in a quasimagical fashion to bring about some desired end. When plague struck the monastery of Selsey, the brothers observed a three-day fast in order to seek God's mercy, which they obtained (iv. 14). More striking perhaps is the battle between the heathen Saxons and Picts and the Christian Britons, led by Bishop Germanus of Auxerre. Germanus and his fellow priests shouted "Alleluia" three times. The army repeated the shout and the Saxons and Picts, terrified that heaven and earth were falling, fled in panic (i. 20). (Compare with this the plague story in which a little boy of about three years of age, who was at the point of death, called out the name of his nurse three times. Both he and she died on that very day and entered the heavenly kingdom (iv. 8).)

Bede's rhetoric gave him an economical means of infusing the simplest and sparest of narratives with a wealth of meaning and emotion. An interaction of metaphor and numerical symbol with Biblical allusion could lay open the experience of faith. Two narratives, which are related through their basis in a curious incident in the life of St. Paul, will serve to illustrate.

Bede begins the story of Abbess Hild by calling attention to the numerical patterns in her life. Hild died at the age of sixty-six. This span was divided into two equal parts of thirty-three years each, the first devoted to secular life, the second to her monastic vocation (iv. 21[23]). That thirty-three is the sacred number that corresponds to the number of years Christ lived on earth is taken for granted.[37] Furthermore, Hild suffered from a prolonged illness of seven years before she died. The illness was sent by the Lord "so that, like the apostle, her strength might be made perfect in weakness, [*ut iuxta exemplum apostoli uirtus eius in infirmitate perficeretur*]" (pp. 410–411).

---

37. Augustine records (*Conf.* ix) that he was 33 when Monica died; her fatal illness lasted nine days. Gregory responds to a question of Augustine of Canterbury: "When a woman has been delivered, after how many days ought she to enter the church? You know by the teaching of the Old Testament that she should keep away for thirty-three days if the child is a boy and sixty-six days if it is a girl. *This, however, must be understood figuratively*" (i. 27: p. 91 [emphasis added]).

Just as the seven years of Hild's illness mirror the perfection she achieved, so, by a slight variation, do the nine years of illness which the nun Torhtgyth suffered in Abbess Æthelburh's monastery at Barking. "Now in order that her strength," Bede reports, "like the apostle's, might be made perfect in weakness [*Cuius ut uirtus, iuxta Apostolum, in infirmitate perficeretur*], she was suddenly afflicted with a most serious bodily disease and for nine years was sorely tried, . . . so that any traces of sin . . . might be burnt away by the fires of prolonged suffering" (iv. 9: pp. 360–361).

Illnesses in saints provide occasions for miracles of healing. When such persons fail to recover, the failure will raise doubts about their sanctity, or about their powers as healers, or even about the validity of the religion they practice. St. Paul's semi-mocking account in 2 *Corinthians* xii of his own failure to get relief[38] after thrice praying for it is the *locus classicus*. He claims that his affliction was sent lest he be exalted by the number of revelations he has had. His affliction then is itself a sign of his worthiness, and at the same time illustrates the theme of Christian strength in weakness, which is readily transposed to purification through suffering. The phrase that Bede alludes to twice is, as Paul reports it, actually God's negative answer to Paul's prayers for relief. God says to him, "My grace is sufficient for you, for strength is made perfect in weakness [*nam virtus in infirmitate perficitur*]" (2 *Cor.* xii:9). God validates Paul's apostleship by means of a direct verbal communication and provides a gloss, which, when Hild and Torhtgyth recapitulate Paul's experience, serves also to explain the meaning of their suffering and death.

The allusion to 2 *Cor.* xii:9 is a formula which belongs to the narrative of the illness and death of a saint; the formula provides the spiritual meaning of the event; and the theme of the perfection of strength through weakness is reinforced by the use of a "perfect" number for the years of suffering. Torhtgyth's disease is a metaphorical fire that burns away her sins. She undergoes an earthly purgatory in order to enter heaven directly. The fever which attacks Hild wearies her by its sharp fire (*acri ardore*, p. 410). Two observations may be made about this image. First, its latent symbolism is identical with the metaphorical fire that burns Torhtgyth. Second, the line of demarcation between literal and metaphorical description is not easy

---

38. Relief from what is unclear, though it was and is generally assumed to have been illness; Paul speaks of a goad (*stimulus*), an Angel of Satan who boxed his ears (*colaphizet*).

to find. Does the phrase *acri ardore* represent the pains of fever literally or figuratively? In either case the image is a sign. Suffering calls forth the image of the "fire" that causes it. Fire has both its literal sense and the figurative meaning of purgatory. Or, we can reverse the direction of the signs and say that purgatorial suffering is the "thing" that calls forth the signs that figure it, including the "fires" and the earthly diseases of the saints. The medieval universe begins with the Word, which is made flesh. "Things" in Bede's historical recreation of the world are in part generated by the symbolic structure of his rhetoric, which is a mirror of God's symbolic universe.

These stories share with the chapter in 2 *Corinthians* not only an interest in the meaning of human suffering but equally an interest in the visionary experience. This is Paul's main topic. Using curiously oblique language, he claims that he was himself caught up to the third heaven and into paradise (2 *Cor.* xii:1–4). Paul was, uniquely, a living witness of the beatific vision—the goal of every medieval Christian on the pilgrimage through life. Despite their common elements, the stories of Torhtgyth and Hild are utilized for different narrative purposes. Torhtgyth's is an adjunct to the story of Æthelburh, the point being that Torhtgyth was worthy of receiving a vision of Æthelburh's death and entrance into the heavenly kingdom. Hild, on the other hand, is at the center of a cluster of subordinate stories (including the incomparable one of Caedmon). But there happens to have been a nun named Begu, a virgin dedicated to the Lord "for thirty or more years" (iv. 21[23]: p. 413), who was granted a vision of Hild's death and ascent into heaven, as Torhtgyth was of Æthelburh's. The allusions to 2 *Cor.* xii recall the single, dramatic testimonial in the Scriptures to the reality of the experience that Æthelburh and Hild hope to have after death, while the visions of Torhtgyth and Begu testify that their hope has been achieved. Similarly, Bishop Chad's translation to heaven is confirmed by the story of a vision that came to his friend Egbert, who was an exile for the sake of the Lord (*peregrinus pro Domino*) in Ireland at the time of Chad's death. As Egbert told it: " 'I know a man [*scio hominem*] in this island, still in the flesh, who saw the soul of Chad's brother Cedd descend from the sky with a host of angels and return to the heavenly kingdom, taking Chad's soul with him.' Whether he was speaking of himself or of another [Bede adds] is uncertain, but what cannot be uncertain is that whatever such a man said must be true" (iv. 3: pp. 344–345). The imitation of Paul (*scio hominem* etc., 2

Cor. xii:2–3) is clearly deliberate. (Bede's expressed uncertainty as to the identity of the visionary is consistent with the obliquity of Paul's language.)

In what is very nearly the last chapter of the *History* (v. 21), Bede incorporates Ceolfrith's letter to King Nechtan on the Catholic observance of Easter. Bede's editors agree that the composition is Ceolfrith's in name only; Bede was the principal author.[39] The controversy over the correct date of the Easter celebration had been a matter of passionate concern to him all his life. He could not avoid the subject in writing the history of the English Church. The rules for calculating the date of Easter were based on events in the Old and the New Testaments which were linked allegorically. When all the churches of the world, which made up the one Church, celebrated Easter at the same time, the celebration was an imitation filled with metaphoric and numerical symbolism. The divisions of earthly existence were overcome. "So at last we duly celebrate our Easter feast to show that we are not, with the ancients, celebrating the throwing off of the yoke of Egyptian bondage but, with devout faith and love, venerating the redemption of the whole world, which, being prefigured by the liberation of the ancient people of God, is completed in the resurrection of Christ; we also signify that we rejoice in the sure and certain hope of our own resurrection . . ." (p. 545). The purpose of the narratives of the *History* is, through the rhetoric of faith, to make the hope of the beatific vision, in which all the contradictions of the human experience are to be resolved and its limitations transcended —a hope which goes beyond the literal resources of language—a meaningful reality. Placed as it is, the letter to Nechtan reveals the convergence of this rhetorical purpose with the sacramental meaning of Easter.

---

39. Plummer, II, 332; Colgrave, p. 534, note 1.

Adaptation of Classical Rhetoric in Old English Literature

JACKSON J. CAMPBELL

BEOWULF is once described as *wis wordcwida* (wise of word-speech), a description any classical *rhetor* would also have coveted. The Old English poet wished to praise his hero's eloquence as much as he did his physical prowess, since both were necessary to a leader living in a civilized society. Skill with words, the art of *bene dicendi*, was prized and fostered in Anglo-Saxon England, although in order to fit new situations in a new era, it had naturally changed and developed in a way which might have made Isocrates shudder. After their conversion to Christianity during the course of the seventh century, the Angles and the Saxons who were at all bookish distinctly felt themselves to be in the Roman tradition stemming from the old Empire, and they carried on that tradition in their particular way. It was now, however, a Roman-Christian tradition, and the utility of things coming from the past was judged in terms of Christian philosophy. Classical rhetoric was by no means rejected as useless, but parts of it were apparently considered less useful than others. Anglo-Saxon law and government were so different from those of the time of Quintilian or Cicero that forensic rhetoric, as applied to legal proceedings, public speaking before the Senate and the like, was almost ignored in its purest form, although there is ample evidence that it had been adapted to other types of public address. In modified guise it appeared in sermons and poems, where persuasion and influencing an audience were still matters of dedicated concern.

173

One must, of course, always keep in mind that the study of
vernacular literature in England cannot be separated from the
study of the total learned culture, which was by definition a form
of Latin Christian culture. There was constant influence between
Latin and vernacular literature extending throughout the period
we call Anglo-Saxon, and there are few works indeed which do
not evince some coloration from a well-developed Latin culture.
Beginning with Aldhelm in the late seventh century and Bede
in the early eighth, we have good evidence of the extensive
knowledge of classical learning in England, and also of the free
adaptation and modification of that learning to fit the English
situation. In a manner perhaps emblematic of the larger English
cultural picture at the time, Aldhelm drew much of his early
classical learning from Irish sources. Though contemporary Irish
testimony is scanty, nearly all modern researchers agree that the
Irish monks valued, read and copied manuscripts of Roman poets,
grammarians and rhetoricians. This interest in earlier Latin writers,
whether pagan or Christian, they sometimes passed on to the
English students and scholars they influenced, although the English seemed slightly more suspicious of the pagan Romans than
the Irish.[1] Nevertheless, the textual history of many writers such
as Juvenal, Ovid, Persius, Priscian, Cicero (*De inventione*) and
Martianus Capella often reveals that some of the earliest manuscripts we possess were written in insular script, whether Irish or
Anglo-Saxon, all of which indicates that men in the British Isles
not only had these books but thought enough of them to copy
them.

It is by now well known that in late Roman times, certainly
by the fourth century, the teachers of language and poetry, called
grammatici, had appropriated parts of the discipline of the
rhetores. Especially the aspects of language manipulation and
figurative thought, which orators had long considered part of
elocutio, were found to be useful to grammarians, who were
concerned with a full understanding of poetry. Grammar books

---

1. The flavor of this wariness can be felt in a passage of Bede's commentary on a
portion of *Esdras*: *Sal in palatio comedunt Samaritani cum haeretici sapore mun-
danae philosophiae cum suavitate rhetoricae, cum versutia dialecticae artis instituunt.*
Quoted by Pierre Riché, *Education et culture dans l'Occident barbare, VIe-VIIIe
siècles* (Paris, 1973), p. 439. Riché grants that Aldhelm, Bede and Boniface fostered
grammar and poetry, but they were wary of studies that became enmeshed with
pagan philosophy.

from the *Ars Maior* of Aelius Donatus forward frequently contained sections expounding the proper use of the rhetorical phenomena called *schemata* and *tropi*. The schools founded in England during the seventh and eighth centuries, at Canterbury, Monkwearmouth, York and numerous less famous places, found it essential to begin education of youngsters with grammar before they went on to rhetoric and other subjects of the trivium and quadrivium. Englishmen needed first of all to learn the Latin language as well as a method for understanding the thought of the Scriptures and other Christian writing. Support for learning the rhetorical figures came from Augustine's *De doctrina christiana*, Cassiodorus' *Institutiones*, Isidore's *Etymologiae* and elsewhere,[2] and English education from the first was undoubtedly established on the general lines laid down by these works.[3] The best grammarian from the past, Priscian, was well known in England from the seventh century onward, and although he included no separate section corresponding to Donatus' *Barbarismus*,[4] Priscian constantly quotes classical poets whose language necessitates knowledge of rhetorical figures. Aldhelm, the earliest of a group of writers who contributed to a small renaissance in eighth-century England, demonstrates an extraordinary variety and scope of grammatical learning. His original works, *De virginitate, De laudibus virginibus, Epistola ad Acircium* and some letters, borrow from Priscian, Donatus, and from a flock of grammarians who commented on Donatus' book—Servius, Sergius, Pompeius and Julian of Toledo.[5] Aldhelm may possibly have used another work of Priscian, the *Praeexercitamina*, which is an adaptation of a rhetorical book of Hermogenes, explaining such things as *fabula, narratio, descriptio, sententia, expolitio* (*usus*), *loci communes*

---

2. E. R. Curtius, *European Literature and the Latin Middle Ages*, trans. by W. R. Trask (New York, 1953), pp. 40 ff.

3. J. J. Campbell, "Knowledge of Rhetorical Figures in Anglo-Saxon England," *JEGP* 66 (1967), pp. 3–9.

4. The latter part of Donatus' *Ars Maior* is found in some medieval manuscripts separated from the early section on the eight parts of speech. This portion is usually called the *Barbarismus*, though it not only discusses barbarisms, solecisms and the like, but gives a full presentation of the *schemata lexeos*, those rhetorical figures which grammarians thought useful in analyzing poetry. See J. J. Murphy, "The Rhetorical Lore of the *Boceras* in Byhrtferth's [sic] Manual," *Philological Essays in Old and Middle English Language and Literature in Honour of Herbert Meritt*, ed. by J. L. Rosier (The Hague, 1970), pp. 111–124.

5. M. Manitius, "Zu Aldhelm und Beda," *Wiener Sitzungsberichte* 113 (1886): 591–600.

and the like.[6] In fact Aldhelm's poems are so full of the fruits of his study of rhetorical manipulations of language that many modern critics find him tedious and difficult to read, but of course twentieth century anti-rhetorical criticism is inappropriate when assessing a writer whose epoch obviously admired and imitated the most ornate and rhetorical Latin poets.

Bede followed Aldhelm by a few years, and although his interest in rhetoric was less ostentatious, it was no less strong. Not satisfied merely to use and teach Donatus' *Barbarismus,* he rewrote part of it and published it as *De schematibus et tropis.* Bede's little work was designed to assure the proper understanding of sacred texts, and he found it essential that to this end all students should be conscious of the various unusual configurations of language and meaning which the grammar and rhetoric textbooks had categorized and codified. Furthermore, the classical grammarians had also had the study of poetic metrics in their domain, so following this tradition Bede also wrote a *De arte metrica.*[7] Although his extensive, total *oeuvre* was largely exegetical, scientific and historical, Bede apparently remained a teacher of the young much of his life and insisted that they learn grammar and rhetoric at an early stage, as well as psalms and prayers.

Three other Englishmen wrote grammar books during the eighth century, but undoubtedly the most important was the great teacher Alcuin. His learning was wide-ranging and varied; in a pleasant, informal poem he left us an idea of the extremely broad scope of the library holdings at York, where he was educated. He mentions the *rhetor Tullius* as one of the authors on the shelves, but we cannot be sure, of course, which book or books of Cicero he meant. When he came to write his own book on rhetoric, however, his chief source was *De inventione,* supplemented by materials from Julius Victor and others.[8] He casts his treatise in the form of a dialogue between Charlemagne and himself (Albinus), and the

---

6. D. L. Clark, "Rhetoric and Literature in the Middle Ages," *QJS* 45 (1959): 19–28.

7. Aldhelm had also written an account of Latin metrics to which he had appended a large collection of riddles illustrating various metrical patterns (*Epistola ad Acircium*). Thus he also might be thought to fulfill the complete role of a *grammaticus.*

8. For a summary of sources, see W. S. Howell, ed., *The Rhetoric of Alcuin and Charlemagne* (New York, 1965). Additional sources are added with certain demurrers in L. Wallach, *Alcuin and Charlemagne* (Ithaca, N. Y., 1968), pp. 36–47.

substance of the five divisions of Ciceronian rhetoric is expounded in the course of questions, answers and comments between the two. One Ciceronian idea Alcuin develops in a unique way, namely that the good rhetorician must also be a good man promoting truth rather than sophistry: Alcuin ends his book with a short treatise on the four classical virtues necessary for the complete orator, but in his hands they are made components of Christ's summation of the commandments (Matthew 22, 37–40).[9] Of the theoretical materials concerned with rhetoric in the Anglo-Saxon period, Alcuin's rhetoric, written after he had moved to the continent, is the only one chiefly concerned with judicial causes. Such material would seem to be intractable since the Roman legal system on which classical doctrine was based had largely disappeared. However, a recent scholar, Luitpold Wallach, has shown that Alcuin cleverly modified his precepts in the direction of Frankish law prevailing in Charlemagne's kingdom at the end of the eighth century.[10] As to content, Alcuin's book at least touches on *inventio, dispositio, elocutio, memoria* and *pronuntiatio,* but it must be said that his treatment of invention is far more complete than that of any other element. The components of *elocutio* which so interested the grammarians were given short shrift, and memory was granted a bare nod.

The works of early scholars such as Aldhelm, Bede, Boniface, Tatwine, and Alcuin give us many clues as to the older books which were available in their libraries and consequently available to other unknown Englishmen from the eighth century forward. The fact that original authors on rhetorical subjects did not appear in the ninth and tenth centuries should not make us think that simple students and devout readers did not study the books at their disposal even though they did not presume to write new books to supplement or supercede the standard authors. The most standard of all was probably Isidore of Seville's *Etymologiae.* The usefulness of this great compendium, with its brief and clear summary of the entire disciplines of grammar, rhetoric, dialectic and the other liberal arts, was apparently recognized soon after it was written. The English were using it long before the seventh

9. The full title usually associated with this book is *Disputatio de rhetorica et de virtutibus.*

10. Wallach, pp. 73–82 and 99–101. An interesting idea is further suggested by Wallach: the entire dialogue which provides the bulk of the rhetoric is couched in the same epistolary form which later writers on the *artes dictaminis* propounded, including an *invocatio, captatio benevolentiae* and *conclusio.* See pp. 48–59.

century ended. One of Isidore's main sources had been Cassiodorus' *Institutiones*, a book which also sketched out a complete
education in the liberal arts. This, too, was present in some
English libraries. The English made more use, however, of another
of Cassiodorus' works, the *Commentary on the Psalms*. This
valuable treatise contains large quantities of rhetorical information
scattered among the explanations of individual lines and sentences
in the psalter. Alcuin's student Rabanus Maurus continued the
liberal arts tradition in the ninth century, and his *De institutione
clericorum* is very explicit regarding the Christian uses to which
any learning is to be put.[11] Grammar books of Priscian and
Donatus were also omnipresent,[12] as well as those of many other
grammarians such as Diomedes, Charisius and Probus, whose
books are almost forgotten today. Many Englishmen who were
educated from such theoretical textbooks apparently used their
education merely to understand sacred texts rather than to write
new works imitating or explicating them, but during the ninth,
tenth and eleventh centuries we find a great body of vernacular
literature which would probably not be as it is unless its authors
had studied Latin grammar and rhetoric.

The public discourse most prevalent in Old English seems to
have been the sermon or homily. Of course this situation may be
more apparent than real, for it is perfectly possible that *scops*
composing poetry in halls like Hrothgar's, or even while riding
on horseback, reached a larger audience and reached it more
frequently than did the preachers. The proof of such a proposition is mostly conjectural, whereas the sheer quantity and scope
of homilectic literature still extant gives clear indication of its

---

11. See J. J. Murphy, "Saint Augustine and Rabanus Maurus: The Genesis of
Medieval Rhetoric," *Western Speech* 31 (1967): 88–96. The overt apologia for rhetoric in Augustine's terms appears first in Rabanus, although the same attitude had
been implicit in Bede's and Alcuin's and even Isidore's treatment of rhetoric.

12. Aelfric, in writing his bilingual grammar in the late tenth century, claims
to be following Priscian. However, at the end of the body of the work, where indeed
he had made much use of Priscian, he adds brief mention of the thirty divisions of
grammar in the tradition of Donatus. It is interesting, though, that he was actually
using Isidore's adaptation of the *Ars Maior* in the *Etymologiae*, which includes such
topics as *prosa, metra, fabula* and *historia* which were not covered by Donatus. For
a detailed study of Aelfric's grammar, see D. A. Bullough, "The Educational Tradition in England from Alfred to Aelfric: Teaching *Utriusque Linguae*," *La Scuola
nell'occidente latino dell'alto medioevo, Settimane di studio del Centro italiano di
studi sull'alto medioevo* 19 (1972): 453–494.

pervasive presence in Old English culture. The patristic models most frequently copied were the homilies of St. Augustine and St. Gregory, but new composition both in Latin and the vernacular went on during all four centuries of the Old English period.

For the preacher, the problems of *inventio* were partially simplified, since his main goal was usually instruction in the facts, meaning and morality of the Bible. Ingenuity of mind was naturally still required, but passable sermons could be produced with either a little or a lot of that quality. The *dispositio* presented slightly more difficult challenges, since no set form or structure had been established by Old English times to serve as a safe and secure guide. The *artes praedicandi* which were written in the later Middle Ages were doubtless comforting to preachers in that they provided prescribed norms which one could learn and follow with assurance. In Old English times, the thematic sermon described by the *artes* was occasionally written and delivered, but there is no evidence that its rules of disposition were more prized than any other. Also the structural distinctions made in more recent times between homilies and sermons were apparently not noticed during the period. *Sermo* appears in some manuscripts as a rubric before things we might call homilies, and collections which modern editions label homilies often contain many works of the sermon type. To Old English preachers, as to the writers of the patristic period, *homilia* was simply the Greek word for a sermon, with no reference to special structure or content. In practice, the Old English homilists pursued their art in close imitation of such earlier homilists as Ambrose, Augustine, Caesarius and Gregory. Some Old English homilies are direct translations of a Latin source, while many, perhaps most, are made up of selective borrowings translated or paraphrased from patristic sermons.[13] Thus the notions Old English preachers had of arrangement or structure of their material probably came as much from *imitatio* as from study of rhetoric books, though of course both avenues of learning were open to them.

A thorough study of *dispositio* in homiletic writing has yet to be made, and it is devoutly to be desired, but a number of

---

13. For an enlightening discussion of some methods of translation and adaptation, see J. E. Cross, "The Literate Anglo-Saxon—On Sources and Dissemination," *Proceedings of the British Academy* 58 (1972): 67–100.

valuable beginnings have been made. Marcia Dalbey, in a study
of the Blickling Homilies, found that the typical pattern of arrangement was: *exordium, narratio, argumentum* and *peroratio*.[14]
She uses the term *argumentum* for the body of the homily because the *confirmatio* usually exists without any trace of a balancing *refutatio*. Naturally a preaching situation seldom produced
a need for *refutatio*, as a legal proceeding might. Ms. Dalbey
finds that in nearly all cases the *narratio* is quite simple, usually
no more than a reading of a Biblical text in translation, and the
argumentum consists often in simply amplifying and expanding
the ideas of the text. The *peroratio* in the particular homilies she
studies usually takes the form of an earnest exhortation and
application of the moral ideas previously developed to the immediate audience. At the beginning, there is very often no more
to the *exordium* than an *invocatio, Men þa leofostan,* and almost
never is there an extensive effort to do what the classical rhetoric
books might call *captare benevolentiam*. Again this is easily
explained in terms of adapting rhetoric to the preaching situation:
a well-disposed audience was probably assumed by the Old English homilist. Actually the *Rhetorica ad Herennium* had taught
that the artful capturing of goodwill was most necessary in the
type of *principium* called *insinuatio,* where a skeptical audience
was expected.

The Anglo-Saxon writer who left the largest, most varied and most
skillful collection of homilies was Aelfric, whose works demand a
slightly fuller discussion. A recent scholar, Peter Clemoes, claims
that "Aelfric owed to a training in Latin rhetorical methods traditional techniques of arranging his material and applying formal
stylistic devices."[15] Doubtless this is true, and probably the best
evidence of his total mastery of rhetoric is that he ignores the textbook precepts when he wishes and uses them freely when they serve
his purposes. Aelfric seldom begins with a normal *exordium*; even
a simple address such as *Men þa leofostan* or *leofan men* is often
omitted. In this matter he was possibly following the practice of
some patristic homilists, for St. Augustine's homilies seldom begin

---

14. Marcia Dalbey, *Structure and Style in the Blickling Homilies for the Tem-
porale,* Diss. (University of Illinois 1968), p. 11.
15. Peter Clemoes, "Aelfric," in *Continuations and Beginnings,* ed. by E. G.
Stanley (London, 1966), p. 193.

with an *invocatio*, and Bede sometimes inserts his *Fratres carissimi* in the middle of his first sentence and sometimes neglects it altogether.

A somewhat exceptional case in the Aelfric canon is found at the beginning of the homily *De falsis diis*.[16] Following a Latin text, he begins with an opening greeting, then continues with a statement about the unity of God (based on *Ephesians* IV), which looks very much like the protheme of the university sermon described by the *artes praedicandi* in the thirteenth and fourteenth centuries. This is followed by a brief prayer—*sy him wuldor a to worulde, amen*—which again fits the pattern for the opening of a thematic sermon. As his development of the *argumentum* begins, however, he departs widely from the prescribed form for the university sermon, though it must be said that his own rhetorical structure is cogent and unified, producing one of his more elaborate and effective sermons.

An Aelfrician homily often begins directly with a *narratio*, either explaining the feast being celebrated that particular day or translating the portion of Scripture which serves as the pericope for the day. The *confirmatio* or *argumentum* follows hard upon, usually tied to the Biblical passage either closely (sometimes with methodical verse-by-verse explanation) or loosely, developing ideas stemming in some way from the pericope. Frequently Aelfric stops to explicate the *tacnas* or figures which require allegorical interpretation, for he is often conscious that his audience will misunderstand unless he clarifies the *gastlice andgit* of his material. Even more frequently, however, he introduces *amplificatio* consisting of direct application of the overt ideas in the narrative to his audience and their lives. Although Aelfric may omit any attempt at capturing the sympathy and good feeling of his hearers at the beginning of the homily, throughout the *confirmatio* he constantly speaks in a fatherly and loving tone which accomplishes the process of creating responsiveness from the audience in a continuing and pervasive way.

Although the bulk of an Aelfrician sermon is devoted to the *confirmatio*, one cannot easily dogmatize about its content. In the homily on the passion of St. Stephen Protomartyr, the *confirmatio* deals with the difficult matter of how to achieve the sort

---

16. John C. Pope, ed., *Homilies of Aelfric*, Early English Text Society 260 (London, 1968), II: 677.

of boundless love which allows one to love one's enemies. At one point Aelfric decides to use the technique of *confutatio,* thus:

> Nu cwyð sum man ongean ðas rædinge, Ne mæg ic minne feond lufian, ðone ðe ic dæghwonlice wælhreowne togeanes me geseo. Eala ðu man, þu sceawast hwæt ðin broðor þe dyde, and ðu ne sceawast hwæt ðu Gode gedydest.[17]

Aelfric then proceeds to remind this unidentified man of his earlier sins which had been forgiven. The imagined doubter continues:

> Micel gedeorf bið me þæt ic minne feond lufie, and for ðone gebidde þe me hearmes cepð. Ne wiðcweðe we þæt hit micel gedeorf sy; ac gif hit is hefigtime on ðyssere worulde, hit becymð to micelre mede on ðære toweardan. Witodlice þurh ðines feondes lufe þu bist Godes freond.

This management of *refutatio* also demonstrates his command of the technique of *concessio* as well as neat verbal antithesis. His use of figures of thought as well as figures of diction is always sure and discreet. Although he sometimes borrows them directly from the Latin homily he is adapting, at others he supplies them in his original composition where they did not occur in his source, and at still other times he eschews elaborate rhetoric completely in favor of direct, simple statement. Peter Clemoes shows that Aelfric's mastery of the arts of discourse was so complete that he knew exactly when to copy Latin devices and when not to; above all, he "never made the mistake of trying to make English behave like Latin," especially with regard to syntax.[18]

Unlike his relaxed and varied treatment of the *exordium* and *confirmatio,* Aelfric never neglects the *peroratio.* To be sure, sometimes it may be very brief; the end of the homily dedicating a church to St. Michael[19] consists only of the words, *se ðe leofað and rixað a on ecnesse. Amen,* tacked onto a declarative sentence which forms part of the *confirmatio.* Far more often, however, he is less laconic. Fairly typical is the *peroratio* of the homily for the seventeenth Sunday after Pentecost:

> Uton we biddan þone Aelmihtigan Fæder, seðe us þurh his wisdom geworhte, and þurh his Halgan Gast geliffæste, þæt he ðurh ðone ylcan

---

17. Benjamin Thorpe, ed. *The Homilies of the Anglo-Saxon Church* (London, 1894), I: 54. This passage is also quoted by Clemoes, p. 192.

18. Clemoes, p. 202.

19. Thorpe, I: 518.

Gast us do ure synna forgyfennysse, swa swa he us ðurh his ænne an-
cennedan Sunu fram deofles ðeowte alysde.

Sy lof and wuldor þam ecan Fæder, seðe næfre ne ongann, and his anum
Bearne, seðe æfre of him is, and þam Halgan Gaste, seðe æfre is of him
bam, hi ðry an Aelmihtig God untodæledlic, a on ecnysse rixigende.
Amen.[20]

Towards the end of this homily, which is earlier about the raising
of the dead boy at Naim, Aelfric is drawn into a discussion of
the Trinity, its nature and operation. We can see that his trini-
tarian emphasis continues throughout the exhortation of the
extended *peroratio.*

There were great divergences from rhetorical norms in the wide
variety of patristic sources imitated by Aelfric. He knew and used
constantly homilies of St. Augustine, Ambrose, Bede and Caesarius of Arles, as well as those of several Carolingian homilists.
Augustine of course had been an extremely skilled rhetorician
and quite consciously had made an adaptation of classical precepts, which he partially explains in the fourth book of *De
doctrina christiana.* In his homilies he very judiciously used the
three styles, *gravis, mediocris* and *adtenuata,* at appropriate
times,[21] and virtually all the *exornationes* discussed by the rhetoricians appear from time to time in his writing.[22] Bede also used
his rhetoric in this Augustinian way, always directing it solely
toward strengthening a doctrinal idea. A fairly typical Bedan
homily is *Homelia I, 7* on a *lectio* from St. Luke 2, 15–20.[23] He
omits the opening address, as Augustine usually did, but throughout the homily he often speaks intimately to *fratres dilectissimi*
or *fratres mei.* A combined *exordium* and *narratio* paraphrases
the story of the shepherds' visit at the Nativity, noting its mystical
as well as literal meaning. In the *confirmatio* he gives a step-by-
step explication of the six verses of the pericope, using a number
of other passages from the Bible to clarify phrases such as *verbum
videntes* and others. His *conclusio* is an earnest exhortation to

---

20. Thorpe, I: 500.

21. See J. B. Eskridge, *The Influence of Cicero upon Augustine* (Menasha, Wisc.,
1912).

22. See Sister M. Inviolata Barry, *St. Augustine, The Orator,* Catholic University
of America, Patristic Studies 6 (Washington, D. C., 1924).

23. *Bedae Venerabilis Opera, Pars III,* Corpus Christianorum, Series Latina 122
(Turnholt, 1955), pp. 46–51.

virtue, ending with the *qui vivit et regnat* formula. Both the arrangement and the diction of this homily are simple to the point of austerity. He did, of course, use a number of different techniques in other homilies; Philip West notes that in Bede's four Christmas homilies, one is in a style which could be called *adtenuata,* while three are well developed with *amplificatio* and *exornationes,* even including a use of *refutatio* along with *confirmatio,*[24] as indeed Aelfric was later to do in the St. Stephen homily. Thus the models used by the Abbot of Eynsham encourage the same kind of freedom of choice which he habitually employed.

Aelfric's varied practices in the *dispositio* of his homilies can nearly always be paralleled in one place or another in the earlier homilists he used as sources, although there is one case where he departs markedly from a normal rhetorical structure as it was presented in the textbooks. The homily which begins the first series of Catholic Homiles is called *De initio creaturae,* and consists essentially of an extremely long *narratio.* With occasional comments on doctrinal and figurative matters, he tells in cursive, chronological form the events from the creation of the world through the fall of the rebellious angels, the defection of Adam, the story of Noah, the exodus from Egypt, the birth of Christ, his ministry and crucifixion, to his resurrection and ascension. At the end, there is a very brief, hortatory *conclusio.* Despite its peculiarities, this work must have been used and delivered as the other homilies were, although it certainly would have lengthened the service considerably. It has been pointed out that even here his general inspiration was probably Augustinian, though not strictly homilectic; precisely this kind of extended *narratio* was recommended as the first step in instruction by Augustine's *De catechizandis rudibus.*[25] Furthermore, it should be mentioned that Aelfric's narration throughout is interesting and extremely skillful from the point of view of verbal rhetoric.

Aelfric has often been praised for his use of language in creating smooth and graceful prose. Lavish encomiums as well as specific analyses of his style abound. Although he would sometimes use rather elaborate figures of speech, virtually all critics emphasize his

---

24. Philip J. West, "Liturgical Style and Structure in Bede's Christmas Homilies," *American Benedictine Review* 23 (1972), pp. 424–438.

25. Virginia Day, "The Influence of the Catechetical *narratio* on Old English and some other medieval literature," *Anglo-Saxon England* 3 (1974): 51–61.

preference for simple, unaffected speech. Ann Nichols has recently demonstrated how consciously he chose the "brief style," characterized by more *abbreviatio* than *amplificatio*, by closely scrutinizing Aelfric's statement in his Latin preface to the *Lives of the Saints*.[26] The technical rhetorical terms he uses make clear his realization of the various stylistic paths open to him. Ms. Nichols' claim that he consistently avoided *amplificatio*, however, must be modified slightly in that he often expanded material and ideas from his sources for purposes of clarity. She is certainly right of course that he regularly eschews inflation of words. It is rare indeed to find even a short passage in Aelfric which one would consider *oratio gravis*.

Several scholars have used a homily on St. Agnes, which Aelfric translated from the work of St. Ambrose, for purposes of studying his rhetorical practices. Dorothy Bethurum's study concludes that he was very cautious in copying verbal effects; although he sometimes does imitate Ambrose's rhetorical locutions, he more often converts them into more natural, straightforward English.[27] Similar conclusions were developed in some detail by Frances Lipp.[28] Here is a passage from Ambrose's homily which Ms. Lipp juxtaposes with Aelfric's translation:

> Dii autem tui aut aerei sunt,
>   ex quibus cacabi melius fiunt ad usus hominum:
> aut lapidei,
>   ex quibus plateae melius sternuntur ad evadendum lutum.
> Divinitas autem non in lapidibus vanis habitat,
>   sed in coelis:
> non in aere aut aliquo metallo,
>   sed in regno superno consistit.

> þine godas syndon   agotene of are,
> of þam ðe man wyrcð   wynsume fate,
> oððe hi synd stænene   mid þam þe man stræta wyrcð.
> Nis na godes wonung   on ðam grægum stanum,
> ne on ærenum wecgum,   ac he wunað on heofonum.[29]

Although Ms. Lipp uses this comparison for slightly different purposes, one can readily see that Ambrose carefully constructed his idea out of two long cola governed by chiasmus and antithesis, using

---

26. Ann E. Nichols, "Aelfric and the Brief Style," *JEGP* 70 (1971): 1–12.
27. Dorothy Bethurum, "The Form of Aelfric's Lives of the Saints," *SP* 29 (1932): 515–533.
28. Frances R. Lipp, "Aelfric's Old English Prose Style," *SP* 66 (1969): 689–718.
29. Lipp, p. 706.

repeated anaphora and homoeoptoton. Aelfric's English rendering copies the chiasmus and antithesis but ignores the anaphora; he adds, however, alliteration and much more homoeoptoton of dative case endings. As Ms. Lipp points out elsewhere, Aelfric frequently uses homoeoptoton to emphasize pauses and reinforce parallelism. One can certainly agree with her that "Aelfric's indebtedness to Latin prose for many of his habits of style is unquestionable,"[30] and he had learned its techniques so well that he could freely reject them in copying sources or supply them from his own fund whenever he wished.

A striking aural effect of Aelfric's prose which has been much discussed is its strongly rhythmic nature. Not always, but often, Aelfric constructs units of speech which seem to fall naturally into two roughly equal parts, and sometimes the two parts are connected by alliterating words. Some years ago, G. H. Gerould suggested that Aelfric consciously used the Latin techniques of *cursus* in creating endings for his rhythmic units in English.[31] Several later writers have demurred from this idea, most notably Sherman Kuhn.[32] Although such artificial and formalized clause endings do sometimes occur, Kuhn successfully shows that their appearance is rather sporadic and even then the rhythmic patterns produced are quite natural to normal Old English linguistic practice and doubtless could be produced by speakers not attempting rhetorical ornamentation.

Much of the rhythmic effect of Aelfric's consciously controlled periods and cola is produced by the alliteration which adds emphasis and cohesion to his two-member units. Long ago it was noted that these units are somewhat similar to the two members of the classic Old English poetic line. Recently John Pope has discussed the matter in detail,[33] concluding that Aelfric's alliteration is indeed governed by patterns that are not quite fixed rules. It does not seem to depend on any suggestion about the use of *paromoeon* in the rhetoric or grammar books, and it is not nearly so regularized as the alliterative demands of the verse system.

---

30. Lipp, p. 718.

31. G. H. Gerould, "Abbot Aelfric's Rhythmic Prose," *MP* 22 (1924–25): 353–366.

32. Sherman Kuhn, "Cursus in Old English: Rhetorical Ornament or Linguistic Phenomenon?" *Speculum* 47 (1972): 188–206.

33. Pope, I, pp. 123 ff.

Although the rhythms Aelfric creates in sentence after sentence may well have been distantly influenced by the sounds of poetic units,[34] they are nearly always much more expansive and far freer in the use of unstressed syllables, even when (infrequently) the alliteration might correspond to poetic practice.

Another Old English homilist whose prose has been much admired and studied is Wulfstan, Archbishop of York and Bishop of Worcester. Wulfstan was also inordinately fond of alliteration, and he quite often arranged his syntax into two-member cola. It is interesting, however, that even when he used techniques similar to Aelfric's, his alliterative patterns and also his rhythmic units differ markedly from those of the West Saxon abbot. There are cases where we can demonstrate that Wulfstan had a homily of Aelfric's before him as he adapted it for his own delivery, yet he changed wording liberally to produce his own particular style of rhythmic, alliterative prose.[35]

Wulfstan's most famous homily, *Sermo ad Anglos,* has been exhaustively discussed by scholars; it is remarkable for its mixture of elaborate rhetoric fused with real passion on the part of the preacher. None of his other homilies show such concentrated and effective use of persuasive homiletic skill, yet all the extant writing of Wulfstan, legal as well as homiletic, shows a profound grasp of technical rhetoric. Dorothy Bethurum has studied this aspect of his style better than anyone else up to the present, and she concludes:

> Indeed Wulfstan shows himself to be a trained rhetorician familiar with the manuals of rhetoric available in his time—Cicero's *Orator* and *De Oratore,* the *Rhetorica ad Herennium* which from the fourth century until recently was attributed to Cicero, Alcuin's *De Rhetorica et de Virtutibus,* and Augustine's *De Doctrina Christiana,* Book IV, besides Bede's *De Arte Metrica* and *De Schematibus et Tropis Scripturae Liber,* Isidore's epitome in *Etymologiae* II, 1–21, and Rabanus' *De Clericorum Institutione.* It is not possible to say just which manuals he studied, but his practice leaves no doubt about his training.[36]

Even if Ms. Bethurum's list is slightly overenthusiastic (and that

---

34. See also Lipp, p. 718.

35. See Angus McIntosh, "Wulfstan's Prose," *Proceedings of the British Academy* 35 (1949): 109–142.

36. Dorothy Bethurum, "Wulfstan," *Continuations and Beginnings,* ed. by E. G. Stanley (London, 1966), p. 230.

last sentence tends to dampen its effect), she goes on to demonstrate convincingly his sophisticated use of the three styles. He used the medium far more frequently than the grand or the humble, but he delighted in such stylistic figures as *traductio, conversio, similiter cadens* and *similiter desinens, contentio, gradatio,* and many others. Ms. Bethurum's edition of Wulfstan's homilies contains many explanatory notes discussing specific passages where he uses diverse schemes and tropes.

One homily of Wulfstan's is unusual in the corpus of Old English prose in that it contains a clear case of the use of *partitio* in its structure. *Be Cristendome,* homily Xc in Bethurum's edition, makes use of a number of sources, including works of Amalarius of Metz and St. Pirmin, yet the final arrangement and wording are his own. He begins with the terse *invocatio, Leofan Men,* and a brief *exordium* stating the great need for all men to follow the precepts of Christianity and to know what it means to claim the name Christian. The *narratio* is also extremely brief—a quotation from the first epistle of St. John II, 6—with a translation. There follows a statement which indeed turns out to be a foreshadowing of the divisions of the *confirmatio,* which forms the bulk of the homily:

> And ðeah hwa cweðe þæt he on Crist rihtlice gelyfe 7 nele his larum ne his lagum folgian, he lihð him sylfum; 7 Crist sylf eac on his godspelle swyttollice þus spæc: *Si diligitis me, mandata mea seruate.* Gyf ge me lufian, he cwæð, folgiað minum larum, forðam se me ne lufiað na þe nele minum larum rihtlice fyligean. Nu age we þearfe þe cristene syndon þæt we georne his larum 7 his lagum fyligean.[37]

The extended *confirmatio* which follows takes up in turn the laws of Christ, including the Ten Commandments, the love of Christ and the belief by which one participates in the *ecclesia,* the sins possible to those who follow the devil's lore rather than Christ's, the path of repentance for those sinners who eagerly wish to forswear error and reform themselves by loving Christ truly. We have here the positive aspects of calling oneself Christian, the negative aspects, then a return to the positive. It seems clear that the *partitio* adumbrated the arrangement which Wulfstan later followed. Furthermore, the homily comes fairly close to being con-

37. Dorothy Bethurum, ed., *The Homilies of Wulfstan,* Oxford, 1957, pp. 200–201.

structed in the manner prescribed by the later medieval *artes praedicandi*. Incidentally, toward the end, immediately before the hortatory *conclusio*, a brief passage on Christ's mercy to sinners looks very much like the sort of *digressio* mentioned in Robert of Basevorn's *Forma praedicandi*. It grows naturally out of the previous discussion and leads smoothly into the *peroratio* which follows. Wulfstan the man led an extremely busy life and had many duties as legal writer and counsellor as well as homilist; thus some of his homilies may seem brief and almost perfunctory. Yet when he used his full powers, as in *Be Cristendome* and *Sermo Lupi*, his rhetorical skill allowed him to construct moving and convincing sermons.

When we turn to Old English poetry with rhetoric in mind, we must avoid a number of pitfalls. Some aspects of the Germanic poetic form distinctly did not owe anything to classical Greek and Roman learning. The traditional unrimed, alliterative, four-stress line, for instance, undoubtedly came from a tradition untouched by Mediterranean influence. Various stylistic techniques such as parallelism or variation and the peculiar type of metaphor known as the kenning also have often been claimed as "purely" Germanic. Much has been made of the oral nature of Germanic poetics, with its formulaic phrases which were supposedly learned by unlettered *scops* for ease in composing poems extempore. Such may well have been the mode of composition in prehistoric times, but scholars now seem to agree that by the time of the extant poetry, the formulaic style was by no means incompatible with written composition accomplished silently by erudite men in a scriptorium.

Many Old English poets, including Cynewulf, had Latin educations, with all the training in grammar and rhetoric which that would imply. Men like Aldhelm and Alcuin wrote their verse in Latin itself, imitating the forms of earlier Roman and Christian poets. Other poets translated Latin works, both prose and poetry, into good Old English verse, displaying complete command of both the native formulaic verse system and the learned techniques of rhetoric. The factor of imitation is not to be discounted in this connection, for doubtless the educated poets learned as much about style by reading poems of Prudentius, Sedulius, Virgil and Persius as they did from theoretical techniques taught by the manuals of Donatus and Isidore. Once a poet had learned the craft of writing, however, he would almost inevitably use all his skill from whatever source, whether he was paraphrasing a saint's life or retelling an ancient heroic tale.

The kind of poetic seen in the *artes poetriae* of the twelfth century had not yet developed in the Old English period, but definite moves were being made toward it. There is in Old English poetry no very good evidence that poets embraced many elements of forensic rhetoric, since many of its techniques tended toward dialectic and logic. It is difficult to demonstrate, for instance, that the rules of *dispositio* were followed at all closely. Poems do indeed have clearly defined beginnings, middles and ends, which might possibly be called *exordia, confirmationes* and *perorationes,* but beyond this, rhetorical structure is doubtful. Naturally enough, poets were more interested in poetry than in prose speeches, and they found that the late Roman grammarians had already skimmed off the elements from the discipline of rhetoric which were most useful to poets. Moreover, Bede had isolated that section of Donatus which spoke most directly to imaginative Christian writing in his *De schematibus,* even updating it for medieval use by adding a fuller treatment of *allegoria.*[38] It is in the area of figurative language and figurative thought that rhetoric entered the mainstream of the Old English poetic tradition.

Yet here there is another pitfall. We must realize that factors of figurative language can usually be found operating in the language in its most natural state; that is, a completely untutored person competent in his own language has the resources for producing practically all the *figurae verborum* and *figurae sententiarum.* Originators of the study of rhetoric, before or after Aristotle, had invented very little; rather they had described phenomena which they found in the speech of the "best" speakers. Of course, people who are naturally endowed with quick and imaginative minds invent more colorful speech and ingenious thoughts than clods do, but their raw material always lies in the linguistic structures they have inherited. Thus in analyzing the schemes and tropes one finds in Old English poetry, there is always the possibility that a given figure may equally well be the result of the poet's instinctive use of his native linguistic tradition as the product of his following learned precepts acquired during his education. For example, an omnipresent feature of Old English poetic style is often labeled "variation"; one type manifests itself in

---

38. It has been insufficiently recognized that Bede's additions toward the end of his book reflect concepts which grew up in exegesis during the fourth, fifth and sixth centuries and which are quite foreign to classical precepts.

multiple appositives—words or phrases meaning roughly the same thing, and syntactically parallel, but differing slightly in specific reference and certainly in connotation. Books like Isidore's *Etymologiae* or Donatus' *Barbarismus* might use the terms *synonomia* or *schesis onomaton* for this phenomenon, but it could easily be argued that an Old English poet learned the technique from the Germanic tradition stretching back into prehistory long before there was any contact with Latin learning. Thus variation may have, in some cases, nothing whatsoever to do with the poet's education in rhetoric.

Solid proof for an exact description of the untouched, native Germanic tradition is difficult to come by, but probably most modern scholars feel, with or without proof, that variation existed in the Old English poetic style independent of Latin learning. Similar arguments can be adduced for many other schemes and tropes, but it must be admitted that some of them represent rare locutions which very seldom occur in natural, unstudied speech. When a number of such figures appear in the same poem, quite obviously used with conscious skill to create impressive literature, the likelihood of the poet's having a background of Latin education is tremendously increased, although at our present stage of knowledge any dogmatic or extravagant claims are unwise.[39] Ms. Bethurum, for instance, has found extremely interesting evidence of alliteration and parallelism in some very dry Anglo-Saxon laws describing ancient legal practices, and it is unlikely that *paromoeon* or *synonomia* have any pertinence to them.[40]

In a bilingual culture such as that of the Anglo-Saxons, where many English poets had Latin educations, we have some avenues of testing influence, since the poets often translated Latin prose and poetry into English verse. There is a tiny poem in two different manuscripts, where a Latin version and its English equivalent are placed side by side:

---

39. Since this was written, an article of J. H. Bonner has come to hand: "Toward a Unified Critical Approach to Old English Poetic Composition," *MP* 73 (1976): 219–228. Mr. Bonner's claim that certain rhetorical devices existed in Germanic poetry without influence from Latin is plausible, but much weakened by his total lack of evidence and the substitution of pure speculation as to what the "native" poetic consisted in. He points out a problem in the definition of the term "rhetorical," which is real, though irremediable. Far more semantic confusion would result if the term "grammatical" were substituted. What we now call "style" was treated in both rhetoric and grammar books, but modern connotations for the word "grammar" would distort the medieval facts.

40. Dorothy Bethurum, "Stylistic Features of the Old English Laws," *MLR* 27 (1932): 263–279.

> Ardor frigescit,   nitor squalescit,
> Amor abolescit,   lux obtenebrescit.
> Senescunt omnia,   que ęterna non sunt.
>
> Hat acolað,   hwit asolað,
> leof alaðaþ,   leoht aðystrað,
> æghwæt forealdað   þæs þe ece ne byð.[41]

The Latin is quite obviously a *sententia* constructed with an epigrammatic eye for rhetoric. The first four phrases are measured into neat isocolon, with antithesis as the principle figure of thought. The third person inflectional endings produce the sound effect of *homeoteleuton* in an insistent way, and the final sententious statement is emphasized by its departure from the established pattern. The Old English translator, following the English poetic requirements, created the proper alliterative pattern which did not exist in the Latin and produced an effective rhythmic sequence by writing five lines in A type accentuation, varying it at the end with a B line ending in a strong accent. He was also extremely conscious of the rhetorical effects, to the extent that he imitated the isocolon, antithesis and *homeoteleuton,* even though he had to mistranslate the phrase ''Amor abolescit'' slightly in order to do it. The theme of mutability remains intact, but at the same time the poet attempted with real success to reproduce in Old English the rather artificial rhetorical manipulations of the Latin.

More weighty examples of imitation of *schemata* can be found in studying many passages from the Old English *Phoenix.* The poem was translated and much expanded from a poem of Lactantius, *De ave phoenice,* whose diction and syntax were artfully elegant in the best late Roman manner. The Old English poet was highly sensitive to the rhetorical manoeuvres of the Latin poet; not only did he imitate many schemes and tropes from the original, but he had so far assimilated rhetorical techniques that he constructed complex passages at will, even when they were not suggested by the Latin he was translating. For example, consider lines 15–18 of Lactantius' poem:

> non huc exsangues Morbi, non aegra Senectus,
> nec Mors crudelis nec Metus asper adest;

---

41. E. V. K. Dobbie, ed., *The Anglo-Saxon Minor Poems,* ASPR 6 (New York, 1942), p. 109. It is just possible that the translation process went the other way, from English to Latin. In either case, the sophistication of the English poet in rhetorical writing is clear.

nec Scelus infandum nec opum vesana Cupido
huc meat aut ardens caedis amore Furor.[42]

Here we have a series of phrases connected by repeated negatives in the manner of *polysyndeton,* each phrase beginning with an anaphoric word, *non* or *nec.* The first part of the series in lines 15 and 16 is suspended by *zeugma* until the verb *adest* appears. Lines 17 and 18 vary this technique by putting the verb *meat* in the middle of the series of nominatives, producing syntax which rhetoricians would call *coniunctio.* The repeated *m*'s are unquestionably intentional *paromoeon,* and the *-um* endings on *infandum* and opum seem suspiciously like *homeoteleuton.*

The Old English poet not only imitates these figures, but expands them with the addition of vivid additional details and images:

Nis þær on þam londe   laðgeniðla,   50
ne wop ne wracu,   weatacen nan,
yldu ne yrmðu   ne se enga deað,
ne lyfes lyre,   ne laþes cyme,
ne synn ne sacu   ne sarwracu,
ne wædle gewin,   ne welan onsyn,   55
ne sorg ne slæp   ne swar leger,
ne wintergeweorp,   ne wedra gebregd,
hreoh under heofonum,   ne se hearda forst,
caldum cylegicelum,   cynseð ænigne.[43]

Keeping the references to age and death, he moves into other types of sorrow, such as poverty, fighting, vengeance and bitter weather. The rhetorical structure of the expanded series, though, is still based on anaphora, *polysyndeton* and *zeugma.* Actually, the series also involves *apo koinou* (a rhetorical term clearly defined by Cassiodorus in his *Commentary on the Psalms,* though missing in most of the standard Latin manuals), since the parallel nominatives stretching from line 51 to line 58 can equally well be the subjects of *cnyseð* in line 59 as of *Nis* in line 50. This impressive figure, so easy to achieve in oral poetry, is usually obscured by modern printed punctuation. The *Phoenix* poet apparently liked the emotional emphasis made possible by this type of controlled, anaphoric series, and he constructed an even more elaborate one with the same anaphora, *polysyndeton*

---

42. Mary C. Fitzpatrick, ed., *Lactanti de ave phoenice* (Philadelphia, 1933), p. 40.
43. G. P. Krapp and E. V. K. Dobbie, eds., *The Exeter Book,* ASPR 3 (New York, 1936), p. 95.

and *homeoptoton* in lines 14 to 20 of his poem, where no such elaborate rhetoric exists in the Latin.[44]

The anaphoric series, often accompanied by *zeugma,* was a favorite device of many Old English poets. Examples occur in poem after poem. Negative series such as

> Ne mæg him þonne se flæschoma,   þonne him þæt feorg losað,
> ne swete forswelgan   ne sar gefelan,
> ne hond onhreran   ne mid hyge þencan.   (*Seafarer* 94–96)

are especially prevalent. Likewise the *sum* series found in *The Gifts of Men,*

>   . . . his giefe bryttað
> sumum on cystum,   sumum on cræftum,
> sumum on wlite,   sumum on wige,
> sumum he syleð monna   milde heortan . . .   (105–108)

can be paralleled in a number of poems. Indeed the anaphora on the word *sum* provides in both *The Gifts of Men* and *The Fates of Men* a structuring principle which also becomes the very theme of the poem. The poem which begins the collection of riddles in the Exeter Book uses the word *Hwilum* anaphorically to demark sections or shifts of idea in the poem, and then uses it climactically toward the end to summarize those sections:

> Swa ic þrymful þeow   þragum winne,
> hwilum under eorþan,   hwilum yþa sceal
> hean underhnigan,   hwilum holm ufan
> streamas styrge,   hwilum stige up . . .[45]

An especially moving use of this technique appears in *The Wanderer,* where anaphora is used for a passionate statement of the *ubi sunt* motif, and is couched in *interrogatio*:

> Hwær cwom mearg? Hwær cwom mago? Hwær cwom maþþumgyfa?
> Hwær cwom symbla gesetu?   Hwær sindon seledreamas?   (92–93)

These rhetorical questions are followed immediately by another passage of anaphora, cast in the even more emotional figure of *exclamatio*:

---

44. The above material is reduced from a fuller discussion in J. J. Campbell, "Learned Rhetoric in Old English Poetry," *MP* 63 (1966): 196–197.

45. For a fuller discussion, see J. J. Campbell, "A Certain Power," *Neophilologus* 59 (1975): 128–138. The recurrence of *hwilum* in other poems is discussed briefly in Adeline C. Bartlett, *The Larger Rhetorical Patterns in Anglo-Saxon Poetry* (New York, 1935), pp. 40–42.

Eala beorht bune! Eala byrnwiga!
Eala þeodnes þrym! (94–95)

Much of the poetic effectiveness of many Old English poems derives from the consummate skill with which poets wedded skillful rhetorical manipulation to strong emotion and meaningful ideas.

The device of *prosopopoeia* was also a recurrent favorite in the Old English poetic. It provides the basic fiction for many of the riddles in the Exeter Book,[46] where a group of different poets (apparently) found ingenious ways to create speaking inanimate characters to convey ideas, to stimulate questions or simply to mystify. Some years ago Margaret Schlauch pointed out that one of the finest poems in Old English, *The Dream of the Rood*, was constructed on the principle of *prosopopoeia*, adducing antecedents as far back as Ovid's *De nuce*.[47] She incidentally points out that such techniques as *concessio* and *purgatio* were also consciously used by the poet.

Word play, both simple and complex, in Old English poetry has recently been brilliantly studied by Roberta Frank.[48] *Paronomasia* as defined by Bede's *De schematibus* was a tiny shift of sound which changed the meaning of the word without radically changing the general sound. Using as material a large segment of the extant poetry and some prose, Ms. Frank finds many different types of *paronomasia*, some of which Bede and the other rhetoricians would not accept as such. However, her evidence of conscious word play by many poets between such words as *rod* and *rodor*, *word* and *wyrd* is highly convincing, and the doctrinal sophistication behind some of the concepts for which certain poets used this word play is nothing less than astounding. An interesting example of sheer ingenuity is quoted from the prose *Solomon and Saturn*; to translate the etymology of the Latin word for sky,[49] *caelum a celando superiora*, the

---

46. See Marie Nelson, "The Rhetoric of the Exeter Book Riddles," *Speculum* 49 (1974): 421–440. Ms. Nelson also is especially perceptive in her analysis of anaphora, antithesis and *homoeoptoton* as they appear at key points in certain riddles.

47. Margaret Schlauch, "The 'Dream of the Rood' as *Prosopopoeia*," *Essays and Studies in Honor of Carleton Brown* (New York, 1940), pp. 23–34. More recently Whitney Bolton has pointed out that the riddle tradition much closer to home could have provided both the technique and the general subject matter of the poem: "Tatwine's *De Cruce Christi* and The Dream of the Rood," *Archiv* 200 (1963): 344–346.

48. Roberta Frank, "Some Uses of Paronomasia in Old English Scriptural Verse," *Speculum* 47 (1972): 207–226.

49. Using other examples, F. N. Robinson has recently studied the Old English penchant for adapting etymology, both from Isidore and elsewhere, for a variety of *amplificatio*. See "The Significance of Names in Old English Literature," *Anglia* 86 (1968): 14–58.

196 JACKSON J. CAMPBELL

Old English writer explains that *heofon* is the English word, *forþon he behelaþ eal þæt him be ufan biþ.* He not only conveys the meaning of the Latin word play, but creates a similar one in the very different English phonetic and semantic system. *Paronomasia* was not, however, confined to the use of learned Christian poets translating scriptural or didactic material, for the secular poets were also aware of its effectiveness. The poet of the Battle of Maldon recounts that Byrhtnoð *rad ond rædde* among his troops, and the phrase surely did not pop out in such neat form without his knowing what he was doing.[50]

Virtually all the schemes and tropes can similarly be found as common tools for Old English poets. A recent study by Dorothy Jehle catalogues most of them in the poetry of Cynewulf.[51] Since he was usually translating Latin sources, and was undoubtedly a learned writer with a sophisticated sense of style, this is not especially surprising. But Ms. Jehle demonstrates that often Cynewulf uses rather complex rhetorical devices in passages where he departed from his source or amplified it. The smoothness of his style, which some have called "classical" in the sense that Aelfric's prose style is classical, undoubtedly stems from the decorum and moderation with which he used figures, managing to make even complicated language patterns appear to grow naturally out of his narrative and thematic material.

It has been debated for many years whether the author of *Beowulf* knew Virgil's *Aeneid.* One does not, however, have to accept all the parallel passages proposed by Friedrich Klaeber[52] to feel that an influence of some kind from the Latin poetic tradition was working on the Old English poet. George Engelhardt is the only scholar who has thoroughly addressed the problem in rhetorical terms and his results proved extremely interesting.[53] On the stylistic level, *expolitio* is a term which might possibly describe certain types of the omnipresent variation in poetic writing. Its analogue in larger patterns,

---

50. Ann S. Johnson has analyzed another definitely secular poem: "The Rhetoric of *Brunanburh,*" *PQ* 47 (1968): 487–493. "The Wanderer," which probably is equally "Germanic" and "learned," has also recently been discussed in connection with *paronomasia*: E. R. Kintgen, "Word Play in 'The Wanderer'," *Neophilologus* 59 (1975): 119–127.
51. Dorothy M. Jehle, *Latin Rhetoric in the Signed Poems of Cynewulf,* Diss. (Loyola University of Chicago, 1973).
52. F. Klaeber, "Aeneis und Beowulf," *Archiv* 126 (1911): 40–48.
53. G. J. Engelhardt, *"Beowulf:* A Study in Dilation," *PMLA* 70 (1955): 825–852.

amplificatio, was studied by Engelhardt in detail with reference to *Beowulf.* The leisurely expansiveness of the poem contrasts sharply with the economy of short Germanic lays like the *Hildebrantslied,* and Engelhardt finds that much of the expansion can be explained by techniques of *peribole* and *epimone* which are often used to dilate the contrasting *effectio* and *corruptio* of the characters and tribes of the poem. He discusses numerous rhetorical *loci* as he systematically applies ingenious and knowledgeable analysis to the structure of the narration. The technical terms he uses come mainly from Priscian's translation of Hermogenes' *Progymnasmata* and Boethius' *De differentiis topicis,* whose currency in Anglo-Saxon England might possibly be questioned, yet the weight of his careful study is finally so impressive that it cannot be ignored. The *Beowulf* poet is universally credited with poetic power and imaginative genius, but there is a clear possibility that he had also thoroughly assimilated the disciplines of the Latin poetic and rhetorical tradition. A poet like Cynewulf, who was completely within the learned Christian tradition, can easily be believed to have been well trained and practiced in rhetoric. But the *Beowulf* poet had perhaps gone a step further—had so thoroughly absorbed his education and mingled it so unobtrusively with his innate talent that his poem achieves a state where art subsumes artfulness. The rhetoric informing both the small and large details of the poem has its profound effect without ostentatiously calling attention to itself.

The careful study of Old English literature from the point of view of classical rhetoric has little more than begun. Much more research and contemplation need to be done and unquestionably will be done. Knowledge of the grammatical and rhetorical tradition from the seventh century forward is clearly established, but many detailed investigations are required before we have a complete picture of the kind of unique adaptation and modification of the tradition made by individual Old English writers. The elements of rhetoric they did not choose to employ are often as interesting as those they did use. Yet it is now beyond doubt that the English were in the main stream of civilized Christian learning, accepting their heritage from the past and expressing their own perceptions, ideas and emotions about man's destiny with intelligence, sincerity and skill.

Rhetoric and Dialectic in
The Owl and the Nightingale

JAMES J. MURPHY

IT REQUIRES some temerity to add another analysis of a very famous Middle English poem which has already been examined by so very many famous modern English scholars. It is a bit like adding one more word about Shakespeare, or about Chaucer. Consider, for a moment, the scholars who have examined this poem that A.C. Baugh calls "A truly amazing phenomenon," and that others have termed "outstanding" or "remarkable." Eric G. Stanley points out that it has poetic virtues not seen again in Middle English until Chaucer. The roster of commentators is considerable: J.W.H. Atkins, John E. Wells, C.T. Onions, R.M. Wilson, Robert M. Lumiansky, Douglas Peterson, Neil Ker, C.L. Wrenn, G.G. Coulton, J.C. Russell, W.W. Greg, Frederick Tupper, Edmond Reiss, Morton Bloomfield, Francis Magoun, A.C. Cawley, B.J. Whiting, Mortimer Donovan, Constance Hieatt—to name a few.[1]

This list is important, not as an epic catalogue for the sake of literary form, but as a reminder that much has already been said about this poem—a poem of only 1794 lines. Surely, then, no one should lightly embark on a new set of studies without some good reason.

There have been the usual scholarly approaches to the poem. Some have seen it as an allegory, though there has been little agreement about the meaning intended by the author; many have commented

---

1. A convenient summary of recent scholarship may be found in Kathryn Hume, *The Owl and the Nightingale: The Poem and Its Critics* (Toronto, 1975), especially chapter one (pp. 3–14). For a more extensive survey, see Francis Lee Utley, "Dialogues, Debates, and Catechisms," in *A Manual of the Writings in Middle English, 1050-1500, by Members of the Middle English Group of the Modern Language Association*, vol. 3, ed. Albert E. Hartung (New Haven, 1972), pp. 716–720 and 874–882.

on the Christian themes, as might be expected; others have looked into the background of beast fables, though no one seems yet to have uncovered the precise direct source or sources of this particular story; those who have probed the background of medieval literary debate have contributed a number of footnotes to the matter but have not yet produced a comprehensive critical approach to the poem; some have seen echoes of canon law terms and canon law procedures; the problem of authorship has naturally engaged the attention of a good many scholars, with some feeling that the poem was written to secure preferment or employment; a few have noted that the poem possibly had a French version in addition to the Middle English one, since the monastic library at Titchfield records a French work with the same title. As for date, many feel that it was composed in the late 1180's or early 1190's, though others note that the thirteenth-century provenance of the two surviving manuscripts raises the possibility of composition as much as a century later than that.[2]

What seems to be lacking so far in this galaxy of opinions about *The Owl and the Nightingale* is a careful consideration of what can best be termed the "environment of discourse" in twelfth-century Europe—that is, the role played by the so-called *trivium* of grammar, rhetoric, and dialectic in shaping the *forma* of writings both fictional and nonfictional. This essay discusses that environment of discourse as a means of providing a better understanding of the poem. To that end it proposes a dialectical-rhetorical biography of the author, which in turn illuminates some key passages in the poem. Finally, it advances what can only be seen as a sad and depressing conjecture about the welfare of Middle English literature in the two centuries following the poem.

I do not intend to drag the reader through a catalogue of rhetorical figures to be found in *The Owl and the Nightingale*—Herbert Hässler has already drawn up a partial list for us.[3] Angela Carson has already

---

2. The question about the date of composition is no mere antiquarian search for scholarly perfection or a mere attempt to wrap up loose ends about the text. Critical judgments are at stake. If the poem was indeed written about 1182–1183 (as Huganir proposes), it then stands alone in its time as a little masterpiece of early Middle English; its near-contemporary Ormulum, for instance, would offer a painful artistic contrast. If on the other hand it was composed in the 1270's or 1280's, after another century of development in Middle English, we might not then be so prepared to hail its virtuosity.

3. Herbert Hässler, *'The Owl and the Nightingale' und die literarischen Bestrebungen des 12. und 13. Jahrhunderts*. Frankfurt am Main, 1942. For instance Hässler (p. 43) finds nine figures in *O&N* vv. 556–582, and (p. 64) identifies several examples of anaphora (vv. 1641–1650: pu/an, vv. 1771–1778: pat/an). See also Eric

argued for the presence of the three ancient rhetorical genres in the poem.[4] Nor do I intend to provide a systematic analysis of the argument and counterargument in the poem based on the 200 *Loci*, or "Topics," outlined in the basic medieval textbook in dialectic (Aristotle's *Topics*); no one has yet made this systematic study, and it deserves to be done, but this is not the place for it.

In other words this study does not intend to be either purely rhetorical or purely dialectical. Instead, the primary concern is to demonstrate that no satisfactory understanding of the poem is possible until we comprehend the author's early medieval understanding of the relation between grammar, rhetoric and dialectic as being simply different points on a continuum of discourse. Until we understand this, we will continue to distress ourselves with such questions as whether foxes really do climb trees, and we will never even know enough to ask ourselves why at the end of the poem, after all that bitter controversy, the nightingale quite meekly agrees to let the owl repeat the whole set of speeches to their judge, Nicholas. After all, why should the nightingale trust the memory of her opponent?

Its compositional environment, in other words, can help us understand *The Owl and the Nightingale*.

THE TWELFTH-CENTURY ENVIRONMENT OF DISCOURSE

The twelfth century may well have been the happiest of centuries as far as the *trivium* was concerned. We happen to know a good deal about it from the writings of men like John of Salisbury, William Fitzstephen, Alexander Neckham, Hugh of Saint Victor, and even such adopted Englishmen as Peter of Blois. Grammar was taught with the ancient textbooks of Donatus and Priscian, both of which encouraged the student to look to classical models;[5] the dominant

---

G. Stanley, "Some Aspects of the Poem's Rhetoric," in his "Introduction" to *The Owl and the Nightingale* ed. Eric G. Stanley. Revised Edition. (Manchester University Press, 1972), pp. 33–35.

4. M. Angela Carson O.S.U., "Rhetorical Structure in *The Owl and the Nightingale*," *Speculum* 42 (1967), 92–103. She sees the poem "as an example of oratorical rhetoric according to the three genera of argument: forensic, epideictic, and deliberative." (93) There are some factual errors (e.g. listing Cicero's *De oratore* as a text which was influential in the twelfth century); for a treatment of classical rhetorical texts in the Middle Ages see James J. Murphy, *Rhetoric in the Middle Ages* (University of California Press, 1974), esp. pp. 89–130. Carson's study is mainly designed to show that examples of the three genera can be found in selected passages, rather than to show that the author used them to shape the poem.

5. It must be remembered that the medieval *ars grammatica* was a far broader subject than that indicated by most modern meanings of the term "grammar." It

textbooks in rhetoric were the youthful *De inventione* of Cicero (his
so-called "First Rhetoric"), the Pseudo-Ciceronian *Rhetorica ad
Herennium* (called Cicero's "Second Rhetoric" or "New Rhetoric")
with its full treatment of 64 tropes and figures, and their twelfth-
century commentaries.[6] In the year 1128 Jacob of Venice translated
into Latin four logical works of Aristotle to form what was called
"The New Logic": The *Prior Analytics, Posterior Analytics, Topics,*
and *On Sophistical Refutations.* These four works, added to the "Old
Logic" of Aristotle's *Categories* and *On Interpretations* (both through
Boethius), and the *Isagoge* of Porphyry, made up the complete set of
logical works we know as the "Organon" of Aristotle.[7]

The translation of Aristotle's *Topics* and *Sophistical Refutations*
was undoubtedly one of the most significant intellectual events in
the twelfth century. The reason is that these two books provided a
highly sophisticated groundwork for dialectical processes which in
many ways shaped the educational process of Europe for centuries to
come. As Peter Cantor, a twelfth-century teacher at Paris, expressed
it, "A teaching master has three duties; to lecture, to preach, and to
dispute."[8] The pedagogy of the medieval university, after all, was
built around a framework of *disputatio.* Disputation was used for
instruction, for testing, for public display, for the advancement of
new ideas, and ultimately for the form of written didactic works like
the *Summa Theologica* of Thomas Aquinas.[9]

---

included not only the "rules" of syntax, but also much of what we would ordinarily
include today under "literature." See below, pp. 208–209.

6. See Murphy, *Rhetoric in the Middle Ages,* pp. 106–123; and John O. Ward,
"The Date of the Commentary on Cicero's 'De inventione' by Thierry of Chartres
(ca. 1095–1160) and The Cornifician Attack on the Liberal Arts," *Viator* 3 (1972),
219–273.

7. For a useful guide to the medieval translations of Aristotle's works, see George
Lacombe, *Aristoteles Latinus,* Corpus Philosophorum Medii Aevi, 2 vols. (I, Rome,
1939; II, Cambridge, 1955).

8. Petrus Cantor, *Verbum abbreviatum,* ed. J.P. Migne, *Patrologia Latina,* vol.
205, col. 25.

9. For a treatment of the historical development of the general disputation mode,
see Martin Grabmann, *Die Geschichte der scholastischen Methode,* 2 vols. (Freiburg
im Breisgau, 1909–11), esp. II.17ff. For an excellent summary of the typical disputation process, however, see A.G. Little and F. Pelster, *Oxford Theology and Theologians, A.D. 1282–1302* (Oxford, 1934), 29–56 and 246–248; another survey may
be found in Palémon Glorieux, *Répertoire des maîtres,* I.15–35; also Pierre Man-
donnet, *Siger de Brabant* (Louvain, 1911). Recent scholarship has brought into print
the disputation reports of a number of individual masters; these "transcripts"
usually bear the mark of editing after the fact and must be reviewed critically
insofar as actual content is concerned. It is nevertheless true that they probably

Modern scholars have generally studied the medieval *disputatio* in terms of its use in the universities—perhaps because its university use is so well documented—but there is also clear indication that during the twelfth century, at least, it was also a feature of education for young boys at what might be called an "elementary level" of schooling. For instance there is the famous account of William Fitz-stephen, the biographer of Thomas à Becket, who describes a scene in a London church yard about the year 1170; the boys are apparently twelve to fourteen years of age:

> The scholars dispute, some in demonstrative rhetoric, others in dialectic. Some 'hurtle enthymemes,' others with greater skill employ perfect syllogisms. Boys of different schools strive against one another in verse, or contend concerning the principles of grammar, or the rules concerning past and future. There are others who employ the old art of the crossroads in epigrams, rhymes, and metre.[10]

Earlier in the century Hugh of St. Victor describes a view of classroom activity. In his dialogue *On the Vanity of the World*, Discipulus is being given a survey of the world by Magister. They observe students at work:

> "Turn again and look," says Magister, "and what do you see?" "I see the schools of learners. There is a great crowd, and of all ages, boys and youths, men young and old. They study various things. Some practice their rude tongue at the alphabet and at words new to them. Others listen to the inflection of words, their composition and derivation; then by reciting and repeating them they try to commit them to memory. Others furrow the waxen tablets with a stylus. Others, guiding the feathered quill (calamus) with a learned hand, draw figures of different shapes and sizes on parchments. Still others with sharper zeal seem to dispute on graver matters and try to trip each other with twistings and impossibilities."[11]

Here, again, young boys are seen "disputing." Dialectic, with its schoolroom format, the *disputatio*, has become a twelfth-century

---

represent the *form* of the disputation process, which would be more easily remembered than the precise language of the actual encounter. See the collections by Glorieux, *La Littèrature quodlibetique de 1260 à 1320* 2 vols., Bibliothèque Thomiste, V and XXI (Paris, 1925 and 1935).

10. Quoted in Nicholas Orme, *English Schools in the Middle Ages* (London, 1973), p. 131. We do know some of the "different schools" to which Fitzstephen refers—there were at least three of them: Saint Paul's, St. Mary Arches, a peculiar of the Archbishop of Canterbury, and St. Martin-le-Grand, a royal free chapel. For all of twelfth-century England, about 30 such schools are known by name; for France and Germany, perhaps ten; for Italy, another dozen or so.

11. Trans. A.O. Taylor, *The Medieval Mind* (two vols.; Harvard University Press, 1959), II, 137–138.

staple. The Chartrean schoolmaster, Thierry, dutifully includes dialectic (including Aristotle's *Topics* and *Sophistical Refutations*) in his *Heptateuchon*, or survey of the seven liberal arts.[12]

But it is essential for us to note that this lore of dialectic operated in twelfth-century education to overlay a basically Quintilianistic foundation which had previously made grammar and rhetoric the core of the elementary curriculum. John of Salisbury's *Metalogicon* (1159)[13] shows us exactly how this happened. It is usually said that John is attempting to defend the whole *trivium* in this book. But history has shown that John instead helped collapse the Quintilianistic approach to language by his well-expressed praise of the two books that embodied the dialectical method—Aristotle's *Topics* and *Sophistical Refutations*. Quintilian, who is quoted frequently by John, had his students begin with basic grammatical rules followed by exercises like the rephrasing of Aesop's fables or the imitation of epic style, or the style of a historian. Rhetorical study then followed grammar. Bernard of Chartres, according to John, used exactly this method: it is fair to conclude that other schools at places like Bec, Dunstable, London and Beauvais did exactly the same in the twelfth century. Here is John's description of the grammatical-rhetorical training he recalled from his time with Bernard:

> Bernard of Chartres, the greatest font of literary learning in Gaul in recent times, used to teach grammar in the following way. He would point out, in reading the authors, what was simple and according to rule. On the other hand, he would explain grammatical figures, rhetorical embellishment, and sophistical quibbling, as well as the relation of given passages to other studies. He would do so, however, without trying to teach everything at one time. On the contrary, he would dispense his instruction to his hearers gradually, in a manner commensurate with their powers of assimilation. And since diction is lustrous either because the words are well chosen, and the adjectives and verbs admirably suited to the nouns with which they are used, or because of the employment of metaphors, whereby speech is transferred to some beyond-the-ordinary meaning for sufficient reason, Bernard used to inculcate this in the minds of his hearers whenever he had the opportunity. In view of the fact that exercise both strengthens and sharpens our mind, Bernard would bend every effort to bring his students to imitate what they were hearing. In some cases he would rely on exhortation, in others he would resort to

12. Still unedited. See the outline in A. Clerval, *Les Écoles de Chartres au moyen âge* (Paris, 1895; reprinted Frankfurt am Main, 1965), pp. 222–223.

13. *The Metalogicon of John of Salisbury: A Twelfth Century Defense of the Verbal and Logical Arts of The Trivium*, trans. Daniel D. McGarry (University of California Press, 1955).

punishments, such as flogging. Each student was daily required to recite part of what he had heard on the previous day. Some would recite more, others less. Each succeeding day thus became the disciple of his predecessor. The evening exercise, known as the "declination," was so replete with grammatical instruction that if anyone were to take part in it for an entire year, provided he were not a dullard, he would become thoroughly familiar with the [correct] method of speaking and writing, and would not be at a loss to comprehend expressions in general use. Since, however, it is not right to allow any school or day to be without religion, subject matter was presented to foster faith, to build up morals, and to inspire those present at this quasicollation to perform good works. This [evening] "declination," or philosophical collation, closed with the pious commendation of the souls of the departed to their Redeemer, by the devout recitation of the Sixth Penitential Psalm and the Lord's Prayer. He [Bernard] would also explain the poets and orators who were to serve as models for the boys in their introductory exercises in imitating prose and poetry. Pointing out how the diction of the authors was so skillfully connected, and what they had to say was so elegantly concluded, he would admonish his students to follow their example. And if, to embellish his work, someone had sewed on a patch of cloth filched from an external source, Bernard, on discovering this, would rebuke him for his plagiary, but would generally refrain from punishing him. After he had reproved the student, if an unsuitable theme had invited this, he would, with modest indulgence, bid the boy to rise to real imitation of the [classical authors], and would bring about that he who had imitated his predecessors would come to be deserving of imitation by his successors. He would also inculcate as fundamental, and impress on the minds of his listeners, what virtue exists in economy; what things are to be commended by facts and what ones by choice of words, where concise and, so to speak, frugal speech is in order, and where fuller, more copious expression is appropriate; as well as where speech is excessive, and wherein consists just measure in all cases. Bernard used also to admonish his students that stories and poems should be read thoroughly, and not as though the reader were being precipitated to flight by spurs. Wherefor he diligently and insistently demanded from each, as a daily debt, something committed to memory. At the same time, he said that we should shun what is superfluous. According to him, the works of distinguished authors suffice. As a matter of fact, to study everything that everyone, no matter how insignificant, has ever said, is either to be excessively humble and cautious, or overly vain and ostentatious. It also deters and stifles minds that would better be freed to go on to other things. That which preëmpts the place of something that is better is, for this reason, disadvantageous, and does not deserve to be called "good." To examine and pore over everything that has been written, regardless of whether it is worth reading, is as pointless as to fritter away one's time with old wives' tales. As Augustine says in his book *On Order*: "Who is there who will bear that a man who has never heard that Daedalus flew should [therefore] be considered unlearned? And, on the contrary, who will not agree that one who says that Daedalus did fly should be branded a liar; one who believes it, a fool; and one who questions [anyone] about it, impudent? I am wont to have profound pity for those of my associates who are accused of ignorance because they do not know the name of the mother of Euryalus, yet who dare not call those who ask such questions 'conceited and pedantic busy-bodies.' " Augustine summarizes the matter aptly and with truth. The ancients correctly reckoned that to ignore certain things constituted one of the marks of a good grammarian. A further feature of Bernard's method was to have his disciples compose prose and poetry every day, and exercise their faculties in mutual conferences, for nothing is more useful in introductory training than actually to accustom one's students to practice the art they are studying. Nothing serves better to foster the acquisition of eloquence and the attainment of knowledge than such conferences, which also have a salutary influence on practical conduct, provided that charity moderates enthusiasm, and that humility is not lost during progress in learning.[14]

This systematic medieval educational program has roots in Christian monasticism,[15] and in the basic teaching of Latin as a foreign language,[16] but there is nothing in it which would be inconsistent with the even more systematic program which had been laid out much earlier by the Roman schoolmaster Quintilian in the first two books of his *Institutio oratoria* and then re-presented to Western Europe in the early twelfth century.[17] As we have seen, John of Salisbury says his tutor Bernard of Chartres made explicit use of Quintilian in teaching "grammar." But whether or not that particular Roman book was explicitly cited by others, there is a clear pattern of elementary education for a twelfth-century boy in grammar and rhetoric. If he was in a monastic foundation he heard Latin long before he studied its grammar, so that the sounds of Psalter, Mass, and Hours

14. *Metalogicon* I, 24 (pp. 67–70).
15. Charles W. Jones has an excellent concise description of this background in his Preface to *Bedae Venerabilis Opera: Pars I: Opera Didascalica*, Corpus Christianorum Series Latina CXXII A (Turnholti: Typographi Brepols Editores Pontifici, 1975), pp. v–xvi. See also Jean Leclercq, O.S.B., *The Love of Learning and the Desire for God: A Study of Monastic Culture*, trans. by Catharine Misrahi (Mentor Omega Books; New York, 1961), esp. pp. 116 ff.
16. This fundamental fact of medieval cultural life has so far gone virtually unexplored. Medieval Latin, a language "cut off from the spoken word" (Eric Auerbach) and increasingly distant from everyday discourse as the various vernaculars supplanted it, was for all medieval writers a "foreign" language. The implications of this surely require further study.
17. The varying fortunes of Quintilian's *Institutio* in the Middle Ages are outlined in Murphy, *Rhetoric in the Middle Ages*, pp. 123–130.

accustomed his ear to the *clausulae* he would later see analyzed in
Donatus and Priscian; the metrics of Scripture were impressed upon
him through *declinatio*—the intensive analysis of verse, every word
by case or mood or tense or number—supplemented by notations
on which locutions constituted this or that "trope" or "figure."[18]
If the boy was in a nonmonastic school—we know of some 30 such
in twelfth-century England—the aural background would be somewhat different but the pedagogical devices were apparently the same.
Language facility was promoted through an adroit combination of
model-reading, model-analysis, rule-learning (and even memoriza-
tion), model-imitation, written and oral composition, classroom
recitation, and classroom criticism by both peers and masters. The
student product, when all went well, could be an Abelard or a
Becket.

We have seen that John of Salisbury is deeply aware that he is a
beneficiary of this rhetorical-grammatical progymnasmatic tradition.
His praise of his master, Bernard, tells us that. It is only modern
readers who find puzzling his equal enthusiasm for dialectic, and
especially for Aristotle's two dialectical textbooks, *Topics* and *On
Sophistical Refutations*. No intelligent twelfth-century reader would
have been surprised. If it is clear that Hugh of Saint Victor, Thierry
of Chartres, Bishop Fulbert, Bernard of Chartres and a host of other
twelfth-century figures admired the commingling of rhetoric and
grammar in elementary education, it is equally clear that all of them
also took dialectic for granted. Those schoolboys in William Fitz-
stephen's London churchyard reconfirm that for us.

What is interesting about John of Salisbury's defense of the three
arts of the *trivium* is that for grammar and rhetoric he lauds the
process by which they are taught—but for dialectic he praises *two
new textbooks*. In other words, he takes dialectical disputation itself
for granted. His main effort in Books Three and Four of the *Metalogicon* is to show how these recently available Aristotelian texts make

---

18. It is precisely for this reason that the Venerable Bede appends to his *De arte
metrica* a treatise on the tropes and figures of Donatus; Bede substitutes 122 Scriptural examples for the classical pagan examples Donatus had used. For Bede, and
the monastic educators after him, an intimate familiarity with versification was a
Christian duty—was not God, after all, the Creator of meters? On this point see
Jones, *Bedae. . . . opera didascalica,* p. xi. Bede's *De arte metrica* is found in
Heinrich Keil (ed.), *Grammatici latini* (Leipzig, 1880), VII, 227–260; *The De schematibus et tropis* is in Carolus Halm (ed.), *Rhetores latini minores* (Leipzig, 1863),
607–618 (a translation by Gussie Hecht Tanenhaus appears in *Quarterly Journal
of Speech* 48[1962], 237–253).

the prevailing disputation more effective. There is never a question of whether *disputatio* should take place; he and his twelfth-century readers already knew that schoolboys had to be dialectical as well as grammatical and rhetorical. (Bernard of Chartres' evening *collationes,* for instance, obviously went far beyond mere parsing of sentences.)

It is therefore well worth our while to try to understand these two books of Aristotle as John and his contemporaries would have understood them. This involves an understanding of the *disputatio* itself.

A medieval *disputatio* was a formal discussion of a subject by two people who took opposite sides of the issue, speaking in dialogue order. While the internal format of the argument/reply sequence might differ from time to time, it was customary for a third party to offer at the end a *determinatio,* or approved answer to resolve the issue.

John first praises the *Topics,* saying (III. 10) that "without this book one disputes by chance, not by art." He continues:

> Since dialectic is carried on between two persons, this book teaches the matched contestants whom it trains and provides with reasons and topics, to handle their proper weapons and engage in verbal, rather than physical conflict. It instills into its disciples such astute skill that one may clearly see that it is the principal source of the rules of all eloquence, for which it serves as a sort of primary fountainhead. It is undoubtedly true, as Cicero and Quintilian acknowledge, that this work has not merely been helpful to rhetoricians, but has also, for both them and writers on the arts, even served as the initial starting point for the study of rhetoric, which subsequently expanded and acquired its own particular rules.

The *Topics* is divided into eight books covering 200 separate suggested modes of argument; the eighth book, moreover, is a set of directions for conducting what Aristotle calls "Contentious Reasonings"—i.e. dialectical debates or disputations. It is a mixture of rhetorical and logical advice—that for instance it is poor psychology in a disputation to act as if your opponent has advanced an argument you cannot answer (a caution which the nightingale observes on two occasions by the way), or that you should advance your premises in random order, so that your opponent will not at first see how they all fit together—it is interesting to note that a number of scholars have criticized the poet for not having his birds speak out in purely logical order.

As for the book *On Sophistical Refutations,* John declares that a systematic study of sophistry is useful to avoid being entrapped by false arguers: "I would be reluctant to say that any other study could

be more beneficial to the young." Our own examination of these two
books can confirm John's judgments. The Preamble to the *Topics*
states: "Our treatise proposes to find a line of inquiry whereby we
shall be able to reason from opinions that are generally accepted
about every problem propounded to us, and also shall ourselves,
when standing up to an argument, avoid saying anything that will
obstruct us." (I. 1. 100)[19] The final part of the *Topics*, Book Eight, is
a set of specific directions for conducting a disputation with an opponent ("respondent"). The book *On Sophistical Refutations* has
as one purpose "to speak of arguments used in competitions and
contests" (ii. 165[b]), and Aristotle concludes by noting that "We have
shown, moreover, how to question or arrange the questioning as a
whole." (xxxiv. 183[b]) It is no wonder, then, that a society already
employing *disputatio* might well find these books useful—and, indeed, find them perfectly compatible with other aspects of twelfth-
century education.

This artistic compatibility is sometimes hard for a modern reader
to understand. Whenever modern students of medieval culture attempt to find parallels or influences in literary works, they should
remember that the primary objective of ancient and medieval grammar, rhetoric and dialectic was not to teach a boy a large number of
formulae which he could plug into a poem whenever he needed
something to say. Instead, the objective was to achieve the mastery
of a facility, of a talent, or a capability—what the ancients called an
"art." All the petty drills of the rhetorician Quintilian or the grammarian Priscian are for the purpose of practicing the little details so
that the writer or speaker will be able to make intelligent linguistic
judgments in each given case. Indeed Aristotle told the medieval
reader about this in his famous example of the shoes, at the conclusion of his book *On Sophistical Refutations.* He criticizes those
teachers who try to give a student a set speech to memorize for each
separate occasion:

> For the training given by the paid professors of contentious arguments
> was like the treatment of the matter by Gorgias. For they used to hand
> out speeches to be learned by heart, some rhetorical, others in the form
> of question and answer, each side supposing that their arguments on

---

19. Quotations here from these two works are from the translation of W.A.
Richard-Cambridge in *The Works of Aristotle*, ed. W.D. Ross (Oxford, 1949–1956),
Vol. 1 (1955). The reconstitution of the medieval Latin texts of Aristotle's works,
under way for some years under the direction of Lorenzo Minio-Paluello and others
in the *Aristoteles Latinus* project, has not yet produced versions of these two treatises.

either side generally fall among them. And therefore the teaching they gave their pupils was ready but rough. For they used to suppose that they trained people by imparting to them not the art but its products, as though any one professing that he would impart a form of knowledge to obviate any pain in the feet, were then not to teach a man the art of shoe-making or the sources whence he can acquire anything of the kind, but were to present him with several kinds of shoes of all sorts: for he has helped him to meet his need, but has not imparted an art to him.[20]

This insistence upon "art"—as opposed to *formulae* or *materia*—helps to explain why John of Salisbury and his contemporaries saw no inherent conflict in this easy intermingling of the three arts of the *trivium*. In that all three arts promoted essentially the same inner ability in a student, John would naturally place the dialectical skills of these two books of Aristotle right alongside the normal training in grammar and rhetoric based on Donatus, Priscian, Cicero, and Quintilian.[21]

One further element remains to be considered. By the year 1170, as we have seen, there are accounts of boys engaged in exercises in all three arts of the *trivium*, including not only the tropes and figures but "sophisms" and formal disputations. Presumably this was all in Latin. But of course a good many twelfth-century English figures were trilingual (English, French, Latin), Thomas à Becket and John of Salisbury among them. Was all their schooling in just one language? Certainly the school teachers were aware of the problem of vernacular languages in respect to the teaching of Latin. In the year 1199 we find evidence of that in Alexander de Villedieu's *Doctrinale*, the hexameter grammar textbook that eventually replaced Priscian in the schools. Alexander not only brings Latin syntax up to date and includes some Latinized Germanic words, but he quite explicitly

---

20. *On Sophistical Refutations*, 184[a]. In the seventeenth century Francis Bacon's retort to this passage (*Advancement of Learning*, II.xiii.6–7) was to be that Aristotle "would have us exchange a rich wardrobe for a pair of shoes."
21. It was the university curriculum, after all, which destroyed the concept of the *trivium* as a coordinated set of progymnasmatic processes to promote sophisticated language use. By 1215 Oxford is requiring the *Topics* and *On Sophistical Refutations* for first year university students along with the advanced grammar of Priscian. Ultimately this curricular sorting-out led to a two-tier educational system, at least in England, in which the most elementary schools taught only basic grammar (and sometimes song), leaving dialectic and advanced grammar to the universities. Rhetoric was thus squeezed out, to reappear in the university only in the fifteenth century. For the curriculum of 1215 see Hastings Rashdall, *Universities of Europe in the Middle Ages*, 3 vols., new ed. F.M. Powicke and A.B. Emden (Oxford, 1936), I, 440. Also see Murphy, *Rhetoric in the Middle Ages*, esp. pp. 94–95.

reminds his school master readers in his prefatory remarks that they are dealing with students who already have another language—*lingua laica*:

> I am about to write the *Doctrinale* for young clerics
> And I add my own writings to those of many teachers.
> Now instead of the trifles of Maximianus the boys will read
> What the ancients used to refuse to reveal to their dear
>   companions.
> May the grace of the Holy Spirit attend this work
> And assist me and make me bring it about that it is useful.
> If the boys at first fail to grasp it fully,
> Let him listen, who, taking on the function of teacher,
> Reveals it to the boys, lecturing to them in their own
>   language (*laica lingua*);
> Even to the boys most of it will be clear.
>   Alexander de Villedieu, *Doctrinale,* vv. 1–10.[22]

In other words, the well-educated Englishman of the twelfth century would not only have been drilled in all three arts of the *trivium,* but would have undergone this training in at least two languages—English and Latin—with perhaps French as a third possibility depending on his travels. Or a well-educated Englishman, for instance, could get to the continent to study, say, canon law with a considerable background in language *facilitas* already in his possession.

Now, what might all this mean to the conjectural educational biography of the poet of *The Owl and the Nightingale*? Very probably he was born an Englishman, studied on the continent, and returned to England as an adult. Perhaps it was around 1176 when Henry II recalled from the continent the scholars who had benefices in England but had been studying on the continent. Perhaps it was later, depending upon how one chooses to interpret line 1091 about the possible death of King Henry. He may well have been trilingual, which would make interesting the possibility that he did indeed com-

---

22.   Scribere clericulis paro Doctrinale novellis,
                 pluraque doctorum sociabo scripta meorum.
                 iamque legent pueri pro nugis Maximiani
                 quae veteres sociis nolebant pandere caris.
                 praesens huic operi sit gratia Pneumatis almi;
                 me iuvet et faciat complere quod utile fiat.
                 si pueri primo nequeant attendere plene,
                 hic tamen attendet, qui doctoris vice fungens,
                 atque legens pueris laica lingua reserabit;
                 et pueris etiam pars maxima plana patebit.

Das Doctrinale des Alexander de Villa-Dei, ed. Dietrich Reichling, *Monumenta Germaniae paedogogica* 12 (Berlin, 1893), p. 1. For an analysis of the *Doctrinale* see Murphy, *Rhetoric in the Middle Ages,* pp. 146–151.

pose another version in French which shows up in the Titchfield catalogue.[23] The author would have learned the Latin grammar of Donatus and Priscian and the inventional and dispositional love of Cicero, would have been exposed to the rhetorical figures of the Pseudo-Cicero, and the disputational exercises of the schools based on the dialectic of Aristotle. He would thus have acquired a considerable *facilitas* in language, to use Quintilian's term. That *facilitas* certainly did not have to be limited to one language, since it was intended to be an art resident in the person himself, and not merely a set of *formulae* in one specific language like English or Latin. A medieval rhetorician or grammarian would have seen no problem there.

THE DEBATE IN THE POEM

Let us look briefly at the poem itself. More than ten percent of the verses deal with the argumentative frame itself, including two fairly lengthy discussions by the author of the nightingale's problems in replying to the owl (659–706, 933–954). A number of the proverbs refer to dialectical problems of this nature, including one attributed to "Alfred" (1072–1074) about speaking well being the same as fighting well, which has no located material source. (This same idea appears in Aristotle's *Rhetoric*, I. i., but this book was unknown to twelfth-century readers and in any case the idea was probably a well known dialectical commonplace.)

No clear idea of any debate can be secured until the opposing arguments are arranged against each other. For the reader as well as the attacker/defender, the argument as a whole ought to proceed in some definite order,[24] and one good way for a reader to examine this order of battle is to strip away amplifying verbiage in search of the contestants' own outline. Before commenting on the poem in light of its "environment of discourse," it will be useful to analyze the *Owl and Nightingale* into its argumentative parts, in the order in which the poet presents them. The text used is that of Stanley (1972).

---

23. See Hume, *The Owl and the Nightingale*, p. 12n. The Titchfield catalogue uses the phrase *in gallico*.

24. So begins Aristotle's advice to disputants in Book Eight of *Topics*: "Next there fall to be discussed the problems of arrangement and method in putting questions. Anyone who intends to frame questions must, first of all, select the ground from which he should make his attack; secondly, he must frame them and arrange them one by one to himself; thirdly and lastly, he must proceed actually to put them to the other party."

Verses	Nightingale	Owl	Comments
Title			*Altercacio* appears in ms. J. [Titchfield catalogue lists "altercaciones inter . . ."] Plait (v. 5), plaiding (v. 12) = law suit or pleading
1–12	[Setting and Introduction]		
13	"þe Niȝtingale bigon þe speche"		
14–33	Description of scene (no quoted song)		
33–40	'get away' speech		
40–45		Owl waits until eve	
46–54		Look out if I catch you	
55–138	Personal abuse speech 98–126; *exemplum* (Vorbisne) 98. (See also 244, 637.) —127–138 ("bispel" of it: moral)		Build-up toward violence
139–149		Owl is furious "Fly up here"	
150–152			
153–186	"No, . . . scharpe clawe" —proverb flight/fly (176) —we disagree, but must fight with words not force (w/o strife or battle—183)		vv.5—182 to establish conflict Salisbury, *Metalogicon*, III, 190: "verbal rather than physical conflict"
187–188		Who shall judge us?	
189–198	I know Nichole of Guildeforde —praise (192–198)		

Verses	Nightingale	Owl	Comments
199–214		OK—he'll never fall for "þe fals dom deme" (210)	
215–252	Owl, why do you do what "unwi3tis" do? (list) —Alfred proverb (236)		
253–390		Angry: "Galegale" —why I have beak, etc. —Alfred proverb (299) —is hawk worse? —you say I can't sing (310) —attacks N's singing —Alfred proverb (349ff.) —flies at night (365)	A perceptive insight by the poet: the Nightingale here is afraid not of the Owl, but of doing badly in the debate. Cf. Aristotle, *Topica* VIII 159ª20, on making mistakes.
391–410	Thinks, decides to be bold though afraid to "alegge" —for he spoke right and sense (396) (Vor he spac boþe ri3t an red)		
410–465	You sing bad things —winter (412) —rejoice in evil (417–429) —sing in snow (430–432) —I sing bliss (433–443) ⌣men glad ⌣flowers, trees ⌣rose greets my song		*post hoc* argument (a fallacy)

OUTLINE OF *The Owl and the Nightingale* Continued

Verses	Nightingale	Owl	Comments
	⌣but not overlong (450–466) (wisdom to do)		
467–472		Owl thought well, for those "aferd of plaites wrenche"	Foreshadowing of "sate" *topos*
473–542		You ask why I sing	
		—good custom for me to have friends in house especially at Xmas	
		—I help him.	
		—And I think of other than to play or sing—I have answer prepared (488)	= trick [sophism?]. Only Owl repeats the charge Many doublets, vv. 479–488
		—For summer is too wanton (*wlonc*) and misreckons man's thinking	
		—nought of clanesse	
		—steeds in stud, and you there among "of golnesse is al þi song" (498)	
		—sing worse than hedge-sparrow	
		—pipe like titmouse	
		—I sing of home, not winter (532–539)	
		—"Hu þincþ þe? Artu ȝut inume, / artu mid riȝte overcum?" (541–542)	Recap question (dialectical process) (inume = refuted/captured [legal])

Verses	Nightingale	Owl	Comments
543–548	"Nay, nay"—with one bare word" I'll make your speech ruined		Denial that issue is settled
549–555		That isn't right—you made a charge and I have to give you an answer. —if we are to seek judgment I'll speak to you as you speak to me, and you answer me if you can (ȝif þu miȝt) (555)	*Topos* of fair play Owl professes to choose *same* mode of reply but does not do it —choosing his own ground (i.e., "use" is the standard to be set up)
556–576		—do you have any other use besides a shrill voice? So how can you be of use to man? —you cry out as if mad —Alfred says song is not enough for worth	—(doesn't *ask*, just assumes agreement and goes on)
577–592		Things you are not ⌣fair ⌢strong ⌢thick ⌣long ⌣fair ⌣clene	—return to personal attack
593–598		—You sing behind seat of privy yet despise my food	
599–601		—And you eat worms and spiders	—comparison
602–655		—I clean mouse from church and help man	—contrast

OUTLINE OF *The Owl and the Nightingale* Continued

Verses	Nightingale	Owl	Comments
		—My house is evergreen	—allegory of evergreen/ivy?
		—Yours disappears in winter cold (624)	
		—Yet you say nest is unclean ⌣ox, child	
		—I answer; come look how strong and neat ⌣My birds go to privy at end	—challenge?
656–658		—Sit thou stille!	—pun on privy seat? [Nere þu never ibunde uastre]
		—"Never thou't be bound faster"	
		—"You'll never find answer"	—Taunt that Nightingale cannot answer him (see same process above, vv. 541–542)
		—"Hang up þin ax!"	
659–700	Author's comment on Nightingale's need-problem of replying		—Nightingale admits premise? (See above, comment on vv. 556–576)
	—well-nigh out of *rede* become		
	—tried to think of something else good besides singing		
	—hard to fight against the truth and right ⌣needs ingenuity when opponent must be answered ⌣it is easy to make mistakes with words		A key passage: The reference to the disputative situation ("An þ man mot on oþer segge") is generalized to any contention, not just this

Verses	Nightingale	Owl	Comments
	∽but wit is keener in need ∽Alfred proverb (when calamity highest, remedy is next) ∽repeated (699–700)		debate. cf. Aristotle *De sophisticis elenchis* 170[b] 10 on ease of using wrong words.
701–706	Nightingale had found good answer in her hard time		
707–710	Owl, you ask if I do anything but sing in the summer		Admits premise but qualifies with "in summer" by analogy to songs of priests, canons, etc., and begins *Topos* of One Better than Many
711–746	—My one talent is better than all of thine —I sing like priests, etc. who sing men to God ∽sing with them ∽gladden them ∽"I warni men to here gode" (739) ∽This is not mere "chattering" —If we go to Pope of Rome, he'd agree		To lead men to God (enthymeme) Canon law echo? The sense is that the Nightingale is so sure of being right that she'd be willing to refer the case to Rome for judgment.
747–750	And I have another argument you can't withstand		False transition, since it is actually a continuation of the same *topos*, not 'another' one
751–808	Why criticize my size and weakness? —cunning better ∽Alfred proverb ∽horse is strong		—evasion of issue? —authority —analogy

Outline of *The Owl and the Nightingale* Continued

Verses	Nightingale	Owl	Comments
	—but one good thing is better than many —wrestling (795–804) —my one is better than all of yours (807–808)		—cf. Edward Wilson, *Notes and Queries* (January, 1976), 3. See above, v. 711–712, and below, v. 836
809–836	—fox and cat fable ''Betere is min on pan pine twelve'' (836)		Aesop's fable, see Quintilian, *Institutio oratoria*, I..9 (cf. *Metalogicon*, I, 24–25.) (Note on line 816: Magoon declares that the fox's ''hanging from bough'' ruins the point; Stanley thinks it an error in poet's narrative. The line reads: ''An he kan hongi bi þe boȝe'').
837–838		''Abid! Abid!'' (repeated 845). Your words are trickery (''Swikelede'').	
839–844		All your words you gloss over (''bileist'') so that they seem truth, and, so made decent and made pleasing . . . all them that hear, they deem that you speak truth.	Accusation of sophistry. cf. Aristotle, *De sophisticis elenchis* 171^{b}30: ''a certain appearance of wisdom without the reality'', Transition
845–848		Abid! Abid! now we'll see you've lied.	

Verses	Nightingale	Owl	Comments
849–855		You say you sing to help man home, but you lie	Beginning of reply to One-is-Better-than-Many argument
856–874		—My song reminds of true guilt	Proverbial antithesis?
875–892		—If right go forth, and back come wrong, then better is my woe than your song.	Comparison
893–902		—you sing only of ''golnesse''	Contrast
903–933		—I sing everywhere, not you	
933–954	Nightingale pondered, in weeds where men go to their need, to calm herself —vexed, ashamed —for Alfred says the wrathful do not speak well (943–44)		cf. Aristotle, *De sophisticis elenchis* 174ª15: "for when agitated everybody is less able to take care of himself." Also, *Topica* VIII, 161ª20.
955–1042	Listen—I sing where Lord/Lady lie, beside lovers' bed —I sing joy, you gloom —is it better man be blithe or sad? (991–992) —(repetitions) —other lands are grim/wild so I don't go there —proverb: mad to sow and never reap		(disorganized section) Reflecting Nightingale's discomfiture? Rhetorical question Overlong, little new, not systematic

OUTLINE OF *The Owl and the Nightingale* Continued

Verses	Nightingale	Owl	Comments
1043–1066		Owl (wroth) ready to strife (*to cheste rad*) with flashing eyes —you say you know "lours', bours" —once you lured, got caught, were sentenced to be drawn by wild horses —you'll get caught again!	Eager, not angry? Ready to pounce on an error New evidence?
1067–1174	Nightingale would have fought with sword or spear at this —pondered her speech: "who speaks well fights well" (song-Alfred) (1072) —not my shame for jealous husband —King Henry (d. 1189?) judged the matter and banished the knight and fined 100 pounds —now my race can sing —but you are hunted and hated —made scarecrow —you sing of griefs (so it's right to hate you) —list (1151–1164)		"Past fact" accusation Nightingale begins to recover her composure No other record of proverb "Iesus his soule do merci" (1092). Possible clue to date. King Henry's judgment: foreshadowing of *determinatio* by Nicholas (see below, comment on vv. 1789–1794). Accusation-list. Note Aristotle, *Topics* VIII 157ª1: "It is well to expand the argument and insert

Verses	Nightingale	Owl	Comments
	—messengers of woe (*and* "all wearing linen cloth") are cursed (evil befall)		things that it does not require at all. . . for in the multitude of details the whereabouts of the fallacy is obscured."
1175–1290		Owl gave quick reply —have you been ordained, so you can curse? —matching list of what owl knows —future: (foresee things that are fated, but not responsible for what is foreseen) (1233–1242) —everything you say to dishonor me turns shame on you: the stroke that fells thee is thine own (1286)	Clergy? Boast-list to counter Nightingale's accusation-list. Boethius, *Consolatio*?
1291–1330	Nightingale sighed, pondered, for all the points the owl had made (1294) —only witches know future —you are cursed (need no priest to make it worse) because men hate you —you don't know stars (ape can turn book)		Another reflection on the disputative situation. See above, vv. 659–700. Non sequitur

OUTLINE OF *The Owl and the Nightingale* Continued

Verses	Nightingale	Owl	Comments
1331–1510	—I sing only of true love		Reversal of Owl's Boethius echo?
	∿not my fault if women (not man) do wrong?		
	∿anything may be used for evil—my song too		Restatement and example (money/weapons)
	∿do you condemn love itself?		Love = sex
	∿women are frail, their flesh is weak, drive men mad		Diatribe? Confessional?
	∿my song teaches such love does not last long		
	∿my song is short, falls with hot breath		
	∿don't try to break marriage bonds		Analogy (sophism)
	∿adultery is a shame		
	∿but maybe husbands fault?		
1511–1602		The Owl sensed victory	Causality again (this passage of some 180 lines is the longest argument on a single subject in the poem)
		—Wives have troubles, and they come to me	
		∿husbands cheat	Long rambling defense
		∿wives mourn, my heart breaks for them	Picture of good marriage

Verses	Nightingale	Owl	Comments
		—yet you have me sore vexed that my heart is well nigh paralyzed that I may hardly speak; and yet I will further wreak —repeats his charges: hated, pelted with stones, scarecrow	Pathos? No, this much-misunderstood passage is probably a stratagem: cf. Aristotle, *Topica* VIII 156^{b}18: "It is a good rule also, occasionally to bring an objection against oneself: for answerers are put off their guard against those who appear to be arguing impartially."
		—so I do good by my death —your death does nothing, nor your life	Reversal of Nightingale's claim about good her song does (admits the charge, though) *And* capitalizes on Nightingale's claim "any good thing can be used for bad"
1635–1666	Nightingale heard this, hopped on a blossoming branch —owl, beware, I debate no more with you, because ∼you brag you're hated ∼I think you've lost! ∼you yield your own shame —Nightingale stopped speaking, started singing ∼other birds gathered, as men gather to jeer at one who's lost game		Colorful description of presumed audience gathering about apparent victor "Game," not "debate" (Compare with owl's battlefield analogy below, vv. 1712–1716)

Outline of *The Owl and the Nightingale* Continued

Verses	Nightingale	Owl	Comments
1667–1716		Owl: have you called army to fight? —I can call mine too —But one agreed to ajudge. —will you break word? —I'll fight you all —Owl spoke audaciously to try plan of talking Nightingale down, as boasters do on a battle-field —agree to go to a judge —you agreed to do it.	Shifting of ground Return to "judge" *topos* (they've been debating *each other* so far) Disrespect for rules? Note that the Nightingale has been described (by the author) at times as fairly discomfited or perplexed; here, the poet seems to imply that the Owl is actually dishonest, by contrast.

End of Debate: All after line 1716 is procedural: intervention of the Wren, reiteration of earlier agreement to seek a third party, justification of Nicholas as suitable to render judgment, and agreement that Owl would prepare the summary.

1717–1738		(Wren intervenes) The Wren came with the dawn to help Nightingale —clever, loved of men	The literal dawn? or to stop the drama?

Verses	Nightingale	Owl	Comments
		—nurtured among men and not in woods —could speak anywhere even before king She said: will you break peace and harm the king?	Allegory of what? *Not* "plead" in law sense, but "speke" [Date: 1194–1198 when Justiciar Hubert Walter kept peace while Richard I was abroad? But note that neither ms. actually contains the word "king" in line 1731.]
		"lateþ dom þis plaid tobreke"	*Determinatio?*
1739–1749	Yes, but for the law and not for thy *tale*, Wren —I'm not afraid of judgment (*dome*). —I still want Nicholas —Where might we find him?		Self-righteous? When the Wren uses the singular (3[5]) address above it could be construed as an admonition to the Owl, who has just spoken. The Nightingale, however, is the one who answers the Wren.
1750–1768		*Wren*: at Portisham in Dorsetshire "þar he demeþ manie riȝte dom An diht and writ mani wisdom" —he is easy to find, for he has but one house— "þat his bischopen muchel schame" —why don't they give him rent and place?	A Judge? One house only—fault of bishops and others who know his worth. Stanley (21): this proves Nicholas not author, for he wouldn't dare criticize potential benefactors.

OUTLINE OF *The Owl and the Nightingale* Continued

Verses	Nightingale	Owl	Comments
1769–1780		*Owl*: it is true that rich men misdo when they ignore his talents and give rents to unfit men, or to children. —so let us go to his *dom*	Again, further indication of the "rules" governing such debates. Compare this speech with the Owl's angry preceding one.
1781–1783	Let us do so, but who will recount our arguments?		
1784–1788		I will, and you correct me if I err.	Surprising concession by Nightingale? No, a normal procedure.
1789–1794 (end)	Author: They flew away and arrived at Portisham —but if you ask how it thrived, I cannot say—there is no more of this story.		Typical of postponed *determinatio* in disputation, but adds to drama here

Explicit

THE NATURE OF THE DEBATE

To begin with, the whole tone of the poem of course depends upon the contestants' agreement to fight with words and not physical weapons. At line 183, for instance, the nightingale reminds the owl that they must oppose each other "Mid fayre worde / Witute cheste and bute fiȝte"; compare this with John of Salisbury's praise of the *Topics* of Aristotle: "Since dialectic is carried on between two persons, this book teaches the matched contestants whom it trains and provides with reasons and topics, to handle their proper weapons and engage in verbal rather than physical conflict." At the end of the poem, you will recall, the owl accuses the nightingale of breaking this agreement by bringing in the wren and the other birds, and of course the nightingale gets so angry at one point that she would have fought with weapons if she had been a man, as the author so slyly phrases it.

Perhaps the most significant passage in the whole poem, from the dialectical-rhetorical point of view, is lines 659–706 in which the nightingale ponders her problem of replying to the owl's best speech (lines 549–658) in which *eight* arguments are laid out. The nightingale's reflections are virtually a paraphrase of the opening of Book Eight of Aristotle's *Topics* dealing with problems of choosing methods of reply. I cannot recall any other passage in Middle English, even in Chaucer, which so directly takes up the interpersonal problems of reply and attack. The nightingale's reply is then built around two selected questions she chooses from the eight thrust at her by the owl—her singing, and her cunning as opposed to the owl's size. The owl then accuses her of sophistry (*Swikelede*) because she has lumped together all his arguments, linking the true with the false and making all the words seem alike so that all will seem true: in the schools they would have called this a fallacy of amphiboly and ambiguity, to use the dialectical jargon, or would have called it a sham enthymeme to use the technical rhetorical term.

This particular exchange, which runs altogether from line 659 to line 933, is rich in dialectical and rhetorical lore. The author must have had a very good time composing it, and we can hope that his audience relished it as well. It is well worth a rereading in light of what we know about twelfth-century schools. The point, of course, is not that Aristotle's *Topica* or some such textbook was a "source" for this or that line of verse; the poet's experience was.

A part of the nightingale's actual reply, incidentally, is the much-discussed account of Aesop's fable of the cat and the fox. We moderns tend to take the Middle Ages much too seriously. But Aesop tells a simple story of a cat with only one trick—climbing trees—which turns out to be better than the fox's hundred tricks for escaping the hounds, because the fox simply cannot make up his mind which of the hundred to choose, so that the hounds catch him. Now, a number of people have done research into medieval foxes and have discovered that indeed there seems to be some evidence that some foxes can indeed climb trees (as the poet says in line 816). Francis Magoun asserts that this ruins the point of the story, and Eric Stanley concludes (rather sadly) that "it is a blunder in the art of narrative."

But this particular fable of Aesop was a rhetorical commonplace in schools even in Quintilian's time—he specifically describes how they are to be used in writing exercises (*Inst.* I.9)—and of course his set of exercises was taken up by Bernard of Chartres in the twelfth century. One of Bernard's pupils, John of Salisbury (I. 24–25) quotes many passages from Quintilian about these exercises though he does not mention this particular fablist by name. In any case, the point is that schoolboys were drilled in composition by being asked to rewrite Aesop's fable, and Bernard evidently had his students doing this kind of rewriting in both prose and verse. Was this little story left over from the author's school days?[25]

As for ruining the point of the story, consider for a moment why it would be a useful school exercise. It is a good school exercise precisely because it has at least *two* solutions to the problem. There is evidence from the very early Middle Ages—the times of Augustine or Isidore—that students were asked to support *either* the cat or the fox. Because one point can be made that decision is important, and this is Aesop's original point; but another point can be made that a cat is helpless unless he is near a tree, and therefore a good speaker should be prepared with many tricks for many possible situations. If I had been in the audience to hear the poem, I would have agreed that showing the fox can climb trees is a way to heighten the emphasis.

As it turns out in the poem, the owl is too smart to be caught arguing about examples, and he interrupts the nightingale with his

---

25. It is interesting to note that other twelfth-century writers also re-work Aesop's fables. For instance Marie de France's handling of the Cat and the Fox story is summarized by Stanley, *Owl and Nightingale*, Appendix p. 164.

accusation of sophistry. So we never hear his reply to the challenge that "Betere is min on pen pine twelve" (836).[26]

One last item from the poem: why does the nightingale allow the owl at the end of the poem to be the one to repeat the arguments before the judge, Nicholas of Guildford? At first glance this seems out of character, given the angry tone of earlier exchanges between the two birds. The answer lies in the format of the medieval disputation. It had several steps: first the statement of a question, then the opposing arguments of the contestants, and finally the *determinatio,* or resolution by *magister* or other third party. In the schools this was usually the master, or what we would call the faculty member. But this could only happen on the spot when the master was physically present. When he was not present, or when participants wished to have a *determinatio* by some one geographically removed, it sometimes occurred that one of the parties—by mutual consent—would draw up a summary of arguments for transmission by messenger. The poet knows this, of course, and so inserts in the poem this little piece of stage business that for us may seem quite unusual. It was not unusual in the twelfth century. So the whole debate is not to be restaged for Nicholas when they arrive at Portisham in Dorsetshire, but only the abstract of it.

A CONCLUSION

There is a depressing inference to be drawn from the chronology of all this. Obviously the "owl and nightingale" poet is happily at home with both rhetoric and dialectic, delighted at his opportunity to play games with birds and readers. He is a master of his four-stress couplet. Eric Stanley concludes the introduction to his fine edition of the poem with these words: ". . . the poet gives the impression of true ease in writing. It is a studied virtue, and one would give much to know who were his masters, and what was the nature of his training."

It is one of the great tragedies of English literature, it seems to me, that this "studied virtue," as Stanley calls it, virtually disappeared

---

26. Edward Wilson (*Notes and Queries,* January, 1976, p. 3) suggests that Seneca's *De beneficiis* is a more likely source than Quintilian's *Institutio* for the "wraslinge" passage immediately preceding the cat-and-fox story. But in this case, also, the *topos* is "One Good Trick Better Than Many." Whether the details might have come from Seneca or Quintilian or someone else, of course, the *topos* makes a good composition exercise. It is the *facilitas* in comparison that counts.

for two centuries until the time of Chaucer. We do happen to know
the nature of the training of the poet of *The Owl and the Nightingale*
even if we do not know the names of his masters. The poet is a literary
brother of John of Salisbury, sharing in his educational biography at
least.[27] This happy marriage of rhetoric and dialectic, based on grammar, makes this poem the delight that it is. Though John did not
know it, he had himself, in his *Metalogicon,* helped to introduce
the sharpness of dialectic into direct competition with the efferves-
cence of literary invention founded on rhetoric and grammar.

The history of what came afterward is clear but sad. Dialectic
dominated the University, driving rhetoric out. The ''dialectical
establishment'' triumphed. Since dialectic was a basic university subject, after about 1200 it was no longer taught in the lower schools of
England. So the schoolboys of thirteenth- and fourteenth-century
England became ''grammar school'' students, with neither rhetoric
nor dialectic to enrich their basic knowledge. Where in all this was
there room for the humane advice of Quintilian about the values of
literature? Where was there opportunity for a happy jointure of all
three arts of the *trivium*?

The Owl and the Nightingale, then, is not a literary anachronism,
born two hundred years before its time. The poem is a true product
of the enlightened environment of discourse of the twelfth century.
It is not in the spirit of the thirteenth. The author is not a *Pearl*-poet
born too early. Instead, he is an exceptionally fine product of his own
age, when the rigid decisions of university curriculum makers had
not yet shattered the continuum of discourse that we know as the
trivium. We can only conclude that his work shows us what might
have been.

27. We might well look more carefully at the career of another literary brother,
Alexander Neckham (1157–1217). He wrote his *Corrogationes Promethei,* a Latin
treatise designed to display his literary talents, apparently to recommend himself
for some unnamed position. The ''Prometheus'' in the title refers to Alexander,
seen as chained looking up and unable to rise in the world. He studied in his native
England, taught at Dunstable then, 1180–1186, in Paris (which he disliked) and
returned to England. He died as Abbot of Cirencester. The text of the *Corrogationes*
is in Paul Meyer, *Notice sur Les Corrogationes Promethei d'Alexandre Neckham* in
Notices et Extraits 35(1897), 2ᵉ partie, pp. 641–682. For a general discussion of his
career see J. Reginald O'Donnell, ''The Liberal Arts in the Twelfth Century with
Special Reference to Alexander Nequam (1157–1217),'' in *Arts Libéraux et philosophie au moyen âge,* Actes du quatrième congrès international de philosophie médiévale (Montréal et Paris, 1969), pp. 127–135.

Topical Invention in Medieval French Literature

DOUGLAS KELLY

RHETORIC had a vast and profound influence during the four to five hundred years when medieval French was a literary language. The variety of authors and works, the diversity of kinds and forms of literary expression make it difficult to indicate briefly the scope of that influence. Romance, *chanson de geste,* and fabliau; troubadours, trouvères, and poets of the Second Rhetoric; religious and secular writings; allegorical and historical verse—such variety is in part the result of rhetorical influence and inspiration. Some prominent authors demand by themselves special consideration, just as would Cicero, Horace, and Vergil in the history of Latin rhetoric and poetics: Chrétien de Troyes and Thomas d'Angleterre; Rutebeuf and Guillaume de Machaut, the two parts of the *Roman de la rose*; Villon, Charles d'Orléans. Unfortunately, the influence of rhetoric on such eminent writers as these has scarcely received any serious attention. It therefore seems best in this discussion to suggest what misunderstandings regarding rhetoric account for its relative neglect in medieval French scholarship, and then to show how certain features of rhetorical invention may further the interpretation and appreciation of the best authors in medieval French, as well as the hosts of lesser writers that thrived alongside them.

The foundation for most scholarship and criticism touching on rhetoric in medieval French literature has been the work of E. Faral[1] and E. R. Curtius.[2] Their studies stress a broad schematization of

1. *Les arts poétiques du XIIe et du XIIIe siècle: recherches et documents sur la technique littéraire du moyen âge* (Paris 1924, 1958); *Recherches sur les sources latines des contes et romans courtois du moyen âge* (Paris 1913).
2. *Europäische Literatur und lateinisches Mittelalter,* 2nd ed. (Bern 1954); on pp. 565–566, see the bibliography of Curtius' more specialized studies that prepare

rhetoric. It includes on the one hand the principal phases of composition: invention, disposition, ornamentation, memory, and gesture. In addition, the kinds of eloquence are identified as judicial, deliberative, and epideictic or panegyric; medieval French literature underwent the influence principally of epideictic oratory and literature. Specific medieval adaptations of classical rhetoric also come in for consideration. This includes foremost the principle of amplification and abbreviation of a given source. Another medieval adaptation that is notable is the development of the concept of Material Style, which makes stylistic distinctions according to the quality of vocabulary—that is, the reflection in vocabulary of the social class of the most prominent personages in a given subject matter.

The application of this knowledge to the interpretation of French literature has been unsatisfactory, with the prominent, and recent, exception of the troubadours. Modern criticism tends to emphasize "creation" and "structure," terms most closely related to rhetoric's invention and disposition. Yet these very phases of composition seem to offer little that is applicable to literary composition, even when they are discussed in the medieval arts of poetry like those of Matthew of Vendôme, Geoffrey of Vinsauf, and John of Garland. Consequently, there has been a tendency to neglect the influence of rhetoric on medieval French literature. In particular, this has meant that scholars have not pondered and assimilated the significance of medieval notions of invention, disposition, and ornamentation.[3]

The neglect has been justified by three principal arguments. First, medieval grammars and rhetorics, including the arts of poetry, give little relevant instruction on composition beyond ornamentation by tropes and figures. Second, the treatises are too elementary to be of use in the interpretation of serious literature. Third, vernacular

for this volume. English trans. W. R. Trask as *European Literature and the Latin Middle Ages* (New York 1953); special bibliography, pp. 597–598. See also Curtius' *Gesammelte Aufsätze zur romanischen Philologie* (Bern, Munich 1960).

3. On the aptness of these subjects for French romance, see D. Kelly, "Theory of Composition in Medieval Narrative Poetry and Geoffrey of Vinsauf's *Poetria Nova*," *Mediaeval Studies*, XXXI (1969), 117–148. In general, see C. S. Baldwin, *Medieval Rhetoric and Poetic (to 1400)* (New York 1928); and, for the later period, W. F. Patterson, *Three Centuries of French Poetic Theory: A Critical History of the Chief Arts of Poetry in France (1328–1660)*, 2 vols. (Ann Arbor 1935). The best study is still H. Brinkmann, *Zu Wesen und Form mittelalterlicher Dichtung* (Halle 1928). Also useful: J. W. H. Atkins, *English Literary Criticism: The Medieval Phase*, 2 vols. (London, New York 1952); J. J. Murphy, *Rhetoric in the Middle Ages* (Berkeley and Los Angeles 1974); P. Zumthor, "Rhétorique et poétique latines et romanes," in the *Grundriß der romanischen Literaturen des Mittelalters* (Heidelberg, 1972), I, 57–91.

writers tend to use compositional principles and methods independent of the rhetorical tradition illustrated in the arts of poetry; two
examples are the influence of the oral tradition on the *chanson de
geste,* and that of popular verse forms and techniques on the fixed
forms that emerged in the northern French *puys* and in the Second
Rhetoric.

INVENTION OF *TOPOI*

Invention is the technique whereby material is identified as suitable for treatment in the literary work; it also covers the adaptation of
that material to authorial intention. It therefore includes both raw
source material (*materia remota*) and authorial changes in, and adaptation of, that material (*materia propinqua*).[4] The choice of the
source material is as arbitrary as the facts of the case an orator may
choose to defend. Indeed, if the source is imposed upon an author,
either by a patron or some tradition, there is little real difference
between his *matiere* and that of the orator. If the material chosen is
good and the author has the talent or insight needed to exploit its
potentialities, his adaptation will be successful.

Prior to the identification of source material, however, the author
identifies what Geoffrey of Vinsauf calls an "archetype" (*Poetria
nova,* v. 48)[5] or mental conception of the work he proposes to write.
This conception provides a context that gives meaning to the source
material and indicates where and how it might be adapted to the
author's intention. "In poeticae facultatis exercitio, praecedit imagi-
natio sensus, sequitur sermo interpres intellectus, deinde ordinatio
in qualitate tractatus."[6] In composition in medieval French, this
technique is a conscious departure from the oral tradition. As Chrétien de Troyes points out in the Prologue to his *Erec et Enide,* the
writer progresses from *matiere* that previous *conteurs* tended to
"depecier et corronpre" towards a "molt bele conjointure."[7] Or, as
his contemporary Marie de France puts it, the writer's predecessors
"Assez oscurement diseient," whereas the adaptor discovers and

---

4. Terminology from Konrad of Mure, *Summa de arte prosandi,* ed. W. Kronbichler (Zürich 1968), pp. 66–67. Konrad knew Geoffrey of Vinsauf, and his treatment of the terminology parallels the *domus construenda* image Geoffrey uses to
describe invention; see Kronbichler, pp. 14–15.

5. Ed. E. Faral, in *Les arts poétiques.*

6. *Ars versificatoria,* ed. Faral, in *Les arts poétiques,* p. 180 § 52. Cf. J. de
Ghellinck, "Imitari, imitatio," *ALMA (Bulletin du Cange),* XV (1940–41), 151–159.

7. Ed. M. Roques, CFMA (Paris 1955), vv. 14 and 21.

elicits from that obscurity "ceo k'i ert."[8] Even in the later Middle Ages this conception of composition prevails, as we may read in the Commentary to the *Echecs amoureux*:

> Et c'est choses samblable es choses que nous veons par art faittes ou nous veons que l'ouvrier qui voelt aulcunnes choses raisonnablement faire entent premierement et conchoit par devant en sa pensee la fourme de la chose qu'il voelt faire, et puis vient apres la fantasie ou la fourme dessus-ditte est inprimee et pourtraite, et puis la main et la doloire apres ou le pincel qui la chose parfait en la vertu des choses dessusdittes. Car . . . la doloire du carpentier ou le pincel du paintre se met a la similitude de la main qui l'adresce, et la main le remeult a la similitude de la fantasie et la fantasie oultre aussi a la similitude de la figure ou de la fourme que l'ouvrier principal entent.[9]

This conception of artistry is congruent with adaptation of *matiere* by the invention of topoi—that is, in Marie de France's words, the discovery of "ceo k'i ert."

The invention of *topoi* has not always been understood. The origin of the misunderstanding is the imprecise distinction made between historical topics and invention of *topoi*. The two ways to envisage *topoi* correspond neither in purpose nor in object of investigation. "Historical topics" stresses the frequency and regularity of topical material as indicative of historical and even psychic mentalities and changes in mentality. It thus seeks the commonplace in medieval literature over various spans of time. As such it is a branch of modern scholarship. But in rhetoric and poetics the invention of *topoi* is an art. The artist in invention seeks to identify places (*loci*) in his *matiere* that are suitable for elaboration or elucidation in conformity with context. Context is the meaning the author gives to his work. The actual material that fills the place is an *argumentum*. Such *argumenta* are the commonplaces that become the object of investigation in historical topics.[10] For critical appreciation of the given work, it is

---

8. *Les Lais*, ed. J. Rychner, CFMA (Paris 1968), Prologue vv. 12 and 22.

9. Bibliothèque Nationale ms. fr. 9197, fol. 16 r. Cf. the *Poetria Nova*, vv. 43–70.

10. On this distinction, see M. Baeumer, *Toposforschung* (Darmstadt 1973), especially pp. vii and 299–300. The distinction is well known in classical scholarship. See also the chapter by M. Leff (above) on Boethius' *De differentiis topicis* for the distinction between topoi in rhetoric and topoi in logic. Also, see Curtius, *Europäische Literatur*, pp. 89–92; E. Gallo, *The 'Poetria Nova' and Its Sources in Early Rhetorical Doctrine* (The Hague, Paris 1971), pp. 152–154; and his "Matthew of Vendôme: Introductory Treatise on the Art of Poetry," *Proceedings of the American Philosophical Society*, CXVIII (1974), 53.

not enough to know what commonplaces are used. It is just as important to understand where the *loci* are, how they are expressed, and what functions they serve.

That historical topics is a modern science is indicated by the absence in antiquity and the Middle Ages of catalogues of *topoi*. If we go back to the medieval sources, Cicero and Quintilian, we discover instruction on how to invent *topoi*.[11] These techniques, or formulae, correspond to those used by Matthew of Vendôme for the description of persons and things.[12] As formulae for topical invention, they help the writer invent credible arguments and verisimilar illustrations.[13] Where Cicero may be anxious to convince judges or his audience of the rights of heirs to paternal inheritance, Matthew of Vendôme would render the loves of a god plausible. He is thus close to the concerns of the troubadours and trouvères as well as of the authors of courtly romance and dream visions.

The perception of general truth inherent or implicit in the specific *matiere*—"ceo k'i ert," in Marie de France's expression—does not entail imposition of preconceived commonplaces on recalcitrant matter, but rather the elucidation of the *matiere* by what amounts to generic definition—that is, the identification of the qualities or paramount characteristics appropriate to the *matiere* and the context chosen for it. The elucidation derives from the formulae which address specific questions to the specific *matiere*. The author is not to apply the formulae indiscriminately. Cicero, for example, distinguishes between the abundance of formulae he proposes in his *Topica* and their judicious application in specific works.[14] Similarly, Matthew of Vendôme enjoins his students to master the techniques first by exercises in using the formulae (instruction on *descriptio*), then by learning to apply them judiciously in actual literary compositions (instruction on *exsecutio materiae*).[15] Such preliminary

---

11. See the *De inventione*, ed. E. Stroebel (Leipzig 1915), pp. 96^b–97^b; Quintilian, *Institutio oratoria*, ed. L. Radermacher (Leipzig 1959), I, 253.

12. *Ars versificatoria*, pp. 118–151. See also Gallo, *Proceedings*, CXVIII, 53; and F. P. Knapp, "Vergleich und Exempel in der lateinischen Rhetorik und Poetik von der Mitte des 12. bis zur Mitte des 13. Jahrhunderts," *Studi Medievali*, ser. 3, XIV (1973), 468–469; L. J. Friedman, "Occulta cordis," *Romance Philology*, XI (1957–58), 103–119.

13. Murphy, *Rhetoric*, pp. 68–69.

14. In *Rhetorica*, ed. A. S. Wilkins, 2 vols. (Oxford 1902–03), 21.79 and 23.87–24.90.

15. Cf. the outline to the *Ars versificatoria* that Faral gives in *Les arts poétiques*, pp. 106–108; and the *Ars versificatoria* itself, pp. 179–180.

exercises, known as *praeexercitamina* in antiquity, survive in the
student exercises contained in a manuscript part of which has been
published by Faral, and part, more recently, by B. Harbert.[16]

INVENTION AND MATERIAL STYLE: CHARACTER AND GENRE

The writer's choice of epithets is as much a feature of his invention
of *topoi* as his use of traditional, readily identifiable descriptions or
digressions.[17] They indicate the intention that inspired the topical
description or digression. For example, Paul Zumthor's statistical
surveys of the vocabulary in trouvère Chansons underscore topical
features as Matthew of Vendôme sets them forth: choice of epithet,
of characteristic vocabulary consistent with context and thus with
authorial intention.[18] Such elaboration provides the work's Material
Style.

Material Style is a medieval adaptation of the classical *genera dicendi*, or high, middle, and low styles.[19] Originally, the high style
used metaphorical language, the middle style figurative language
(figures of speech and figures of thought), and the low style common,
vulgar, or colloquial speech. During the transition from antiquity
to the High Middle Ages, these distinctions shifted to the designation
of characteristic types of persons and their attendant paraphernalia
and actions. A broad scheme includes high or aristocratic subjects,
middle or bourgeois subjects, and low, humble, or rural subjects.

---

16. On the *praeexercitamina*, see Curtius, *Europäische Literatur*, p. 440; and
W. Trimpi, "The Quality of Fiction: the Rhetorical Transmission of Literary Theory," *Traditio*, XXX (1974), 75–81. On the medieval school exercises, see Faral,
"Le manuscrit 511 du 'Hunterian Museum' de Glasgow: notes sur le mouvement
poétique et l'histoire des études littéraires en France et en Angleterre entre les années
1150 et 1225," *Studi medievali*, n.s. IX (1936), 18–121; B. Harbert, *A Thirteenth-
Century Anthology of Rhetorical Poems: Glasgow Ms Hunterian V.8.14* (Toronto
1975).

17. See the *Ars versificatoria*, pp. 120, § 44; and 132–134, §§ 60–71.

18. *Essai de poétique médiévale* (Paris 1972); *Langue, texte, énigme* (Paris 1975).
See also his "Charles d'Orléans et le langage de l'allégorie," *Mélanges Rita Lejeune*,
2 vols. (Gembloux 1969), II, 1481–1502; and "Recherches sur les topiques dans la
poésie lyrique des XIIe et XIIIe siècles," *Cahiers de civilisation médiévale*, II (1959),
409–427.

19. On the development of the concept of Material Style, see F. Quadlbauer, *Die
antike Theorie der 'genera dicendi' im lateinischen Mittelalter*, Österreichische
Akademie der Wissenschaften. Philologisch-historische Klasse. Sitzungsberichte,
CCXLI, 2 (Graz, Vienna, Cologne 1962). See also F. P. Knapp, *Studi medievali*,
ser. 3, XIV, 505–511.

John of Garland provided a schematic representation of the three
kinds of Material Style in "Vergil's Wheel." John makes the three
Vergilian works—the *Aeneid*, the *Georgics*, and the *Eclogues*—illustrate, respectively, aristocratic, bourgeois, and rural types.[20] The
inapplicability of the scheme to Vergil's poems is patent, and reveal-
ing. Not the illustration but the principle of illustration demands
within each of the three classes a variety of types—species within
genera, as John calls them[21]—and each type demands its own vocabulary. This corresponds to Matthew of Vendôme's instruction
on the ways by which the properties of persons may be chosen and
represented. The distinctions assure correct generic representation of
persons, their attendant accoutrements, and their actions. Horace
calls this the *colores operum*, and the arts of poetry borrow the
expression from him and apply it to Material Style.[22] The identification of such properties aids the reader in finding the work's context,
and through the context the author's intention in inventing it. Since
Material Style encompasses not merely the three social classes, but
the variety of subclasses, professions, offices, and characters within
those classes, a truly broad spectrum of many colors appears in the
mind's eye, like the pilgrims described in the General Prologue to
The Canterbury Tales. Matthew's stress on the paramount trait that
excludes other individual characteristics serves the same purpose of
typical identification of personages. Such types are the subject of
most medieval French literature.

Material distinctions of this sort are pertinent to the truth of a given
matiere. Jehan Bodel recognized this in the *Chanson des Saisnes*
when he established the tripartite distinction between the *matieres*
of France, Rome, and Britain.[23] The distinction corresponds to the
three most common kinds of medieval French romance, including
the *chansons de geste*, especially those like the *Saisnes* that were
written after 1175.

> N'en sont que trois materes à nul home entendant:
> De France et de Bretaigne et de Romme la grant;
> Ne de ces trois materes n'i a nule samblant.

20. *The 'Parisiana Poetria'*, ed. T. Lawler (New Haven, London 1974), pp. 40–41.
21. P. 36 (II.83–86).
22. *Opera*, eds. E. C. Wickham and H. W. Garrod, 2nd ed. (Oxford 1901), v. 86.
On this interpretation in the Middle Ages, see Matthew of Vendôme, *Ars versificatoria*, p. 120, § 46; and the *Scholia Vindobonensia ad Horati artem poeticam*, ed.
J. Zechmeister (Vienna 1877), p. 11.
23. *Saxenlied*, eds. F. Menzel and E. Stengel (Marburg 1906–09).

> Li conte de Bretaigne s'il sont vain et plaisant
> Et cil de Romme sage et de sens aprendant,
> Cil de France sont voir chascun jour aparant.
> Et de ces trois materes tieng la plus voir disant.
>   (vv. 6–12)

The distinction is founded on veracity.

However, it is not historical fact that determines Jehan Bodel's preference for the matter of France; his own *Saisnes* makes that obvious enough. Nor is he denying relative truth to the two other *matieres*. He may of course be alluding to the chronicler sources of French material, presumably more reliable than Roman epic or British legend and oral traditions (vv. 1–5, 33–34). But these *matieres* also had sources that were allegedly eyewitness accounts, the most reliable kind of source for medieval historians.[24] Jehan Bodel's truth is the truth of topical invention as Material Style, a truth whose validity is determined by established social typology rather than by documentation. That typology recognizes established hierarchies like those evident in Vergil's Wheel.

> La coronne de France doit estre si avant,
> Que tout autre roi doivent estre à li apendant
> De la loi chrestienne qui en dieu sont creant.
>   (vv. 13–15)

Indeed, the superiority of the *Saisnes* over the versions of ordinary jongleurs resides in its topical arguments: "Seignor, ceste chançons ne muet pas de fabliaus, Mais de chevalerie d'amours et de cembiaus" (vv. 25–26). This is the subject matter of medieval romance, and many a *locus* expands to contain it. The superiority of French subjects relies on hierarchical presuppositions which, in argument, are meaningful and credible to Frenchmen. Jehan Bodel parallels Chrétien de Troyes' elevation of French civilization above that of Greece and Rome in the *Cliges* Prologue.[25] Where Chrétien's topical *translatio* extols French *chevalerie* and *clergie*, Jehan Bodel lauds French *matiere* as the preeminent medium for the expression of *chevalerie, amours,* and *cembiaus.* These abstractions color the work,

---

24. M. Schulz, *Die Lehre von der historischen Methode bei den Geschichtsschreibern des Mittelalters* (Berlin 1909), pp. 16–23; B. Lacroix, *L'historien au moyen âge* (Montreal, Paris 1971), pp. 45–49.

25. Ed. A. Micha (Paris 1957), vv. 28–42. Though no doubt "vain," the Arthurian tales express a truth by pleasing exemplification.

in Horace's sense, affecting thereby the way the author represents the ideals, heroes and heroines, and actions and circumstances in his romance.

Within the narrower format of the courtly Chanson and the fixed forms of the Second Rhetoric, similar adherence to the demands of Material Style is evident. Dante made a fundamental distinction akin to Jehan Bodel's when he pronounced the subjects of the most excellent verse to be prowess in arms, love, and moral fortitude.[26] These abstractions provide the archetypes, in Geoffrey of Vinsauf's sense, for the writings of the troubadours and trouvères which Dante makes exemplary of the best writing.

The principal types or characters thus serve to designate the *matiere*, and we may understand why Matthew of Vendôme attached so much importance to their proper representation and careful, clear characterization. The individual was a type. The type could be established by convention, as Horace maintained for standard mythological and legendary personages.[27] New types could also be invented, and we thus see in the Middle Ages the Tristan, the Lancelot, the Galahad, the Pygmalion. Contrasting types were also prominent, like Charlemagne and his often deceptive or fearful son Louis in French *matiere*, or Dinadan as opposed to the other knights of the Round Table in the prose romances.[28] But, in conformity with Marie de France's method of illuminating obscurities in source *matiere*, the author could restate a given character's attributes and conduct in conformity with his understanding of the *matiere* and the context he finds suitable to it. The technique is obvious among the troubadours and trouvères. In romance, the Lancelot in Chrétien de Troyes' *Charrette*, who appears as an exemplary courtly lover and knight, is adapted to a new type in the Vulgate and the post-Vulgate cycles in

---

26. Dante Alighieri, *De vulgari eloquentia*, ed. P. V. Mengaldo (Padua 1968), pp. 35–36. Excellent illustrations of topical amplification and hierarchical discrimination are given in R. Rohr, "Zur Skala der ritterlichen Tugenden in der altprovenzalischen und altfranzösischen höfischen Dichtung," *Zeitschrift für romanische Philologie*, LXXVIII (1962), 292–325.

27. Vv. 120–130.

28. See the beginning of the *Couronnement de Louis,* ed. E. Langlois, CFMA (Paris 1969), especially vv. 80–159. For the romances, see E. Vinaver, "Un chevalier errant à la recherche du sens du monde: quelques remarques sur le caractère de Dinadan dans le *Tristan* en prose," *Mélanges Maurice Delbouille*, 2 vols. (Gembloux 1964), II, 677–686; and C. Kleinhenz, "Tristan in Italy: the Birth or Rebirth of a Legend," *Studies in Medieval Culture*, V (1975), 145–158.

which his love is a sin. The same is true for Tristan and Iseut in the different adaptations of their legend in the *version commune,* the *version courtoise,* and the prose romances.

INVENTION AND SEMANTIC ADAPTATION

Material Style makes semantics a significant feature of topical invention. The abstraction is closest to the archetype from which the work is made to derive. The latter is usually elaborated by fragmentation into a constellation or configuration of subordinate or derivative abstractions that may exist by themselves, as personifications, or as attributes of persons and things in the *matiere.* However, the abstractions do not constitute a terminology as such. Rather they are potentially capable of expressing all or any of the connotations that fall within their semantic fields. This accounts for "the complexity of . . . semantic problems created by medieval thought processes";[29] and G. S. Burgess offers an astute explanation of such complexity:

> When situated carefully within its context and viewed in conceptual terms, an abstract word rarely allows us to pinpoint its meaning with certainty. The inadequacy of modern terminology to convey not just a nuance but the very scope or range of a word becomes more and more apparent. Faced with the impossibility of translating with accuracy a given term, we can but select from its semantic field the most appropriate and pronounced element.

This is precisely how medieval theoreticians conceived of semantic elaboration of their work: "oportet versificatorem esse exercitatum in verborum significatione cognita et consignificatione. . . . Ignota enim verborum significatio ad nocendum est efficacior ceteris doctrinae offendiculis".[30] Matthew's instruction regarding epithets provides for semantic adaptation to context—that is, of adapting the qualities of personages to their representations in description and in narrative. It is also evident in Geoffrey of Vinsauf's instruction on conversion of parts of speech in order to find the most expressive form. Through such instruction, a close link exists between topical invention and its particular variety as Material Style. Attention to semantic adaptability precludes reductionism and inaccuracy: "necesse est versificatorem esse exercitatum in verborum significatione,

29. G. S. Burgess, "*Talent* in Early Old French (to 1150)," *Romania,* XCV (1974), 466.
30. *Ars versificatoria,* p. 186, § 25.

ne dictiones audeat conjugare, quae propter mutuam significationum repugnantiam ad discidium quasi anhelantes nullo patiuntur copulari matrimonio".[31] A multitude of cognates produces clarity, evokes nuances, and assures wholeness.

The widespread use of abstractions and abstract personifications in medieval French comes from Latin influence in the schools.[32] This is especially true for courtly literature, where the influence of the rhetorical tradition is particularly strong from the beginnings.[33] The use of abstractions tends to conform to the rhetorical devices *interpretatio* and *frequentatio*. *Interpretatio*, and its related device *expolitio*, elicits meaning from a given abstraction or subject by synonymic or incremental repetition.[34] Within the author's imposed context, the word expands into its semantic potentialities, and this expansion realizes in a clear and precise manner effective communication. Description with personification, as well as the medieval propensity to use etymology as a rhetorical device to discover the real or invented sources of the word's signification,[35] are the principal means by which *interpretatio* is effective.

Frequentatio is the analysis of a given abstraction into its attributes. Thus a poet may analyze the goodness or beauty of the loved one by naming the special qualities that make up his or her goodness or beauty. The whole thus acquires integrity by means of the following three operations: meaningful semantic correlations among the different abstract attributes, hierarchical classification of the attributes based on the relative value and dependency they show with respect to one another, and contextual control of the meaning of the attributes and the abstraction which is their source by careful juxtaposition and interrelation of discrete attributes. Some recent studies of the troubadours show that attention to semantic range and context reveals in their poetry greater subtlety of expression and more variety

---

31. *Ars versificatoria*, p. 166, § 42.

32. R. Glasser, "Abstractum agens und Allegorie im älteren Französisch," *Zeitschrift für romanische Philologie*, LXIX (1953), 43–122.

33. S. Heinimann, *Das Abstraktum in der französischen Literatursprache des Mittelalters*, Romanica Helvetica, LXXIII (Bern 1963).

34. Faral, *Arts poétiques*, pp. 63–67. On the philosophical sources of this instruction, see B. Stock, *Myth and Science in the Twelfth Century: A Study of Bernard Silvester* (Princeton 1972), pp. 156–157.

35. Faral, *Les arts poétiques*, pp. 65–67; R. Klinck, *Die lateinische Etymologie des Mittelalters* (Munich 1970); M. F. Nims, "*Translatio*: 'Difficult Statement' in Medieval Poetic Theory," *University of Toronto Quarterly*, XLIII (1974), 215–230.

in treatment of common abstractions than was previously recognized.[36] The widespread use of common abstractions in *frequentatio* finally led to their loss of semantic potential in the later Middle Ages.[37] For this reason, personification and abstract configurations representing hierarchical systems of abstractions gave way to greater reliance on concrete exemplary material. The outline of such material served as a literal pattern for allegorical constellations in which abstractions express the sense of the total image. This is prominent in bestiaries, moral and courtly Ovidian mythographies, and dream visions.

The epideictic intent to praise or blame introduces into semantic usage an affective value which is basic to the rhetorical character of medieval literature. Medieval writers call attention to this intent, particularly in the verse forms of a more intimate, even epistolary, nature. Matthew of Vendôme insists that the affective intent of the speaker rather than the definition or denotation of the given word is more important in the choice of attributes.[38] The tendency to underscore the typical (to the exclusion of individual characteristics that detract from the typical) unites with epideictic eloquence to make most medieval French literature hyperbolic. But hyperbole is not meant to deceive. Rather it makes clear the author's viewpoint and interpretation, and it tends to sway the reader by its emotional impact.

ARRANGEMENT OF LETTER AND SENSE

The arts of poetry maintain the traditional distinction between natural and artificial order. Natural order relates events or circumstances in the order they actually or ideally follow. Artificial order revises this order, either by rearranging events or circumstances into a sequence that is not real or normal, or by adding some device like a prologue, interpretive commentary, or transposition of the subject into another mode (as when a dream vision is made to precede or anticipate a historical narrative). In his chapter on Geoffrey of

---

36. R. Rohr, "Zur Interpretation der altprovenzalischen Lyrik: Hauptrichtungen der Forschung (1952–1962)," *Romanistisches Jahrbuch,* XIII (1962), especially 62–73. See also G. M. Cropp, *Le vocabulaire courtois des troubadours de l'époque classique* (Geneva 1975); G. S. Burgess, *Contribution à l'étude du vocabulaire pré-courtois* (Geneva 1970); J. Frappier, " 'D'amors', 'par amors'," *Romania,* LXXXVIII (1967), 433–474.

37. R. Glasser, *Zeitschrift für romanische Philologie,* LXIX, 88–93.

38. *Ars versificatoria,* pp. 132, § 60; and 150, § 115.

Vinsauf, E. Gallo uses commentaries on Vergil's *Aeneid* to show that order may obtain both in the *matiere* and on the level of the meaning or interpretation of that *matiere*. Traditionally the books of the *Aeneid* exemplify artificial order because the narrative relates the fall of Troy and Aeneas' search for Italy after the sea storm and the arrival in Carthage, although, chronologically, the latter follow the former. But medieval commentators distinguish between the artificial literal order and the natural order in which the moral improvement and ascent of Aeneas emerges allegorically from the narrative. Thus the *Aeneid* becomes a complex interlace of historical and interpretive levels of reading. The arrangement of matter and meaning in the work is a feature of its composition after invention.

The arrangement of source material and topical inventions gives rhetorical meaning to problems of linking, juxtaposition, blending, and interlace which scholarship has come to subsume under Chrétien de Troyes' term *conjointure*. *Conjointure* is an expansion of Horace's use of *iunctura* in the *Art of Poetry*.[39] The medieval word preserves Horace's notion of the combination of parts into an original whole expressive of a truth about the *matiere*. Fundamentally, *conjointure* serves to elicit new meaning from old *matiere* by original arrangement: "dixeris egregie notum si callida verbum Reddiderit iunctura novum" (vv. 47–48). Such a *iunctura* is a deflection from an established speech pattern. As such, it brings up the problem of beginning, middle, and end, as well as their arrangement. Geoffrey's *Poetria nova* includes such considerations in the discussion of invention and disposition. Concern for the location and linking of parts precedes the artful arrangement of the natural or normal beginning, middle, and end.

Horace's use of *iunctura* in v. 48 anticipates its appearance in v. 242: "tantum series iuncturaque pollet, Tantum de medio sumptis

---

39. D. Kelly, "The Source and Meaning of *conjointure* in Chrétien's *Erec* 14," *Viator*, I (1970), 179–200. T. Hunt has questioned the derivation of Chrétien's *conjointure* from Horace's *iunctura*; see "Tradition and Originality in the Prologues of Chrestien de Troyes," *Forum for Modern Language Studies*, VIII (1972), 338–339, note 4. He follows C. O. Brink, who has recently argued in support of Bentley's emendation of the order of lines in the Horace manuscripts containing the "callida iunctura" passage to vv. 45–47–46–48; see Brink, *Horace on Poetry*, 2 vols. (Cambridge, 1963–71), II, 134–135. This may well be true. But it is not likely that Chrétien and his contemporaries knew the original order. No extant manuscript contains the postulated order, nor do any of the published commentaries on Horace. All follow the order vv. 45–46–47–48. If that represents a garbled source, it is nonetheless a source.

accedit honoris." This statement covers not only the linking of parts, but the texture of the parts.[40] Texture in medieval French literature comes either from metaphorical mode of representation or from correct Material Style. Metaphorical adaptation may be either allegorical (*verba translata*) or metonymic (*verba immutata*).[41] The two may in fact be combined, as in the following passage from Froissart's *Prison amoureuse*:

> je vous envoie une exposition faite et arestee sus cesti songe parmi l'aÿde de Dieu et d'une ymagination que j'ai eü. Et premiers, j'entens par le lit et la cambre aournee de toute honneur ou vous dormiés, quant les trois dames par samblance vous esvillierent, la douce pensee, gaie et amoureuse, qui est dedens vous encorporee, et, pour esvillier ceste pensee, j'entens par les trois dames, Justice, Pité et Raison, trois vertus principaus qui sont en vostre souverainne: bonté, biauté et maniere bien arree.[42]

Froissart's reading reinterprets the metonymic letter with an allegorical sense, and in effect forces a rereading of the work that the narrator himself effects in an exemplary manner.

> Des foelles lisi jusqu'a sis
> Et puis recommenchai mon tour
> A la premiere page, pour
> Mieuls concevoir et cler entendre
> A quoi la matere poet tendre.
> (vv. 2241–45)

Similar compositional correction of the narrative occurs in the *Lancelot-Graal* prose cycle. The literal account of Lancelot's achievements follows the natural order. But the reinterpretation of his life and the condemnation of his sinful love for Guenevere in the *Queste del saint graal,* almost at the end of the cycle, forces the reader to make a complete reexamination and reinterpretation of his life in the earlier parts. The effect on Lancelot is tragic, in the strict sense that in seeking the Grail, he is to discover his own sinfulness. The discovery brands his conduct as unworthy since he first saw Guenevere and

---

40. Brink, *Horace,* II, 290.

41. H. Lausberg, *Handbuch der literarischen Rhetorik,* 2 vols. (Munich 1960), § 566.

42. Jean Froissart, *La prison amoureuse,* ed. A. Fourrier (Paris 1974), p. 151, 11. 14–24. On the coherence of letter and meaning in the *Ovide moralisé,* see P. Demats, *Fabula: trois études de mythographie antique et médiévale* (Geneva 1973), especially pp. 61–105; and P. Haidu, *Aesthetic Distance in Chrétien de Troyes: Irony and Comedy in 'Cligès' and 'Perceval'* (Geneva 1968).

loved her. The need to reread the literal praise of Lancelot as false makes the order of sense in the cycle artificial.

ORNAMENTATION AS AMPLIFICATION

Amplification, or dilation by means of tropical or figural devices, provides the author with modal or formal techniques by which to achieve topical invention. Geoffrey of Vinsauf enjoys a dubious notoriety for his list of devices for amplification, dubious because it has led to stress on the sterile device rather than the productive process. Amplification is the extension of tropes and figures, just as allegory is an extended metaphor. Since there was no general agreement on the definition, number, and classification of tropes and figures in antiquity and the Middle Ages, there was none for amplificatory devices as extended tropes and figures. However, the principle common to both ornamentation and amplification is deflection from direct discourse. As set forth by Quintilian, there are four kinds of deflection:[43] (1) *incrementum,* or incremental sequence of descriptive statements of the subject; (2) *comparatio,* or comparison; (3) *ratiocinatio,* or conjectural amplification of circumstances preceding, attendant upon, or following the subject; and (4) *congeries,* or synonymous accumulation. The formal or modal application of each kind of deflection requires the adaptation of specific tropical or figural devices to the *matiere* and its topical additions.

An old prejudice that has had a curious survival value—curious given the findings of modern psychoanalysis and anthropology—is that topical amplification, by the schematic and abstract character of its *argumenta,* bleeds literature of life, and persons and events of reality and credibility. Reality receives its due in the Middle Ages by reference to, and analysis of, generally received experience. The definition of that experience in the specific work was the purpose of topical invention. The task was difficult and required ingenuity and subtlety in the choice of devices: "Nam fere non difficile invenire quid sit causae adiumento, difficillimum vero est inventum expolire et expedite pronuntiare."[44] The devices are the various kinds of amplification that we commonly associate with rhetoric, the figures and tropes.

43. Lausberg, *Handbuch,* pp. 221–224, Knapp, *Studi medievali,* ser. 3, XIV, 461–468.
44. *Rhetorica ad Herennium,* ed. H. Caplan (Cambridge, Mass., London 1954), p. 106.

The identification of tropes and figures is an established subdivision of medieval French scholarship.[45] The inventory is the rule, especially in some early critical editions and a few manuals illustrating the devices as ornamentation. These are catalogues and possess as such little critical value. The function of the specific device is lost in excision and classification. And the catalogues foster the erroneous notion that identification and definition of the device explain its function in context. This runs counter to methodology in classical and medieval grammar and rhetoric. There was some discussion as to the quality and function of various tropes and figures.[46] The illustrations used in the treatises were to bring the student back to the texts, both in his own reading and by original composition. Thus he could observe and experiment with the quality of tropical and figural deflection from direct speech. The modern classifications do not take these practical features of rhetorical instruction into consideration.

Some applications have been gratifying, both in their awareness of the function of amplification and ornamentation in composition, and in their felicitous interpretation of medieval writing in the light of that awareness. This applies especially to recent studies of the troubadours and the trouvères. Scholars like R. Dragonetti, U. Mölk, and L. M. Paterson show an intelligent appreciation of the relation and distinction between *ars* and *exercitatio*, technique and text.[47]

---

45. For example, see E. M. Warren, "Some Features of Style in Early French Narrative Poetry (1150–70)," *Modern Philology*, III (1905–06), 179–209, 513–539; IV (1906–07), 655–675; V. Bertolucci, "Commento retorico all'*Erec* e al *Cliges*," *Studi mediolatini e volgari*, VIII (1960), 9–51; V. Bertolucci-Pizzorusso, "La retorica nel *Tristano* di Thomas," *Studi mediolatini e volgari*, VI–VII (1959), 25–61. For early work, see Faral, *Les arts poétiques*, p. xi, note 1.

46. Cf. Lausberg, *Handbuch*, pp. 308–309.

47. See U. Mölk, ed. *Französische Literarästhetik des 12. und 13. Jahrhunderts*, Sammlung romanischer Übungstexte, LIV (Tübingen 1969); Mölk, *Trobar clus trobar leu: Studien zur Dichtungstheorie der Trobadors* (Munich 1968); R. Dragonetti, *La technique poétique des trouvères dans la chanson courtoise: contribution à l'étude de la rhétorique médiévale* (Bruges 1960); L. M. Paterson, *Troubadours and Eloquence* (Oxford 1975); C. Leube-Fey, *Bild und Funktion der 'dompna' in der Lyrik der Trobadors*, Studia romanica, XXI (Heidelberg 1971); A. M. F. Gunn, *The Mirror of Love. A Reinterpretation of 'The Romance of the Rose'* (Lubbock 1952); A. M. Colby, *The Portrait in Twelfth-Century French Literature: An Example of the Stylistic Originality of Chrétien de Troyes* (Geneva 1965); N. F. Regalado, *Poetic Patterns in Rutebeuf: A Study in Noncourtly Poetic Modes of the Thirteenth Century*, Yale Romantic Studies, 2nd ser., XXI (New Haven, London 1970); D. Thoss, *Studien zum 'locus amoenus' im Mittelalter*, Wiener romanistische Arbeiten, X (Vienna, Stuttgart 1972). Thoss suggests that the vernacular tradition was distinct from the Latin tradition in topical elaboration of the *locus amoenus* image.

These studies suggest the flexibility rather than the constraints of rhetoric in composition.

A COMPOSITE ILLUSTRATION:
THOMAS D'ANGLETERRE'S *TRISTAN ET ISEUT*

The key to medieval writing influenced by the rhetorical tradition is topical invention. Topical invention encompasses authorial interpretation of *matiere*, disposition of parts, amplification, and choice of ornamental devices and vocabulary. It gives to the notions of natural and artificial order a meaning the terms already possessed in all artful sentence structure departing from direct, simple expression. It provides insight into the qualities of medieval literature. The topical *argumenta* reveal artistry, intention, and adaptation; and they help us recognize originality and uniqueness in the artistic quest to represent chivalry, love, or a life pleasing to God.

Thomas d'Angleterre's *Tristan et Iseut* can illustrate succinctly how readily applicable the compositional techniques discussed above are to the interpretation of literature. There appears to have been a rich and varied tradition of Tristan material in the twelfth century, and Thomas himself refers to it.[48] In addition he singles out a version which he considered authoritative, and made his adaptation conform to it when it was impossible to reconcile it with other versions.[49] His passage from *materia remota* to *materia propinqua* included a choice of features that would be as complete, but also as verisimilar, as possible. Thus he suppressed contradictions among different versions, excessive repetitions, and abrupt, paratactic transitions like those in the more primitive versions of Beroul and Eilhart von Oberg (the latter based on a lost French original).[50] Thus he made the different parts of his *materia propinqua* into an arrangement that was coherent and thematically consistent. It is a *bele conjointure* in Chrétien de Troyes' sense of that expression.

Topical invention facilitated the adaptation of Thomas' *matiere*. His original intention—his archetypal vision, in Geoffrey of Vinsauf's words—was to make *fin'amors* the subject of a work pleasing and consolatory to lovers (Sneyd², vv. 820–839). For him, this required

---

48. A. Vàrvaro, "La teoria dell'archetipo tristaniano," *Romania*, LXXXVIII (1967), 13–58; D. Kelly, *"En uni dire (Tristan* Douce 839) and the Composition of Thomas's *Tristan,"* *Modern Philology*, LXVI (1969–70), 9–17.

49. Ed. B. H. Wind, *Les fragments du Roman de Tristan* (Leiden 1950).

50. E. Vinaver, *A la recherche d'une poétique médiévale* (Paris 1970), pp. 75–104; A. Vàrvaro, *Il 'Roman de Tristran' di Béroul* (Turin 1963).

a conception of love allowing for human choice and decision rather than a supernatural invasion of the mind and emotions which the love potion represented in versions previous to his.[51] Therefore, Thomas makes the love of Tristan and Iseut begin prior to the drinking of the potion. To do so, he counters the natural hatred between Tristan and Iseut, because Tristan had killed Iseut's uncle the Morholt, by a love that begins with sight and advances through the *gradus amoris*[52] towards the consummation that occurs with the drinking of the potion. The love potion is therefore an image representing their love rather than its supernatural cause. The topical adaptation thus imposes a new conception of love onto the Morholt-potion-love death without which the legend of Tristan and Iseut could not exist as such. But the conception of that love precedes the discovery of Thomas' *matiere*. The *materia propinqua* results from the discovery of the topical potential of the Tristan legend, particularly in the version Thomas says he follows, for the expression of that love. Like Marie de France, Thomas found in his *matiere* "ceo k'i ert."

The elaboration of his *matiere* by topical interpretation continues in the separate and distinct episodes. Tristan's monologues upon his marriage to Iseut White Hands are topical inquiries into the meaning of the love he and Iseut the Blond share. Iseut the Blond is faithful to Tristan during their separation, yet she continues to live and bed with Marc. There arises from this situation a debate in Tristan's mind. He seeks to analyze and understand her feelings through his own by an extensive and intricate *interpretatio*. Tristan's problem is semantic, as he considers and analyzes the words *pooir, voloir,* and *desir* in an effort to clarify the function of capacity, will, and desire in love. The lengthy description of his interior monologue, in direct and indirect discourse, is a brilliant flourish of credible thought and figurative amplification and elaboration.[53]

In despair at his inability to understand Iseut, Tristan decides to duplicate the Marc-Iseut the Blond marriage by a mirror image: a

51. On what follows, see J. Frappier, "Structure et sens du *Tristan*: version commune, version courtoise," *Cahiers de civilisation médiévale*, VI (1963), 255–280, 441–454; and "Sur le mot 'raison' dans le *Tristan* de Thomas d'Angleterre," *Linguistic and Literary Studies Helmut A. Hatzfeld* (Washington, D. C. 1964), pp. 163–176.

52. Cf. L. J. Friedman, "Gradus amoris," *Romance Philology*, XIX (1965–66), 167–177.

53. See V. Bertolucci-Pizzorusso, *Studi mediolatini e volgari*, VI–VII, especially 28–38.

Tristan-Iseut White Hands marriage. Tristan's reconstruction of the Marc-Iseut marriage preserves the name, marriage, and separation from the lover. The mirror inverts the image, however. Tristan is in Iseut's place, and their sexes are different. When Tristan discovers his own impotence (by will, or desire it matters not)—that is, his own inability to enjoy his wife as Marc does his—he understands that, like him, Iseut shares no pleasure with her spouse. *Pooir* depends on *desir,* not an act of *voloir,* and this is Tristan's new knowledge of his and his lady's love (*savoir*). It is a carnal knowledge, one derived by abstinence and made comprehensible by topical elaboration of the situation by semantic analysis and illustration of abstractions characteristic of that love, but in need of interpretation in terms of the author's understanding. That is the realization of his artistic intention and originality.

> Sa nature proveir se volt,
> La raison se tient a Ysolt [= the Blond].
> Le desir qu'il ad vers la reïne
> Tolt le voleir vers la meschine;
> Le desir lui tolt le voleir,
> Que nature n'i ad poeir.
> Amur e raisun le destraint,
> E le voleir de sun cors vaint.
> (Sneyd[1], vv. 595–602)

For both Tristan and Iseut, no magic force or natural obligation can prevail over love. Thomas has shown by topical invention that Tristan's unconsummated marriage to Iseut White Hands is a triumph of love over the senses. This makes his version so distinct from others contemporary with him that literary historians have established the meaningful distinction between his *version courtoise* and the *version commune* found in French versions not influenced by Thomas. Other works—*Cligès, Amadas et Ydoine*—would attempt to bring the body and soul more into harmony. But in each case, the author subjects his *matiere* to specific questions that, as topical formulae, elicit variant answers in conformity with authorial intention. The answers become the amplification of the *matiere* at appropriate places (*loci*) as argument (*argumentum*). The completed work is a meaningful adaptation.

CONCLUSION

Invention is the hidden fount of medieval poetry, and the arts of poetry identify it as such. By invention, the artist imitates God himself. Geoffrey of Vinsauf borrows the well known *domus con-struenda* image from religious writing to describe invention in the *Poetria nova*.[54] A progressive verbalization ensues, from the general subject to the determination of *matiere*. The accommodation of subject to matter—the construction of the building, as it were, for what it is to house—is essentially the rhetorical conjunction of the facts of a case and judgment or interpretation of the case (*casus* and *quaestio infinita*). The paradigm for such composition in scholastic exercises is the *chria*, which is the combination of *sententia* and narrative material to express a credible truth by exemplification. The resultant "subject-matter" is the contents of the work. In succeeding stages, the subject-matter will be arranged, in its entirety and in its parts, in natural or artificial order; that order will take into account the parallel functions of matter and meaning. Finally, amplification or abbreviation will apply specific tropical and figural devices to the elaboration of meaning in a suitable and convincing form or mode.

The most important phase in composition is the realization of *materia propinqua* as the combination of *materia*, topical additions, and links that eliminate lacunae.[55] It yields the content and natural order of the work, and it contains the ideas the author wishes to show forth. Since the procedure is rhetorical, it is inherently argumentative, entailing either the praise or blame of persons, things, and actions. The care required to avoid incongruities does not preclude the adaptation of designated persons by change of properties that in effect change character. We have seen this in Thomas' adaptation of the Tristan legend to his own conception of courtly love.

There is a tendency in topical invention to divest a person, thing, or action of properties found perhaps in the source but not conducive to the Material Style chosen by the author; this often results in hyperbole when combined with the epideictic requirement to praise or blame. Dante recognized this in the *De vulgari eloquentia* when he insisted on only what is "most excellent" for the best poetry. Thus, extremes are the rule in romance and the chanson, since they show most clearly the qualities the author feels paramount in his work. *Narratio* in literature was since classical times the account of the extraordinary; this accounts for the preference for the *merveilleux* in the *matiere* chosen for topical interpretation.[56] Interlace and care-

---

54. Kelly, *Mediaeval Studies*, XXXI, 126–127. Cf. H. de Lubac, *Exégèse médiévale: les quatre sens de l'écriture*, 4 vols. (Paris 1959–64), II.2, 41–60.
55. Kelly, *Mediaeval Studies*, XXXI, 130.
56. See Faral, *Recherches*; M. W. Bloomfield, "Episodic Motivation and Marvels

ful linking preserved the artistic integrity of the new work. And topical adaptations gave it significance by hyperbolic representation of the typical. The union of hyperbole and *merveille* as the account of the extraordinary required the common designation of elements that Material Style made possible. Material Style is of course associated with generic distinctions, both by its social and character classification, and by its relation to the classical *genera dicendi*. But its import is different. Whereas emphasis on genre tends to subordinate the work to a type, medieval writing, as adaptation, underscores the work's autonomy: it is a unique adaptation of an idea and a source.

---

in Epic and Romance," in *Essays and Explorations: Studies in Ideas, Language, and Literature* (Cambridge, Mass. 1970), pp. 96–128; Kelly, "*Matiere* and *genera dicendi* in Medieval Romance," *Yale French Studies*, LI (1974), 148–150. On *narratio* in rhetoric as it was known in the Middle Ages, see K. Barwick, "Die Gliederung der *narratio* in der rhetorischen Theorie und seine Bedeutung für die Geschichte des antiken Romans," *Hermes*, LXIII (1928), 261–287.

Dante and the Rhetorical Theory of Sentence Structure

ALDO SCAGLIONE

THE *De vulgari eloquentia* opens with the blunt claim that the author is doing a thoroughly novel piece of work: "Cum neminem ante nos de vulgaris eloquentie doctrina quicquam inveniamus tractasse." It is indeed new in its treatment of the vernacular according to the time-tested theories traditionally reserved for Latin, and in its doing so with methodic sweep and broad scope. It is also new for its philosophical delving into the nature and requirements of the poet's work. The book posits and answers basic questions as to the causes of linguistic phenomena in a spirit of inquiry that makes it an unprecedented treatise of philosophy of language applied to the vernacular. To grammar and rhetoric the treatise adds poetics, essentially understood, as it generally was in the Middle Ages, as the direct assimilation to verse of the rules and principles devised by traditional rhetoric for prose.

Aside from these novelties of execution, the treatise does hark back to the tradition, and in particular to such close, though pitifully more limited, manuals as the Catalan Raimon Vidal's *Razos de trobar* (ca. 1200), Girolamo Terramagnino da Pisa's *Doctrina de cort* (a paraphrase of the former, of around 1270), Jaufré de Foxa's *Continuación del trobar* (i.e. Vidal's *Trobar,* of ca. 1290), Uc Faidit's *Donat proensal* (ca. 1250), and especially Brunetto Latini's rhetoric from the third book of his *Trésor.* To all these must then be added the medieval "poetics" and the *artes dictandi* and *praedicandi*; in particular Matthew of Vendôme, Geoffrey of Vinsauf, John of Garland, Bene da Firenze's *Candelabrum,* and perhaps Guido Faba's *Summa dictaminis.*

In Book 2, Chapter 6, Dante enters his famous discussion of the *gradus constructionis,* levels of compositional style. He distinguishes four of them: briefly, the unsavory, the savory, the elegant, and the supreme—*insipidus, sapidus, venustus,* and *excelsus,* each incorporating the qualities of the preceding ones. He then proceeds to submit made-up examples of each in Latin, while as further examples of the last one, the one worthy of the *vulgare illustre,* he cites eleven *canzoni (cantiones),* by Provençal, French, and Italian poets. He adds in the end that the reading of the excellent Latin poets *and* prose writers will greatly contribute to our command of such a style.

The reader should be particularly intrigued by this chapter because it provides, as it were, a microcosm of many issues appearing within the larger confines of the treatise. It seems to contain everything that is important for the artistic use of the *vulgare illustre.* Students of Dante have often stressed the point that it is not possible to understand the full context of his literary ideas without a good knowledge of medieval stylistic theories, but no one has yet provided a comprehensive and detailed analysis of Dante's technical background.[1] Furthermore, the close analysis of Dante's own stylistic practice still remains rather tentative and fragmentary. To anticipate the directives of such a study, and its likely conclusions on the basis of available knowledge, I should like to quote a general statement by Don Francesco Di Capua, one of the most consistent students of medieval stylistic doctrines and practices. "In all the works of Dante, from those of his youth to those of his maturity, the impact of medieval stylistics and rhetoric is conspicuously evident. The secret of his greatness does not lie in an effort of liberation from or rebellion against the precepts and prejudices of the past, whether they be stylistic or moral, historical or religious, but in the full acceptance of them in order to dominate them and, by using them, attain his own ends."[2]

To return to our text, an elect *constructio* is one of the four

---

1. A good start is found in Patrick Boyde, *Dante's Style in His Lyric Poetry* (Cambridge, Eng.: Cambridge U. Press, 1971), within the limits indicated in the title. Pp. 188–208 cover inversion and word order. The whole study is conducted on the basis of the traditional rhetorical categories, methodically yet rather mechanically, or positivistically, applied.

2. F. Di Capua, *Scritti minori* (2 vols., Rome, 1957), II, 239 (from *Studi in o. di F. Torraca,* 1922). Trans. mine. Also reprinted in this vol. the student can find the most elaborate and extensive analysis of this chapter of the *De v. e.,* namely Di Capua's ch. "I gradi della costruzione," pp. 326–339, from his *Insegnamenti retorici medievali e dottrine estetiche moderne nel* De vulgari eloquentia *di Dante* (Naples, 1945). Di Capua's judgment which I have just quoted is implicitly confirmed in the able Introduction to P. V. Mengaldo's ed. of *De v. e.* (Padua: Antenore, 1968), I, where the absence of the medieval Latin poets is also stressed (see esp. p. L).

ingredients of the tragic style, the style to be used in treating the themes of *salus, amor,* and *virtus*—salvation, love, and virtue. The other ingredients are depth of thought, splendor of verse, and excellence of vocabulary. "Stylo equidem tragico tunc uti videmur, quando cum gravitate sententie tam superbia carminum quam constructionis elatio et excellentia vocabulorum concordat" (II, 4, 7). The reference to verse would obviously correspond to an apt use of harmony or oratorical rhythm if Dante had gone on to treat the use of the *illustre* in prose. This possibility is not excluded by his specific assignment of the *illustre* to the *canzone*. It is, indeed, implicitly confirmed in this very chapter by his reference to the *altissimas prosas* of the Latins as appropriate propaedeutic schooling for the pursuer of *vulgare illustre.*[3] This consideration is, on the other hand, really unnecessary, since the first sentence of Book 2 explicitly assigns the use of *illustre* to both verse *and* prose—"Latium vulgare illustre tam prosayce quam metrice decere proferri."

Commentators are rather vague on the meaning of Dante's *constructio.* They adduce, principally, Priscian, Hugh of St. Victor, Bene da Firenze, Guido Faba, and first and foremost, the Auctor ad Herennium. The identification of Dante's sources is a crucial decision, and in the case of the *De vulgari eloquentia* it seems clear that Dante's technical background reflects above all his exposure to the Bologna school circles.[4]

Now *constructio* was Priscian's term for syntax (Books 17 and 18 of his *Institutions,* or, in the Middle Ages, *Priscianus minor*), but, since ancient syntax hardly covered any aspect of *syntaxe de la période,* which is precisely Dante's concern here, Dante is using *constructio* to mean *compositio,* which indeed was the traditional way of referring to sentence structure. *Compositio,* however, was not part of grammar,

---

3. *Convivio* I, x, 13 deals with *artificialis constructio,* and III, ix, 2 as well as III, x, 6 with *ornatus* in prose.

4. Cf. *De v. e.,* ed. Mengaldo, I,, pp. xxxvi-1, "Cultura e teorie retoriche," and particularly p. xxxvii: "Dunque un ventaglio piuttosto ampio di esperienze, che valicano Firenze in direzione di Bologna e si allacciano pure alle fondamentali *poetrie* transalpine, una cui larga conoscenza è, in generale, meglio supponibile nei paraggi della cultura bolognese che di quella fiorentina." A. Marigo's commentary on II, 6 (*De v. e.,* Florence, 1938, 1957) brings in Priscian VIII (definition of *constructio*), Hugh of St. Victor (*constructio propria, secundum proprietatem,* i.e. using tropes and schemata, which Marigo regards as Dante's elect construction, but it is emphatically grammatical in Hugh; *contra proprietatem,* i.e. barbarisms and solecisms); Thurot 83. And for *ordo vel compositio artificialis* Marigo adduces *Rhetorica ad Herennium* cited by Thurot, text p. 344, the *Candelabrum,* and Guido Faba's *Summa dictaminis,* Gaudenzi ed.

as *constructio* was, but of rhetoric, and precisely a major subdivision
of the theory of elocution—usually divided into diction or vocabulary,
composition, and *ornatus* (theory of figures). This is characteristic
of Dante's original and, to an extent, idiosyncratic way of bringing
together traditional *grammatica, rhetorica,* and *poetica* or *poetria.*
Some degree of syncretism was more frequent than one might think,
but it usually involved no more than two disciplines, and in a partial
manner. What Dante achieved in the *De vulgari eloquentia* was a
bold and unprecedented fusion of these three disciplines, which he,
furthermore, applied to both Latin and the vernaculars, both verse
and prose. No one had ever attempted to do so much in so little
space, and no one followed his example until the sixteenth century,
starting with Bembo. A cogent and coherent synthesis of these
separate and somewhat divergent disciplines, with such disparate
applications, required no less than his genius, and presented numerous terminological and ideological problems.

Of particular interest is the broad interplay of two apparently conflicting criteria: the belief in the priority of poetry over prose, the
latter deriving patterns from the former as its "model" ("Sed quia
ipsum [vulgare illustre] prosaycantes ab avientibus magis accipiunt et
quia quod avietum est prosaycantibus permanere videtur exemplar"
—II, 1, 1), even while Dante specifically applies to poetry a circumscribed set of norms taken over from the rhetorical analysis of prose,
namely the norms of sentence structure and word order (= *compositio*). Although this theoretical reduction of both verse and prose
to a common denominator is a signal achievement of the *De vulgari
eloquentia,* even this was by itself hardly a novelty, since, without
mentioning the transference of rhetoric to verse which characterized
the medieval *poetriae,* the attempt to offer under a single cover a
rhetoric valid for both poetry and prose was already a *fait accompli* in
the Italian *artes dictandi,* including those of Brunetto and the Bolognese masters. There remained in this tradition a problematic
uncertainty: Buoncompagno asserted the absolute superiority of
prose, *artium mater*;[5] Bene opted instead for verse, and to verse
Dante gave primacy, *primatum,* both chronologically and in terms
of value or exemplar. Dante proceeded to treat the metrical forms

---

5. Buoncompagno da Signa, *Palma*: "[prosaycum dictamen] non debet dici ars,
immo artium mater, quia tota scriptura trahit originem a prosa." Cf. Carl Sutter,
Aus Leben und Schriften des Magisters Boncompagno (Freiburg i. B.—Leipzig,
1894), p. 106. See, on all this, Mengaldo's ed., p. xl.

first, i.e. poetry, precisely because, he says, prose writers derive their
patterns from poets.[6]

Elsewhere I have tried to show how Dante's poetic language distinguished itself on the syntactical level for the introduction of functional periodicity.[7] Book 2, Chapter 6, of *De v. e.* underlines Dante's
theoretical awareness of the importance of mastering complex periodic structures in the excellent use of poetic, and implicitly prosaic,
speech. It is interesting to note that in all the examples adduced here
by Dante from Provençal, French, and Italian, the structure of the
poems shines for the command of complex periodicity—with the
sole exceptions, perhaps, of the *cansos* of Aimeric de Pegulha and
Gace Brulé. And it deserves to be underlined that such examples
came, not only from ancient Latin poetry *and* prose, but especially
from the troubadours. In concluding his scrutiny of existing models
Dante gives us an important clue for understanding his exclusion
of Guittone from the company of practitioners of a "sweet new
style," namely when he sharply rebukes the admirers of Guittone
who, he claims, never ceased to remain plebeian *in vocabulo atque
constructione*—this meaning, we should here interpret, that he
lacked a smooth, perfectly polished, elegant mastery of diction and
syntax, rather than elect vocabulary and complex periodicity *per se*.

Of all the disciplines which Dante synthesized, rhetoric was the
most weighty and pervasive. This is clearly reflected, after all, even

---

6. Cf. *Dante e Bologna nei tempi di Dante* (Bologna, 1967): G. Vecchi, "Giovanni del Virgilio e Dante," and other essays in the volume. Mario Pazzaglia, *Il
verso e l'arte della canzone nel De vulgari eloquentia* (Florence: La Nuova Italia,
1967) analyzes "the syntactic-architectonic ideal of Dante's canzone," pp. 202–204,
and concludes (p. 204): "this ideal of a poetry nourished with profound doctrine
and organized around solid meditative and expressive structures (namely, the philosophical treatment of love) prompts Dante to propose as a model for poets even
the excellent prose of Livy, Frontinus, Pliny, and Orosius (II, 6, 7), and to consider,
as Leopardi will also do, prose as a nurse to poetry." Pazzaglia concludes that the
Convivio parallels the *De v. e.* by exemplifying the periodic construction in prose.
On the question of derivation of patterns from poetry to prose (in rhetorical theory),
cf. my study *The Classical Theory of Composition, from Its Origins to the Present*,
N. C. Studies in Comparative Literature, 53 (Chapel Hill: U.N.C. Press, 1972),
pp. 34 and 37–38. The idea that poetry *permanere videtur exemplar* to prose (II, 1,
1) was transmitted to medieval readers by Isidore, *Etymologiae*, I, 38, 2: "Tam apud
Graecos quam apud Latinos longe antiquiorem curam fuisse carminum quam prosae.
Omnia enim prius versibus condebantur; prosae autem studium sero viguit." Cf.
Panvini, ed. cited below, p. 96 fn. Here the notion of chronological priority of verse
is not specifically applied to the derivation of rhythmic artistic patterns (especially
the Gorgianic), but this latter idea was common among ancient rhetoricians.

7. See my "Periodic Syntax and Flexible Meter in the *Divina Commedia*," *RPh*,
XXI, 1 (1967), pp. 1–22.

in his definition of poetry (II, 4) as 'nothing else than imaginative fiction textured with eloquence in rhythmic form': "[poesis] nichil aliud est quam fictio rhetorica musicaque poita."[8] We will then do well to keep the rhetorical categories firmly in mind while analyzing his examples. But, to begin with, even though he was here dealing with rhetorical composition, he did use the grammatical term 'construction.' And construction must perforce be, first of all, 'grammatical,' since illiterates incapable of mastering grammatical forms are to be laughed at like a blind man who would presume to discern colors—"non aliter deridemus quam cecum de coloribus distinguentem"—an absurdity which, unfortunately, is not without example, since some quasi-illiterates presume to attempt even the noblest of all forms, the *canzone*—"pudeat ergo, pudeat ydiotas tantum audere deinceps, ut ad cantiones prorumpant."

The first grade of acceptable, grammatical construction, *congrua constructio*, is the *insipidus*, the artless one, which belongs to those with a barely rudimentary education: *insipidus qui est rudium*. An example would be: *Petrus amat multum dominam Bertam*. It is usually assumed that Dante is referring to the 'style' of the man of the street, to wit, 'spoken Latin.' But the only contact with spoken, popular Latin here is (together with the position of *multum*, of which more later) the particular coloring given to this example by the use of the popular name *Berta*. Otherwise the example is linguistically and stylistically on the same level as the preceding one, which sounded learned though not elegant: *Aristotiles phylosophatus est tempore Alexandri*—an example designed to illustrate the very meaning of appropriate construction: "constructionem vocamus regulatam compaginem dictionum, ut *Aristotiles* etc." Dante adds immediately after this example: these five words are tied together according to the rules of grammatical art, and they make one and only one sentence— "et unam faciunt constructionem." We have here the narrowest meaning of the term in Dante's context: *constructio* = sentence.[9]

---

8. See Marigo's ed., p. 188.

9. Marigo, p. 206, holds that Dante's *compago* and *una constructio* add "a concept of logical structure" and "unity" to Priscian's definition "constructio est dictionum congrua in oratione ordinatio" (*Inst.* VIII); but Dante could have found such concepts clearly implied in another passage of Priscian (*Inst.* II, 15), which he might have had before him: "oratio est ordinatio dictionum congrua, sententiam perfectam demonstrans," but which might also, and better, have reached him through the phrasing of the *Glosa Admirantes* to the *Doctrinale*: "Est constructio congrua constructibilium unio ex modo significandi causata" (Ch. Thurot, *Notices et extraits* . . . , "Notices et extraits de la Bibliothèque Impériale," t. XXII, 2, Paris,

This is a purely grammatical acceptation, but it is not Dante's invention, as implied by Marigo. It is rather common in medieval usage starting perhaps around the year 1000.[10] A third meaning of *constructio*—inextricably bound with, yet distinct from, the preceding—was the practical school exercise of "construing" or parsing, an exercise designed to explicate difficult constructions by placing words in a 'normal,' analytical order. This meaning had made its appearance in Priscian, but it became current only in the later Middle Ages.[11] It is particularly relevant to our discussion because it directly refers to the medieval theory of the two orders, *ordo naturalis* and *ordo artificialis,* which are precisely one of the ingredients of Dante's distinction of stylistic grades.

Not an imitation or parody of popular, current speech, Dante's example *Petrus amat multum dominam Bertam* is, rather, a standard type which regularly occurs in medieval treatments of 'natural order.' Faba's *Summa dictaminis* entered an example *Ego amo te* for the *constructio naturalis,* perspicaciously submitting that this mode serves didactic purposes (*ad expositionem*), while the *artificialis* is the one actually used in composition (*compositio ad dictationem*). At a much earlier time, however, a single text reproduced by Thurot and assigned by him to the eleventh century entered the following sequence of examples, designed to show how one must order the elements of the clause by placing them logically or analytically: namely, first the agent (subject); then the act (predicate); finally, the patient (object), while the 'adjectives' tend to precede the parts they modify—unless they have taken the form of complements or govern complements. Note the Aristotelian framework of this reasoning: the subject comes first because it expresses the agent; then come the act and the patient. The examples are: *Fortis Johannes multum percussit debilem Petrum*; *Johannes fortis brachium vel dignus laude percussit Petrum multae audacitatis cum virga*; *Johannes manibus apprehendit Petrum fugientem pedibus*; *Johannes magnae virtutis multum percussit Petrum hodie in ecclesia ob furtum*; finally, the most complex and comprehensive: *Johannes ideo scripsit librum, quem Priscianus, volens relin-*

1868, anast. repr. Frankfurt, 1964, pp. 83, 218–219). Di Capua, *Scritti minori,* II, p. 326, has suggested that the substitution of *constructio* for *compositio* may have come from *Rhetorica ad Herennium,* IV, 12, 18: "Compositio est verborum constructio quae facit omnes partes orationis aequabiliter perpolitas"—a definition, I should add, which was often repeated or echoed in medieval treatises.

10. Cf. Scaglione, *The Classical Theory of Composition,* p. 106.
11. Ibid.

quere exemplum aliis, composuit, quoniam exinde accepit precium.[12]
These examples are interesting in more than one respect. Note,
however, that Dante's example differs from these in the postposition
of the adverb *multum*. This gives his clause a strong flavor of spoken
Latin—indeed, it sounds very vernacular—, even while it contradicts
the above rule that adjectives (adverbs were regarded as adjectives
to the verb) tend to precede their terms. This difference is due to
the early date of our manuscript. Later manuals reflect the greater
closeness of current—or analytical, 'scientific'—Latin to the modes of
the vernaculars. As a matter of fact, Dante's position of the adverb
is in keeping with the rule adopted in the famous *Doctrinale* of
Alexander de Villadei (Villedieu), whose rule for adverbs stands out
curiously because it reminds us of the prevailing trend in the Romance languages. According to this, the most successful of all medieval grammars, first should come the nominative (preceded, if the
case be, by the vocative), then the personal verb (to wit, in finite
mood, which will be first if the aforementioned is lacking, just as the
impersonal verb comes first). Afterwards the adverbs, if any; otherwise, the dative (indirect object) and the accusative (direct object),
in this order. The genitive follows immediately its regimen (i.e., the
modifier follows the modified). Prepositions accompany, apparently
in the final places of the clause, either an accusative or an ablative.

The original is worth quoting *in extenso* as a picturesque instance
of this splendid text, all in memorial verses, of which we have extant
250 mss., and which went through about 250 printed editions. The
memory of this best seller of all times will make the mouth water of
many an author of college textbooks.

> Construe sic: casum, si sit, praepone vocantem;
> Mox rectum pones; hinc personale locabis
> Verbum, quod primo statues, si cetera desint.
> Tertius hinc casus et quartus saepe sequuntur,
> Aut verbo subdes adverbia. Subde secundum
> Casum rectori. Debet vox praepositiva
> Praeiungi quarto vel sexto, quem regit illa.
> *Doctrinale*, ch. ix, 11. 1390–96

Although these precepts were meant to be taken as an explanatory
method, the *Glosa Admirantes* referred to them as "debita et communis forma constructionis, . . . communis modus in contextu partium orationis," and it soon became easy to infer, if one did not

---

12. Ibid., p. 108.

already do so by the time of Alexander, that what is good for scholastic explanations must also be good for direct plain speaking and writing. A host of didactic writers began to do just that.[13] Furthermore, the very notion of 'natural' or 'right' order, whether used for pedagogic reasons in the school or assigned in theory and practice to scientific speech, necessarily and naturally implied that this order was inherently good and valid. This order was later called direct or analytical and it conspicuously corresponded to the natural trend of the Romance vernaculars. Indeed, it was Priscian who established the view that the 'right' order is the 'natural'—right because natural, and natural because 'logical.' In this he was following a long, continuous trend of thought which bore the clear imprint of Stoic logic.[14] Dante's two examples of a simple, correct and plain sentence structure show, through their word order, the impact of the tradition of construing by 'natural' order.

Dante's general theory of styles derives essentially from the *Rhetorica ad Herennium,* where *constructio* was also used to mean composition, and where the kinds of style were defined as three: the *gravis,* the *mediocris,* and the *attenuatus* or *extenuatus.* "Gravis est quae constat ex verborum gravium magna et ornata constructione. . . ." "Attenuata est quae demissa est usque ad *usitatissimam puri* consuetudinem sermonis."[15] [Emphasis mine.]

Now if Dante comes closest to the *usitatissimus* mode in describing the first *gradus,* it shall not surprise us if he does not mention the requirement of purity included in the *ad Herennium* passage. *Puritas,* or *latinitas,* was the first virtue demanded of style, and as such it was

---

13. Ibid., p. 110.

14. Ibid., p. 399 and relevant passages in Ch. 1.

15. *Rhetorica ad Her.,* IV, 8. Alfredo Schiaffini, *Lettura del De vulgari eloquentia di Dante* (Rome: Edizioni dell'Ateneo, anno accademico 1958–59, litho.), p. 287, stresses Dante's derivation from the Auctor ad Herennium for his theory of styles. These lecture notes offer a close, punctual reading of the text of *De v. e.* in a way that synthesizes the best recent commentaries (Mengaldo's notes to the text will appear in the second vol. of his edition, and promise to be substantive). See pp. 325–339 for a comprehensive analysis of the section on the four *gradus constructionis.* See, also, the close philological and rhetorical reading in Bruno Panvini's ed. of *De v. e.* (Palermo: Andò, 1968).

In I, 19, 3 Dante promises that he will lastly turn to the *inferiora vulgaria* and their uses, namely the low style. In II, 4, 1 he announces that in his as yet unwritten Book 4 he will deal with *vulgare mediocre* and its use in *ballatae* and *sonitus* (and then with the lowest vernacular and its use in *alii illegitimi et irregulares modi,* II, 3, 2). According to II, 4, 5–6 the *illustre* goes with *tragedia,* the mixture of *mediocre* and *humile* with *comedia,* the *humile* alone with the *elegia.* Both comedy and elegy were to be treated in Book 4.

held to belong to the elementary, grammatical, prerhetorical level of formation. It could mean grammatical correctness or national purity of vocabulary, or both. Obviously, no pre-Renaissance author could be a good judge of this latter requirement for Latin; hence, Dante speaks only of congruence and grammaticalness, morphological and syntactical—not of purity. He reserves this requirement to the vernacular, of which he is supreme judge: he will apply it there with total dedication yet only implicitly, without using the term.

If sheer *constructio*—to wit, the *regulata* or *congrua compago dictionum*, the syntactic congruence of words—is only the grammatical foundation of style, though a necessary one, the elect, ornate construction, on the other hand, is brought about by *urbanitas*, i.e. the artistic arrangement of words which distinguishes the speech of the cultivated urban circles (II, 6). The *gradus pure* (= 'merely') *sapidus*, first of the three 'urban' grades and second of the four literate ones, is that of the schoolmen at their best—a didactic and technical style which therefore is also, essentially, the style of the *De vulgari eloquentia* itself (and, for a roughly contemporary example, Francesco da Barberino's *Documenta amoris*, as Marigo points out).[16] The example is: *Piget me, cunctis pietate maiorem, quicunque in exilio tabescentes patriam tantum sompniando revisunt*—'I, who am more than any other affected by pity, deeply sympathize with all those who, languishing in exile, can revisit their country only in their dreams.' Note here the disjunction of the attribute *maiorem* from *me*, the anteposition of *cunctis pietate* to *maiorem* of which it is a complement, and the end-positioning of the subordinate verb *revisunt*. Briefly, this *gradus* is characterized by *ordo artificialis*, inversion and hyperbaton; and the syntax becomes in it hypotactic, *constructio composita*. Furthermore, it has *cursus*, three cases of it, according to the *stylus curiae romanae*, to wit: *pietate maiorem* (*cursus planus*), *exilio tabescentes* (*cursus velox*), and *sompniando revisunt* (*c. planus*).[17] On the other hand, it lacks an artistic use of vocabulary, since the words have their literal meaning: the *elocutio* does not contain *ornatus*.

The third *gradus*, *sapidus et venustus*, has congruence, *cursus*, *compositio* complex and artificial (in word order), *and* figures of speech (*ornatus*). *Laudabilis discretio marchionis Estensis, / et sua*

---

16. Marigo, p. 208.
17. For a detailed analysis of *cursus* in these examples, see Di Capua, *Scritti minori*, II, pp. 332–337.

magnificentia preparata / cunctis illum facit esse dilectum. Again a succession of three *cursus,* a *planus,* a *velox* and a *planus.* The *ornatus* is the new factor here, but it is of the lower kind, mere irony, not a very noble figure: the example satirizes Azzo VIII of Este, who is praised for being discreet and loved by all for his magnificence, whereas he was known to be the opposite, a petty tyrant and a miser.

The fourth grade, *sapidus et venustus et excelsus,* goes one step further and attains to the summit of the art by adding *ornatus* of the higher kind, the *ornatus difficilis* or *transumptio,* plus a truly excellent periodic complexity of the more artful variety. The splendid example, once again made up by Dante, reads: *Eiecta maxima parte florum / de sino tuo, Florentia, / nequicquam Trinacriam / Totila secundus adivit*—'Charles of Valois, the new Totila, succeeded in casting out of thy bosom the greatest part of thy flowers, o Florence, but then he failed in his assault on Sicily.' There are four cursus cadences: *velox, tardus, tardus, planus.* Note the inverted form of the sentence, on which hinges the effective periodic suspension. The subject and its predicate are withheld until the end, and are preceded, in this order, by the object *Trinacriam* and the opening ablative absolute, which in particular contributes to the period through its hammered-out conceptual brevity. The period is articulated into four isocola, or members of similar length, set off by the four wisely varied cadences. It is made dramatic by the metaphorical elements of the best citizens as flowers of the city and Charles of Valois as a new leader of a barbarian tribe. These metaphors are enhanced by the linking of the first to its referent, *Florentia,* through the *figura etymologica "florum-Florentia,"* while *Florentia* appears as a personification in the form of antonomasia. Such a concentration of figures is conclusively tied together and set off, as it were, by the antithetic arrangements of the two main statements in the sentence. The reader was undoubtedly prompt to perceive this antithesis, since the two undertakings and their clashing outcomes are just as antithetically expressed in the sarcastic popular judgment related by Villani: "E così per contradio si disse per motto: Messer Carlo venne in Toscana per paciaro, e lasciò il paese in guerra; e andò in Cicilia per fare guerra, e reconne vergognosa pace."[18] The two main images

---

18. Marigo, p. 212. A. Viscardi, *Le Origini* (Milan: Vallardi, 1953³), pp. 364ff., reminds us that Dante's *gradus constructionis excelsus* appeared to include the degree of structural complication which the Provençal troubadours called *entrebescamen.* Cf. Bernard Marti: *Aisi vauc entrebescan / Los motz e'l son afinan.* The

are intimately related: the laying waste of Florence's garden by Charles (*Florentia-flores*) recalls to Dante's mind the former destruction of his city by Totila. This is a case of supermetaphor called *metalepsis* by Quintilian and *transumptio* by Geoffrey of Vinsauf.[19] The images echo one another. Curiously enough, both Dante's and Villani's dicta have taken on the form of what the ancients called a square period, made of four balanced members.

Now that we have looked at some aspects of Dante's theory of style, we may wonder how they relate to his practice. As of yet, no one has placed Dante's syntactic practices within the broad context of the peculiar traditions of medieval writing. Both Giuseppe Lisio's 1902 pioneer study and Cesare Segre's excellent 1952 monograph implicitly assume that a sufficient assessment of Dante's achievements can be obtained by moving almost exclusively within the limited confines of early experimentation in the Italian vernacular.[20] Likewise, a more recent book on Dante's language by Christoph Schwarze, a young German linguist, makes too little of the medieval Latin heritage, the true creative background without which the expressive habits of a man like Dante cannot be properly understood, broadly steeped as he was in all the available cultural traditions.[21] The most comprehensive analysis available to this date is perhaps to be found in the numerous essays of Francesco Di Capua, published between 1912 and 1951. For further study I can do no more here than hint at some of the questions which I believe ought to be raised in this connection.

The more striking characteristics of medieval sentence structure, both in Latin and in the vernaculars, lie perhaps in the widespread tendency to conceive by coordination or by clumsy and only apparent subordination. About this, however, it is difficult to generalize. A recent linguistic study of OF brilliantly argues the point that the ratio of parataxis and hypotaxis is more a matter of literary style and formal traditions (genres) than of historical linguistic transition from a more

hermetic practitioners of *trobar clus* could twist the *entrebescar* beyond recognition, namely when the excess of inversion would reach the intolerable degree called *synchysis* (see *Classical Theory of Composition*, esp. pp. 118–122).

19. Cf. Di Capua, op. cit., I, pp. 337–338.

20. Giuseppe Lisio, *L'arte del periodo nelle opere volgari di Dante Alighieri e del sec. XIII: Saggio di critica e di storia letteraria* (Bologna, 1902); Cesare Segre, *La sintassi del periodo nei primi prosatori italiani (Guittone, Brunetto, Dante)*, Atti dell'Acc. Naz. dei Lincei, Sc. morali, IV, 2 (Rome, 1952), repr. in *Lingua, stile e società: Studi sulla storia della prosa italiana* (Milan, 1963).

21. C. Schwarze, *Untersuchungen zum syntaktischen Stil der italienischen Dichtungssprache bei Dante* (Bad Homburg v. d. H., 1970).

primitive to a more advanced stage.[22] Thus it would be incorrect to infer that French was syntactically less developed at the time of the *Chanson de Roland* than at that of the *Roman de Thèbes* BECAUSE the percentage of subordinate clauses jumps from 20 in the former to 30 in the latter, since one finds 30 percent to be the case in the earlier *Alexis* and even 75 percent in the *Serments de Strasbourg*. In other words, we can only legitimately conclude from that comparison that the language of the epic differs from that of the courtly romance. Indeed, one is bound to infer—on the ground of that kind of evidence—that OF is not inherently more paratactic than classical Latin, if one remains within the sphere of the epic, since 20% also happens to be the rate of incidence of hypotaxis in the *Aeneid*.

Basic devices and forms of sentence structure appear at different times and places in the function, as it were, of eternal constants. This makes it difficult to characterize individual styles on those terms and to identify specific influences and sources. Yet whenever these constants come to the surface, they acquire unique complections which are conditioned by particular historical circumstances. This is also true with the medieval sentence, both Latin and vernacular. Greek and Roman speculation about literary composition constantly revolved around the following basic notions. Art prose (Norden's *Kunstprosa*) was supposed to have found its method with the Sophist Gorgias, who introduced the so-called Gorgianic figures. These were based on the assumption that beautiful prose must resemble and imitate verse, therefore be essentially symmetrical. Symmetry or, in Latin, *concinnitas* (in English, properly 'balance') was clearly a matter of sound, therefore its figures or schemes were sound or verbal schemes. Figures of thought, on the other hand, such as metaphor, irony, allegory, witticisms, were on principle separable from the above. They were often advocated by the enemies of the grand style and partisans of the plain style. We may agree to refer to these thought figures as "tropes." The sentence, finally, as first theorized by Aristotle, could be basically loose, unstructured (as most plain writers and the Atticists wanted it), or periodic, this latter being usually described as a circular or square arrangement. Its parts or

---

22. On this and the following, see *The Classical Theory of Composition*, pp. 361–3, parts of which are repeated here as necessary background to the tentative statistical calculation of Dante's forms, that follows. The study referred to is W.-D. Stempel, "Untersuchungen zur Satzverknüpfung im Altfranzösischen," *Archiv für das Studium der neueren Sprachen und Literaturen*, Beiheft I (Braunschweig, 1964), esp. pp. 32–96.

members were conceived as units of delivery, not identical with, yet similar to, our notions of clause and phrase.

Now if we consider it legitimate, as we well might, to invoke the three characters of periodicity, symmetry, and looseness, and attribute circularity to the first, schematism to the second (in the sense of relying on the verbal schemes), and tropicality to the third, we shall find the following. The use of symmetrical sound schemes (essentially isocolon, parison, and paromoion) is rare in antiquity outside the period; even within the period it is always kept in check, especially in the good authors (like Isocrates, the canonical master of periodic balance), by the sobering constraint of good taste and tempered by the sustained study of variety in both form and rhythm. This variety also graces the members within the period, which, as in Cicero, where it is the normal unit, is circular and cumulative. On the other hand the medieval sentence has, by and large, no true periodicity and can be either loose (with or without tropes) or symmetrical (schematic). In the latter case it tends to use the schemes without preoccupation for any sense of measure and with rather exacting uniformity, heightened by the sharpness of its short members. Instead of being shunned, uniformity was sought.

This last pattern begins to be found among the Fathers of the Church of the Silver Age and, as Croll has demonstrated,[23] survives from the churchly literature of the Middle Ages well into the Renaissance and the early seventeenth century in the various forms of *estilo culto* (as in Antonio de Guevara, John Lyly, and some courtly literature). Whereas in classical prose the schemes had the function of underscoring the rhythm, in the medieval writers they became the chief source of a new, "schematic" rhythm, which occasionally achieves a repetitive singsong of magic incantation. The fountainheads of the schematic style were the imperial and papal courts, the *aula* and the *curia*, where the direct child of the *ars dictandi*, the *oratio aulica* emanating from the official chanceries or secretarial bureaux, pervaded even the more mundane and literary productions gravitating around them. It may not be out of place to recall here that Dante's *vulgare illustre* is required to be both *aulicum* and *curiale*. To the *aulici* the humanists opposed themselves as *eruditi*, starting as early as Petrarch, in an attack which eventually brought the humanists to take control of the courts and change their style.

---

23. Croll, "The Sources of the Euphuistic Rhetoric," in M. W. Croll and H. Clemons, eds., John Lily, *Euphues . . .* (London and New York, 1916).

This triumph was gradual; in Italy, where it began with Petrarch's successor Coluccio Salutati, it became widespread in the fifteenth century, but it never proceeded very far afield in some more peripheral countries, such as England.[24] Again, what the Middle Ages cultivated as the 'grand style' was essentially schematic composition, while the 'humble style' was little else than the loose. Dante theorized a language as well as a style which were meant to be illustrious (noble), courtly (aulico-aristocratic), and artificial (*curiale* like the language of the ecclesiastical bureaucracy); Boccaccio tried to rediscover the ancient circularity. But both remained essentially in the medieval tradition, in the senses just indicated, regardless of the unique features of their individual genius.

The classical theory of *compositio* (for Dante, *constructio*) was principally concerned with sentence structure and word order. Let us now turn our attention briefly to the latter. We have seen that Dante was clearly aware of the importance of *ordo artificialis*. How did he practice it? His vernacular shows even from the *Vita nuova* an extraordinary sensitivity to the potential inherent in the use of the most precious sorts of hyperbata, what the medieval rhetoricians called *transgressio* and *trajectio* (Geoffrey of Vinsauf's *perversio*). Allow me only to cite his practice of separating participles and infinitives from the governing verbs or auxiliaries, as, most typically, in *l'ora ne la quale m'era questa visione apparita*; . . . *era la quarta della notte stata*; . . . *ciò che io avea nel mio sonno veduto* (*VN* iii, 8–9); *non sofferse lo nome de la mia donna stare* (vi, 2). Such practices were literary yet frequent, but Dante turns them into delicate modes of suspension and magic unreality. An analogous occurrence was that of separating and end-positioning adjectives with predicative (or quasi-adverbial) connotation, such as: *e li sospiri m'assalivano grandissimi e angosciosi* (*VN* xxxvii, 3); *andavano, secondo che mi parve, molto angosciosi* (xl, 2); *povero mi pareva lo servigio e nudo* (xxxiii, 1), this last being a particularly sophisticated, but far from unusual, case of separation, and all of the preceding being quite typical trademarks of Dante's juvenile prose (of a particularly expressive type, through emphasis).[25]

But what about Dante's Latin? How does it relate to medieval and

---

24. Ibid., pp. 272 and 284 in the reprinting of the study in J.M. Patrick and R.O. Evans, *Style, Rhetoric, and Rhythm. Essays by M. W. Croll* (Princeton, 1966).

25. *Theory of Composition*, p. 122; cf. B. Terracini, *Pagine e appunti di linguistica storica* (Florence, 1957), pp. 247–263 and 264–272.

to ancient practice? Can his word order in this language be used as a decisive factor in characterizing his style? An assessment of this important question is more problematic than ever at this point because the conventional view of such matters, which was established as early as 1903 in a fundamental study by the Viennese Romance philologist, Elise Richter, has been recently challenged from several angles.

Richter believed she had proved the thesis that word order in the Romance languages was little more than the consequence of an evolution which had been taking place within Latin itself. By the year 400 A.D. spoken Latin had already begun to show a basically Romance movement, namely S + V + Complements. A number of German scholars such as Linde, Haida, Stempel, and Koll have since shown that the real picture is much more complex and even contradictory. To make a long story short, we are confronted, first of all, with the striking fact that the evolution of word order in ancient literary Latin is far from homogeneous. Not only does it follow an uneven course, but it varies by author and, within the same author, by genres, as does the ratio of coordination and subordination, as we have just seen. Thus the end-position of the verb which is found in 84 percent of the main clauses and 93 percent of the dependent clauses in Caesar's *De bello gallico*, does decline to 37 and 63 percent respectively in Victor Vitensis, an author of the late fifth century. But the ratio not only also declines when we go further back than Caesar (it is 70 and 86 percent in Cato's *De agricultura*) but, most strikingly, it is as low as 35 and 61 percent in Cicero's *De republica* (lower than in Victor Vitensis!).

In the Middle Ages the pattern also varies considerably from time to time, author to author, and text to text. One possible interpretation, brilliantly and cogently argued by Hans-Georg Koll, is that the most important single factor is the pressure of scriptural writings, all based as they were on Greek plain style texts, which displayed a considerably more analytical word order than classical Latin. Thus Christian authors in the late Roman empire show a strong drift toward Romance word order, whereas pagan, literarily-oriented writers, cling determinedly and rigidly to uniformly "inverted" patterns. A most important consideration in drawing statistical accounts of such trends and mutations is that the end-position of the verb *per se* is much less meaningful than the position of the verb vis-à-vis the object, wherever they might be placed in the clause as a whole.[26]

---

26. *Theory of Composition*, pp. 364–366, with pertinent bibliographic references.

My own statistical analysis of the whole of *De v. e.* Book I, plus Book II, 4, conducted on Koll's principles, has yielded the following figures: 81.25 percent of Ob + V sequences in main clauses versus 18.75 of V + Ob sequences, and 79.03 percent versus 20.97 percent in secondary clauses.[27] This pattern strikes me as somewhat personal and idiosyncratic both for Dante's time and for preceding centuries. It would appear to come closest to, say, such authors as Gregory of Tours (fl. 550–573) and, even more, Cicero in *De legibus*—only, however, if one considers the ratio in main clauses alone. The slightly lower incidence of Ob + V positions in secondary clauses than in main clauses is strange and is paralleled only in the Bible and such a text as the *Chronicae Fredegarii*, of A.D. 613–768 (which happens to give 90.3/9.7::75/25). By itself, of the texts tabulated by Koll, Tacitus' *Annales* II would appear to offer a close enough average for comparison. Of course only a comparison with late medieval authors would make such tabulations truly meaningful.

Furthermore, if we use the plainer method of analysis as observed in Linde's computations, we find that Dante's *De v. e.* shows an incidence of 56.25 percent and 72.30 percent of end-position of the verb respectively in main and secondary clauses, which would place him in the relative neighborhood of Seneca, Firmicus Maternus, and also what Linde gives as the "approximate average of Cato, Cicero, Sallust"—generally closer, at any rate, to the authors of Golden Latinity than to those of Silver Latinity, and unlike the patterns found both in proto-Christian and popular or scholastic writings of the medieval period.[28]

The tentative conclusion I would feel tempted to advance is that Dante appears to be a conspicuous heir to the classical tradition (so that his praises of the ancient prose writers as models are far from idle). He is also remarkably free from a close association with the didactic style of his time (except for his vocabulary). On the other hand, one must remain acutely aware of the fact that, when analyzed case by case, his adoption of natural or artificial order eminently represents a functional choice of the most expressive possibility available, without ever sounding like a routine yielding to mechanical patterns, *even* in his more didactic, scholastic moods.

---

27. I have excluded interrogative clauses starting with pronoun, relative clauses, objective infinitive clauses, as well as split objects (*turpissimum habent vulgare*) and split verbs (*venati saltus et pasqua sumus*).

28. Cf. tables in *Theory of Composition*, pp. 364 and 366.

The point of all this is that Dante's style, both Latin and vernacular, both in prose and verse, still remains largely unexplored, and that a close study is bound to confirm how thoroughly original and incomparably sophisticated it was when measured by the standards of its own time. And I wish to emphasize that all this is true particularly of his didactic passages, since the merits of his lyrical ones do not need stressing in this context.

Chaucer's Realization of Himself as Rhetor

ROBERT O. PAYNE

In 1963 I wrote in the introduction to a study of Chaucer's poetry in the context of the medieval *artes poetriae*:

> The relationship between [Chaucer's] poetic practice and the body of orthodox theory with which my study begins is variously experimental. Consequently, one has always to speak of the poems in this connection as tentative ways of realizing the terms, ideas, and theoretical prescripts of the traditional poetic in immediately practical compositional situations, or as ways of testing the usefulness of the theories.[1]

Since J. M. Manly's seminal essay "Chaucer and the Rhetoricians"[2] in 1926, most of the discussion of such experimentation has focussed on style—the relationships between Chaucer's poetry and tabulations of figures like Geoffrey of Vinsauf's *Summa de coloribus* or the sections on *elocutio* in the school rhetorics. In a sense, that is as it should be, given the heavy weighting of *elocutio* in the school treatises themselves and the considerable overlap between *grammatica* and *rhetorica* as essentially linguistically oriented school disciplines.[3] It has been observed from time to time, however, that there is danger of a rather sterile circularity in combing through Chaucer's works and tabulating the figures in them that are also listed and described in the manuals. In fact, two of the earliest

---

1. Robert O. Payne, *The Key of Remembrance: A Study of Chaucer's Poetics* (New Haven: Yale University Press, 1963), pp. 6–7.
2. *Proceedings of the British Academy*, 12 (London, 1926).
3. In fact, the most recent historian of medieval rhetorical theory, James J. Murphy, treats the school *artes poetriae* under the chapter heading "Preceptive Grammar, or the Rhetoric of Verse-Writing," in *Rhetoric in the Middle Ages* (Berkeley: University of California Press, 1974), pp. 135 ff.

investigators of Chaucer's rhetoric, Manly and Traugott Naunin,[4] after making just such extensive tabulations, concluded that the most important relationship between Chaucer and the school rhetoricians was his gradual disengagement from their influence, and that they could never have taught him anything of real aesthetic value anyway.

However, since my chapter on "Chaucer and the Art of Rhetoric" in *Companion to Chaucer Studies*[5] provides a recent survey in some detail of the accumulated half century of relevant scholarship, I shall not repeat it here but rather explore a different kind of relationship between Chaucer's work and traditional rhetorical theory—an exploration which may open some new possibilities for future work on Chaucer and the rhetoricians.

At the end of *The Key of Remembrance*,[6] I argued for a quite different definition of "Chaucer's rhetoric" from the one that seems implied by most of the work centered on stylistic and figural analysis:

> All of these things—consciousness of a situation in which speaker confronts audience, awareness of an element of pretense as necessary to communication in the situation, agreement to tolerate specified artifices

4. *Der Einfluss der mittelalterlichen Rhetorik auf Chaucer's Dichtung* (Bonn University Dissertations, 21, 1929).

5. Beryl Rowland, ed., *Companion to Chaucer Studies* (Toronto, New York and London: Oxford University Press, 1968), pp. 38–57. Since that essay was written, however, there have been several interesting additions to the discussion, most notably: Judson B. Allen, *The Friar as Critic* (Nashville: Vanderbilt University Press, 1971); Jane Baltzell, "Rhetorical 'Amplification' and the Structure of Medieval Narrative," *PCP* 2 (1967), 32–39; Paul M. Clogan, "The Figural Style and Meaning of *The Second Nun's Prologue and Tale*," *M and H*, NS 3 (1972), 213–40; Robert W. Frank, Jr., "*Troilus and Criseyde*: The Art of Amplification," in *Medieval Literature and Folklore Studies in Honor of Francis Lee Utley*, ed. Jerome Mandel and Bruce A. Rosenberg (New Brunswick: Rutgers University Press, 1970); John H. Fisher, "The Three Styles of Fragment I of the *Canterbury Tales*," *ChauR* 8 (1973), 119–27; David V. Harrington, "Chaucer's *Man of Law's Tale*: Rhetoric and Emotion," *MSpr* 61 (1967), 353–62; Stephen Knight, "Rhetoric and Poetry in the Franklin's Tale," *ChauR* 4 (1970), 14–30; Charles Koban, "Hearing Chaucer Out: The Art of Persuasion in the *Wife of Bath's Tale*," *ChauR* 5 (1971), 225–39; Allen C. Koretsky, "Chaucer's Use of the Apostrophe in *Troilus and Criseyde*," *ChauR* 4 (1970), 81–84; John Nist, "Chaucer's Apostrophic Mode in *The Canterbury Tales*," *TSL* 15 (1970), 85–98; Glending Olson, "Deschamps' *Art de dictier* and Chaucer's Literary Environment," *Speculum* 48 (1973), 714–23; and J. S. Simmons, "The Place of the Poet in Chaucer's *House of Fame*," *MLQ* 27 (1966), 125–35. Browsing through *Dissertation Abstracts*, I notice also that there has been considerable concern with Chaucer's rhetoric among the new Ph.D.'s in the past six or seven years, with six or eight dissertation titles listed specifically on rhetorical subjects in Chaucer's poetry.

6. P. 231.

to keep the pretense working, identification of similarities and differences in speaker's and audience's reactions to a subject, the search for a larger ground of agreement between them (i.e. persuasion)—all of these things constitute a large part of what we mean by the term "rhetorical," even when it is used in a limited historical sense. In all these ways, a good deal more than simply in the configurations of its style, *Troilus and Criseyde* is a highly rhetorical poem . . . [and it] engages us in a continuing dialectic with the narrator which defines and locates both poet and audience. That is a kind of appeal from *ethos* which Aristotle's *Rhetoric* never foresaw, and of which no other English poet has made such capital.

It is from that model—the poem as central element in a whole rhetorical situation—that I want to begin here, because one of the most interesting aspects of the gradual evolution of one branch of *rhetorica* into *poetria* in the Middle Ages is first the blurring and then the redefining of the ways language mediates between speaker and audience. In the school manuals of the late twelfth and early thirteenth centuries, in many of which *rhetorica* and *poetria* seem to have become nearly synonymous, the speaker seems indeed to have disappeared from the discussion altogether. And although discussions of the levels of style and of the different kinds and effects of figurative language necessarily imply a psychology of audience response, none of the schoolmen ever actually articulates one.[7] To put it a bit differently, the almost completely linguistic (or "literary") reorientation of *rhetorica*, which Murphy notes,[8] turns the classical rhetoricians' three-way relationship among speaker / language / audience into a two-way relationship between idea and poem. It is the problem of explicating a decorum for that relationship to which the school manuals regularly address themselves—the Christian poet's problem of coordinating man's emotional and rational natures by correlating the invented structures of language with the given structure of ideas.

The great difficulty for the modern historical critic (and I suspect for Chaucer also) is that even in the best and fullest of the treatises—Geoffrey's *Poetria nova* or John of Garland's *De arte prosayca, metrica, et rithmica*—the basic ethical, psychological, and epistemological issues are so quickly lost in the sheer tabulation of the patterns of verbal invention. In fact, after a couple of generations, the tabulations themselves had so ossified that the patterns of verbal invention became almost as "given," almost as beyond the need for exploratory

---

7. Cf. above, pp. 70–73, Ernest Gallo's argument that for Geoffrey of Vinsauf, a poem is a linguistic projection of an *archetypus*.
8. See n. 3, above.

analysis, as the structure of ideas was initially. It is precisely that terminal rigor, and the basic dysfunction of which it is symptomatic, that Chaucer satirizes so neatly in the Nun's Priest's parody of one of Geoffrey of Vinsauf's own poems.[9]

Still, Chaucer and his fellow medieval poets had seriously to deal with the problem of decorum, and the implication in the very idea of decorum that there must be a hierarchy of beauty and worth inherent in language just as in the ideas poetry conveyed. If decorum is to have any reasonable meaning at all, it must depend on the adjustment of two different hierarchical orders, idea and language, so that they correspond precisely. Yet the analysis of language that we get in medieval rhetorical-poetic theory is usually so obsessed with the figural topography of language that the correspondence is blurred and distorted.

At the same time, Chaucer keeps reminding us (and we would know it anyway) that he *has* his purposes and expects his style to accomplish them. But in the repeated representations Chaucer gives us of himself struggling with the old poets,[10] he seems to have the same problems with them as we have with him. In a particular poem, how do we determine the specific and unique effects of its verbal decor? Or, when the narrator gives us variant and apparently incompatible versions of his intentions, how can we judge the "fitness" of style to idea until we have resolved the question of the poem's ideas by deriving them from its style? And does that not reduce the notion of decorum to a tautology? Finally, I think some combination of Chaucer's self-consciousness as a poet and his study of the rhetorical treatises produced in him a rather different mode of awareness as he sought to answer those questions. When he looked at the old books, he not only saw (or tried to see) the decorous verbal projection of an archetype which Geoffrey of Vinsauf had instructed him to look for; he also heard a voice, the voice of a man like and unlike himself. And by this sea change, the idea/language model which *rhetorica*-turned-*poetria* had generated became again something much more like the speaker/language/audience one of earlier rhetoric.

The difference has important consequences almost everywhere in

---

9. *CT,* VII, 3338–54. All references to Chaucer's poetry are to F. N. Robinson, *The Works of Geoffrey Chaucer,* 2nd ed. (Boston: Houghton Mifflin, 1957).

10. Ovid in *BD*; Cicero in *PF*; Vergil (and others) in *HF*; "Lollius" (and others) in *T&C*; the French love poets in *Prol. LGW,* etc.

Chaucer's poetry, but we may as well begin with the clear, familiar, but still illuminating example of the Pardoner. If Socrates had known the *Pardoner's Tale,* he would surely have worked it into his humiliation of Gorgias, for the Pardoner goes bluntly and directly to the heart of the question of Sophistic rhetoric:

> Thus kan I preche agayn that same vice
> Which that I use and that is avarice.
> But though myself be gilty in that synne,
> Yet kan I maken oother folk to twynne
> From avarice, and soore to repente.
>
> .   .   .   .
>
> By God, I hope I shal yow telle a thyng
> That shal by reson been at your likyng.
> For though myself be a ful vicious man,
> A moral tale yet I yow telle kan,
> Which I am wont to preche for to wynne.
> (*CT,* VI, 427–31; 457–61)

Chaucer, of course, would have put the issue not in Platonic terms, but in Christian ones: can a corrupt officer perform a good office? But the case of the Pardoner surely has strong rhetorical overtones for Chaucer as well, for he is only a few generations removed from the emergence of the preaching orders and the concurrent appearance of the *artes praedicandi.*[11]

For obvious reasons, the *artes praedicandi* follow the speaker/language/audience model for rhetoric a good deal more closely than do the *artes poetriae,* but they have very little to say about the tactics of the Pardoner—namely, the deliberate use of images (in the old rhetorical sense) to create an "image" (in the modern, Madison Avenue sense). There are occasional admonitions to preachers to approach their audiences persuasively,[12] but few traces survive in the manuals for preachers of the true Aristotelian appeal from *ethos,* the rhetor's calculated representation of his own character as a part of his material for persuasion.

The other preacher on the Canterbury pilgrimage, in fact, raises the same issue, but from the opposite point of view. The Parson's rather surly refusal to accept any of the responsibility for persuading

---

11. See above, Margaret Jennings, "The Preacher's Rhetoric: Ralph Higden," pp. 112–126.

12. Jennings, above, pp. 116–117, especially her citation of Alain de Lille's injunction: "praedicator debet captare benevolentiam auditorum . . . per humilitatem et a rei quam proponit utilitate."

his audience of course clears him at once of the Pardoner's sophism, but it also suggests that he may frequently have preached to a slumbering congregation.

> This Persoun answerde, al atones,
> "Thou getest fable noon ytold for me;
> For Paul, that writeth unto Thymothee,
> Repreveth hem that weyven soothfastnesse,
> And tellen fables and swich wrecchednesse.
> Why sholde I sowen draf out of my fest,
> When I may sowen whete, if that me lest?
> For which I seye, if that yow list to heere
> Moralitee and vertuous mateere,
> And thanne that ye wol yeve me audience,
> I wol ful fayn, at Cristes reverence,
> Do yow pleasaunce leefful, as I can.
> But trusteth wel, I am a Southren man,
> I kan nat geeste 'rum, ram, ruf,' by lettre,
> Ne, God woot, rym holde I but litel bettre;
> And therfore, if yow list—I wol nat glose—
> I wol yow telle a myrie tale in prose
> To knytte up al this feeste, and make an ende."
>   (*CT*, X, 30–47)

Unfortunately, the fragmented state in which the framework of the *Canterbury Tales* has survived (which may well only reflect the state in which Chaucer left it) makes it extremely hazardous to speculate on the relationship between the Pardoner and the Parson *as figures in a deliberate poetic construct*. And perhaps even more unfortunately, the very modern notion that probably a medieval audience would have found the Parson's sermon gratifyingly persuasive, and therefore we should substitute their putative response for our own analysis of the text, further embarrasses discussion of the suggestion I wish to advance here. Nevertheless, the Pardoner, whom we all know to be a rogue, *does* live up to his boast and preach a sermon (or tell a tale) which the concensus of nearly six hundred years judges to be one of the best of the surviving twenty-four. The good Parson, over the same span of time, seems to have persuaded only a small coterie of neo-exegetes of the past twenty-five or thirty years that his "myrie tale in prose" really does "knytte up al this feeste." I suggest that within the framework of the *Canterbury Tales*, dimly and uncertainly as we may be able to perceive it, there exists a real and illuminating possibility of placing the Pardoner and the Parson at the opposite ends of a continuum which defines Chaucer's sense of the problem of rhetoric—and at the same time a good part of his sense of the problem of poetry.

The bad Pardoner, by his superlative command of precisely those skills recommended in the *artes praedicandi* and the *artes poetriae,* also produces the result they recommend. He persuades his audiences for their own benefit.[13] We have no comparable criteria by which to judge the Parson as a preacher, except that to centuries of readers his tale has seemed one of the dullest. The good man who began his sermon by abjuring persuasion made a self-fulfilling prophecy. But we must also note that both men at the same time do something else: they present images of themselves. And we know the Pardoner's *persona* to be completely false, the Parson's to be completely true. At one pole, we have the bad man whose superlative skills not only work but produce good results; at the other, the good man whose unwillingness to falsify himself by any art vitiates his good intentions. The illusion succeeds better than the reality.

This is not an issue which gets much consideration in any of the medieval branches of rhetoric, although Guibert de Nogent, early in the twelfth century, raises it and, startlingly, confronts it head-on:

> Individuals have different ideas about preaching, however. Some refuse to do it out of pride, some out of laziness, and some out of envy. Some, I say, despise it because of pride: they see that many preachers display themselves arrogantly and for the sake of vanity, and they wish to avoid the epithet "sermonizers," which describes so contemptible a breed, a class which Gregory Nazianzen called "ventriloquists, because they speak for the belly's sake *(pro suo ventre loquuntur)*." They despise all preachers as of this unspeakable type.
>
> If a comparison between the two is justified, however, the man who preaches out of a desire for praise does the more good and harms only himself. He at least proclaims to others the teachings they need; the other vilely conceals matter he knows to be useful, and so neither benefits others nor does anything to help himself.[14]

Guibert could scarcely have known it, but in that passage he aligns himself with Gorgias against Socrates[15] and, in so doing, reconstructs

---

13. The audience of Canterbury pilgrims, however, has to be excluded from this evaluation. The Pardoner does not really preach his sermon to them; rather he includes it as an example in his lecture to them on the art of his kind of rhetoric.

14. *Liber quo ordine sermo fieri debeat, PL* 156, 11–21. Translation by Joseph M. Miller in *Readings in Medieval Rhetoric,* ed. Joseph M. Miller, Michael H. Prosser, and Thomas W. Benson (Bloomington and London: Indiana University Press, 1973), p. 163.

15. Cf. *Gorgias,* 454 ff. in *The Dialogues of Plato,* trans. B. Jowett (New York: Random House, 1937), pp. 512–13:

perhaps the oldest form of the controversy over persuasion by deliberate artifice. In the *Gorgias,* Plato glances only obliquely at the
character of the orator. It is the audience, and its determination of
the rhetor's procedures, on which Socrates concentrates his anti-
rhetorical fire:

> In my opinion then, Gorgias, the whole of which rhetoric is a part is not
> an art at all, but the habit of a bold and ready wit, which knows how to
> manage mankind: this habit I sum up under the word 'flattery;' . . .[16]

In the *Republic,* however, the rhetorician/poet *in propria persona*
receives an even more hostile treatment than the vulgar audience he
manipulates had received in the *Gorgias.*[17] First, in Book III, Socrates
(still pretending to want to save something of poetry for the citizens
of his ideal state) makes a distinction which, although it is theoretical,
is essentially the same as the practical one the Parson makes in the
preamble to his tale. Socrates says

> Now as far as these lines, "And he prayed all the Greeks, but especially
> the two sons of Atreus, the chiefs of the people," the poet is speaking in
> his own person; he never leads us to suppose that he is anyone else. But
> in what follows he takes the person of Chryses, and then he does all that
> he can to make us believe that the speaker is not Homer, but the aged
> priest himself.[18]

Gor. I answer, Socrates, that rhetoric is the art of persuasion in courts of law and
other assemblies, as I was just now saying, and about the just and the unjust.
.   .   .   .

Soc. And which sort of persuasion does rhetoric create in courts of law and other
assemblies about the just and unjust, the sort of persuasion which gives belief
without knowledge, or that which gives knowledge?
Gor. Clearly, Socrates, that which only gives belief.
Soc. Then rhetoric, as would appear, is the artificer of a persuasion which creates
belief about the just and unjust, but gives no instruction about them?

16. Jowett, p. 521.
17. Plato, we should remember, had early made the identification of poetry with
rhetoric which was to be unmade by Aristotle and the Roman rhetoricians, and then
to reemerge in the Middle Ages. It occurs explicitly in *Gorgias* (Jowett, p. 564):

Soc. Well now, suppose that we strip all poetry of song and rhythm and metre,
there will remain speech?
Cal. To be sure.
Soc. And this speech is addressed to a crowd of people?
Cal. Yes.
Soc. Then poetry is a sort of rhetoric?
Cal. True.

The passage is an interesting anticipation, but with the valuation reversed, of Dante's
famous dictum that a poem is "a piece of rhetoric set to music." (*De vulgari
eloquentia,* liber secundus, III, 16–20.)
18. Jowett, p. 656.

Finally, in the famous passages in Book X, he banishes poets altogether, on the grounds that both the poet, through his "impersonations," and the audience's perception of his poem, are illusions —artifices—images rather than realities.

I know of no early discussion, other than Plato's, of the possibilities and hazards of the deliberate creation of a *persona* by the orator or poet. But some of the most perceptive criticism of Chaucer's poetry in recent years has grown out of a concern for his various representations of himself in his poems, and it is my contention here that that hallmark of his work is a consequence of his rediscovery and exploitation of a rhetorical issue which had been sharp and lively in ancient Greece, but which had blurred, changed form, and receded far into the background of most medieval rhetorical discourse.

The change begins with Aristotle, and at first it might seem that his *Rhetoric* will put the whole development on a new track, because he is able to define logic, rhetoric, and poetry as three quite distinct and separate and equally justifiable uses of the mind and language. For all his respect for systematic logic and his faith in it, it seemed self-evident to Aristotle that much of what men had to resolve in the daily course of living was simply beyond the power of logic (or of any other systematic science known to him).[19] Rhetoric became the art necessary to men in areas where science wouldn't serve, and poetry was no longer a matter of persuasion or deliberation at all. The consequence I am most interested in here is that such distinctions take most of the ethical pressure off of the appeal from ethos, and Aristotle can simply discuss it objectively as one of the important artifices of persuasion. He makes his case unmistakably clear at the outset:

> Of the modes of persuasion furnished by the spoken word there are three kinds. The first kind depends on the personal character of the speaker; the second on putting the audience into a certain frame of mind; the third on the proof, or apparent proof, provided by the words of the speech itself. Persuasion is achieved by the speaker's personal character when the speech is so spoken as to make us think him credible. We believe good men more fully and more readily than others: this is true generally whatever the question is, and absolutely true where exact certainty is impossible and opinions are divided. *This kind of persuasion, like the others, should be achieved by what the speaker says, not by what people think of his character before he begins to speak.*[20]

---

19. An Orosius or a Martianus Capella might even have called this Aristotle's way of acknowledging original sin.

20. *Rhetorica*, Bk. I.2, 1356ᵃ, trans. W. Rhys Roberts in *The Works of Aristotle*, ed. W. D. Ross (Oxford: The Clarendon Press, 1946), vol. XI. Italics mine.

But Aristotle's insistence that the speaker must re-create his character in each new speech apparently did not close the debate. Cicero never clearly raises the question, but for Quintilian, it is a central and recurrent theme throughout the *Institutio oratoria*; and he reaches conclusions precisely opposite to Aristotle's. Even though the complete text of the *Institutio* was not rediscovered until the fifteenth century,[21] it is Quintilian's way of resolving the difficulty that predominates in medieval rhetoric whenever the issue is raised at all.

Like Aristotle, Quintilian asserts his position flatly at the beginning of his treatise:

> I hold that no one can be a true orator unless he is also a good man and even if he could be, I would not have it so.[22]

In Book II, he acknowledges that the matter has been much debated, but holds his ground firmly:

> The first and chief disagreement on the subject is found in the fact that some think that even bad men may be called orators, while others, of whom I am one, restrict the name of orator and the art itself to those who are good.[23]

There is an interesting but very brief passage in Book III.viii in which Quintilian picks up the question of impersonation that had so bothered Plato in the *Republic*, but he concludes by simply accepting it as a technique to be employed by poets and orators. It is clear that he does not relate the technique to his larger concern with the good character which all the orator's speeches must project, and toward which all his education and training are aimed. Rather, throughout the *Institutio*, Quintilian seems either unaware of, or unconcerned with, the potential conflict between the orator's need to preserve and project his own good character and his need to appear favorably to varying audiences. That the former need will override all others in the true orator is the simple, unambiguous assertion of his account of Socrates, who could have saved himself by a clever defense but refused to do so because it didn't fit his character.

---

21. See Murphy, pp. 357 ff.

22. "Neque enim esse oratorem nisi bonum virum iudico, et fieri etiamsi potest nolo." Bk. I.ii.3. H. E. Butler, ed., *The Institutio oratoria of Quintilian, With an English Translation* (London and Cambridge, Mass.: The Loeb Classical Library, 1958). Subsequent references to the *Institutio* are to this edition.

23. "Prima atque praecipua opinionum circa hoc differentia, quod alii malos quoque viros posse oratores dici putant; alii, quorum nos sententiae accedimus, nomen hoc artemque, de qua loquimur, bonis demum tribui volunt." Bk. II.xv.2–3.

This instance alone shows that the end which the orator must keep in view is not persuasion, but speaking well, since there are occasions when to persuade would be a blot upon his honor.[24]

So we arrive at the dawn of the Christian Middle Ages with the old Platonic debate still apparently going on, but with Aristotle's argument that the speaker must reinvent himself for each new audience now lost in the wreckage of the second sophistic, and with Quintilian's wholly ethical reorientation of *rhetorica* preparing the way for Boethius and Augustine.[25]

It is, as we all know, extremely difficult to make out the extent to which Augustine intended to outline a general Christian aesthetic, or a general theory of discourse, or even a rudimentary *ars praedicandi*.[26] But I think it can be taken as generally agreed that, as the inheritor of a fused Platonic-Aristotelian-Sophistic rhetorical tradition, he puzzled at some length over the difficulties of fallen men conveying Christian truth to other fallen men. In mulling over that question, he seems to be most often concerned with the audience—with the risk of artfully ordering language so that it will attract them to truth. In that, he seems to me (especially in the second and fourth books of *De doctrina christiana*) closer to Aristotle than to Quintilian in his willingness to admit the risk and accept it as simply a given in the human condition. Preachers—and perhaps poets—find their justifiable business in the invention of those "reasonable lies" which deceive weak and illusion-prone men into true perception by making them feel good about it.

However, there is a passage near the end of *De magistro* which really sets the whole matter in quite a different light, and which I suspect is one of the earliest adumbrations of the shift in later medieval rhetoric / poetics from the speaker / language / audience model to the idea / language one.

> Do teachers profess that it is their thoughts that are learned and retained, and not the disciplines which they imagine they transmit by their speaking? Who is so foolishly curious as to send his son to school to learn what the teacher thinks? When the teachers have expounded by means of

---

24. "Quo vel solo patet non persuadendi sed bene dicendi finem in oratore servandum, cum interim persuadere deforme sit." Bk. XI.i.11.

25. See above, Michael Leff, "The Logician's Rhetoric: Boethius," for a discussion of the way in which Boethius' definitions of rhetoric and dialectic share Quintilian's ethical orientation and more or less rule out the kind of Platonic-Aristotelian concerns which Chaucer revivifies.

26. See Murphy, pp. 47 ff.

words all the disciplines which they profess to teach, the disciplines also of virtue and wisdom, then their pupils take thought within themselves whether what they have been told is true, looking to the inward truth, that is to say, so far as they are able. In this way they learn. And when they find inwardly that what they have been told is true, they praise their teachers, not knowing that they really praise not teachers but learned men, if the teachers really knew what they express in words.[27]

Now, if we may force Augustine's "teacher" enough to include more or less anyone who uses words systematically for deliberate communication, this passage might be paraphrased: "The character a speech *really* displays is not that of its orator, but of its subject." And with that we are well on the way to Geoffrey of Vinsauf.

But it is Chaucer who sees straight to the heart of the old Augustinian paradox—knows that it belongs to the poet himself even more than to his language or his audience—and then invents, as a poetic concretion of his perception, that most interesting and most recurrent of all the great Chaucerian characters, the first-person narrator of all the major poems. Chaucer shares with the Pardoner and Aristotle the perception that every effective speech must to some degree invent (simulate) the character of its speaker; he shares with the Parson and Augustine the conviction that moral disaster for the speaker lies that way. Consequently, from the *Book of the Duchess* all the way through to the *Parson's Tale,* the docent who conducts us into, through, and back out of all those various dreams and fictions is a series of variations on a basic, invented *ethos*: the doubtfully hopeful minor academic writer trying his best to recover from his most recent disaster because he really does have something to say to us, even though neither his love life nor his bibliography would make that seem very probable.

Perhaps a different alignment of this Chaucerian narrator with his creator's heritage of Christian rhetoric will help clarify matters. In every one of Chaucer's poems except the *Canterbury Tales,* the first character we see is the narrator struggling in his inadequacies to cope with the language and art—the "sentence and solas"—of some antique book, just as he knows we will eventually have to cope with the book he is about to write. That is, the reader/narrator compresses into a single dramatic image all three of the central issues of ancient rhetoric: persuader, audience, and the language that links them; and

---

27. Trans. J. H. S. Burleigh, in *Augustine: Earlier Writings,* The Library of Christian Classics, Vol. VI (Philadelphia: The Westminster Press, 1953), p. 100.

all three of the cautionary categories Augustine had imposed on Sophistic rhetoric: the mortal fallibility of persuaders, the dangerous volatility of emotional audiences, and the temporal corruptibility of language. And in that tense, comic, wonderfully incisive image of the bumbling old poet reading even older poets just as we will try to read him, all the apparent technical overconfidence of the thirteenth-century rhetoricians from whom Chaucer learned so much simply disappears, and we are left at last with a clear and persuasive insight into what they had all along been trying to tell us about what it means for mortals to try to make poetry.

But as Bertrand Bronson[28] has perhaps overemphasized, Chaucer not only wrote for readers, he also spoke for present audiences. The corollary, as I suggested early in this essay, is that when he read old books, he became an audience and heard a speaker's voice. That, in turn, led him—particularly in the *House of Fame*—into a different entanglement which should be very interesting to those of us who are concerned with what it means to call Chaucer's work "rhetorical."

The change of model[29] from text/reader to speaker/hearer has two closely related and important consequences for much of Chaucer's poetry. First, the old Platonic-Aristotelian problem becomes immediate again. If the speaker has invented a character, the audience must re-create it from his speech and must evaluate it as part of the process of persuasion. That, as even Quintilian admits, is a tricky and difficult process. But how much more difficult it is for Chaucer to hear the "voice" and assess the "character" of an old Roman poet, rather than sit with Quintilian in the forum hearing an orator. He must identify the voice, find the character, in the language of the old book. But in any speech, not only *ethos* but *pathos* is involved. A listener has to find in the language a good deal of himself as well as of the speaker. Wimsatt and Beardsley did not invent the "intentional fallacy"; it was there all the time, hidden in the implications of rhetorical poetics.

Second, none of the rhetorics we have been considering has anything to say about a "speech" in which speaker and audience are separated by scores or hundreds of years (Chaucer is always reading *old* books). For that to occur, the speaker must truly "survive in the valley of his own saying," as Auden puts it; or, in an extension of

---

28. *In Search of Chaucer* (Toronto: University of Toronto Press, 1960).

29. Perhaps I should emphasize that, like Chaucer, I use these formulae as conceptual models; I am not particularly concerned with their situational literalness.

Aristotle's admonition, he must create himself in the language of his work in order that the invented, artificial speaker can survive the mortal, natural one. And given language change and all the difficulties of historical understanding (of which Chaucer shows considerable awareness),[30] that process, too, is beset with perils to both speaker and hearer. It is really to explore just such issues that Chaucer makes his marvelous trip to the house of Fame.

The encyclopedic aquiline pedagogue who conducts Jeffrey to "fames hous" puts it with a nice precision at mid-flight:

> Loo, this sentence ys knowen kouth
> Of every philosophres mouth,
> As Aristotle and daun Platon,
> And other clerkys many oon;
> And to confirme my resoun,
> Thou wost wel this, that spech is soun,
> Or elles no man myghte hyt here;
> Now herke what y wol the lere.
>   Soun ys nought but eyr ybroken,
> And every speche that ys spoken,
> Lowd or pryvee, foul or fair,
> In his substaunce ys but air;
> For as flaumbe ys but lyghted smoke,
> Right soo soun is air ybroke.
>
> . . . .
>
> Eke, whan men harpe-strynges smyte,
> Whether hit be moche or lyte,
> Loo, with the strok the ayr tobreketh;
> And ryght so breketh it when men speketh.
>   (HF, 757–70, 777–80)

That is, Jeffrey, as a mortal consumer of the literary tradition, has all along actually been hearing speeches; but since mortal Jeffrey hears them only after they have echoed down through time, he now needs to visit the record library where they are preserved as first spoken— and at the same time, to identify (as he will in the allegory of Book III) the particular individual speakers who made the speeches. *Elocutio* and *ethos*, after the Eagle's introductory lecture in Book II, will merge in the figures of the ancient writers Jeffrey sees (and partly hears) in Book III.

An understanding of what Chaucer is about in the *House of Fame*

---

30. See Morton W. Bloomfield, "Chaucer's Sense of History," *JEGP*, 51 (1952), 301–13.

depends to a considerable degree upon our perception of the Eagle's reopening of the old Sophistic quarrel, with his punning image of "speech" as "broken air." If, for instance, Jeffrey perceives Vergil (as he does in Book I) in terms of the text/reader conceptual model, then the *Aeneid* crystalizes into the permanent, eternal "table of bras" on the walls of the Temple of Venus.[31] If, on the other hand, Jeffrey is to perceive the *Aeneid* in terms of the Eagle's explication of the speaker/speech/hearer model, then he hears a very mortal Vergil breaking wind down the centuries. And as eloquence verges into flatulence and authority into *ethos,* so the solemn, stately procession of authorities in the Great Tradition fragments under Fame's whimsical ordinance, turns back upon itself, and dizzily spins into the whirling house of Rumor. The result, almost at the end of the third book of Chaucer's first attempt to write his own *ars poetriae,* is a compelling image of his perception of what it means to conceive of poetry as a speech made by a speaker to an audience:

> And somtyme saugh I thoo at ones
> A lesyng and a sad soth sawe,
> That gonne of aventure drawe
> Out at a wyndowe for to pace;
> And when they metten in that place,
> They were achekked bothe two,
> And neyther of hem moste out goo
> For other, so they gonne crowde,
> Til ech of hem gan crien lowde,
> "Lat me go first!" "Nay, but let me!
> And here I wol ensuren the
> Wyth the nones that thou wolt do so,
> That I shal never fro the go,
> But be thyn owne sworen brother!
> We wil medle us ech with other,
> That no man, be they never so wrothe,
> Shal han on of us two, but bothe
> At ones, al besyde his leve,
> Come we a-morwe or on eve,
> Be we cried or stille yrouned."
> Thus saugh I fals and soth compouned
> Togeder fle for oo tydynge.
>   (*HF,* 2088–2109)

---

31. Nevertheless, it remains a fascinating problem for the historical critic that he and Chaucer must know that what Jeffrey sees in the "table of bras" is a serious distortion of Vergil's poem.

There, especially in the concluding two lines, is the opposition and paradox that had troubled rhetoricians and their critics from the beginning: Socrates' belief without instruction; Aristotle's persuasion where knowledge is unavailable; Quintilian's good man sworn to persuade only rightly; Augustine's "reasonable lies"; Horace's *dulce et utile* and Jeffrey's "sentence and solas"; and the Parson's "whete" and "draf."

In an important and influential book,[32] Robert M. Jordan has argued that post-Coleridgean "organic" theories of poetics do not serve very well as bases for analyzing Chaucer's poems. We should rather, according to Jordan, work from such "inorganic" analogues as Gothic architecture. However useful Jordan's perceptions may be for realizing the inner structures of individual poems, they do not seem to me to reach to another very useful possible application of Coleridge's notion of the literary organism—an application which I hope follows directly from my own argument in the preceding pages. Chaucer's revivification of the speaker/language/audience model for the poetic process, in the context of his unquestionably Christian notions of time and reality, produces a *very* organic notion of the poem. That is, the Chaucerian speech/poem, like all those the Eagle showed him in the *House of Fame,* is an initially invented construct which, once committed to time, carries into the stream of time some seeds of its speaker and its topics which germinate, grow, bear fruit, and reseed themselves in successive generations of hearer/readers.[33]

Indeed, one of the major functions of the *persona* Chaucer invents to guide his *Troilus and Criseyde* down the stream of time and criticism is to discuss with us, his readers, how we might share with him—and all his precedent *auctores*—the invention and maintenance of his poem.

---

32. *Chaucer and the Shape of Creation: The Aesthetic Possibilities of Inorganic Structure* (Cambridge, Mass.: Harvard University Press, 1967).

33. My image is one of the most reiterative of Chaucer's images for keeping this awareness alive in his own poems. One of many possible examples will serve to specify it here:

> For wel I wot that folk han here-beforn
> Of makyng ropen, and lad awey the corn;
> And I come after, glenynge here and there,
> And am ful glad if I may fynde an ere
> Of any goodly word that they had left.
>
> (*Prol. LGW,* G, 61–65)

> But soth is, though I kan nat tellen al,
> As kan myn auctour, of his excellence,
> Yet have I seyd, and God toforn, and shal
> In every thyng, al holy his sentence;
> And if that ich, at Loves reverence
> Have any word in eched for the beste,
> Doth therwithal right as youreselven leste.
>
> For myne wordes, heere and every part,
> I speke hem alle under correccioun
> Of yow that felyng han in loves art
> And putte it al in your discrecioun
> To encresse or maken dymynucioun
> Of my langage, and that I yow biseche.
>   (*T&C*, III, 1324-36)

To many of us modern historical critics, such a distillation of Chaucer's vital awareness of the poetic potential of a traditional rhetorical dilemma is but one more (though it is probably also the best) indication that *rhetorica*—limited, partial, and insufficiently articulate though it may have been in the twelfth and thirteenth centuries—was struggling with the same fundamental issues that the best critical theorists of our own time are again centrally concerned with.

Surely, in the context of the ancient and medieval rhetoricians I have been quoting here, the words of Norman Holland[34] will have familiar resonances:

> Indeed, the only way one can ever discover unity in texts or identity in selves is by creating them from one's own inner style, for we are all caught up in the general principle that identity creates and recreates itself as each of us discovers and achieves the world in his own mind. Whenever, as a critic, I engage a writer or his work, I do so through my own identity theme. My act of perception is also an act of creation in which I partake of the artist's gift. I find in myself what Freud called the writer's "innermost secret: the essential *ars poetica*," that is, the ability to break through the repulsion associated with "the barriers that rise between each single ego and the others."

Never mind that what generated Holland's theoretical generalizations was a discussion of Robert Frost. His attention to Frost's poems leads him to an image nearly identical with Chaucer's: of the poem not as fixed linguistic projection of an archetype, but as a flexible linguistic

---

34. "UNITY IDENTITY TEXT SELF," *PMLA*, 90 (1975), p. 820. See also his *Five Readers Reading* (New Haven: Yale University Press, 1975).

medium between speaker/poet and hearer/critic, and partly shaped by both,[35] as well as by its passage through time.

Finally, the most important consequence of Chaucer's realization of himself as rhetor is that it affords him that superbly rich, ironic, time-defeating device of impersonating himself in order to continue to participate in our continuing re-creation of his poetry.

> Wherfore I nyl have neither thank ne blame
> Of al this werk, but prey yow mekely,
> Disblameth me, if any word be lame,
> For as myn auctor seyde, so sey I.
> Ek though I speeke of love unfelyngly,
> No wondre is, for it nothyng of newe is;
> A blynd man kan nat juggen wel in hewis.
>
> Ye knowe ek that in forme of speche is chaunge
> Withinne a thousand yeer, and wordes tho
> That hadden pris, now wonder nyce and straunge
> Us thinketh hem, and yet thei spake hem so,
> And spedde as wel in love as men now do;
> Ek for to wynnen love in sondry ages,
> In sondry londes, sondry ben usages.
>
> And forthi if it happe in any wyse,
> That there be any lovere in this place
> That herkneth, as the story wol devise,
> How Troilus com to his lady grace,
> And thenketh, "so nold I nat love purchace,"
> Or wondreth on his speche or his doynge,
> I noot; but it is me no wonderynge.
>
> (T&C, II, 15–35)

But it is surely a great "wonderynge" to all of us that out of that long historical tangle of persuasion and persiflage and ethos and equivocation and "sentence and solas," Chaucer made such poetry.

---

35. Cf. also Walter J. Ong, "The Writer's Audience is Always a Fiction," *PMLA*, 90 (1975), pp. 9–21.

Gottfried von Strassburg and the Rhetoric of History

SAMUEL JAFFE

THIS ESSAY represents something more like a preliminary study toward an interpretation of Gottfried von Strassburg's *Tristan*-prologue than a full interpretation of the prologue itself. In spite of the attention which has been devoted to the *Tristan*-prologue and, in particular, despite the general impression in the current scholarly literature that the rhetorical aspects of the prologue have been thoroughly illuminated, much more remains to be done before rhetorical analysis may serve as a secure and useful basis for an interpretation of the meaning, structure, and function of the prologue as a whole. In the following, I shall offer a critique of the rhetorical analysis of the *Tristan*-prologue which, in recent years, has gained what seems to amount to almost universal credence in the scholarly literature. Then I shall present a few comments of my own on selected rhetorical features of the *Tristan*-prologue.

If any work in the Middle High German vernacular may be qualified as rhetorical in character, then surely it is Gottfried von Strassburg's *Tristan*. If any part of *Tristan* may be regarded as susceptible of rhetorical analysis, then surely it is *Tristan*'s enigmatically clear and clearly enigmatic prologue. If any scholar has had a decisive influence upon current rhetorically oriented interpretations of the *Tristan*-prologue, then surely it is Hennig Brinkmann. I propose to consider Brinkmann's rhetorical theory of "the medieval prologue as a literary phenomenon,"[1] in its application to Gottfried's *Tristan*-prologue,

---

1. Hennig Brinkmann, "Der Prolog im Mittelalter als literarische Erscheinung: Bau und Aussage," *Wirkendes Wort* 14 (1964), 1–21; esp. 13–16. Also in Hennig Brinkmann, *Studien zur Geschichte der deutschen Sprache und Literatur* II (Düsseldorf, 1966), pp. 79–105; esp. pp. 94–98. I cite according to *Wirkendes Wort*; all translations are my own. For two recent interpretations of the *Tristan*-prologue

under four heads: (1) the bipartite analysis of the *Tristan*-prologue; (2) the interpretation of the *Tristan*-prologue as an *insinuatio*, defined by Cicero and the *Rhetorica ad Herennium* as a subtle form of introduction for use in discreditable or difficult cases; (3) the derivation of Gottfried's sententious opening from the artificial beginning with a proverb discussed in the *artes poetriae* of the late twelfth and early thirteenth centuries, specifically in Geoffrey of Vinsauf's *Poetria nova*; (4) the suggestion of a significant influence of the Roman historian Sallust upon the *Tristan*-prologue. Of these four propositions it is only the last, I would argue, which is truly valuable, even though Brinkmann's own development of it was very slight indeed and it seems, unlike the preceding three, to have been totally neglected by subsequent *Tristan* scholarship.

Brinkmann's thesis, that the prologues to Middle High German "courtly epics" are divided into two parts, in the first of which, the "Prooemium," the author "opens a conversation with his audience" and then, in the second, the "Prologus," "introduces his work," draws—insofar as it seeks further substantiation in rhetorical and grammatical doctrine—upon no more than two sources, Conrad of Hirsau (ca. 1070–ca. 1150) and John of Garland (ca. 1195–ca. 1272). Brinkmann presents the following interpretation of John of Garland's remarks on various sorts of openings:

> In one passage (Mari p. 909), specifically in connection with instructions for the composition of epistolary openings (p. 907–909), John of Garland gives a review of the kinds of openings in general. He distinguishes *exordium* in the broader and in the narrower sense. In the broader sense the *exordium* is everything which precedes the *narratio*; in the narrower sense it is a *proverbium* (or what stands in place of a *proverbium*). The sermon begins with a *thema*, religious poetry with a *praefatio*. An introduction, which at the same time develops the *causa* and the way it will be treated, is called an *epigramma*. With the terms *prooemium* and *prologus* he apparently distinguishes parts of the prologue: the *prologus* is an introduction to the work which follows (*prologus est sermo inductivus subsequentis operis*); the *prooemium*, as *praeordinatio libri*, precedes the prologue. This seems to refer to the bipartite division which we actually find in the prologues of medieval literature.[2]

---

strongly influenced by Brinkmann cf. C. Stephen Jaeger, "The 'Strophic' Prologue to Gottfried's *Tristan*," *Germanic Review* 47 (1972), 5–19; and Günter Eifler, "Publikumsbeeinflussung im strophischen Prolog zum Tristan Gottfrieds von Strassburg," in: *Festschrift für Karl Bischoff zum 70. Geburtstag,* ed. Günter Bellmann, Günter Eifler, and Wolfgang Kleiber (Köln, 1975), pp. 357–389.

2. Brinkmann, "Prolog," p. 7.

But there is nothing in the passage to which Brinkmann refers to suggest that *prooemium* and *prologus* are regarded by John as "parts of the prologue" rather than as *kinds* of openings (*principia*), just as the terms *exordium, proverbium, epigramma, thema,* and *prefacio* are all employed to denote not parts, but *kinds* of openings.[3]

To be sure, according to John the *prologus* may contain proems or "prooemial matter," but it may also not contain such proems or "prooemial matter."[4] Nowhere does John state that "the *prooemium,* as *praeordinatio libri,* precedes the prologue." Finally, Brinkmann seems to have misunderstood John's definition of *prooemium* as *preordinacio libri ad instruendum*; he seems to understand it somewhat in the sense of a presentation of the book to the reader to be instructed, whereas Traugott Lawler's recent translation, "an advance outline of a book's contents, whose purpose is instruction," is undoubtedly more accurate. This misinterpretation seems to lead to a further distortion: in John's definition of *prologus* as *sermo inductivus subsequentis operis* Brinkmann seems to see only the relation to the work which follows and to exclude the possibility that such a *prologus,* as "an introductory discussion to the work which follows it," might actually address itself more to the reader than to the contents of the work. The end result is a reversal of John's terminology. What John would undoubtedly have called a *prooemium,* "an advance outline of a book's contents, whose purpose is instruction," Brinkmann calls the *prologus*; what John probably would have called a *prologus,* "an introductory discussion to the work which follows it," Brinkmann calls the *prooemium.*

Brinkmann's interpretation of Conrad of Hirsau, whom he adduces to confirm his thesis of bipartite structure in the Middle High German epic prologue, seems no less open to question than his reading of John of Garland:

> It [i.e. the thesis of bipartite structure S.J.] is confirmed by Conrad of Hirsau. He calls the prologue: *quaedam ante sermonem praelocutio* (ed. Huygens p. 16), which strives to gain the favor of the listener through justification (*apollogeticus*) or commendation (*commendaticius*). In connection with his discussion of Sallust he distinguishes (ed. Huygens p. 41)

---

3. Cf. *Poetria magistri Johannis anglici de arte prosayca metrica et rithmica,* ed. Giovanni Mari, *Romanische Forschungen* 13 (1902), 909. Brinkmann used Mari's text. Cf. also *The Parisiana Poetria of John of Garland,* ed. and trans. Traugott Lawler, Yale Studies in English 182 (New Haven and London, 1974), p. 63, upon which I have drawn.

4. Mari reads *proemia* from the Munich MS. Lawler, who used all six manuscripts, reads *prohemialia* and lists *prehemia* as variant from the Munich MS.

a *prologus ante rem* and *praeter rem*. Sallust is said to employ the *prologus praeter rem*, in order to defend himself against the reproach of idleness and to commend his work (this applies to the prologue to Catiline but something similar is said about the prologue to Jugurtha as well). Sallust is said to have wanted to show in his *prologus excusatorius*: *tutius et praepollentius esse aliorum facta scribere quam factis scribenda aliis relinquere*. After the *prologus praeter rem* follows, according to Conrad, the *prologus ante rem, ubi summam totius operis sequentis enuntiat.*[5]

If this interpretation is compared with the text to be interpreted, Conrad's discussion of the prologue to Sallust's *Bellum Catilinae*, little justification can be found for Brinkmann's reading. Once again, Brinkmann seems to regard as two parts of the one (in this case Sallustian) prologue what the author intends to distinguish as two different kinds of prologue (the one peculiarly Sallustian, the other apparently not at all). Once again, Brinkmann seems—without substantiation from the text—to ascribe to this author a particular view of the sequence in which these alleged parts of the prologue are ordered.

Conrad's commentary on Sallust's prologue to the *Bellum Catilinae* is, I would maintain, highly significant for interpretation of the prologue in Middle High German narrative literature and for the interpretation of Gottfried's *Tristan*-prologue in particular—but not for the reasons alleged by Brinkmann. Crucial for the rhetorical-grammatical substantiation of Brinkmann's analysis of the epic prologue into two parts is Conrad's statement: "Dicitur autem prologus et ante rem et preter rem."[6] I have attempted to translate it as neutrally as possible: "Moreover, prologues are described both as introductory to the subject matter and as going beyond the subject matter." But what does this mean? Does it mean: "Any prologue may be described as both introductory to the subject matter and as going beyond the subject matter"? Or does it mean: "Any prologue may be described either as introductory to the subject matter or as going beyond the subject matter"? The former interpretation, substantiating Brinkmann's conception of the two-part prologue, seems definitely excluded by Conrad's clarification of *prologus ante rem* and *prologus preter rem*: "Ante rem quidem, ubi summam totius operis sequentis enuntiat, preter rem, cum nequaquam de opere

---

5. Brinkmann, "Prolog," p. 7–8. Brinkmann cited from R.B.C. Huygens' first edition of Conrad's *Dialogus super auctores*.

6. Cf. Conrad of Hirsau, *Dialogus super auctores*, ed. R.B.C. Huygens, Collection Latomus 17 (Berchem-Bruxelles, 1955). I have used Huygens' second (revised) edition (1970).

sequenti agit, ut hic Salustius facit: respondet enim adversariis
suis."[7] A prologue is *ante rem*, says Conrad, when it is introductory
to the subject matter in the sense that "it presents the main contents
of the whole work to follow"; a prologue is *preter rem*, according to
Conrad, when it goes beyond the subject matter in the sense that *"it
does not deal in any way with the following work."* And Conrad
interprets Sallust's prologue to the *Bellum Catilinae* as belonging to
this latter category, for he adds to his clarification of the *prologus
preter rem*: "as Sallust in this particular case: for he responds to his
adversaries" (*ut hic Salustius facit: respondet enim adversariis suis*).
Indeed, the remainder of Conrad's discussion is devoted to corrobo-
rating his view of Sallust's introduction to the *Bellum Catilinae* as a
prologus preter rem, in which the author does not deal at all with the
following work but is concerned only to reply to his adversaries. Such
corroboration seems to be the burden of Conrad's discussion of "the
matter which is the object of Sallust's intention in this prologue"
(*causa intentionis eius in hoc prologo*) and "the material of the
prologue itself" (*materia ipsius prologi*). Both are defined by Conrad
in terms of Sallust's central concern, as he understands it,—response
to the adversaries. The matter which is the object of Sallust's intention in this prologue is simply "the injury inflicted upon him by his
detractors" (*iniuria irrogata detrahentium*);[8] the material of the
prologue itself, the product of Sallust's intention, consists of nothing
more than "those arguments with which he removes from himself
the aspersion of idleness" (*rationes illae . . . quibus a se removet
nomen inertiae*).[9]

It is in the light of this view of Conrad's interpretation that the
final sentences of his prologue commentary fit in with the discussion
which precedes them. They represent Conrad's response to a possible
objection. If the prologue is taken to include the brief general characterization of Lucius Catilina's morals in *Cat.* V, 1–8, then it might
be urged, contrary to Conrad's analysis, that the prologue does indeed "present the main contents of the whole work to follow"
(*summam totius operis sequentis enuntiat*) in the fashion of the
prologus ante rem. Conrad makes a special point, therefore, that this
description is not to be subsumed under the prologue, but forms
instead the natural order of narration: Sallust digresses a little from
this natural opening, i.e. the description of Catiline, but then returns

7. *Ibid.*, p. 104.   8. *Ibid.*
9. *Ibid.*

to the historical narration of Catiline's deeds. Since the description of Catiline's moral character has been interpreted as Sallust's natural opening, Conrad's view of the prologue as *prologus preter rem*, which does not deal in any way with the following work, has been confirmed and he can conclude his commentary with: "In the prologue, however [*vero* S.J.], he justifies and commends himself."[10]

Thus, there seems to be no evidence at all in Conrad's discussion to support Brinkmann's thesis that the *prologus ante rem* and *prologus preter rem* represent two parts of the Sallustian prologue, let alone any trace of a statement to the effect that "after the *prologus praeter rem* follows . . . the *prologus ante rem.*" Quite to the contrary, Conrad sees the *prologus ante rem* and the *prologus preter rem* as two distinct kinds of prologue; and it is the latter which he identifies with the Sallustian prologue. The question might be raised, of course, whether Conrad's view of the matter is correct, whether it is possible for Sallust or any author to justify or commend in a prologue without dealing in any way with the work which follows the prologue. The answer to these questions probably depends upon what is meant by "dealing in any way with the work which follows the prologue." If we interpret "dealing in any way with the work which follows the prologue" in the sense undoubtedly intended by Conrad, i.e. as doing no less than presenting the main contents of the whole work to follow, then Conrad is certainly right. It is possible to justify or commend in a prologue without presenting the main contents of the following work; and Sallust does precisely this, for his brief mention of the conspiracy of Catiline at the very end of the prologue (*Cat.* IV, 3–5) can hardly qualify as such a presentation. If there is this sort of presentation, it is contained in the general view of Lucius Catilina's moral character (*Cat.* V, 1–8) which, as we have seen, Conrad explicitly separates from the prologue and, as an opening in the style of the *ordo naturalis,* ascribes to the historical narrative itself.

Conrad's few remarks about the prologue to the *Bellum Iugurthinum* suggest an interpretation of that prologue corresponding exactly to his interpretation of the prologue to the *Bellum Catilinae.* Conrad seems to have a unified view of the two Sallustian prologues as, on the one hand, Sallust's self-justification and self-commendation and, on the other hand, a commendation of virtue and condemnation of vice—virtue seen as activity of the soul in pursuit of

---

10. *Ibid.: In prologo vero et se excusat et commendat.*

what is praiseworthy and just, vice seen as idleness of the soul and surrender to evil. Thus, in his brief commentary on the *Iugurtha*-prologue, Conrad explicitly equates the goals of the two prologues:

> Finally, the prologue to the second book [*Bellum Iugurthinum* S.J.], where he says that the human race complains without reason of its nature on the grounds that it is fragile and weak, just as in the first, so also in the second he seems to persuade the soul's virtue and to dissuade its idleness.[11]

It comes as no surprise that Brinkmann's bipartite analysis of the prologue, supported only by a misreading of John of Garland and Conrad of Hirsau and—perhaps—already prejudiced by Brinkmann's view of the very poetic practice which it purports to interpret, can be adjusted to fit the structure of Gottfried's *Tristan*-prologue only with the greatest difficulty. Brinkmann distinguishes within the *Tristan*-prologue two major parts, a "Prooemium" (*Tristan* 1–120, = John of Garland's *prooemium* according to Brinkmann's misinterpretation, = Conrad of Hirsau's *prologus preter rem*) and a "Prologus" (*Tristan* 125–240, = John of Garland's *prologus* according to Brinkmann's misinterpretation, = Conrad of Hirsau's *prologus ante rem*). Between these two parts (*Tristan* 1–120 and 125–240) Brinkmann postulates a transitional group of four lines (*Tristan* 121–124):

> Gottfried's prologue to Tristan is, like the prologue to Parzival, bipartite. The first part, the prooemium, brings the author's discussion with his readers, the creation of a situation of dialogue (1–120). That is the *prologus praeter rem*, which does not yet explicitly deal with the content of the work. The latter occurs in the prologue properly speaking, the *prologus ante rem*, which illuminates the work, its significance and value (121–240). The first part ends with an emotional assertion in the rhyme *tot: not* (previously already in 61/62 *not: tot*), corresponding to the four-fold rhyme *brot: tot* which concludes the second part. With lines 125ff. (*ich wil iu wol bemaeren / von edelen senedaeren* . . .) Gottfried introduces his work directly, after having previously prepared its reception.[12]

There is a certain ambiguity in Brinkmann's description, but his statement that "the prooemium as a whole is in turn linked with the following prologus (by 121–124),"[13] his allusion to lines 121/122 "in

---

11. *Ibid.*, p. 105: *Denique prologus secundi libri, ubi dicit genus humanum falso conqueri de natura sua quod fragilis et imbecilla sit, sicut in primo, sic et in secundo animi virtutem videtur persuadere, desidiam dissuadere.*

12. Brinkmann, "Prolog," p. 13.

13. *Ibid.*, p. 14.

the transition from the prooemium to the prologus,''[14] and his references to ''the first part of the actual prologue (125–172)''[15] and ''the second part of the prologus (173–240)''[16] seem to settle the issue. In addition to these divisions, Brinkmann refers to two sections within the ''prooemium'' which are distinguished ''in terms of content'' (1–40 and 41–120).[17] The fact that Brinkmann finds a *major* division in Gottfried's prologue at the end of line 120, in the middle of what is, by general agreement, a syntactic and semantic unit— Brinkmann's division coincides with a colon in most editions—immediately raises most serious doubts. These doubts are strengthened, if not confirmed, by the observation that *none* of Brinkmann's principal divisions within the prologue, except for the alleged break in content after line 40, corresponds to divisions actually marked by initials or by changes in verse form. Finally our doubts are confirmed, if not rendered unshakable, by three observations: (1) Neither in Brinkmann's ''prooemium'' nor in his ''prologus'' is there anything very like what Conrad of Hirsau might have regarded as an introduction *ante rem,* i.e. a presentation of the main contents of the whole work to follow; (2) in Brinkmann's ''prooemium'' there is extensive if very general reference to content, which ''illuminates the work, its significance and value'' *as well as* ''the author's discussion with his readers''; (3) in Brinkmann's ''prologus'' there is a continuation of this discussion or ''situation of dialogue,'' *as well as* additional reference to content, which ''illuminates the work, its significance and value.'' In fine, the whole of the *Tristan*-prologue seems to commend and justify its author's work; and the largely undetailed references to content, which are dispersed throughout the prologue, seem to serve those ends. Appeal to an audience, be it subtle or open, covert or overt, mediate or immediate, appears throughout Gottfried's prologue along with such general references to content; accordingly it is very difficult to distinguish, in Brinkmann's vague and ill-substantiated terms, ''prooemium'' and ''prologus.''

In recent work on the *Tristan*-prologue Brinkmann's theory of bipartite structure has been almost surpassed in popularity by his view of Gottfried's introduction as an insinuation (*insinuatio*) in the Ciceronian sense. According to Cicero (*De inventione* I, xv, 20–21):

> Insinuation is an address which by dissimulation and indirection unobtrusively steals into the mind of the auditor.

---

14. *Ibid.*   15. *Ibid.,* p. 16.
16. *Ibid.*   17. *Ibid.,* p. 14.

In the difficult case, if the auditors are not completely hostile, it will be permissible to try to win their good-will by an introduction; if they are violently opposed it will be necessary to have recourse to the insinuation. For if amity and good-will are sought from auditors who are in a rage, not only is the desired result not obtained, but their hatred is increased and fanned into a flame.[18]

Cicero's further discussion of *insinuatio* concerns "the proper method of handling insinuations" (*De inventione* I, xvii, 23–25). Here he distinguishes three cases, according to three reasons why "the spirit of the audience is hostile" (*animus auditoris infestus est*) in a "difficult case" (*admirabile genus causae*).

Brinkmann's formulation of his thesis concerning *insinuatio* seems to follow Cicero, but it remains quite vague in comparison with Cicero's rather precise delineation of the ends and means of insinuation:

> The *causa* of the Tristan-theme falls within the realm of the *genus admirabile*, which, because of its subject, is not immediately appealing to the reader, but rather can expect to meet with rejection. Therefore it has need of *insinuatio* to win over the reader. The subject could alienate author and reader from one another, but for Gottfried what matters most is to overcome this tension and create a harmony between his work and his readers. That is accomplished with means furnished by the arts of language.[19]

That any renewal of the *Tristan*-theme would necessarily provoke the sort of hostility to which Cicero refers, or indeed any degree of hostility at all, in Gottfried's audience, involves, it seems to me, some rather large assumptions about that audience. Be that as it may, Brinkmann's application of the concept of *insinuatio* to the *Tristan*-prologue remains, on the one hand, almost empty with respect to traditional rhetorical doctrine, and on the other hand, quite remote from Gottfried's text; for Brinkmann never really specifies those "means furnished by the arts of language" which are employed in the *Tristan*-prologue to overcome *per insinuationem* the estrangement of author and reader inherent, at least potentially, in this particular choice of subject matter. He mentions *insinuatio* explicitly in connection with no more than two features of the *Tristan*-prologue, and it remains unclear which of the other features he touches upon are seen specifically as means of *insinuatio* and which as stylistic

---

18. Translations of the *De inventione* are from the Loeb edition. Cf. Cicero, *De inventione*, trans. H.M. Hubbell (Cambridge, Mass. and London, 1960).

19. Brinkmann, "Prolog," pp. 13–14.

phenomena common to all prologues. Referring to the second strophe of the prologue, Brinkmann writes:

> The following strophe separates those who create and those who receive and, at the same time, brings them together: what the good man (*der guote man*, according to the traditional terminology of rhetoric, can be identical, as *vir bonus*, with the *orator*!) with good intentions does for the good of the world, should be received with good will. Thus he who creates in *guot* and he who receives in *guot* become one (they are identified with one another through the word-repetition). That their identification occurs through *guot*, characterizes the *insinuatio*, which has to introduce a subject from the realm of the *genus admirabile*.[20]

Here Brinkmann seems to consider identification of author and reader, accomplished through repetition of a laudatory epithet, as a means of *insinuatio*. At a later point in the discussion Brinkmann writes:

> The second part of the prologus (173–240) completes the *insinuatio* through demonstration of the significance attaching to the story of Tristan and Isolde.[21]

Here Brinkmann seems to consider a means of *insinuatio* the prologue's demonstration that the work which it introduces has significance. But certainly neither of the two procedures explicitly categorized by Brinkmann as means of *insinuatio* deserves to be regarded as such. If, with Cicero, we understand insinuation as "an address which by dissimulation and indirection unobtrusively steals into the mind of the auditor," it is difficult to see in what sense a prologue's identification of author and reader, accomplished through repetition of a laudatory epithet, or demonstration that the work introduced by a prologue has significance, may be said to steal unobtrusively into the mind of the auditor by dissimulation and indirection. More significantly, neither of these two devices is to be found among the means of *insinuatio* listed by Cicero or expounded and exemplified elsewhere within the rhetorical tradition.

Although Brinkmann does not make it explicit, insofar as his case for the *Tristan*-prologue as *insinuatio* goes beyond a mere assertion that the *Tristan*-theme belongs to the *genus admirabile* (i.e. is a difficult sort of case) and points to specific persuasive remedies of a dissimulatory or indirect nature, it seems to stand or fall with his interpretation of the opening generalities and their development in the "strophic prologue" (*Tristan* 1–44). But here again, the use of

---

20. *Ibid.*, p. 15.   21. *Ibid.*, p. 16.

sententiae, let alone such an elaborate sententious development as is found in the "strophic prologue," does not appear among the means ascribed to insinuation by classical or medieval theoreticians of the prologue. Cicero (*De inventione* I, xviii, 25) says that "the *exordium* ought to be sententious to a marked degree and of a high serious-ness" (*exordium sententiarum et gravitatis plurimum debet habere*), but this applies to the ordinary introduction (*principium*) and the insinuation (*insinuatio*) alike.

Indeed, on the one hand, Brinkmann seems tacitly to associate the sententious and the insinuatory openings; on the other hand, unable to document *Tristan*'s sentential opening as a means of insinuation, he derives it from a tradition of rhetorical doctrine in which it is unquestionably *not* described as a means of insinuation, i.e. the poetics (*artes poetriae*) of the late twelfth and early thirteenth cen-turies. In the *artes* of Matthew of Vendôme (ca. 1175), Geoffrey of Vinsauf (ca. 1210) and Eberhard the German (ca. 1212–1280), there is no hint that their recommendation of the artificial opening with a proverb (*principium artificiale sumptum a proverbio*) aims at an insinuatory courting of the reader's favor, by dissimulation or indirec-tion, for a subject from the realm of difficult cases (*admirabile genus causae*). If Gottfried's sententious opening does not seem to derive from the theory and practice of insinuation as delineated and exem-plified in traditional rhetorical doctrine, neither does it appear to be related, as Brinkmann would have us believe, to the theory presented and illustrated in the *artes poetriae*. Indeed, Brinkmann manages to discover in Gottfried's prologue not only the sententious opening (*principium artificiale sumptum a proverbio*) but also the continua-tion (*continuatio*) recommended by Geoffrey of Vinsauf. It is the transitional four-line group *Tristan* 121–124, by means of which "the prooemium as a whole is in turn linked with the following prologus," that Brinkmann interprets as an example of continuation after the artificial opening with a proverb, as expounded by Geoffrey of Vinsauf in his *Instruction in the Method and Art of Composing and Versifying (Documentum de modo et arte dictandi et versificandi).* The sentential opening of the *Tristan*-prologue is associated, in corresponding fashion, with Geoffrey's prescriptions (*Poetria nova* 126–133):

> The transition from the first ["prooemium" S.J.] to the second part ["prologus" S.J.] is (as in the works of Chrétien and Wolfram and others) gradual; the poetics explicitly prescribed (Galfredus, Documentum II,

1ff.) a *continuatio,* just as they also explicitly require (Poetria nova V, 126 ff.) that an opening *sententia* not mention its actual object but have it in view nonetheless.[22]

However, a look at the *Documentum* and the *Poetria nova* will suffice to convince us that neither the technique of *continuatio* described in the former nor—even more significantly—the sort of opening with a *sententia* or *proverbium* described in both the former and the latter has very much in common with the *Tristan*-opening and its continuation. The four lines (*Tristan* 121–124) which Brinkmann seems to regard as a *continuatio* are the following: "The noble lover, he loves tales of love. Therefore whoever desires a love-tale, let him go no further than here."[23] Immediately preceding is, of course, no *sententia* or *proverbium* but rather the statement of a particular situation (*Tristan* 119–120): "I know it as sure as death and have learned it from this same anguish." This statement is separated from the elaborate sententious development of Gottfried's "strophic prologue" by 73 lines the content of which is not merely particular as opposed to the generalities of the "strophic prologue"; it is also particular in the special sense of being dominated by references to the author's own person. By contrast, what Geoffrey means by a continuation (*continuatio*) after the artificial opening with a proverb (*principium artificiale sumptum a proverbio*) is given by the following rule:

> If an artistic opening is formed with a proverb, it should be continued by means of the following verbs: *reveals, teaches, shows, bears witness to,* or through equivalent statements and in the same way. For a proverb is a general statement and what is proposed through a general statement "is taught", "is shown", "is supported" by some particular case which is added to it. This will be seen clearly in every sort of proverb, in that which is formed from the middle and in that which is formed from the end. We give examples of each kind.[24]

---

22. *Ibid.,* p. 13.

23. The translations from *Tristan* are drawn, with a few slight modifications of my own, from Gottfried von Strassburg, *Tristan,* trans. with an introduction by A.T. Hatto (Penguin Classics; Harmondsworth, Middlesex, England, 1960). The line numbers are given according to the standard German edition: Gottfried von Strassburg, *Tristan und Isold,* ed. Friedrich Ranke (Berlin, 1958).

24. Cf. Geoffrey of Vinsauf, *Documentum de modo et arte dictandi et versificandi,* in: Edmond Faral, *Les Arts poétiques du XIIᵉ et du XIIIᵉ siècle,* Bibliothèque de l'École des Hautes Études, fasc. 238 (Paris, 1924; repr. Paris, 1958), p. 269: *Si principium artificiale sumptum fuerit a proverbio, continuandum est per haec verba fatetur, docet, probat, attestatur, vel per aequipollentes sententias et hac ratione. Proverbium enim est generalis sententia, et illud quod datur per generalem sententiam*

The examples supplied by Geoffrey make even more clear the radical difference between what he means by this sort of opening and continuation and Gottfried's way of opening and continuing in the *Tristan*-prologue, as shown in the following illustration:

	Prose	*Metrical*
Proverb formed from the beginning	This is a condition of fortune, that it does not suffer the lingering of prosperity, but those things which are pleasanter to the soul threaten to take flight all the more swiftly.	What is more longed for, escapes us all the more, all things pledge their own ruin and bright fortunes plummet the more rapidly to earth.[25]
Continuation	*For this statement we have as proof* Minos, King of Crete, whose fortune's calm swerved down into a whirlwind, its clarity to gloom, its joy to mourning.	A sad fate seeking out the kingdom of Crete, successor to joy, the death of a royal heir, *reveals* this truth.[26]

It is evident that in Geoffrey's rules and examples a relatively brief sententious opening (*proverbium* or *sententia generalis*) is continued immediately by a statement (*continuatio*) showing how some special case (*aliud speciale*) reveals, teaches, shows, bears witness to the truth of the preceding generality. This is obviously not Gottfried's method in the *Tristan*-prologue. His sententious opening is anything but brief; it comprises, in fact, all 44 lines of the "strophic prologue." Nor, as has been noted, are Gottfried's *proverbia* or *sententiae generales* followed immediately by what Brinkmann regards as their continuation (*Tristan* 121–124); quite to the contrary, the former and the latter are separated by 73 lines consisting of particularized state-

---

"*docetur*", "*probatur*", "*perhibetur*" *per aliud speciale, quod subjungitur. Quod liquido apparebit in omni genere proverbii, in illo quod sumitur juxta medium et in illo quod sumitur juxta finem. De singulis supponemus exempla.*

I have also consulted the translation by Roger P. Parr: Geoffrey of Vinsauf, *Instruction in the Method and Art of Speaking and Versifying* (Milwaukee, Wis., 1968), p. 43, but I have felt free to depart from his translation where I thought it could be improved.

25. Cf. Faral, p. 267.
26. *Ibid.*, p. 269.

ments and dominated by the author's personal reference. Finally, the exhortation to the audience regarded by Brinkmann as Gottfried's *continuatio* (*Tristan* 121–124) bears little resemblance to Geoffrey's *continuatio*, which contains no explicit reference to any audience at all. It may be argued that the ultimate goal of Geoffrey's *continuatio*, like that of Gottfried's *exhortatio*, is to commend the work to an audience, the latter proceeding by appeal to an audience defined in quite specific terms, the former by raising the dignity of the narration to follow as a special case (*aliud speciale*) which nonetheless bears witness to some general truth (*sententia generalis* or *proverbium*). But such a comparison would be superficial at best. The whole discussion of openings in the *artes poetriae* is inapplicable to the *Tristan*-prologue, simply because it does not refer to prologues at all but rather to the ways in which narrations are begun, to the *principium narrationis rerum gestarum*. The function of the prologue is not to begin the narration in as brilliant, charming, and elegant a manner as possible (cf. Geoffrey's discussion of the artificial opening with a proverb *Poetria nova* 126ff., esp. 126, 129–130, 142, 144, 145, 147). It is, rather, to prepare the audience to be as attentive, well-disposed, and receptive as possible to the author's work. The prologue is audience oriented in a sense in which Geoffrey's *principium artificiale sumptum a proverbio* is not.

Neither the *insinuatio*, which lacks the specifically sententious quality, nor Geoffrey's artificial beginning with a proverb, which lacks the audience orientation of the *Tristan*-prologue, appears to present a theoretical or practical model adequate to the task of analyzing and describing, in terms of rhetorical doctrine and tradition, the details of Gottfried's introduction. Both fail to take account of too many of the specific features of the *Tristan*-prologue. Both exhibit too many features which the *Tristan*-prologue lacks and lack too many features which the *Tristan*-prologue exhibits. Both of the models which Brinkmann employs, the *insinuatio* and the *principium artificiale sumptum a proverbio*, imply analogies too remote from the generic practice of Gottfried's introduction. The latter is neither the introduction to a judicial speech nor the beginning of a narration; it is the prologue to a narration. It is, moreover, the prologue to a narration presented quite specifically—as historical narrative. Gottfried insists, in differentiating his version of the *Tristan*-tale from those of his predecessors, that, despite their "noblest of intentions . . . they did not tell the tale aright" (*Tristan* 141–147), for "they did not write according to the authentic version as told by Thomas of Britain who was a master-romancer and had read the lives of all those princes in books of the Britons and made them known to us" (*Tristan* 149–154). Gottfried asserts (*Tristan* 155–172) that he himself, on the other hand, has searched out the "true and authentic version of Tristan such as Thomas narrates" and taken pains to present it faithfully and fully to his readers:

> I began to search assiduously both in Romance and Latin books for the true and authentic version of Tristan such as Thomas narrates, and I was at pains to direct the poem along the right path which he had shown. Thus I made many researches till I had read in a book all that he says happened in this story. And now I freely offer the fruits of my reading of this love-tale to all noble hearts to divert them. They will find it a very good reading.

The Middle High German "courtly" narrator in general, and Gottfried in particular, presents himself not as poet (*poeta*), or as contriver (*fictor*) and fashioner (*formator*), who contrives and fashions fabrications (*fabulae*), at best mixing some truth in with his lies, at worst telling lies instead of the truth; he presents himself rather as historian (*historiographus* or *historicus*), whose work faithfully and beneficially (*fideliter et utiliter*) recounts history (*historiae*), observations (*res visae*), and events (*res gestae*), things which have truly occurred (*res verae quae factae sunt*). Many scholars, including Gustav Ehrismann (1919), Stanislaw Sawicki (1932), Bruno Boesch (1936), and, most recently, Carl Lofmark (1972) have emphasized this fact.[27] The historicizing posture, intended as play or earnest or some ambiguous blend of the two, remains characteristic of Gottfried's narrative style throughout *Tristan*. One passage pointed out by Lofmark[28] is particularly telling, in that it reproduces the traditional depreciation of poetic fabrications (*fabulae*) in comparison with historical truth (*historiae* or *res verae quae factae sunt*):

---

27. Gustav Ehrismann, *Studien über Rudolf von Ems: Beiträge zur Geschichte der Rhetorik und Ethik im Mittelalter,* Sitzungsberichte der Heidelberger Akademie der Wissenschaften: Phil.-hist. Klasse, Abh. 8 (Heidelberg, 1919), esp. pp. 19–20; Stanislaw Sawicki, *Gottfried von Strassburg und die Poetik des Mittelalters,* Germanische Studien, Heft 124 (Berlin, 1932), esp. pp. 158–159; Bruno Boesch, *Die Kunstanschauung in der mittelhochdeutschen Dichtung von der Blütezeit bis zum Meistergesang* (Bern and Leipzig, 1936), esp. pp. 75–94 (an excellent study, often overlooked); Carl Lofmark, "Der höfische Dichter als Übersetzer" in: *Probleme mittelhochdeutscher Erzählformen, Marburger Colloquium 1969,* ed. Peter F. Ganz and Werner Schröder (Berlin, 1972), pp. 40–62.
28. Cf. Lofmark, "Übersetzer," p. 57, n. 38. Cf. other valuable references to *Tristan passim.*

He [Tristan S.J.] reaped much success and good fortune in martial affairs and in hazardous enterprises which I shall not mention at length; for were I to give a detailed account of all the deeds ascribed to him in books, this tale would become a monster (*des maeres würde ein wunder*). I shall cast the fables (*fabelen*) on this topic to the winds—since in dealing with the truth (*warheit*) I have a load of work to carry as it is (*Tristan* 18455–18466).

The bounds of "history" are extended, in the Middle Ages, far beyond those limits to which we are accustomed; the bounds of "poetry" are correspondingly narrowed. The claim to present truth as opposed to fabrication, however—*res verae quae factae sunt, warheit,* as opposed to *fabulae, fabelen*—is regularly encountered among medieval authors writing narrative accounts of past events (*res gestae a memoria hominum remotae*), be such accounts Latin or vernacular, prose or verse, sacred or profane. This claim to truthfulness, although it may be encountered at any point in the narrative, is most frequently met with in prologues; it is a regular feature in Middle High German "courtly" narratives, particularly in the prologues of these works. The truth claim is thus a very characteristic detail in the prologues of medieval narrative literature; it is, however, difficult to relate to traditional rhetorical doctrine of the prologue, in which it plays no great role.

The rhetorical model followed by an *"historiographus"* like Gottfried consists, however, not of theoretical precepts but rather of a practical example—the historical prologue as it developed in the Middle Ages, modified by, and itself modifying, the rhetorical tradition according to the specific generic requirements of historiography—without, however, leaving behind more than the scantiest residue of theoretical formulation. In this essay I shall refer principally to three such formulations, documents of the interaction between rhetorical doctrine and the genre of history: (1) a fragment *de historia* from an eighth-century manuscript (Paris MS 7530) edited by Karl Halm in the *Rhetores latini minores*; (2) the discussion of the *Dictaminum radii* (formerly called *Flores rhetorici*) by Alberic of Monte Cassino († shortly before 1115); (3) the Sallust-commentary in *Dialogus super auctores* by Conrad of Hirsau (ca. 1070–ca. 1150).[29] These three formulations of the interaction between rhetoric and

---

29. *Rhetores latini minores*, ed. Karl Halm (Leipzig, 1863; repr. Frankfurt, 1964), pp. 588–589. [all translations of this work are my own]; *Alberici Cassinensis Flores rhetorici*, ed. D.M. Inguanez and H.M. Willard, Miscellanea Cassinese 14 (Montecassino, 1938) [all translations of this work are my own]; for Conrad, *Dialogus*, cf. *supra*, note 6.

historiography are concerned, in whole or in part, with the prologue
and in each Sallust is invoked as a prime authority. I thus return to
Sallust in a context other than that of Brinkmann's bipartite division
of "the medieval prologue as a literary phenomenon."

Brinkmann deserves much credit for pointing out the significance
of Sallust's prologues in the Middle Ages, even though his bipartite
analysis of the prologue to the Middle High German "courtly epic,"
insofar as it seeks substantiation in rhetorical-grammatical doctrine,
seems to be based for the most part on an incorrect reading of John
of Garland's *Parisiana poetria* and Conrad of Hirsau's Sallust-commentary. Although Brinkmann mentions Alberic's use of an example
from Sallust in the *exordium* discussion of the *Dictaminum radii*
(*Flores rhetorici*),[30] he does not analyze the passage and, aside from
a few scattered references to Sallust and the *memoria*-topos, he does
not follow the matter up. Nor have the many scholars who received
Brinkmann's other suggestions with such enthusiasm.

Each of the theoretical formulations adduced has somewhat different implications for the medieval understanding of Sallust's prologues. I shall use them, in conjunction with Sallust's own writings,
as a conceptual framework for some brief comments on selected
passages from the *Tristan*-prologue and their function in the rhetorical structure of the prologue as a whole. Where necessary, other
parallels from the medieval historical prologue will be adduced. The
sense of this procedure is not to suggest in any way that Gottfried
von Strassburg was directly or indirectly influenced by any of the
particular authors and works cited. What is maintained is that Gottfried found a model for his *Tristan*-prologue in some unknown work
or works, Latin or vernacular, in the tradition of the historical prologue. The particular authors and works cited merely serve as a
convenient means to help characterize that tradition by doctrinal
formulation and practical example.

I turn first to the opening *sententia* of the *Tristan*-prologue. I shall
discuss it in relation to Sallust as a model and Alberic of Monte
Cassino's commentary on the Sallustian sententious opening. Significant for the doctrinal interpretation of the prologue, as set forth
in Alberic of Monte Cassino's *Dictaminum radii* (*Flores rhetorici*),
is the fact that there are *two* such interpretations, corresponding, in
fact, to a double analysis of disposition (*dispositio*); the latter of these
two treatments of disposition (*Flores* III, 1–6) is explicitly charac-

---

30. Cf. Brinkmann, "Prolog," p. 8 n. 6.

terized by Alberic as a "rhetorical division of the whole speech" (*orationis totius rhetorica divisio*). It employs the terminology of Isidore, adapted from Ciceronian rhetoric, to designate the four parts of a speech (*quattuor partes orationis*)—introduction (*exordium*), statement of facts (*narratio*), proof (*argumentatio*), and conclusion (*conclusio*). The former of the two discussions of disposition (*Flores* II,1–5) is not explicitly characterized by Alberic, but the terminology used to analyze disposition is not the customary terminology of Ciceronian rhetorical tradition—prologue or proem (*prologus* or *proemium*), narrative account (*historia*), digression (*digressio*), transition (*transitus*); beginning (*principium*), middle (*medium*), extremes, i.e. beginning and end (*extrema*). This terminology, as well as the discussion which employs it, suggests that the model for Alberic's first analysis of disposition is elevated narrative—poetic, historical, discursive. Much of the discussion derives from Horace's *Ars poetica* and the grammatical tradition of *enarratio auctorum*.

The only invariant function of the nonrhetorical prologue (*prologus* or *proemium*) as presented in Alberic's first, grammatically oriented consideration of disposition is to set forth or give a foretaste of the subject matter to follow. The sort of work which is the object of Alberic's discussion often *does* need rhetorical defence, in its prologue or proem, against tacit objections. But this is *not always* the case (consider Alberic's examples—*Augustine, Aeneid, Consolatio philosophiae*), and the discussion of the "colors" (*colores*) which are the means of such defence, i.e. the gaining of attention (*attentio*), goodwill (*benevolentia*), and receptivity (*docilitas*), is deferred to Alberic's second, rhetorically oriented consideration of disposition with its analysis of the rhetorical prologue (*exordium*). In this second treatment of disposition the authority of Sallust (*auctoritas Sallustii*) is invoked to provide an example of the gaining of attention—which is, according to Alberic, simultaneously a gaining of goodwill:

> Now in order that we may confirm what has been said by means of examples, let the authority of Sallust be cited (cf. Iugurth., II,1 [more likely is *Cat.* I,1–4; the following is not intended by Alberic as a direct quote, as Inguanez and Willard indicate, but rather as an authorial question which incorporates a loose periphrase of Sallust. S.J.]). For why does he divide human pursuits from those of dumb animals, which he separates by distinguishing values of the mind and values of the body? When he strives to show that the former are true, the latter false, the latter fleeting, the former abiding, what other end does he pursue than to purchase attention to the matter at hand by ascribing worth and merit?

For by this means he subtly commends intellectual pursuits and in commending them he gains attention.[31]

Alberic addresses himself to a problem which has been controversial
among classical philologists since Quintilian. Why does Sallust begin
his great histories, *The War with Catiline* (*Bellum Catilinae*) and *The
War with Jugurtha* (*Bellum Iugurthinum*), with prologues which
seem to have little connection with the following historical narratives?
And more particularly, what is the significance and function of the
elaborate sententious development which opens each of these prologues (cf. *Cat.* I,1–II,9; *Iug.* I,1–II,4)? One cannot help being
struck, in passing, by the analogy between these problems of Sallust
scholarship and the issues so much debated by *Tristan* scholars—the
"coherence of prologue and narrative" in Gottfried's *Tristan* and
the significance and function of *Tristan*'s elaborately sententious
"strophic prologue."[32] Aside from these parallels between issues in
Sallust scholarship and in *Tristan* scholarship, it will be recalled that
neither the Ciceronian *insinuatio* nor Geoffrey of Vinsauf's *principium artificiale sumptum a proverbio* contains an elaborate development of *sententiae* such as is found at the beginning of Gottfried's
prologue, in the "strophic prologue" (*Tristan* 1–44). Sallust's prologues do contain just such an elaborate development of *sententiae*
and this too suggests a parallel between the Sallustian and the Gottfriedian prologue. The sort of rhetorical interpretation which Alberic
applies to the opening *sententiae* of Sallust's *Bellum Catilinae* (*Cat.*
I,1–4; the same might be said of *Iug.* I,1–4 or *Iug.* II,1–4) can certainly be applied to the generalities of *Tristan*'s "strophic prologue."
A certain kind of human activity is lauded in the most general and
impersonal terms. The covert object of such sententious praise is both
very specific and very personal; it subtly commends, ascribes worth
and merit to the author's own specific personal activity, and so gains
for it the attention (and goodwill) of his audience. But the activity
thus subtly commended is formulated differently in the two cases.
The *sententia* with which Sallust's *Bellum Catilinae* opens (*Cat.* I,1;
cf. *Iug.* I,1 and *Iug.* II,1) commends the totality of human mental
activities as opposed to the physical activities which man shares with
the brutes:

---

31. Cf. Alberic, *Flores*, p. 37.
32. For the former issue cf. H. B. Willson, "Gottfried's Tristan. The coherence
of prologue and narrative," *Modern Language Review* 59 (1964), 595–607. For the
latter cf. the studies by Jaeger and Eifler mentioned *supra* N. 1. Both contain references to "classic" discussions of the "strophic prologue."

It behooves all men who wish to excel the other animals to strive with might and main not to pass through life in silence like the beasts, which Nature has fashioned grovelling and slaves to the belly.[33]

The opening *sententia* of the *Tristan*-prologue (*Tristan* 1-4) and its elaboration refer, on the other hand, not to the totality of man's mental activities, but rather to one special activity—that of benevolent recollection of the source of good deeds:

If men didn't recall with good will that by which good is done for the world, then it would all be as nothing, whatever good is done in the world.

The function of this generality and those which succeed it in Gottfried's "strophic prologue" may be the same as the function of the generalities with which the Sallustian prologue opens—to subtly commend, under the cover of universal statements, the writer's own particular authorial activity; their substance seems to differ—the totality of human mental activity, on the one hand, and benevolent recollection of the source of good deeds, on the other. Actually, however, the substance of Gottfried's opening *sententia* is as Sallustian as its function. It is, in fact, Gottfried's reformulation of a Sallustian generality (*Cat.* VIII,4) well known to late antiquity and the Middle Ages:[34]

Thus the virtue of those who did the deeds is rated as high as brilliant minds have been able to exalt the deeds themselves by words of praise.

---

33. I have used the Latin text and English translation of Sallust in *Sallust*, trans. J.C. Rolfe (Loeb Classical Library; Cambridge and London, 1971). In a few cases I have modified Rolfe's translation slightly.

34. Cf. St. Jerome, *Vita Hilarionis* I, 1; St. Augustine, *De civitate Dei* XVIII, 2; Flavius Vopiscus, *Vita Probi* I, 1-2 (*Historia Augusta*); cf. for medieval variants Gertrud Simon, "Untersuchungen zur Topik der Widmungsbriefe mittelalterlicher Geschichtsschreiber bis zum Ende des 12. Jahrhunderts," *Archiv für Diplomatik* 4 (1958), 82. Gottfried's formulation: "If men didn't recall with good will that by which good is done for the world, then it would all be as nothing, whatever good is done in the world" recalls Otto of Freising's indication that the continued existence of glorious deeds depends upon their historical narration: "Yet of the two evils, so to speak, I have thought it better that my work should be surpassed by the subject (through my deficiency in expression) than that your glorious deeds should be veiled in silence and perish, were I to say nothing of them" (Otto of Freising and Rahewin, *The Deeds of Frederick Barbarossa*, tr. Charles Christopher Mierow (New York, 1953), p. 115. For the Latin text of this passage from the prologue to Book II cf. *Ottonis et Rahewini Gesta Friderici I. Imperatoris*, ed. G. Waitz (Hannover and Leipzig, 1912), p. 102: *Inter duo tamen, ut ita dixerim, mala melius fore iudicavi minus dicendo a materia opus superari quam cuncta tacendo gloriosa facta silentio tecta deperire.*

Ita eorum qui ea fecere virtus tanta habetur, quantum ea verbis potuere
extollere praeclara ingenia.

The opening maxim of Gottfried's prologue thus shares the content of *Cat.* VIII,4; its form, however, as well as its function, aligns
it with *Cat.* I,1. Both opening *sententiae* (*Tristan* 1–4 and *Cat.* I,1)
are basically conditional. The form of Sallust's statement is implicitly
conditional, while the form of Gottfried's statement is explicitly
conditional. As the classical philologist Karl Büchner has observed,
the opening sententia of the *Catiline*-prologue is not only conditional,
it also makes a distinction—*Cat.* I,1 is "distinguirend-hypothe-
tisch."[35] The same is true of *Tristan* 1–4, only more obviously so. The
Sallustian maxim tells us what "it behooves all men" to do "who
wish to excel the other animals," i.e. what it behooves men to do,
if they wish to excel the other animals. Gottfried's maxim tells us
what would happen to "whatever good is done in the world," *if*
"men didn't recall with good will that by which good is done for
the world." Both generalities, conditionally formulated, aim—if we
follow Alberic of Monte Cassino—at a subtle commendation of the
writer's own authorial activity, Sallust's historical pursuits, and Gottfried von Strassburg's benevolent recollection of Tristan and Isolde.
But these generalities do not only state conditions, with antecedents
and consequents ("hypothetisch"); they also draw distinctions ("dis-
tinguirend"). The function of distinguishing lies in the conditional
form. Each conditional distinguishes activities which are commended
and activities which are condemned. For Sallust the former is "to
strive with might and main not to pass through life in silence like
the beasts, which Nature has fashioned grovelling and slaves to the
belly"; the latter is, of course, to pass through life in precisely that
fashion. For Gottfried the former is to "recall with good will that by
which good is done for the world"; the latter is to recall it otherwise
than with goodwill. Furthermore, each conditional not only distinguishes activities commended and activities condemned but also
distinguishes groups of men to be commended or condemned, to
the extent to which they do or do not practice such activities. Both
prologues move from the initial distinction of activities and groups
commended and condemned toward an increasing specification and
differentiation of their attributes. In each prologue this movement
comes to rest essentially at the moment when the narrator begins to
present himself as author, personally and individually (*Tristan* 45 and

35. Karl Büchner, *Sallust* (Heidelberg, 1960), p. 94.

Cat. III,3; cf. *Iug.* IV,2). In this moment the subtle commendation of the narrator as author and condemnation of his detractors—through impersonal generalities—ends, and the direct commendation of the author and condemnation of the detractors begins. This direct commendation and condemnation is accomplished by means of arguments intended to persuade that the author's activities (and hence his affiliations) are of the sort previously commended and his detractors' activities (and hence *their* affiliations) of the sort previously condemned in general and impersonal terms (cf. *Tristan* 1–44 with 45–130; *Cat.* I,1–III,2 with III,3–IV,2; *Iug.* I,1–IV,1 with IV,2–9). The ways in which Sallust and Gottfried proceed to characterize the activities and groups commended and condemned show striking similarities, sometimes extending even to details of formulation.

As a second example of such a similarity—and one which, like the relation between Gottfried's opening *sententia* (*Tristan* 1–4), the Sallustian maxim *Cat.* VIII,4, and Sallust's opening *sententia* (*Cat.* I,1), has structural significance—I should like to compare *Tristan* 45–54 and *Cat.* IV,1:

Tristan 45–54	*Cat.* IV,1
I have undertaken a labor [lit. "unidleness" *unmüezekeit* S.J.] to please the world and solace noble hearts, the hearts to which my heart is devoted, the world to which my heart looks. I do not mean the world of the many which, as I hear, is unable to endure travail and wishes only to swim in joy. God let it live in its joy!	Accordingly, when my mind found peace after many troubles and perils and I had determined that I must pass what was left of my life aloof from public affairs, it was not my intention to waste my precious leisure (*bonum otium*) in indolence (*socordia*) and sloth (*desidia*), nor yet by turning to farming or the chase, to lead a life devoted to slavish employments.

At the very point where each author makes the transition from general, impersonal commendation and condemnation to specific, personal commendation and condemnation, he specifies his own activity not as idleness, but rather as industry—a labor of high devotion to the ideals which he serves, as opposed to a way of life which he rejects. Gottfried here begins his association of the former ideal conduct with a "world" of "noble hearts"; Sallust describes, with his next breath, the world to which his historical labor is devoted as the Roman people (*res gestas populi Romani perscribere*; cf. also *Cat.* III,1: "It is glorious to serve one's country [*rei publicae*] by deeds; even to serve her by words is a thing not to be despised"). At first thought no two "worlds" might seem more remote than these, and yet there is a certain analogy between them. For Sallust does not mean the Roman people and country as they exist contemporaneous with him; he means the Roman people and country in an ideal sense, as they should be and perhaps once were. It is a people and a country of the mind to which he feels bound; and, like Gottfried's "world" of "noble hearts," Sallust's people and country of the mind constitute, in the present, not a "world of the many," but a world of the few. Gottfried characterizes his "world of the many" as totally pleasure-seeking, unable to bear travail; he might, of course, have said "idle" as well. Interestingly, Sallust seems to view the "slavish employments" (*servilibus officiis*) which he rejects as almost tantamount to pure indolence and sloth. Elsewhere Sallust scorns pure pleasure-seeking, as does Gottfried (*Cat.* II,8; cf. also *Iug.* I,4 and II,4), because it represents domination of the mind by the body. The employments which Sallust scorns, farming and hunting, may be the pursuits of the aristocratic "many" of his world, the country gentlemen with whom he found himself in conflict; but from his point of view they are "servile" nonetheless, for their lives exhibit almost total subjugation of the mind by the body, which is expressed as indolence, sloth, and pure pleasure-seeking. *Even* the "useful industry" of the many is vain idleness. Thus, there seem to be broad analogies in ideological content which parallel analogies of rhetorical structure in the Sallustian and Gottfriedian prologues. According to the interpretation of a medieval commentator like Conrad of Hirsau, Sallust "justifies and commends himself" in his prologue(s) in that he seeks to undo the "injury inflicted upon him by his detractors" (*iniuria irrogata detrahentium*), to remove "the aspersion of idleness" (*a se removet nomen inertiae*) cast upon his reputation by these detractors (and enviers, we might add, remembering that in medieval moral theology detraction is one of the five daughters of envy). Sallust's self-justification and self-commendation, his removal of aspersions of idleness cast by envious detraction emanating from "the world of the many," is under way in *Cat.* IV,1; so, I would maintain, is Gottfried's, in *Tristan* 45–54.

A third and final set of passages, which I should like to cite as additional support for my thesis that the *Tristan*-prologue is Sallustian in its rhetorical structure, is perhaps not so significant in terms of content as the preceding:

Tristan 123–130	*Cat.* IV,3
Therefore, whoever desires a love-tale, let him go no further than here. I will betell him well of noble lovers, who gave an example of pure love: a loving man and a loving woman, a man a woman, a woman a man, Tristan Isolt, Isolt Tristan.	I shall therefore write briefly and as truthfully as possible of the conspiracy of Catiline; for I regard that event as worthy of special notice because of the extraordinary nature of the crime and of the danger arising from it. But before beginning my narrative I must say a few words about the man's character.

The *Catiline*-passage concludes Sallust's prologue. In it the actual subject matter of the work to follow is mentioned for the first time with the name of the protagonist, Catiline; the Gottfried passage is similar. There is an extremely compressed statement of the significance of the subject matter, the reasons why this particular matter is worthy of being written down and read; Gottfried proceeds in a similar fashion. Sallust also promises that the historical narrative to follow will be brief and as truthful as possible. One might also conclude from the formulation of the final sentence that he intends to be clear as well as brief (*pauca prius explananda sunt*). Gottfried mentions neither brevity nor clarity in the prologue; his extensive claim to truthfulness follows, at the beginning of his extension of the Sallustian prologue (*Tristan* 131–166). The extraordinarily brief statement of the particular subject matter to be narrated is quite consistent with what has been suggested thus far about the structure of the Sallustian prologue, at least as analyzed from a medieval point of view. It does not commend or justify so much on the basis of arguments about the subject matter of the work to follow (*de materia*) as on the basis of arguments concerning authorial activity (*de persona*)—arguments of a specific and personal sort which are, however, introduced by a "subtle" commendation and exculpation through impersonal generalities on such topics as the nature and value of intellectual activity or the nature and value of historical pursuits (*de historia*). Gottfried's prologue, up to *Tristan* 130, does approximate this pattern.

The categorization of Sallust's prologues, in spite of their elaborate, sententious openings (and in spite of their unelaborate concluding subject matter references), as examples of the personal prologue (the *principium de persona*) is derived from the excerpt *De historia* edited by Karl Halm (*Rhetores latini minores*) from the eighth-century Paris MS 7530:

> There are three sorts of prologues appropriate to history: from the genre of history, from the person of the author, from the matter of the historical work in question. For we either commend the value of history in general, as does Cato, or, in the character of author, we render an account of his reasons for having undertaken this task, as Sallust does in that passage (*Cat.* III,3) where he says: but as a young man I myself, like many others, was at first borne by my zeal into public life, or we show that the matter which we are about to relate is worthy of being written down and read, as Livy does in his history from the founding of the city.

> Principiorum ad historiam pertinentium species sunt tres: de historia, de persona, de materia. Aut enim historiae bonum generaliter commendamus, ut Cato, aut pro persona scribentis rationem eius quod hoc officium adsumpserit reddimus, ut Sallustius eo loco, ubi dicit: sed ego adulescentulus initio, sicuti plerique, studio ad rem publicam latus sum, aut eam rem, quam relaturi sumus, dignam quae et scribatur et legatur ostendimus, ut Livius ab urbe condita.[36]

The aim of the historical prologue is, according to this excerpt's unknown author, to commend the work which it introduces. This is accomplished in three different ways, in three different kinds of prologues. But do these ways and kinds exclude one another? Is "aut" used here in an exclusive sense? A simple reading of the text might suggest that conclusion. But if this analysis of the historical prologue is compared with Sallust's practice, partially delineated in the foregoing discussion, it is evident that the Sallustian prologue combines all three modes of commending and justifying the literary activity of its author. *Cat.* III,1–2 and *Iug.* III,1–IV,1 (as well as *Iug.* IV,5–9) form a commendation and justification *de historia,* in which the value of historical writing is eulogized in general and compared, to its favor, with an alternative species of mental activity, i.e. that of the man of the world (of many), the public office seeker or official. *Cat.* III,3–IV,2 and *Iug.* IV,2–9 represent a commendation and defence *de persona,* in which the author gives an account of the way that he entered upon the leisure of an historian, deprecated by Sallust's detractors as idleness, rather than the vain and self-seeking pursuits of the detractors themselves, seen by Sallust as the true idleness, indolence, and sloth. Finally, *Cat.* IV,3–4 and *Iug.* V,1–2 contain a commendation and justification, however slight, *de materia,* in which Sallust very briefly shows that the particular matter

36. Halm, *Rhetores,* pp. 588–589.

about to be narrated deserves attention. Sallust, of course, extends the first mode considerably by beginning at an even more general level; in the Sallustian prologue the commendation and justification from a particular form of mental activity, i.e. *de historia,* is preceded by a commendation and justification from mental excellence generally, *de virtute animi* (*Cat.* I,1–II,9 and *Iug.* I,1–II,4). However, although all three modes of commendation and justification mentioned in the excerpt from Paris MS 7530 are evident in Sallust's prologues, it is only his use of the second (*de persona*), in which Sallust offers an account of his way to historical writing, that is used to exemplify a type of prologue. Similarly, although the unknown author of the Paris MS 7530 excerpt cites Cato (*Origines*) to exemplify only the opening *de historia,* the commendation and justification of the work introduced through a eulogy of historical writing in general, it seems clear, from the extant tradition, that Cato's prologue to the *Origines* employed the commendation and justification *de persona* as well, an account and justification of his passage from public business (*negotium*) to literary leisure (*otium*).[37] Indeed, if the significance of the last surviving witness to Cato's prologue, the sentence fragment "si ques homines sunt, quos delectat populi Romani gesta discribere"[38] handed down by Pompeius in his Donatus-commentary as an example of the double declension of the indefinite pronoun, lies in its mention of the subject matter of the work to follow (i.e. "populi Romani gesta"), then the commendation and defence *de materia* also may have been involved in Cato's prologue. But the incomplete context may be completed in a variety of ways, some of which, at least, would suggest an interpretation in terms of the opening *de persona* or *de historia* as well. Finally, although the fragment from Paris MS 7530 uses Livy (*Ab urbe condita*) to exemplify the prologue *de materia,* Livy provides (*Praefatio* 10) a formulation of the value of history (*de historia*) and also renders, in the opening sections of his prologue (*Praefatio* 1–6), an account of his personal reasons for undertaking the task at hand (*de persona*). Thus, the prologues of Cato, Sallust, and Livy are used to exemplify prologue types characterized in terms of one mode of commending and defending the work introduced; and yet all three exemplary prologues contain more than one such mode. Indeed, Sallust's prologues seem to contain all three

---

37. M. Porcius Cato, *Das erste Buch der Origines,* ed. Wilt Aden Schröder, Beiträge zur klassischen Philologie 14 (Meisenheim am Glan, 1971), pp. 30, 51–54.

38. *Ibid.,* pp. 29–30, 49–51.

modes and in elaborated form. Clearly, then, in the excerpt from Paris MS 7530 these prologue types are not exclusive; they are classified, rather, according to the mode of commending which is seen as central and dominant, around which the remaining, subordinate parts of the prologue are organized. This central and dominant mode of commendation and justification is, in the case of Sallust, the mode *de persona,* concretized in a eulogy of the historian's "leisure" as a high form of labor and its vituperation of "worldly" labor as a low form of idleness.

All three modes of commending and justifying the historian's activity and its product, which are presented and exemplified in the excerpt *De historia,* may be identified in the *Tristan*-prologue and their extent corresponds almost exactly to the division—according to initials and verse form as well as content—found in Gottfried's introduction. Thus, *Tristan* 1–40, the "strophic prologue" without the transitional eleventh strophe, might well be interpreted as a generalized and impersonal commendation and justification of the author's "work" *de historia,* history here conceived in terms of benevolent recollection and praise of what is good (and, somewhat less prominently, blame of what is bad; cf. *Tristan* 17–20 and 29–32). The division within the "strophic prologue" (*Tristan* 1–20 and 21–40), between Gottfried's most general commendation and justification of benevolent recollection and praise (coupled with condemnation of envy and detraction) and his more specific commendation and justification in relation to art may also represent a structural echo of Sallust. In *Cat.* I,1–II,9 and *Iug.* I,1–II,4 Sallust commends and justifies human mental and intellectual activity in general. In *Cat.* III,1–2 and *Iug.* III,1–IV,1 (as well as *Iug.* IV,5–9) he commends and justifies the mental and intellectual activity of the historian in particular. In the former passages he condemns the domination of the mind by the body and its consequences. In the latter passages he deprecates, if not condemns, the mental and intellectual activity of the man of the world (of many). *Tristan* 37–40, the final strophe of the "strophic prologue," with its statement of the difficulties of excellence (*tugent*), seems paralleled by the statement in *Cat.* III,2: "I regard the writing of history as one of the most difficult tasks" (and thus, he implies in the context, one of the most excellent activities). *Tristan* 41–44 is a transitional strophe. With its initial "T" and its reference to Gottfried's own activity it belongs to the next section; with its strophic form it looks back to the "strophic prologue". Gottfried's delineation of the (possible) consequences of idleness in this strophe parallels Sallust's delineation of the actual consequences of his earlier idleness in *Cat.* III,3–5 (cf. also *Tristan* 41–44 with *Cat.* II,8–9). In terms of its role in the rhetorical structure of the *Tristan*-prologue, viewed according to the Sallustian model, this strophe probably belongs, with its initial, to what follows; its relation to the immediately preceding strophe is antithetical.

What follows is a change in verse form to the rhymed couplets of the "stichic prologue." *Tristan* 45–122 might well be understood as a commendation and justification of the author's work *de persona* through a personal account of his reason for having undertaken what is indeed a productive task or labor ("unidleness" *unmüezekeit*) rather than mere idleness. The reason, it must be noted—and here is a departure from the Sallustian pattern and a certain tradition of historiographic thought which rejects *delectare* as too unserious for the historian—is to please (cf. *Tristan* 46–47, 71–72, 73–76, 97–100).[39] Gottfried, following the contrary tradition of historiographic thought which was not disinclined to *delectare* and attempted to legitimize it in historical writing in terms of consolation, sees the pleasure which his love story will bring as consolation; but, guided as well by his own ethos, Gottfried finally reformulates *delectare* as half-way alleviation or consolation of love's sorrows (*Tristan* 71–76).

Tristan 123–130 would correspond, as noted above, to a commendation and justification *de materia* (from the subject matter) of Gottfried's work as an author, but in the truncated manner of the Sallustian prologue. Had Gottfried's prologue ended here, and it might have, its resemblance to the Sallustian model would have been more apparent.

Tristan 131–244 represents Gottfried's development and elaboration of the Sallustian model. It continues and extends the commendation and justification of Gottfried's work *de materia* far beyond the narrow limits of the truncated Sallustian version of *Tristan* 123–130. The transitional strophe at the beginning (*Tristan* 131–134) with the rhyme scheme *abab* recalls the transitional strophe (*Tristan* 41–44) which introduced Gottfried's "Sallustian prologue" *de persona.* Both hark back to strophes 1–5 of the "strophic prologue" and seem to suggest an emergence of authorial activity, a new beginning. It is

39. Cf. Lukian, *Wie man Geschichte schrieben soll: Griechisch und Deutsch,* ed. and trans. H. Homeyer (Munich, 1965), pp. 104–107, 188–190; Simon, "Widmungsbriefe," 5/6 (1959/60), pp. 109–111.

possible that behind Gottfried's elaboration of the commendation and justification *de materia* stands another authoritative prologue model and that Gottfried is, in fact, engaged in a virtuoso play between two *auctoritates*, or, at least, between two authoritative traditions. The structure of this extended commendation and justification *de materia* might afford some clues about the tradition in which it stands. *Tristan* 131–172 bring Gottfried's claim to truthfulness, together with a claim to historiographic objectivity in the sense of freedom from fear, favor, envy, partiality (*Tristan* 167–170: "What my reading of this love-story was, that I offer now, of my own free will [*miner willekür*], to all noble hearts");[40] *Tristan* 173–205 bring Gottfried's claim that the matter is morally beneficial; *Tristan* 206–240 bring Gottfried's claim that the matter is praiseworthy. These three arguments which point to the conclusion that the matter about to be related "is worthy both to be written and to be read" correspond closely to the topics recommended by Alberic of Monte Cassino—in his treatment of the *exordium* or rhetorical prologue— for gaining the attention (and hence goodwill) of the reader:[41]

> Therefore, if you wish to make the reader attentive (*attentum*), promise him what is true (*vera*), what is praiseworthy (*honesta*), what is beneficial (*utilia*). For if you offer what is false (*falsa*), disgraceful (*turpia*), not beneficial (*non profutura*), you will make your listener negligent and unresponsive, hardly even a listener at all; quite to the contrary, you will create a despiser or a malignant persecutor.

Like much of the doctrine in Alberic's treatment of disposition, the formulation of these three means of gaining attention seems to

---

40. The meaning of Gottfried's *"miner willekür"* as a claim to freedom from the distorting pressures of fear, favor, envy, partiality, i.e. as a claim to objectivity, becomes clear only against the historiographic background. Cf. *Tristan* 167–170: *waz aber min lesen do waere/von disem senemaere:/ daz lege ich miner willekür/ allen edelen herzen vür* with Halm, *Rhetores*, p. 588: *Verae res sunt, si rerum actarum vetustas et obscuritas diligenter exploretur, si explorata libere, id est sine metu aut gratia aut invidia referatur* (Past events are established as true, if their antiquity and obscurity is carefully investigated, if what has been investigated is then freely recounted, i.e. without fear or favor or envy) or with Sallust himself (*Cat.* IV, 2): *Sed a quo incepto studioque me ambitio mala detinuerat, eodem regressus statui res gestas populi Romani carptim, ut quaeque memoria digna videbantur, perscribere; eo magis, quod mihi a spe, metu, partibus rei publicae animus liber erat* (On the contrary, I resolved to return to the beginnings of a pursuit from which base ambition had diverted me, and write a history of the Roman people, selecting such portions as seemed to me worthy of record; and I was confirmed in this resolution by the fact that my mind was free from hope, and fear, and partisanship). Cf. also Simon, "Widmungsbriefe," 5/6 (1959–60), pp. 93–94.

41. Alberic, *Flores*, pp. 36–37.

represent a product of the interaction between rhetoric and histori-ography. Topics traditionally involved in deliberative oratory or suasion (*partes suadendi* or *loci suasoriae*), such as *honestum, utile,* and *necessarium* (cf. Quintilian *Inst. orat.* III,8,22), *honestum, utile, possibile* (cf. Isidore *Etym.* II,4,4), *honestum, utile, possibile,* and *necessarium* (cf. Conrad of Hirsau, *Dialogus*, p. 101) are transferred, in Alberic of Monte Cassino's analysis, to exordial doctrine. The de-liberative speaker, oriented to the problem of *future* choice, might well attempt to gain attention in his prologue by promising to adduce considerations of necessity and/or possibility; the historian, whose task is the recounting of *past* events worthy of recollection, would, on the other hand, attempt to gain the attention of his audience by promising neither the necessary nor the possible, but the true, an example of rhetorical doctrine undergoing modification through interaction with the generic requirements of historical writing. Thus, even Gottfried's unsallustian elaboration of commendation and justification from the subject matter of his work (*de materia*) seems to exhibit in its structure connections with the rhetoric of history.

This essay has attempted to provide, in at least cursory fashion, a critique of the currently accepted rhetorical analysis of Gottfried von Strassburg's *Tristan*-prologue and to suggest, utilizing a few selected textual features, the outlines of an alternative view. Aside from the difficulties inherent in applying (1) a misinterpretation of Conrad of Hirsau's and John of Garland's generic distinction of different kinds of prologues, (2) the Ciceronian concept of *insinuatio,* (3) the artificial beginning with proverb of the *artes poetriae* to the *Tristan*-prologue, an additional argument against the generally accepted rhetorical analysis of Gottfried's introduction lies in is its dead-end quality. The theses of Brinkmann which have gained the most accept-ance seem to have the least implications for an interpretation of the meaning, structure, and function of the prologue and the entire work. On these grounds, as well as for the reasons alluded to above, it seems likely that the rhetorical conventions generally invoked are not those in fact relevant to Gottfried's prologue.

Where rhetorical conventions actually fit a given work, their very conventionality makes it possible for us to discern quite specific individual nuances in the way that they are employed. We are led, dialectically one might say, to an appreciation of stylistic and ideo-logical individuality only against a background of stylistic and ideo-logical conventionality. It has been the thesis of this essay that the rhetorical conventions and conventionality most relevant to Gottfried's introduction are those of the historical prologue, a tradition largely unformulated in theoretical terms but persistently effective through the influence of practical models, in particular the influence of Sallust himself. Perhaps enough evidence has been submitted to render this thesis at least plausible; a fuller substantiation and application to the interpretation of the *Tristan*-prologue must be reserved for another occasion.

Boncompagno of Signa
and The Rhetoric of Love*

JOSEF PURKART

THE title of this brief study suggests a person who can be fixed in place and time: Boncompagno of Signa who lived in Italy from about 1170 to the late 1240's; it suggests an academic discipline which was taught and learned: rhetoric (the *ars oratoria*, sometimes called *rhetorica*, but frequently answering to the name *eloquentia*); and finally, it links both the person and his discipline to an affection which is as old as mankind.

Few scholars have dealt with Boncompagno in recent years, and it is fair to say that their conclusions are still to be considered tentative because of the lack of sufficient texts and editions available to them in print. Professor Murphy in his assessment of the master's achievements within the tradition of the *ars dictandi* concluded: "It is easy to deride a dictaminal buffoon like Boncompagno, with his wild pretensions of outdoing Cicero, but all over Europe hundreds of earnest writers did their best to lay out their subject matter for the use of their fellow men."[1] Professor Dronke, aware of our modern prejudice toward mere rhetoricians, detected the unusual poetic qualities in Boncompagno's letters and called him "an outstanding exception . . . perhaps the greatest of the teachers of rhetoric."[2] In this study I would like to take another look at the master from Bologna, concentrating mainly on previously unedited texts from

---

*A paper delivered at the 10th Annual Conference of the Medieval Association of the Pacific, University of California, Davis; 20–22 February 1976.

1. See James J. Murphy, *Rhetoric in the Middle Ages. A History of Rhetorical Theory from St. Augustine to the Renaissance*. Berkeley and Los Angeles: University of California Press, 1974. Quotation on p. 362.

2. See Peter Dronke, *Medieval Latin and the Rise of European Love-Lyric*. 2 vols., 2d ed. Oxford, 1968. Quotation I, p. 251.

the *Rhetorica antiqua.* I am concerned with the humorous and—for the modern reader—"blasphemous" intellectual game which Boncompagno played with the tradition. This tradition involves the cultural dualism of both pagan and Christian learning, and it includes rhetoric and the dualistic concept of love.

Boncompagno was born in the little town of Signa near Florence.[3] As he put it himself, he drank the milk of his rudimentary education from the breasts of flourishing Florence, and he completed his higher education, presumably grammar, rhetoric and law for openers, at the University of Bologna. Immediately thereafter (around 1190), he joined the faculty of his *alma mater*, where he taught the *ars dictaminis*—the "new rhetoric," which provided instruction in the drafting of personal, diplomatic and legal letters and documents. Boncompagno was more of a *trufator* and *ioculator* than his colleagues would have preferred. A popular and innovative faculty member, he experienced their professional envy and backbiting, and he was unjustly accused of the deadliest of academic sins, plagiarism. At the height of his career which had led him to a number of Italian cities and universities and probably also to Germany, he not only strove to introduce the dictaminal practices of the papal curia in Bologna but also applied for a position at the papal chancery. Yet all of his publications, about fourteen by then, were not strong enough to constitute a dative case.[4] He was to die at the age of about seventy in great want in a hospital in Florence without the aid of Rome's spiritual *medici.*

It should be easier to appreciate Boncompagno's use of the rhetoric of love if we recall some of the inherent characteristics of rhetoric and its place within the cultural heritage of the age.[5]

Rhetoric may generally be characterized as (1) the art of persuasion, (2) artificial eloquence, showiness and elaboration in language and literary style, and (3) craftsmanship in the mastery of words. Yet, in spite of its obvious importance in political, religious and private life, there have always been reasons to be suspicious of rhetoric. For while

---

3. For a fuller account see Boncompagno da Signa: *Rota Veneris.* A Facsimile Reproduction of the Strassburg Incunabulum with Introduction, Translation, and Notes by J. Purkart. Delmar, New York: Scholars' Facsimiles & Reprints, 1975. From here on cited as *Rota Veneris.*

4. The expression is Helen Waddell's, taken from her lively account in *The Wandering Scholars.* 6th ed. New York, 1955, pp. 150–56.

5. I was guided by the excellent brief account in *Der kleine Pauly,* 5 vols., ed. K. Ziegler a.o., Stuttgart, 1964–75; vol. IV, 1396–1410.

rhetoric can be used, it can also be abused. As the art of persuasion, rhetoric relies on the manipulation of the audience's or the individual's emotions, and the effective persuader tends toward a relativism in respect to values, in order to make his own values best serve his cause. Ornateness of style, while on the one hand lending dignity and esthetic flavor to the argument, may on the other hand result in a play with form for form's sake, at the expense of content. Finally, rhetoric requires adequate talent, instruction and imitation. It may therefore put at a distinct disadvantage those who have neither talent nor the opportunity for instruction.

The proper use of rhetoric in the Middle Ages was a volatile question. Not the least reason for this is the old distinction between pagan rhetoric and Christian rhetoric. The pagan cause is man-centered; the Christian cause is God-centered. Pagan rhetoric serves secular concerns, it obeys the laws of secular history, and it promotes the promises of rewards that can be had in this world. This rhetoric is therefore, from the Christian viewpoint, of only temporal value. Christian rhetoric, on the other hand, serves spiritual concerns, it is governed by the laws of the history of salvation (*Heilsgeschichte*), and it promotes the promise of the highest reward that can be obtained partially here but fully in the life to come. This rhetoric is therefore, from the Christian standpoint, the only legitimate one; it is of eternal value and it ought to be used. Pagan rhetoric is concerned with the sound of words and uses words in their *vox* significance to communicate with the gods and with men; Christian rhetoric is concerned not only with the sounds but particularly with the hidden meaning of words, for it presumes that there is some aspect of the divine mystery in the *res* significance, and it thus seeks those *invisibilia Dei*. By finding a higher significance, a spiritual level, under the veil of the word, man can communicate with God.[6]

It is not necessary to dwell on this dualism of the Middle Ages or to describe step by step the process by which the pagan classical legacy of antiquity was incorporated into the new Christian context.[7] It might be characterized as a process of adoption and adaptation. Adoption of pagan material was justified on typological grounds;

---

6. For a fairly recent study, see H. Brinkmann, "Die Zeichenhaftigkeit der Sprache, des Schrifttums und der Welt im Mittelalter," *Zeitschrift für deutsche Philologie* 93 (1974), pp. 1–11.

7. See J. Leclercq, *The Love of Learning and the Desire for God*. Engl. trans. New York, 1961.

adaptation was made possible by reading a spiritual significance into secular works. This process entailed a search for spiritual meaning behind words, events, figures, numbers, and so on, all to serve the illumination of the faith.[8] What is essential to remember is that Christian doctrine operates with the concept of the history of salvation. This "history" is not measurable by human categories of time, nor is it governed by the human expectation of success in this world; rather, it provides for a life in anticipation. Only in this mode of thought does a system of prefiguration and fulfillment make sense, and only *sub specie aeternitatis* was it possible that any analogous stories of secular origin—even though there, too, one finds absolutely no causal link—could be used as an *auctoritas*.[9] Boncompagno turned this Christian tradition around by putting it into an inappropriate context.

All human experience in order to be communicable among men must be put into a system of signs or into a language. The Scriptures also use language to tell, among other things, stories of human experiences such as love. Since any sign, word or text can be interpreted either *in bonam* or *in malam partem*, depending on the context in which it occurs and depending on which or whose cause is to be promoted, Boncompagno, with his usual wit, made his point very clear that there is room, plenty of room in fact, for interpretation. Thus he concluded his *Rota Veneris,* saying:

> However, even though I have set down in this work many things which seem to display lasciviousness, nevertheless one should not think that I was or wished to be lascivious; because Solomon, who was deserving enough to be joined with the assistance of God—that is, with His Wisdom—set down in the *Song of Songs* many things which, if understood literally, could contribute more to the voluptuousness of the flesh than to the moral edification of the spirit. But, in fact, wise men interpret dubious passages in a nobler sense, saying that the bride or friend was the Church, and the spouse Jesus Christ. And, indeed, you ought therefore to believe that Boncompagno did not say these things for any lascivious reason, but that, out of pure friendship, he conceded to the entreaties of his colleagues.[10]

---

8. Most beneficial is the brief treatment by F. Ohly, "Vom geistigen Sinn des Wortes," *Zeitschrift für deutsches Altertum* 89 (1958), pp. 1–23; reprinted as a *separatum*, Darmstadt: Wissenschaftliche Buchgesellschaft, 1966.

9. Cf. E. Auerbach, *Typologische Motive in der mittelalterlichen Literatur*. Krefeld, 1953.

10. Quoted from *Rota Veneris*, p. 95.

The other dualistic trend in the Middle Ages concerns love. In one of his characteristically encyclopedic footnotes Professor Steadman wrote: "Courtly love is sometimes contrasted with divine love as though they were logical contraries. If we are to use these terms at all—to control them instead of being controlled by them—it would be advisable to define them (and their opposites) more exactly. If the opposite of *curteisye* is *vileinye,* then the opposite of courtly love would appear to be churlish or base love. The opposite of divine love would be earthly love. Rational love would be opposed to irrational lust, spiritual to carnal affection, and sacred to profane, etc."[11] And he pointed out that these categories may overlap. Since I have no intention to add to the library of "courtly love," whatever one is inclined to mean by that term, I shall confine myself to the basic distinction between spiritual and carnal love which is found in the influential writings of Origen.[12] He states:

> Est quidam amor carnis a Satana veniens, alius amor spiritus a Deo exordium habens, et nemo potest duobus amoribus possideri.

> There is carnal love which comes from the devil, and spiritual love which has its origin in God; and no one can be possessed by two loves.

The concept of this spiritual love, as Professor Pollmann has shown, is an eschatological bondage between God and Jerusalem, between the soul and Christ, between the individual daughter of Jerusalem and Christ, and so on.[13] The ritualistic imagery of this concept is that of bride and bridegroom, found in a number of Old Testament books, especially in the *Song of Songs* and in Psalm 44. It is also present in the story of the Wise and Foolish Virgins and in the writings of St. John and St. Paul. This tradition of spiritual love which rejects carnal love as the work of the devil and yet expresses itself in the imagery of sexual love, is found in the epistles of St. Jerome and in later monastic literature, and it is also found in Boncompagno. Unlike his saintly predecessors, however, Boncompagno does not always reserve the language of spiritual love for pious nuns and virgin monks.

---

11. John M. Steadman, *Disembodied Laughter, Troilus and the Apotheosis Tradition.* Berkeley and Los Angeles: University of California Press, 1972. Quotation on p. 160 n. 19.

12. Hom. I, 2; ed. O. Rousseau, *Sources Chrétiennes* 37, Paris, 1953, p. 65. Quoted in Pollmann (see next note).

13. L. Pollmann, *Die Liebe in der hochmittelalterlichen Literatur Frankreichs.* Frankfurt am Main, 1966; see esp. pp. 33–46.

324   JOSEF PURKART

Since Boncompagno is thoroughly familiar with the dualism of carnal and spiritual love, his preoccupation with nuns, the brides of Christ, is not surprising. Many of his model letters, both in the *Rhetorica antiqua* and in the *Rota Veneris,* concern themselves with the "love life" of nuns. To show his familiarity with the tradition of letters giving spiritual advice to nuns, or to girls who are about to become nuns, I offer the following excerpts from a serious letter in the *Rhetorica antiqua*:

> Verbum patris quod erat in principio apud Deum, tuorum precedentibus uotis parentum, tibi diuinitus inspirauit, ut eructaret cor tuum uerbum bonum, et diceres opera tua regi. Sed s(c)ire debes, filia, quid sit istud uerbum, et quis rex cui opera tua dixisti. Hoc enim fuit uerbum "Ipsi sum desponsata cui angeli seruiunt," quod per uerbum Dei uirtutem prompsisti, quando sponso celesti tue uirginitatis meruisti famosum titulum dedicare. Profecto rex iste, rex est omnium regum, dominus domina(n)tium, cui celestia et terrestria famulantur. Talis est sponsus tuus, talis est dilectus tuus. Speciosus est forma pre filiis hominum et sponsas diligit que forma clareant et uirtutum meritis renitescent. Hic introduxit te in cubiculum suum, occidens collum tuum lapidibus preciosis, et exornans pectus castitatis armilla, ut in ipsius presentia sicut lilium reflorescas, et uelut odor balsami sis in conspectu eius. Audi ergo, filia, et uide, et inclina aurem tuam et obliuiscere omnium adulationum blanditias uenatiuas et deceptiua mortalium blandimenta . . .[14]

The Word of the Father which was with God in the beginning, has after the prior vows of your parents divinely inspired you so that the noble theme may stir your heart and so that you may utter the song you have made in the king's honor. But you ought to know, O daughter, what that theme is and who the king to whom you uttered your song. For that theme was, "I am espoused to Him Whom the angels serve," since through the Word of God you have brought forth your virtue, when you were worthy to dedicate the beautiful honor of your virginity to the Heavenly Spouse. Indeed he is king, he is king of all kings, lord of all lords. He is Whom heaven and earth serve. Such is your spouse, such is your beloved. He surpasses all sons of man in beauty and loves those brides who shine with beauty and who grow bright with the merits of virtue. He introduced you into his bedchamber, crushing your neck with precious gems and decorating your breast with the necklace of chastity so that in his presence you shall shine forth like a lily, and so that you be like the odor of balsam in his sight. Harken, O daughter, and consider, and incline thine ear, and forget the entrapping flatteries of all adulations and the deceptive blandishments of mortals . . .

---

14. Paris, Bibliothèque Nationale, MS. lat. 7732, fol. 52^r. Punctuation was added, contractions were expanded. For scriptural borrowings cf.: John 1:1; Ps.44; *Rota Veneris*, p. 101f., nn. 51, 52, 70.

Boncompagno goes on to give specific advice to the young girl on how to discourage secular lovers who are trying to storm the wall of her intended chastity. She should gird herself, he says, with the sword of the spirit, namely the word of God and cut down the tempters with the word of her vows, forcefully asserting: "I am espoused to Him Whom the angels serve and therefore I despise any worldly lover." Having described to her the transitoriness of earthly beauty and the torments and trials of married life, he concludes by exhorting her to be like the Wise Virgins so that she will, with her lamp lit, deserve to enter into the gate of the heavenly kingdom to reign forever in the sight of her glorious spouse.

This letter with its ardent devotional style and traditional imagery hardly differs from the letters of St. Jerome or the spiritual advice found in St. Ambrose. What is unique about Boncompagno, however, is that he employs the same rhetoric of persuasion and dissuasion, the same spiritual authorities, and the same imagery to argue the devil's case. What may come as a shock to some is how he turns Holy Writ into horny wit.[15] It is a technique which for the medievalist is both intellectually stimulating and esthetically pleasing, because the modern reader sees, for once, what happens when human categories of thought and logic are applied to Christian doctrine and divine mystery; we see what *Diesseitsstimmung* in the Middle Ages could achieve.

Boncompagno's writings abound with examples. I shall briefly examine the letter of a nun, who is asked for her friendship, and the events that follow. It is from the *Rota Veneris*. The nun responds:

"Since I am betrothed to Him Whom the angels serve, and, in my first vow of ordination, vowed my virginity to the Celestial Spouse, I am surprised that you dare ask me for my friendship, especially since I am wearing the sign of virginity upon my head—namely, the black veil, by which it is indicated that I have assumed a special kind of mortality. Therefore I ought doubtless to be displeasing to you and to everyone else with regard to the delights of the flesh. But, as I can see, the Devil's persuasion has so ensnared you that you would not shy away from defiling the bed of any man, and thus you do not even fear to call away the bride of the Highest. But you should know without delay, and by no means

---

15. A humorous medieval German sermon in which the Pope addresses the virgins and women concludes with a pious prayer to the "horny spirit" (*dar helf uns der geile geist!*). ed. from the MS. Gotha, Landesbibliothek, cod. chart. A 216 (ca. 1400) in F. Vetter, *Lehrhafte Litteratur* (!) *des 14. und 15. Jahrhunderts,* T. 2: Geistliches. Berlin and Stuttgart, 1889, pp. 129–32.

doubt, that your attempts at persuading me shall not prevail. And if you should give what you have and what you could not possibly have, you are laboring in vain and committing your seed to the sand." [16]

The man in his response is not, as one might expect, at a loss for words. On the contrary, he is eager to "avail himself of that selfsame *mortalitas,*" signified by her black veil, along with her, until they could, perhaps, "revive a little together." Nor does the veil bother him, because, says he, "I still suspect that, underneath it, the limbs are whiter than milk." He wants, one may suspect, to get through *ad invisibilia Dei!* Finally, the fact that she asserts betrothal to Him Whom the angels serve and that she has promised Christ her virginity should not, according to him, stand in the way of their union. After all, the Heavenly Spouse longs for her soul, not her body. For, is it not written, he continues: "The heaven hath He given to the Lord of Heaven, but the earth to the sons of man."

The nun writes back, saying: "Your words were sweeter than honey and honeycomb, nor dare I deny what you demand, since you set forth an unavoidable and irrefutable argument." Why are his words sweet and why is his argument irrefutable? The lover's proposal was to assume her "special kind of mortality." To take vows means and has always meant a dying to the world. It is a "requiem" followed by an "alleluia," a burial followed by a wedding ceremony with wreath and ring. Thus his willingness to avail himself of that selfsame mortality might seem sweet to her. Her second argument was that he must have been ensnared by the devil's persuasion. And indeed he was, for he not only shifted the semantic level, so that they could, in fact *"revive* a little together," but he even dared to call upon Holy Writ, Psalm 113:24: "The heaven hath He given to the Lord of Heaven . . ." He thus used an *auctoritas* devoid of its spiritual validity and semantic connotation, because he had removed it from its Christian context. Yet the method—after all, he learned it from the Church fathers—is in the Christian tradition, and thus his argument should be irrefutable. The Old Testament prefiguration of how man was to have his share of God's creation thus finds its fulfillment in Boncompagno's "new testament" of love!

Similarly, in a letter from the *Rhetorica antiqua,* when a *sarabaita,* a monk without rule, who had fled with a nun, is reprimanded, he responds:

---

16. Quoted from *Rota Veneris,* p. 86.

Audiui predicationem ypocrite anpullosam, in qua mihi consulitur, quod sponsam Christi debeam a meo consortio separare. Sed ipsi Christo dixi cum propheta: "Delectasti me, Domine, in factura tua, et in operibus manuum tuarum exultabo." Ceterum firmiter scio[a] et nullatenus dubito, quod ille[b] qui se moniali coniungit Deum non offendit. Inmo cum sancta sanctus erit, cui se incorporare[c] meretur. Quod autem dicitur me sponsam Christi rapuisse, dico non esse uerum, quia de illius consensu processit; nec ego negare debebam, quia scriptum est: "Erit uobis cor unum et anima una." Et alibi: "Omni[d] petenti te, tribue." Unde Christo ad inguriam non[e] redundat inmo ad gloriam et honorem, quia in nomine meo exaltabitur cornu eius.[17]

I heard the bombastic sermon of a hypocrite in which I am advised that I ought to separate the bride of Christ from my fellowship. But I said to Christ himself with the prophet: "Thou hast made me glad through thy work, O Lord, and I shall triumph in the works of thy hands." Furthermore, I know firmly and by no means doubt that he who joins up with a nun does not offend God. In fact, he will be holy with the holy one with whom to unite he is worthy. But when you say that I have raped the bride of Christ, I say it is not true, because it happened with her consent, nor was I supposed to refuse, for it is written: "You shall be one heart and one soul." And elsewhere: "To every man that asketh thee, give." Therefore it does not bring Christ any harm, but rather glory and honor because in my name His horn shall be raised.

Here, then is the ultimate exegetical response. The monk did only what is written, so that it be fulfilled![18] Of scriptural borrowings there are many in this text, but the two central references used here are Act. 4:32 and Luc. 6:30. In the Acts it is written:

Multitudinis autem credentium erat cor unum, et anima una: nec quisquam eorum quae possidebat, aliquid suum esse dicebat, sed erant illis omnia communia.[19]

For our monk this simply means that in this crowd of the faithful

---

17. From MS. lat. 7732, fol. 53[r]. There are a few textual problems: a) MS: sio b) MS: qui ille qui c) MS: in corporale d) MS: eam *instead of* omni e) MS: non *om.* For scriptural borrowings cf.: Ps. 91:5; Ps. 17:26–27; Act. 4:32; Luc. 6:30; Ps. 88:25.

18. In a medieval Latin story which reads very much like a fabliau, the husband returns unexpectedly and surprises an adulterous monk whom he decides to castrate. In his deliberations how to punish the monk and which part of him he should cut off he decides against the head and the limbs, saying: *bonum est resecare superflua que Deum offendunt et homines.* Another MS. has the following addition: *Nam totum corpus suum lucidum erat et factum est ita, ut adimpleretur quod dictum est per prophetam: Percussit eum in posteria dorsi, opprobrium sempiternun dedit ei.* Text in P. Lehmann, *Die Parodie im Mittelalter,* 2d ed. Stuttgart, 1963, pp. 224–31.

19. Vulgate text.

everybody was full of selflessness; everything was common property
and was therefore to be shared. In Luc. 6:30 he found the justification:

> Omni autem petenti te, tribue: et qui aufert quae tua sunt, ne repetas.[20]

Of course, the monk uses this justification also. Why, after all,
shouldn't God Who is Love, give when He is asked, and why should
not He, too, show selflessness by not asking back what has been taken
from Him? In other words, the monk, or rather Boncompagno, treats
the history of salvation as if it were secular history, and thereby the
Christian God is reduced to no less than a pagan god—and those
pagan gods have been known to be seducers themselves! Or was it a
logical question such as: why shouldn't they have meant what they
said when they said it in the Scriptures? This text has been quoted
from time to time, although never in its entirety, as the prime example of Boncompagno's early signs of protohumanism.[21] What is
more important here is to understand the intellectual game which
Boncompagno plays with the Christian rhetoric of love and with
medieval exegesis by subjecting them to "worldly" rules. It is true
that this text sounds blasphemous to modern ears, but I hasten to
add that in the MS I followed (and in most of the others) the letter
is entitled *iocosa responsio* and thus was considered a joke not only
by Boncompagno, but also by later scribes.[22]

An even bolder letter, in the *Rhetorica antiqua,* exhorts a woman
to marry a priest or cleric for the following reason:

> Eris de filiabus Ierusalem si sacerdotem uel clericum receperis in maritum,
> et deificaberis in templo Domini, cum filium paries qui nascetur de
> semine consecrato. Unde sacerdotissa uocaberis uel sacerdos, quando cum
> uiro tuo oleum de cornu altaris exprimes et ita beata eris inter coniugatas.[23]

> You shall be of the daughters of Jerusalem if you take a priest or a cleric
> for a husband, and you shall be deified in the temple of the Lord, for
> you shall bring forth a son who will be born from consecrated seed. Thus
> you shall be called priestess or priest when with your man you press the
> oil out of the horn of the altar and in that way you will be blessed among
> women.

Here Boncompagno speaks like the evangelist who provides the typological framework for the arrival of the Messiah. The woman becomes
a *figura* of the Virgin Mary, espoused to a priest, the earthly repre-

---

20. Vulgate text.
21. See *Rota Veneris,* p. 13.
22. MS. lat. 7732, fol. 53ʳ.
23. MS. lat. 7732, fol. 57ʳ. Cf. Luc. 1; 3 Reg. 1. 39.

sentative of God. She will be deified in the temple of the Lord, the temple which signifies her own body. She will bring forth a son, having been overshadowed by the Holy Spirit, and thus this son will be born *de semine consecrato*. Her rank will be that of *sacerdos*, which in medieval Latin means not only priest but also mediator between God and man. As a priestess who presses the oil out of the horn of the altar, she may be likened to a wise virgin who has enough "oil" for her lamp when she is with her man and thus will be blessed among women.

We have seen earlier how biblical passages were used as *auctoritates*, as "proof" that the persistent lover has a right to love. In this text Boncompagno goes one step further: he does not use biblical quotations to win an argument, but he rewrites the Bible. The stylistic imitation of this new narrative is close enough to its original so that the distortion is unmistakable. Hence the intellectual game of discovery which is a prerequisite both for humor and parody. This technique constitutes a complete reversal of that used by Christian writers and by Boncompagno himself when he writes in a serious vein. Medieval exegetes made use of pagan texts because they discovered a higher meaning in them and thus "moralized" such texts. Boncompagno here used sacred texts because he discovered a lower meaning in them and thus "de-moralized" them.

And he managed to discover not only a set of useful and appropriate sexual metaphors, but whole passages in the Scriptures which could be used in his rhetoric of carnal love, as the following examples from the *Rhetorica novissima* show:[24]

> Quidam qui cognoverat monialem dixit: "Non violavi thorum divinum, sed quia me in sua factura Dominus delectavit, cornu eius studui exaltare." Item posset monialis dicere amatori: "Virga tua et baculus tuus, ipsa me consolata sunt." Item possent dicere suis amatoribus mulieres: "Date nobis de oleo vestro, quia nostre lampades extinguuntur."

> A certain man who had "known" a nun said: "I did not defile God's bed, but because he had made me glad through His work, I was eager to raise his horn." Also, a nun could say to her lover: "Thy rod and thy staff they comfort me." Also, women could say to their lovers: "Give us some of your oil for our lamps are going out."

These three examples all of which impregnate scriptural passages with obscene sexual meanings show that Boncompagno did not reserve

---

24. Quoted from A. Gaudenzi, ed., *Boncompagni Rhetorica novissima*. Bologna, 1892; reprinted Turin, 1962; p. 284.

his horny wit only for ecclesiastics. A study of his theory on *transump-tio* should provide us with a deeper understanding of erotic metaphor and biblical parody not only in medieval Latin texts but also in the vernacular literatures.

In this short study I have tried to show how Boncompagno, with his creative imagination and wit, succeeded in manipulating the two rhetorics and the two loves. I have suggested briefly that the espousal of pagan rhetoric was a delicate business. In order to appreciate Boncompagno's position, we shall have to take a closer look at Christian rhetoric. The Christian rhetorician speaks not in his own interest; rather he speaks for Him Who sent him. He seeks not his own gain but that of the person he addresses. He too manipulates emotions, argues cogently and exaggerates, but it is all for an honest cause. He also makes values relative, but only because they are values of this transitory world. His proofs are based on the supreme *auctoritas*, the Scriptures, and on patristic writings. And if a pagan *auctoritas* is drawn upon, it has more frequently than not been ripped out of its context.[25] It was Boncompagno who put his fictitious, rhetorically gifted lovers and at times himself into the garb of the Christian rhetorician. But they adapt and adopt for their own, frequently rather worldly purposes what they had learned from Christian rhetoric. These persuasive lovers speak in their own interest using the words of the Scriptures; they seek their own gain not that of their addressee's. They manipulate emotions, argue cogently and exaggerate, not out of a Christian concern for a spiritual daughter or friend, not for an honest cause, but for their own success here on earth. They do not even refrain from treating spiritual values as if they were merely values of this world, and their proofs are based on the supreme *auctoritas* but not *sub specie aeternitatis*. As a result, most scriptural *auctoritates* are not only ripped out of their proper context and semantic environment, a method well established and commonly practiced by pious medieval exegetes, but they are treated as if they were nothing but fragments from secular history. One can perhaps, through these texts, imagine Boncompagno's sanctimonious and mischievous grin as he puts the "unscientific" method of Christian rhetoric to a final test in support of the lover's cause. For the

25. See W. Offermanns, *Die Wirkung Ovids auf die literarische Sprache der lateinischen Liebesdichtung des 11. und 12. Jahrhunderts*. Wuppertal, Kastellaun, Düsseldorf, 1970; esp. pp. 11–17; also G. Strunk, *Kunst und Glaube in der lateinischen Heiligenlegende*. Munich, 1970.

letter-writing lover this was apparently a dangerous game as the following *exemplum* from Jacques de Vitry illustrates:[26]

> De clerico, qui verba Scripturarum in epistola
> amatoria scripsit.

In Alimonia (!) clericus quidam monialem peruerso animo diligens consueuerat sibi dulces litteras mittere et scribere, ut animam eius facilius ad peccatum posset trahere. Die ergo quadam, cum litteras sibi mittendas scriberet et in fine litterarum ista uerba inferret: *Tota pulchra es, amica mea, et macula non est in te*, cum uenisset ad illud uerbum: *Labia tua mel et lac . . .* , statim lingua de gutture suo resiluit et vitam morte subita finiuit. Cum astantes de eius repentino interitu mirarentur, cedulam, quam tenebat in manibus, perlegentes cognouerunt, quod ideo fuerat suffocatus, quod verbum spiritualis amoris carnali et immundo amori coaptauerat.

> [About the cleric who wrote scriptural passages
> in a love letter.]

In Germany there once lived a certain cleric who with his perverse mind loved a nun and used to write and send her sweet letters so that he could more easily attract her soul to sin. One day, then, as he was drafting a letter, he added at the end: *Tota pulchra es, amica mea, et macula non est in te* (Cant. 4:71), but when he came to the words: *Labia tua mel et lac* (Cant. 4:11), suddenly the words stuck in his throat and he quickly ended his life with death. As those standing around him wondered about his sudden destruction, they noticed that he was holding a letter in his hands and after they had read it, they realized that he had choked to death because he had mixed the language of spiritual love with that of carnal and foul love.

Boncompagno survived. To any scholar who wants to understand what the Middle Ages meant by "love," he is an indispensable corrective.

---

26. Quoted from J. Klapper, ed., *Exempla aus Handschriften des Mittelalters.* Heidelberg, 1911, p. 52.

Appendix

Concordant Index

A Note to the Reader: While the authors in the volume range over many subjects, covering a vast period of time and a broad geographical area, they are all dealing with a single central subject—rhetoric—in its varied European manifestations during the Middle Ages. Inevitably, a large number of authors, titles, and technical terms will have appeared in these essays.

A reader of several successive essays may well find it difficult, for instance, to grasp at once the extent of the recurrence of certain terms or concepts—say, "artificial order" or "tropes and figures"—even though that reader may have a generalized and almost subconscious impression that such recurrences do occur. The significance of such recurrences surely cannot be appreciated without some reliable method of cross-reference. No mere list could accomplish this.

Therefore the following Concordant Index is constructed with the reader in mind. It lists these elements:

1. Each author cited, whether classical, medieval, or Renaissance.
2. Each work title from these periods, whether cited with author's name or not.
3. Each technical term, including names of individual tropes and figures.
4. Each major concept discussed, even in those cases (e.g., "education" [p. 41]) where the usual technical denotative term may not actually appear on the page listed. When several significant entries for a single term occur, some in English and some in another language (e.g. *paroemion*/alliteration), the basic entry will be the English term to facilitate cross reference.
5. Each contributor's name when used in an essay other than his or her own.

The complex interweavings of medieval rhetorical theory and practice may thus be more apparent to the reader.

342

Doctrina ad inveniendas, incipiendas et formandas materias. See Guido Faba
Doctrina de cort. See Girolamo Terramagnino da Pisa
Doctrinale. See Alexander de Villedieu
Documenta amoris. See Francesco da Barberino
Documentum de arte versificandi. See Geoffrey of Vinsauf
Donat proensal. See Uc Faidit
Donatus, Aelius, 4, 56, 150, 178, 189–190, 200, 206, 209, 211; *Ars maior (Ars grammatica)*, 149, 175n, 178n; *Barbarismus*, 4, 175–176, 191; commentary of Pompeius, 313; tropes and figures of, 206
Donatus, Tiberius Claudius, 73
The Dream of the Rood, prosopopoeia in, 195
Dream visions, 235, 242
Dryhthelm, vision of, 167n
Dualism of Greek thought, 164

Easter, sacramental meaning of, 172
Eberhard the German, 298; *Laborintus*, 69
Echecs amoureux, commentary to, 234
Eclogues. See Vergil
Education, xi, xii, 27, 41, 208; elementary, in grammar and rhetoric, 205–206; in university, 57–58, 61, 208
Educational cadre, 31–32
effectio, 197
Eilhart von Oberg, 247
elocutio, 28, 41, 45, 55, 147–148, 174, 177, 270, 283
Eloquence, 17–18, 63, 173, 205, 284, 320; as Queen of Sciences, 64; epideictic, 232, 242; kinds of, 232
eloquentia, 43, 319; and *sapientia*, relationship between, 43n
enarratio auctorum in grammatical tradition, 305
Enthymeme, 9, 16, 19, 21, 120–121, 202, 217; sham, 227
entrebescamen, 262n
Environment of discourse, xi, 199–200, 211
Eorcenberht of Kent, King, 154n
Epideictic (panegyric) eloquence, 232, 242

epigramma, 289–290
epimone, 197
Epistemology, 18
Epistola ad Acircium. See Aldhelm
Epithet, 240, 297
Erasmus, 69; *De duplici copia*, 71
Eric et Enide. See Chrétien de Troyes
Erotic metaphor, 330
estilo culto, 265
ethopoeia, 148
ethos. See Aristotle, Three forms of persuasion
Etymologiae. See Isidore of Seville
Etymology, 95, 195, 241, 262
Evagatorium Genemy. See Michael of Hungary
Example, 16, 19, 21, 70, 76–77; ancient, 256
excelsus (as style level), 253
Excerpta rhetorica, anonymous, 10n
exclamatio, 194
Excommunicates, 97
exemplum, 331
Exercises: in writing, 228; school, 82
exercitatio and *ars*, distinction between, 246
Exeter Book 195
exordia, collection of, 88
exordium, 51, 53, 88, 97, 104, 107n, 148, 150, 152, 188, 289–290, 304–305, 317; and its *continuatio*, 88; as rhetorical prologue, 316; collection of, 88; in letters, 91–95; in third person, 98; types in Tristan-prologue, 298
Explanation of parts, in preaching, 75
expolitio, 175, 196, 241
exsecutio materiae, 235
Ezekiel, Jerome's prologue to, 129n

Faba, Guido, 85–111; *Arenge*, 88, 91, 193n; *Dictamina rhetorica*, 86, 89–90, 108n; *Doctrina ad inveniendas incipiendas et formandas materias*, 88n; *Gemma purpurea*, 88–91; *Parlamenta et Epistole*, 87n, 90–91; *Petitiones*, 90; *Rota nova*, 87; *Summa dictaminis*, 85–111, 252, 254, 258; *Summa de vitiis et virtutibus*, 88; *Summula magistri Guidonis*, 87n
fabliau, 231
Fable: as rhetorical commonplace, 228; Aesop's, 203, 218

thema, in sermons, 99, 116, 120–121, 125–126, 289–290. *See also* Sermons
Thematic foreshadowing, 75
Themistius, 7, 8n, 13; commentary on Aristotle's *Topics,* 7
Theory, xi, 24; and practice, 111; of genres, 21; of topics, 5–6, 24
Thesis, 10; and hypothesis, 9
Thierry of Chartres, 35, 46, 49n, 50n, 59, 203, 206; attributive commentary on Boethius, 36n; *Heptateuchon,* 203; rhetorical gloss on *Ad Herennium,* 33n, 38; rhetorical gloss on Cicero's *De inventione,* 33n, 38
Thomas à Becket, 209
Thomas d'Angleterre. *See* Thomas of Britain
Thomas of Britain, master romancer, 231, 302; *Tristan et Iseut,* 247–249
Thomas of Salisbury, 113
Thomas of Todi, 113, 121, 124
Three duties of teaching master, 201
Timaeus. See Plato
Time, 168
Topic, as seat (*sedes*) of an argument, 6
Topic (*topos, locus*), 3, 6–8, 12, 16–17, 20–21, 247; defined, 6; dialectical, 6, 9, 12, 17, 19, 22, 42, 50; *differentiae,* in Boethius, 6–7, 9, 13; extrinsic, 8, 13; historical, 234; in French literature, 231–251; intermediate, 8, 13; intrinsic, 7, 12–13; invention, 3, 231–251; principles, in Boethius, 6–8; rhetorical, 3, 9–11, 13, 17, 20, 22–24, 99; rhetorical and dialectical, 11n, 14, 23. *See also locus*
Topics. See Aristotle
Topics (Topica). See Cicero
topos (Topic, *q.v.*), 96n
topos: of Fair Play, 215; of "One Better Than Many," 217–219, 229; of The Judge, 224
Torhtgyth, 170–171
traductio, 188
Transference, 48
transgressio, 266
transitio, 105n
transitus, 305
translatio, ancient legal issue of transference, 47
Translations, Italian, 88, 90

Transumption (*transumptio*), 8, 262–263, 330
Trapezuntius, Georgius, 40–41; *Rhetoricorum libri quinque,* 41n
Traversagni, Lorenzo, 4
Trésor. See Brunetto Latini
Trevet, Nicholas, commentaries on classical authors, 32n
tria genera dicendi, 27, 49n, 50
Tristan and *Bellum Catilinae,* compared, 311, 315
Tristan and Isolde, versions of, 240, 297, 308
Tristan et Iseut. See Thomas of Britain
Tristan-prologue. *See* Gottfried von Strassburg
trivium, arts of, 6, 87, 175, 199, 203, 206, 209–210; dialectic in, 64
Troilus and Criseyde. See Chaucer
Trope (*tropus*), 71, 105, 149, 162–167, 175, 199, 206; in Bible, 149; in semantics, 162; tropes and figures, 209, 232, 246
Troubadours, 84, 231–232, 235, 239, 241, 256, 262n
trouvères, 231, 235, 239; *chansons* of, 236
Truth claim, 303, 311
Typology, 122, 238, 321, 328

Uc Faidit, *Donat proensal,* 252
Ulrich of Bamberg, 45
University, 57–58, 61, 120, 201; dialectic in, 209n
urbanitas, 260

Valla, Lorenzo, 15, 17–18, 40; *Disputationes dialecticae,* 18
Variation, in Old English poetry, 190
velox (type of *cursus*), 101–103, 104n, 106
venustus (as style level), 253
Verbum abbreviatum. See Peter Cantor
Vergil, 47n, 56, 74, 76, 81, 152n, 189, 231, 237, 273n; as philosopher, 76; *Eclogues,* 237; *Georgics,* 69, 157, 237. *See also Aeneid*
Vergil's Wheel, 237–238
Vernacular, 252, 259, 261, 304; as *lingua laica,* 210; criticism of, 82; distinct